THE END OF THE EUROCRATS' DREAM

THE END OF THE EUROCRATS' DREAM

Adjusting to European Diversity

Edited by

D. CHALMERS

M. JACHTENFUCHS

C. JOERGES

CAMBRIDGE
UNIVERSITY PRESS

CAMBRIDGE
UNIVERSITY PRESS

University Printing House, Cambridge CB2 8BS, United Kingdom

Cambridge University Press is part of the University of Cambridge.

It furthers the University's mission by disseminating knowledge in the pursuit of education, learning and research at the highest international levels of excellence.

www.cambridge.org
Information on this title: www.cambridge.org/9781107107182

First published 2016

A catalogue record for this publication is available from the British Library

Library of Congress Cataloguing in Publication data

Names: Chalmers, Damian, editor. | Jachtenfuchs, Markus, 1961- editor. | Joerges, Christian, editor.
Title: The end of the Eurocrats' dream : adjusting to European diversity / edited by D. Chalmers, M. Jachtenfuchs, and C. Joerges.
Description: New York : Cambridge University Press, 2016. | Includes bibliographical references and index.
Identifiers: LCCN 2015031021 | ISBN 9781107107182 (hardback)
Subjects: LCSH: European Union countries—Politics and government—21st century. | European Union countries—Economic conditions—21st century. | Financial crises—European Union countries. | Global Financial Crisis, 2008–2009.
Classification: LCC JN30 .E238 2016 | DDC 341.242/2—dc23
LC record available at http://lccn.loc.gov/2015031021

ISBN 978-1-107-10718-2 Hardback

CONTENTS

TABLES

PREFACE

The editors and the contributors to this book have dedicated a very significant part of their academic lives to the study of the European integration project. They have promoted it and they have profited from it: it was the integration process which generated European-wide discourses, multi-disciplinary and multi-national cooperative communities. This common commitment persists. But it has to address unprecedented challenges. 'The end of the Eurocrats' dream' is meant as a diagnosis and a message. We are, of course, concerned about the state of the European Union. We are, however, also concerned about the prevailing political and academic perceptions of and responses to the multifaceted European crisis. 'Buying time', 'muddling through', 'structural reforms', the management of assumed functional necessities will not suffice to bring Europe 'back on track'. The European Union needs to be concerned about its legitimacy, about solidarity and social justice within and between its member states, its constitutional condition, the integrity of its law. The message which our title seeks to convey concerns also the past. The chances of a sustainable renewal depend upon an understanding of the past. We will have to re-examine what we thought were valid assumptions. We have to explore potential failures in the design of the European project and the conceptual frameworks which have guided its praxis.

Our objectives contrast, hence, with the many efforts to provide quick fixes or long-term solutions to so many topical issues on the political agenda. We do not believe, however, that everybody who supports European integration, as we do, must also support the Union's overall trajectory and its main policy orientations or be called 'anti-European'. Quite the contrary: there is a strong need for a debate about fundamentals, especially among those favouring the European project.

We have pursued our agenda in a sequence of meetings, exchanges of draft papers, their discussion and further elaboration. The first meeting was held at the Hertie School of Governance in Berlin in July 2013. A second one, organised by the Berlin Social Science Center, followed in

December. For a third meeting we convened in London at the London School of Economics and Political Science (LSE) in February 2014. The Institute for Advanced Study in Delmenhorst, Lower Saxony, hosted the group for a concluding workshop in May 2014. It then took a good number of months to finalise the contributions.

Are we too late with the delivery of our product? Throughout the duration of our cooperation, the crisis kept generating spectacular news, anxieties and hectic activities. Now, the tensions within the Union are again rising and the future of European integration is more uncertain than ever. The harsh treatment of Greece and other 'states in financial difficulties' has caused enormous collateral damage. If proof were needed of the deplorable state of the Union, its failure to respond responsibly to the refugee crisis has documented it. The need for fundamental debate is, in our view, irrefutable.

We wish to express our gratitude for the financial and organisational support we received from the Hertie School of Governance, the Berlin Social Science Center, the LSE, and the Institute for Advanced Study in Delmenhorst. We would like to thank Rebecca Roberts, Paul Smith, Elizabeth Spicer and Richard Woodham and everybody else at Cambridge University Press for their great help, support and patience throughout the duration of our project.

Last, but not least, we would like to underline how much we appreciate the commitment and patience of our authors. We dedicate this book to the memory of C. Maxwell Watson, the former Director of the Political Economy of Financial Markets Programme at the European Studies Centre of St Anthony's College in Oxford. His contributions to our deliberations were of invaluable importance. It was a pleasure for us all to work with him, albeit all too briefly.

1

The retransformation of Europe

DAMIAN CHALMERS, MARKUS JACHTENFUCHS AND CHRISTIAN JOERGES

The state of the Union

Prior to the more recent refugee crisis, the 'euro crisis' was the most severe crisis in the history of the EU. As the EU is often written as a history of crisis, such a statement is not made easily. However, the euro crisis occupies this position for six reasons.

First, its scale is more wide-ranging and the consequences more severe than previous crises. The failure of the European Defence Community, the empty chair crisis and the various breakdowns of earlier attempts at monetary integration did not lead to a retrenchment of the EU or to disintegration but merely prevented the EU from going further and temporarily cemented the status quo. The common currency, however, is one of the few exclusive powers of the Union. Of all the exclusive powers, it is the one that most clearly resembles a core state function (Genschel and Jachtenfuchs 2014), with the French Constitutional Council seeing it as 'vital to the exercise of national sovereignty'[1] and the German Constitution Court as a precondition for democracy.[2] A breakup of the euro would amount to a failure of the most ambitious attempt at integration so far, and in a field which is both factually and symbolically of the utmost importance. This is clearly in the minds of policy makers, most famously in Angela Merkel's often-quoted remarks before the German Bundestag: 'Europe fails if the euro fails, Europe succeeds if the euro succeeds.'[3]

Secondly, the crisis is multidimensional. The crisis is often described in this regard as one of public finances in which particular states, through bad luck, unwise choices and/or poor governance, are no longer able to pay their

1 Decision 92-308 DC, *Maastricht I*, Judgment of 9 April 1992, para. 43.

2 *Brunner* v. *TEU* [1994] 1 CMLR 57.

3 Deutscher Bundestag, Plenarprotokolle, 17. Wahlperiode, 160. Sitzung, 27 December 2012, 19078.

way. The badness of the term 'public finances' is itself unhelpful, and conceals more than it reveals. Public finance crises are not merely actuarial deficits. Direct remedial action invariably involves a mixture of cuts in public spending, most obviously to welfare, health, pensions and education; increases in taxes, often in ways which may be regressive; and garnering income through other sources, notably privatisation and the sale of public assets. In addition, international organisations and European Union institutions often perceive deterioration of public finances as a symptom of underlying weaknesses in the public administration or economy of a member state. Further remedial action may be required, therefore, in the organisation of government, labour law, industrial policy and levels of product or service regulation, or professional requirements. Public finance crises touch a multifarious variety of interests, perspectives and values in a way like no other.

This multidimensionality is, to be sure, common to all public finance crises. However, in the case of the euro-area crisis it has been further complicated by the 'sovereign-bank nexus', a vicious circle in which banks finance government debt, governments are lax on banking supervision, and governments must then rescue banks with public finances due to the wider effects on the economy of bank collapse. This nexus not only tied national governments to commercial banks in a suffocating embrace, but national governments to each other. Despite the fact that Greece represented only a small fraction of the Eurozone's gross domestic product, at the onset of the crisis neither the European Council nor the European Central Bank considered its sovereign default a feasible option because they feared a wave of bank breakdowns, bank bailouts and budget imbalances throughout Europe. The financial means involved were enormous. According to a 2012 Commission estimate, more than 4,5 trillion euros of taxpayers' money were used to rescue banks in the EU in the period of the crisis up until then (European Commission 2012a: 3).

Thirdly, the crisis has been marked by high levels of political contestation. Social hardship developed rapidly: according to Eurostat, the unemployment rates increased between 2007 and 2013 in Ireland from 6.4 per cent to 13.1 per cent, in Greece from 8.4 per cent to 27.5 per cent, in Spain from 8.2 per cent to 26.1 per cent, in Italy from 6.1 per cent to 12.2 per cent and in Cyprus from 3.9 per cent to 15.9 per cent.[4] The ability of political institutions to respond effectively was not immediately

4 http://ec.europa.eu/eurostat/statistics-explained/index.php/Unemployment_statistics.

apparent. As Jean-Claude Juncker once remarked, 'We all know what to do but we just don't know how to get re-elected once we have done it' (quoted in Hix and Høyland 2011: 271). At Union level, the crisis increased the politicisation of the Union in a manner which is unlikely to be reversed in the foreseeable future. It has also had dramatic domestic political repercussions: between 2010 and 2013, only four Eurozone governments *remained* in power (Schimmelfennig 2014: 324).

Fourthly, the euro crisis marks the visible end of the standard model of the euro-polity according to which the EU was strong in fields of rather technical and potentially Pareto-improving areas of market regulation and weak in issues relating to large-scale redistribution (Hix 2007; Moravcsik 2002; for a classical treatment of the distinction between regulatory and redistributive politics, see Lowi 1972). Now, the EU is engaged in massive redistribution among member states. This occurs most explicitly through the European Stability Mechanism (ESM), a €700 billion series of guarantees to support euro-area states which can no longer sustain their public finances. It has also occurred indirectly through various forms of European Central Bank (ECB) assistance and intervention (Wilsher 2013), but most dramatically through the commitments by the ECB to purchase both unlimited amounts of securities from euro-area governments which have entered EU sponsored financial support programmes (Outright Monetary Transaction (OMT) Programme)(European Central Bank 2012) and its wider monthly purchases of €60 billion of euro-area public sector securities, which began on 9 March 2015 and is envisaged to last until September 2016 (Public Sector Purchase Programme (PSPP)).[5] These measures not only redistribute wealth between member states but also between private parties. The ESM has secured the position of creditors at the expense of taxpayers and recipients of public expenditure in the debtor state who have to bear the burden of any programme to secure financial support. OMT and PSPP stoke demand for particular assets, thereby benefiting holders of those assets. While regulatory policies can, under certain conditions, be legitimated by their output and be taken by non-majoritarian institutions, the massive involvement of the EU in such redistributive policies has created visible winners and losers, something which has habitually required a strong democratic mandate (Scharpf 1999; Dawson and de Witte 2013).

Fifthly, the crisis has shifted the relationship between the different EU institutions and has further increased the EU's institutional fragmentation

5 Decision ECB/2015/10 on a secondary markets public sector asset purchase programme, Decision of 5 March 2015.

(Genschel and Jachtenfuchs 2016). For many observers, the crisis marked a decisive step for the 'new intergovernmentalism' (Bickerton et al. 2015), which is characterised by the dominance of the European Council and a diminished role for the Commission and the European Parliament, which supersedes and partly replaces the old Community method. In this view, the increased role of the European Council is not merely a phenomenon that accompanied the most dramatic years of the crisis but a long-term structural change which the crisis brought to the forefront. Moreover, the European Council is not the only intergovernmental body to acquire prominence during the crisis. The euro group, comprising the finance ministers of the euro-area states, the ECB President and the Commissioner responsible for economic and financial affairs, has been central to micro-managing many aspects of the crisis, be it draft national budgets or structural reforms, as well, in its guise as the Board of Governors of the ESM, as the central decisions governing financial support for states which have requested it as well as the central conditions surrounding that support. In the case of the Commission, these include supervision of almost all fields of economic and social policy under the guise of preventing and correcting macroeconomic imbalances. The ECB's powers to purchase unlimited amounts of securities have turned it into a lender of last resort (Buiter and Rabari 2012; Wilsher 2013). Beyond the monetary sphere, it has sought to acquire ever more regulatory powers, initially over prudential supervision but also over clearing systems, in the guise of securing monetary stability. This has resulted in new administrative resources, most notably the addition of 1,000 employees to the ECB in 2013–14 to allow it to carry out its new tasks of prudential supervision.

The relative power of these supranational institutions is facilitated by their decision-making dynamics. Despite the build-up of a more permanent administrative structure and a President, the European Council is, in essence, a forum for negotiation and deliberation which meets only several times a year for brief periods, and which has to decide mostly by unanimity. In contrast, the ECB has a fast decision-making structure, independent from direct democratic control and with a substantial administrative backup. This shaped the relative influence and roles of the institutions during the crisis. While the European Council was often divided on the issue and unable thus to make decisions, the ECB stepped in to provide substitutes, most notably financial support to stricken states, and thereby broadened its powers 'through the monetary backdoor' (Schelkle 2014). These overlapping, fluid roles between the European Council, Commission,

ECB and the euro-Group raise questions not only about institutional coordination and cooperation, but also accountability, transparency and representation as this varies significantly between the institutions (Bovens and Curtin in this volume). These issues have been further stirred by the presence of processes which do not have a formal institutional presence but have significant equivalent effects. The most visible of these is the 'Troika' of the International Monetary Fund (IMF), the European Commission and the European Central Bank, which is responsible for negotiating the details and overseeing the implementation of those programmes which are a precondition for ESM financial support. In practice, this has allowed it to impose demands and oversee almost all aspects of those states' economic and social policies in a highly unaccountable manner. It has, thus, become the symbol of far-reaching and deeply intrusive adjustment policies from a technocratic informal association without democratic credentials, with its removal being a central demand of the incoming Greek Syriza government in January 2015.

Sixthly, and finally, the crisis set tremors through domestic constitutional settlements. The only formal requirement was that euro-area states entrench a commitment to balance their budgets 'in provisions of binding force and permanent character, preferably constitutional'.[6] Arguably, a greater transformation is that EU law now claims a continual oversight and legal authority over elements which are at the centre of many domestic constitutions, be these budgetary powers, the social state, or citizenship. As the demands of EU law have intensified and shifted during the crisis, this has, in turn, put corollary pressures on established domestic understandings of sovereignty, citizenship and parliament–executive relations. It is, thus, unsurprising that it has led to a series of responses in national constitutional courts (Chalmers in this volume). Furthermore, the constitutional resettlement taking place is not that advocated by some exponents of European constitutionalism in which the disciplines of EU law or the image of Europe leads domestic settlements to take more account of interests or values historically poorly represented within them (Joerges 2014a). Instead, it is one in which asymmetries of financial power are protected from political correction with private creditors of euro-area states insured against the risk of bad investments and creditor states within the ESM given greater power to dictate policy terms to debtor states (Dawson and de Witte 2013).

6 Article 3(2) TSCG.

The continuation and amplification of structural features of the Union by the crisis

To be sure, the six developments outlined in the previous section transform the European Union. They stretch and challenge the pre-existing modus operandi, set up new constellations of conflicts and make European Union policies a much more salient and divisive presence. However, for all this change, the institutional responses to the crisis represented very much a continuation of a Union way of doing things. By this, we argue that the evolution of the crisis was not merely a result of economic and fiscal policy choices but reflected broader structural features of the European Union construction which the crisis exposed. These structural features are marked by enduring and persistent characteristics. They are not impossible to change or to deal with but evidence frequent potentially powerful and entrenched effects which are endemic to the EU in that they settle and institutionalise their effects. The following seem particularly important to us.

A concern with scale

A recurring feature of Union responses to its challenges – be they realising collective goods, dealing with externalities, strengthening institutional capacity or reimagining political community – is the assumption that sizing upwards will offer solutions that would otherwise not be available. This is most explicit in the subsidiarity principle, which links the justification for Union action to the effects or scale of a problem. It is also present in the granting of significant powers to centralised non-majoritarian institutions, most notably the Commission as the central agenda-setter for law-making and policy, and the ECB as the pre-eminent institution in managing the economic policy of the euro area. The rationales are that these have a purview and a freedom from sectoral or national interests that domestic institutions do not have. It exists within the hierarchy of norms within the Union, whereby international law binds the Union, EU law has primacy over national law, and national governments are assigned responsibility for all that takes place on their territory on the assumption that central domestic legal law can suborn other legal orders within the territory. It is, of course, present territorially, not only in the concern with the expansion of the Union but also in its neighbourhood and other policies which seek to extend the effects of Union norms beyond its frontiers (Lavenex 2014; Scott 2014). Notwithstanding certain benefits, this privileging of scale generates many tensions and conflicts. There are dangers of administrative centralisation, imperfect knowledge, the effects of poor policies being magnified, and insensitivity to local concerns. Furthermore, as Majone has observed in this volume, collective action theory suggests that, the greater the number of participants in an enterprise, the more likely it will be that the agreed outcome will deviate from what is optimal for the majority.

The starkest manifestation of this concern with scale was the Commission's 'blueprint for a deep and genuine economic and monetary union' which acted in many ways as the template for reforms in response to the crisis (European Commission 2012b). This called in particular for a more centralised economic and monetary union. This would include a banking union in which there would be a single Union rulebook for the financial services industry, the ECB would acquire significant powers of prudential supervision, and a European Resolution Authority (now a Single Resolution Board) would establish a recovery and resolution regime for insolvent banks within the euro area. The rationale provided for this are assertions that a lack of strong supranational institutions exacerbated the crisis, led to a reversal of integration and the lack of a level playing field for businesses and households (European Commission 2012b: 9). The blueprint also sought harmonisation of national budgetary laws, increased fiscal capacities for the Union and greater Union oversight of employment and tax law. The rationale was, once again, that lack of supranational oversight and power had led to weak national performance in these fields which had contributed to the crisis (European Commission 2012b: 2–3 and 6). The diagnosis is thinly substantiated, but, even if it were correct, does it warrant the prognosis? All the concerns of capture, amplification of risks of poor decision-making, sub-optimal choice of collective preferences, and poor local knowledge are present in the blueprint. Furthermore, federations experience cycles of power moving upwards or downwards between levels. More than 60 years after its foundation, if the EU were such a federation, a downward cycle would be likely and no fundamental threat. Even such a characterisation does not take account of the current political debate in Europe in which elites and mass public are increasingly attracted by narratives which argue that European integration in general is the problem and not the cure (Majone 2014). This is not to argue that there is not a place for arguing that scale has certain benefits. It is simply to argue that these are neither questioned sufficiently nor are the risks and costs sufficiently thought through.

A weak political centre and administrative system of justice

For all its attempts at legal and administrative consolidation, the European Union has weak central resources relative to its competencies. Compared to other political systems, there are limited central financial resources; a small bureaucracy; no extensive administrative system of justice; weak political authority; and considerable checks and balances hemming in central decision-making. This leads to the Union having to rely strongly on national administrations, legal systems and resources to secure its policies. This results in a double bind. On the one hand, the Union can externalise the costs of applying and implementing its policies onto national actors. Unless it is highly attuned – and this is unlikely – to the extent, incidence and nature of these costs, there will inevitably be a danger that it externalises costs which are seen as excessive, unequally distributed and culturally insensitive. This has led to increased concerns with tools such as impact assessments (European Commission 2009), but the scale and heterogeneity of the Union makes sensitivity to its diversity very difficult indeed. On the other, the independence of national actors becomes a source of suspicion as it can be used to frustrate and negate Union policies. The Union is, thus, marked by a variety of tools used both to police national administrations and to induce them to realise Union policies – be they financial sanctions administered by the Court of Justice; litigation before national courts by private parties affected by non-compliance; naming and shaming; reporting duties; or benchmarking.

To be sure, during the crisis the Union acquired new capacities. Most notably, the ECB's unlimited purchasing power turned it into a de facto lender of last resort. Its weak central authority and resources shaped its dominant strategy to the crisis, which was to adopt a regulatory style. Central long-term goods were set out to be protected, notably fiscal discipline, return to the financial markets, and balanced economic performance. Protection of these goods justifies regulation by non-majoritarian supranational institutions to protect against their being damaged by domestic legislative or governmental excess or neglect. The sacralisation of these goods has been taken furthest in the Treaty on Stability, Co-ordination and Governance (TSCG) stipulation that a duty to balance the budget across the economic cycle should be put in a permanent and binding norm preferably of a constitutional character.[7] This is notwithstanding that there is no tradition since the Second World War of balancing the budgets in

7 Article 3(2) TSCG.

Europe, let alone a constitutional one that elevates it above other imperatives in these fields. As Chalmers observes in this volume, these norms then justify an institutional system of oversight, discipline and sanctions which is analogous to that found in fields where regulatory agencies are deployed. There is no tradition of this in the field of fiscal or welfare policy (Chalmers 2012). It has allowed the Union, however, to externalise the central costs and political responsibilities of adjustment onto national administrations. This has, in turn, proved to be an Achilles Heel for the Union. National administrations both become vehicles for securing its goals and the central impediment to realising them. Having cast them as unreliable actors to justify its intervention in the first place, the crisis led it – in both the 'Six Pack' and 'Two Pack' – to set out ever more detailed legal constraints on the exercise of domestic fiscal and economic policy. However, it has no administrative machinery to enforce these constraints effectively. More powerful states can thus game these constraints by exacting greater leeway as a price for cooperation.

Excessive reliance on government by law

A consequence of these weak central resources is a high dependence on those which remain available to the Union, most notably legal resources, to further its objectives. Law remains the central instrument both for realising integration and for allowing the Union to govern. In this, one sees not so much a Union rule of law. EU legal constraints on Union institutions are often patchy and EU law in a way claims to rule over private activities within the Union (Chalmers and Chaves 2014). Instead, there is government by law. Intervention is, above all, by use of legal instrument. This has resulted in an overstretching of EU law. As EU law is the central tool for the realisation of EU policies, a failure to meet the ambitions of these policies is frequently condemned as an act of illegality because these policies have been formalised within the substantive norms of EU law. This had a number of effects. It has led to an instrumentalisation of EU law, whereby EU legal pre-commitments are not only associated with unpopular or ill-conceived policies but seen as an instrument for masking debate about these behind requirements that the law be observed (Herdegen 1998). It has, in some cases, led to over-formalisation whereby the rigid structures of the law are unable to adapt with sufficient suppleness to the needs of the policy-sector and those affected by it. Finally, it has led to a desiccation of legal authority. In order to manage law's inflexibilities, an ever wider array of legal or quasi-legal instruments has been developed. Alongside the Regulations,

Directives, Decisions and Recommendations mentioned in the original Treaties, a number of other instruments have emerged which include, inter alia, Resolutions, Guidelines, Framework Directives, Action Plans, international agreements, common positions and Declarations. If these are less constraining than EU law, which is formally binding or directly applicable, the central features of law remain intact. It is difficult to change legal instruments, and legal normativity requires conduct not to deviate from the law for legally impermissible reasons. These features constrain the flexibility that can be offered, and it is obtained often at a cost, most notably in the form of uncertainty as to the impact and incidence of non-binding law.

The crisis extrapolated these features through both legal expansion and legal dispersion. It has generated a lot of EU law. The 'Six Pack' and 'Two Pack', the post-crisis secondary legislation governing the budgetary and macroeconomic policies of states, combine to make up seventy pages of *Official Journal*. However, alongside this, there has been a hollowing out of EU law and a move to other forms of law. The former is best seen with regard to assessments of whether a state has a macroeconomic imbalance. This is gauged against a Scoreboard which, in April 2015, comprised 16 headline indicators and 34 auxiliary indicators.[8] None of these indicators can be said to qualify as legal norms. It is difficult to know how they are read by the Commission to guide its assessment, but it is doubtful that it does this through interpreting these indicators as legal texts, although they do, nonetheless, combine to form a legal term, 'excessive macroeconomic imbalance', which can be deployed to act as a trigger for legal procedures and sanctions. The latter, the use of other forms of law to serve Union objectives, is seen most vividly with the three central treaty responses to the crisis. The European Financial Stability Facility (EFSF) Treaty, ESM Treaty and TSCG are all characterised as international agreements between member states which must comply with EU law, notwithstanding that the ESM required an amendment to Article 136 TFEU to allow its ratification[9] and it is anticipated that the TSCG will be integrated into the EU Treaties by 1 January 2018.[10] The implications of this go beyond the formal designation of the legal instrument (Chiti and Texeira 2013; Peers 2013). The ESM Treaty, for example, breaks from the established principle that the member states treat each other as equals by requiring that the granting of financial assistance

8 http://ec.europa.eu/economy_finance/indicators/economic_reforms/eip/#/headline/.

9 Decision 2011/199/EU amending Article 136 of the TFEU with regard to a stability mechanism for member states whose currency is the euro, OJ L 91, 6.4.2011, 1.

10 Article 16 TSCG.

is 'subject to strict conditionality'.[11] The central instrument of government is the 'memorandum of understanding',[12] which sets out the central conditions to be met if a state is to receive financial support. However, the status of these memoranda is unclear. They are certainly not legal instruments and are subject to regular change (Tuori and Tuori 2014: 97–101).

Put most disturbingly, the crisis did not create a greater respect for government by law. If certain actors were subject to heavy legal constraint, this was not true of the EU institutions, which were granted broad discretionary powers to govern on the grounds that the crisis prompted an emergency. This was, in turn, subject to only weak constraint by the Court of Justice.[13] In this volume, Joerges has argued that this led to a de-legalisation of the Union, in which a legal vacuum sits at the foundations of these powers. This de-legalisation is disquieting in itself, but it has also allowed an administrative authoritarianism in which the crisis justifies any number of fiats and impositions (Wilkinson 2015).

The weak management of interdependence and heterogeneity

Interdependence is present both as a standard analytical explanation for the presence of the Union and as a justification for both current and future powers on the grounds that negative externalities should and can be internalised by stronger integration between the respective units. This interdependence in the economic, political and legal spheres was also seen, however, as a goal to be actively promoted. The single market was supposed to lead to increased specialisation, division of labour and competition and overall to more economic growth. This promotion was not only for reasons of economic growth, but to open up the hard shell of the state and increase transnational interactions. It has, however, a downside. Interdependence, first, makes states more vulnerable, depending on their size and their degree of dependence on others (Keohane and Nye 1977). The economic freedoms, thus, limited a state's policy options, which were further restricted by EU legislation. They also have more indirect and unpredictable consequences with EU requirements on the free movement of capital and incorporation limiting the available tax base for states to taxes

11 Article 3(1) ESM.

12 Article 13(3) ESM.

13 The reasoning of this institution in relation to conferred powers is weak both in relation to the ESM and the ECB's powers. See, respectively, *Pringle*, EU:C:2012:756; *Gauweiler*, EU:C:2015:400.

which were centred on immobile actors, leading in turn to general downward pressures in this base (see Menéndez in this volume). The language of interdependence, secondly, unduly fosters functional logic within the legal and political realms. A law becomes necessary to secure the functioning of a particular policy or the market. The challenge with such logic is that it can privilege the securing of the policy or realisation of the market at the expense of other values or interests. It is, in short, too unidimensional. The third challenge with the logic of interdependence is that it provides few tools with which to manage the relationship between it and its equally endemic counterpart, heterogeneity. This relationship can take many forms, as this heterogeneity has a number of dimensions within the Union.

Heterogeneity is substantial in terms of socio-economic development. Per capita GDP of the top group (Netherlands, Ireland, Austria, Sweden, Germany, Denmark and Belgium) is two to two-and-a-half times the per capita GDP of the lowest group (Romania and Bulgaria). Future envisaged enlargements would widen this gap. In corollary fashion, states take different approaches to the role of the market and the private sector in providing welfare and in using the welfare system to redistribute wealth between citizens (see most famously Esping-Andersen 1990). These differences leave them asymmetrically exposed to the encroachment of EU law as it may catch institutions in one state doing a parallel task to those not caught by it in another. Within the context of this collection, heterogeneity is most central in the 'varieties of capitalism' present within the Union. Systems of corporate governance, industrial relations, access to finance, inter-firm relations, and patterns and modes of state intervention differ significantly between member states (Hall and Soskice 2001; Iversen and Soskice 2013). Interdependence obscures these differences and the consequent variable impacts of common legislation on different domestic political economies.

This heterogeneity generates more invidious problems. In particular, member states push for Union regulatory models or policies which align with their own regulatory systems (Héritier et al. 1996) or styles of capitalism. Apparently neutral EU policies have 'beggar thy neighbour' qualities insofar as they extend the features of the systems of certain states at the expense of other states. Hall has noted that this both contributed to the crisis and shaped, in unfortunate ways, the responses to it. He argued that member states broadly fall into two categories. Some states relied on export-led growth with institutions, notably those on wage control, well established to secure this, whilst others relied on demand-led growth with institutions developed around this strategy. Monetary union set out an architecture which required all states to adopt the former strategy: something that was very easy for the first group, but not politically and economically for the second group. It was, correspondingly, largely members of the latter that were most severely hit by the crisis. In offering financial support, the response of the first group was to demand more of the same, namely, that it should be predicated on strategy centred around export-led growth, whilst clamping on something that had historically generated growth, namely, domestic demand (Hall 2014).

Interlocked levels of government

As a multilevel system, the most characteristic feature of the EU is not that the European and the national level are linked, but the specific way in which they are linked. Whereas, in the USA, the federal and the state levels are, at least ideally, independent of each other, with separate jurisdictions and administrations and with independent tax resources, the EU is structured in a fundamentally different way. In stark contrast to the US system, practically no field of activity is immune from EU intervention. Empirical studies reveal the constantly increasing substantive scope and institutional depth of EU involvement (Börzel 2005: 222–23). However, domestic actors, most notably national governments, are central to EU law-making by virtue of the centrality of the Council and have a monopoly, as mentioned earlier, over the enforcement of almost all areas of EU law. This interlocking decision-making results in the Council not necessarily looking for the best solutions. Its central lawmakers, the national governments, will have their own institutional self-interests in mind (Scharpf 1988).

To secure mutual accommodation of these interests, conflict-minimising strategies are often adopted (Falkner 2011; Genschel and Jachtenfuchs, this volume). This can involve decision-making by consensus within the Council. If this seems to favour national autonomy and diversity, there is a bigger risk that it is outweighed by decision-making which favours vested interests, be they of the administrations themselves or of those who hold particular sway over the latter. As the number of veto players within the EU increases, so changing the status quo becomes more difficult. In situations where there is EU legislation combined with the presence of so many veto players, change is difficult (Tsebelis and Garrett 2001). The average piece of EU legislation now takes seven years to amend (Borghetto and Mäder 2014). The other conflict-minimising strategy is the delegation of significant powers to non-majoritarian institutions either directly or through incomplete contract whereby vague legislative terms have to be implemented or interpreted by these institutions. This is, indeed, the basis for much of the powers of the Commission, the Court of Justice and the ECB. In recent years, the capacities of these institutions have not only expanded with their governing more activities, but independent agencies have also both proliferated and acquired more extensive powers with standardisation bodies and private norm-setting bodies, being used much more intensively and extensively (Chalmers and Chaves 2014). Some authors prefer to speak critically of 'technocracy' or 'integration by stealth' (Majone 2005). If this non-majoritarian ethos is deeply engrained in the EU with its initial belief in strong executive institutions autonomous from intergovernmental control (Haas 1964; Dehousse 2011) this technocracy has also become a convenient coping mechanism for evading addressing the conflicts brought about by the increasing heterogeneity of the EU.

The crisis took this integration by stealth to new levels. Mention has already been made of the way that the ECB acquired new powers during the crisis and was better placed to exercise its powers than other EU institutions which relied on unanimity or Qualified Majority Voting (QMV) for decision-making. This transfer was part of a wider shift. The European System of Financial Supervisors (ESFS), three new euro-agencies, was granted extensive powers to regulate the financial services industry. The ECB engaged in 'competence creeping' by seeking regulatory powers beyond the field of prudential supervision to those of clearing systems.[14] In addition, the Commission was granted significantly more influence in the corrective procedures to police states which had run excessive budget deficits or macroeconomic imbalances or significantly deviated from their path towards a balanced budget. As in many cases, it now required a QMV decision by the Council to overrule a Commission decision, rather than, as previously, a QMV vote by the Council to approve it (Chalmers 2012).

Asymmetric integration and the destabilisation of law and legal subjectivities

A feature of European Union integration is that it is partial in its scope. It only covers certain activities and there are few fields where it covers all dimensions of that activity. One consequence is asymmetric integration. Perspectives or policies set out extremely powerfully by the EU (i.e., the single market or monetary policy) cut across policies or perspectives

14 This was struck down in *United Kingdom* v. *ECB*, EU:T:2015:133.

which are either weakly or not governed or articulated by EU law, such as cultural, consumer or health policy. Such 'diagonal conflicts' destabilise both EU and national law (Joerges 2010; Joerges 2014b). As EU law almost never governs all dimensions of a dispute, with national law governing some aspects of the dispute and monopolising the context within which the dispute takes place, it is impossible to talk fully of the primacy of EU law or its pre-empting national law. For it will not fully govern disputes or the surrounding activity, but only some dimensions of these. These limits result invariably in national law acting as a source of disruption for the effectiveness of EU law. Conversely, as national laws combine to govern policy areas, insofar as EU law displaces one or more national law, it has wider rippling effects, as this acts to upset the coherence of the policy field more generally.

This mutual destabilisation arises also in relation to legal subjectivities, namely, how EU and national law conceive their subjects and are to see and understand the world. This is nowhere more evident than with citizenship.

National citizenship acts to destabilise EU citizenship by virtue of the requirement that the latter be additional to it and not replace it.[15] Insofar as citizenship is about membership rights, this suggests that there are some entitlements, political, civil or social, to which only nationals should be entitled. This sits uneasily with the idea at the heart of EU citizenship that EU citizens resident in another member state should have equal access to its entitlements. The tension between these poles is marked by legal fluidity mediated by ambiguous constructs, such as integration requirements[16] or the legitimate interests of the host state,[17] being deployed as preconditions for certain entitlements and by an obscurely restricted remit so that EU citizenship offers only limited protection against discrimination in the private sector.[18] This legal fluidity reflects the wider uncertainty about the position of the EU citizen, which allows many to be seen too easily as second-class denizens within their host societies, with all the racism and marginalisation engendered by this (Isin 2013).

EU law acts, conversely, to destabilise national citizenship. As Colliot-Thélène observes in this volume, national citizenship is marked by a

15 Article 9 TFEU.

16 *Martens*, EU:C:2015:118.

17 *Brey*, EU:C:2013:565.

18 Only workers have wide-ranging protection here, Directive 2014/54/EU on measures facilitating the exercise of rights conferred on workers in the context of freedom of movement for workers, OJ 2014, L 128/8.

facility which allows citizens to slip between private and public roles and individual and collective identities. The boundary between these roles and identities is never demarcated, and this, as well as a sense of balance between these roles and identities, is central to much of the freedom and equality associated with citizenship. It allows citizens to adopt a multiplicity of roles and identities whilst still exercising citizenship. EU law not only does this, it also destabilises national citizenship by cutting across it and putting in question both its indivisibility and the balance central to this. In particular, it puts in play a cleavage between the mobile and the immobile, whereby the mobile have greater private and individual opportunities but less political or collective voice. They have left behind their home society and do not form an equal part of the body politic of their host state. By contrast, the immobile still fully form part of a collective and public identity, but their private and individual status is destabilised, as they bear many of the risks of mobility, be they capital and skills flight from the home state or the pressure on public services and labour markets in host states.

During the crisis, this mutual destabilisation took two forms. As Chalmers notes in his contribution to this volume, national citizenship became a central institution for expressing resistance to EU institutions in those states subject to the memoranda of understanding in exchange for financial support. In both Greece and Portugal, constitutional courts struck down elements of those programmes on the grounds that they violated constitutional provisions on citizenship. Conversely, the lack of a properly constituted public sphere surrounding the ESM became an issue most notably for the German Constitutional Court, which, albeit from a highly one-sided perspective, noted how, unchecked, the administrative quality of its arrangements breached a central tenet of citizenship, namely, no taxation without representation.

Adjusting to European diversity: the approach of this volume

After several years of debate, we understand what happened with the crisis and the reasons behind it (De Grauwe 2013; Eichengreen 2012). If it is also desirable to reflect on its consequences, as Cole reflected in his introduction to Polanyi's Europe Today, it is much less easy to undo these (Polanyi 1937). Some humility is required. At best, we can reflect upon and try to understand the challenges to which the crisis has exposed us. We have already described how structural features of the Union contributed to the crisis, and these are developed more fully in individual chapters. Within the context of these, this volume wants to set out a few ideas about how to address the crisis and how the Union should develop.

Can the Union get 'back on track' to paraphrase the parlance of its crisis managers, regain its legitimacy and maybe even its long-assumed avant-garde potential for the evolution and design of transnational governance? In addition to our concerns about the structural features of the Union, we make use of the work of the American political economist Dani Rodrik. Rodrik (2011) asserts the impossibility of simultaneous pursuit of economic globalisation, democratic politics and national determination (autonomy), highlighting a trilemma in which only two goals can be paired: economic globalisation and democratic politics or democracy and national autonomy. He argues that the Union furnishes a dramatic illustration of this. On the one hand, the EU could transnationalise democracy through federalisation and thereby defend the advantages of the single market; at the same time, however, it would be forced to establish a common European politics to legitimise its necessary assumption of fiscal and social policy, with negative consequences for national sovereignty. In the absence of such a denationalising will, the EU must give up the common currency and accept economic disintegration (Rodrik 2011).

Should Rodrik be right, we are in a very uncomfortable position. The type of 'federalisation' that we have been witnessing during the crisis is anything but democratic. Rodrik himself is by no means confident as to the chances for a realisation of the federal project (Rodrik 2015). To be sure, none other than Germany's leading philosopher and public intellectual keeps designing the contours of a *non-federal* European democracy which would build upon the co-originality of European and national identities (Habermas 2015). Not only do the factual premises of his construction seem profoundly at odds with the impact of Europe's present conflict constellation on the mindsets of Europeans in both the north and the south of Europe, but the normative vision itself is also simply implausible. As Scharpf has pointed out in a comment on these suggestions (Scharpf 2015), the further transfer of essential powers to the Union would, in order to remain democratic, have to be embedded in democratic processes and go hand in hand with profound institutional transformations. Such changes would not only have to transform Union institutions but reach into the institutional infrastructures and fabric of European societies which are inextricably intertwined with the political order of constitutional democracies. For this reason, the persistent diversity of Europe is not only a factual obstacle, but gives rise to normative objections against federal or quasi-federal visions. The varieties of European capitalism and social models are the result of historical processes, often bitter contestation, the formation of preferences and their evaluation, which cannot be undone.

None of the authors believes that the above requires a return to a world where there are nation states enjoying only Westphalian style relations. Notwithstanding these difficulties, the European Union and European integration provide the possibility for realising collective goods and averting harms that could not otherwise be broached: the effective mediation of social conflicts which either transcend the nation state or are not adequately addressed by it, and the re-imagination of political community. This volume is not, therefore, about 'more or less Europe', but rather to argue that the existing trajectories and structures of European integration have become badly misaligned.

Marrying these propositions requires the costs of adjustment be considered in a much more detailed manner as a counterweight to the gains of integration. These include both transaction costs and the potential of the effects on diverse political economies, welfare systems, democratic processes, styles of public policy and local identities. Furthermore, this assessment must take account of European integration not affecting national territories equally with the gains, risks and costs being distributed in uneven and unpredictable ways.

This has a number of immediate implications.

First, the justificatory language of European integration has to be changed. It cannot be centred around perceived functionally defined necessities. This is the language of There Is No Alternative (TINA) and claims that the demands of financial systems or economic spillovers necessarily require particular legal or political solutions. As mentioned earlier, functionalist logic is remorseless and open-ended in its purview. It does not easily admit other forms of reasoning or perspective, let alone give them much weight. As it promises returns which extend indefinitely into the future, it also offers a seductive allure to policies justified by it which rarely materialises, as these policies cannot operate indefinitely along functional tramlines but must inevitably engage with the messy environment surrounding them.

Secondly, there are institutional implications. European integration cannot rely on the outgrowth of the Monnet method, an ever-more powerful technocracy, to guide it. This has become not only normatively highly problematical but is unable to deal constructively with the diversity of European varieties of capitalism and social welfare. Administrative processes struggle to deal with many forms of social conflicts. They do not have the authority to resolve this. They are too easily captured by some interests and insufficiently receptive to others. Too often, they see problem-solving and managerialism as the only style of politics available.

Thirdly, integration has become too asymmetric. Integration has become highly advanced in certain policy areas, notably the single market and monetary policy, but less so in other fields. To realise or preserve the former, other policies, albeit primarily domestic in their institutional make-up, are skewed to allow this. There is a doctrinaire quality to this. Preserving the single market becomes a central imperative of domestic environmental or consumer policies just as securing a stable euro has become an imperative for domestic welfare policies, particularly in those euro-area states receiving financial support. The other dimension to this asymmetry is that the Union often does not have the tools necessary to address the problems facing it. This can lead to delay, policy failure or surreptitious 'competence creeping' when the Union is faced with this. This is seen nowhere more clearly than the crisis where the issue was addressed as one of monetary policy (preserving the euro) and public finances, when the problem was a much wider one including a heterogeneity of macro- and microeconomic issues.

Fourthly, Union legislative and administrative processes have to be much more resilient, pluralist and accessible containers for social conflicts than has hitherto been the case. The current processes are marked by inter-institutional deals, most vividly exemplified by the Trilogue: secret negotiations between the Commission and part of the national administration (be it over enforcement of EU law, transposition or meeting the demands of the Stability and Growth Pact); uneven institutional accountability and weak processes of contestation within the EU institutions. Much of this deal-making between civil servants needs to be revisited and thought given to how voice is provided to historically under-represented institutions and actors within EU processes, notably national parliaments, and these are mobilised to exercise that voice. Most central to the latter is probably the abolition of institutional monopolies over large parts of the legislative and administrative processes which foreclose pluralism and contestation, most notably those of the Commission over agenda-setting, legislative review and enforcement of EU laws and rules.

Fifthly, as products of struggle set within their own constellations of interests and perspectives, it is impossible to re-embed domestic processes and institutions at a pan-Union level, be they constitutional identities, parliamentary processes, the *Sozial Staat* or welfare state, or citizenship.

All these are central to how polities and citizens orient themselves within Europe, and to social justice and constitutional democracy within its territories. As it cannot replace these, all that the Union should do is establish and develop a respectful relationship with them. This is indeed predicated by Article 4(2) TEU which requires the Union to respect not only national identities but their 'fundamental structures, political and constitutional'. Such a respectful relationship entails that the Union must value these processes and institutions. It cannot exist where EU processes or institutions are considered in isolation without regard to their impacts on these domestic institutions and processes. It makes, for example, little sense to talk of EU citizenship without thinking of its impacts and relationship to national citizenship. Similarly, it is equally crude to analyse the democratic qualities of EU law-making without thinking how it relates to domestic law-making. If laws would have been passed by statutory instrument domestically, this is very different from where they would have been passed by an act of parliament. This respectful relationship may be coordinative, experimentalist or a form of mediated agonism in which domestic and EU processes challenge each to reconsider their positions. It cannot be one in which the Union has an a priori entitlement to trump or replace valued domestic institutions or processes.

Finally, the crisis poses a challenge for the academic study of the Union. The asymmetry and technocracy of integration have been matched in both law and political science by both a foreclosure of horizons and a methodological theologising. In political science, study of European integration in recent decades has moved away from grand questions to ever increasing specialisation and sophistication in statistical modelling. Legal scholarship analysed ever more meticulously the steadily growing body of EU law and developed ever more intricate and abstract debates on European constitutionalism and EU governance. Both disciplines were insufficiently sensitive to the fragility of the European Union project, the pressures placed on it by an unstable environment and the content of its policies. They were, consequently, conceptually unprepared for the tsunami that hit it. Furthermore, the economic, social and political crises were and remain interwoven. Combining different disciplines seemed necessary to us in order to grasp this conceptually. This cannot lead to some merger of their disciplines which could then claim some superior authority but it does allow some synthesis of the knowledge and insights different disciplines generate, and some understanding of how their disciplinary limits both enable insights but also restrict their horizons (Kratochwil 2010).

Possibilities for a new European configuration

This book does not set out a common manifesto or programme. There is too much uncertainty and contingency about the European integration and too much diversity and independence amongst our contributors. The editors believe, however, that the contributors have a shared ethos which results in all their contributions addressing a number of the structural features and (misguided) assumptions of the European integration process outlined above. For the contributors to this volume, the old mode of technocratic integration supervised by non-majoritarian institutions and aiming at an ever closer harmonisation among the EU's member states (the 'Eurocrats' dream') is empirically over and normatively unsustainable (if it ever was defensible).

It is possible to cluster the contributions into four headings.

First, a number of contributions focus on the problems posed by the asymmetric nature of the integration process. Scharpf's contribution focuses on this most starkly. If conceived as a macroeconomic regime, economic and monetary union (EMU), he observes, it is highly dysfunctional. In particular, it stripped member states of a central macroeconomic steering capacity, namely, the possibility for central banks to respond to external imbalances or internal booms and recession that occurred on their territories. For Scharpf, the dismantling of this capacity lies at the heart of the crisis. It can only be countered by strong macro- and microeconomic intervention by member states such as wage controls, increasing taxes on tradable goods, or changing the terms of credit for certain sectors. All these actions are likely to be highly contentious politically. In corollary vein, Nicolaïdis and Watson explore the implications of 'demoicracy' for EMU and how it could lead to a less divisive, more resilient and more decentred economic and monetary union. They argue that there should be complementary strengthening of domestic economic and fiscal capacities and stronger incentives for domestic institutions and private banks to internalise the risks of boom and slump cycles. The former involves strengthening domestic capacities to analyse and plan ahead as well as empowering those institutions best able to do this. The latter entails allowing states and banks to go bankrupt. Alongside this, they argue that central action has been too much framed around a creditor mentality. Instead, fiscal coordination should take place to secure appropriate levels of demand and there should be a central lender of last resort but its intervention should be more anchored around a humanitarian justification than is currently the case. Finally, Menéndez explores how monetary union has related to capital movements. He notes that EU law restricted a member state's capacity to tax mobile actors much more extensively and more intensively than is typically thought. This reduction of the tax base has made it increasingly challenging for states to secure social democracy as it has resulted in a diminishing of actors who can be taxed. This became particularly acute during the crisis. He argues that this does not warrant a compensatory EU fiscal capacity. Instead, EU law has to find ways to strengthen national fiscal capacities, by both tempering the economic freedoms to protect fiscal capacity and by providing for much stronger exchange of information between tax authorities.

There is, secondly, a concern that EU decision-making should be much more contestable and accountable than is currently the case. Colliot-Thélène observes that the Union has failed to incorporate the central elements of democratic citizenship and this has come home to roost in the crisis. Citizenship, she notes, sets up the individual as a rightful political actor, on the one hand, and provides the pre-political basis which allows individuals to trust collective institutions as providing the best possibilities for securing their freedom. Democratic citizenship has allowed trust to continue as it provides for dissensus within the public sphere whilst allowing it to take place through the shared significations of this sphere. EU citizenship secures neither trust nor dissensus but has, instead, been rather promoted, she notes, to secure better individual understandings of EU policies and, through mobility and the reallocation of risks, to remind citizens of their shortcomings. This failure did not matter when the Union's policies had limited perceived effects on daily lives. This, of course, changed with the crisis. De Wilde notes that the European Union political system has not yet come to terms with its own politicisation or the implications of crisis politics. He notes that for many years the Union was the beneficiary of crisis politics. Crises allowed policy entrepreneurs to argue the presence of limits in national capacities which could only be rectified through increasing Union power. This has now changed. As a settled and significant presence, the Union now suffers from the difficulties of incumbency. It has struggled to develop alternative narratives, in part because it has not addressed its own politicisation and the wide number of actors with conflicting narratives engaged in Union politics and in part because it still struggles with providing a plausible account of its democratic legitimacy.

Genschel and Jachtenfuchs consider how Union decision-making procedures have contributed to this, notably during the crisis. A hallmark of these procedures is that they seek to minimise conflicts and this has been central to the accretion of Union power over time. This has left the Union particularly exposed to the crisis. On the one hand, it created a blockading effect in which the requirement for consensus both restricted the adoption of possibly more effective options and led to a bias for integration by regulation rather than genuine capacity building as the former does not affect the vertical division of powers between the Union and the member states and often obscures the eventual costs of action. On the other, it led to ratcheting. Those participating in the consensus now had an interest in maintaining the Union status quo with a corollary distaste for radical reform. Bovens and Curtin address the issue of executive accountability following the crisis. They note how the crisis led to a new executive within the Union, comprised of three dominant institutions: the ECB, the Commission and the European Council. Executive power has been exercised reasonably interchangeably between these institutions. In itself, this poses certain challenges for checks and balances on executive power, but Bovens and Curtin note that a more significant challenge is that each institution is marked by different levels of accountability, with the European Council being the least accountable of the three institutions.

The third narrative within this volume is both the need for more differentiation within the Union and for thinking through more carefully the basis for this differentiation and how it is structured. Differentiation already exists. It exists most strikingly between the euro states and those states which do not want to join the euro or are unlikely to be allowed to join the euro within the foreseeable future. However, even within the euro area, there is huge differentiation in the obligations different states have to meet. These exist not simply between states subject to the memoranda of understanding and other states, but between all euro-area states. The obligations required of Germany are very different from those required of Slovenia, partly by dint of their perceived economic performance, but also their economic size. Instead, it is the conditions underpinning this differentiation which is problematical: the concern with scale and functional reasoning. One possibility, an ex ante one, is suggested by Majone. Integration should be based around 'club goods' in which different associations of states club together for particular tasks. Differentiation would thus be the norm with, in his view, participation by all states only occurring where there is evidence of clear benefits for all and popular support in all member states. Grimm suggests an ex post approach. He notes that EU law acts as a constitutional constraint on national action which both limits choices and serves to depoliticise whole fields of activity on the grounds that they are authoritatively determined by EU law. If the constraining qualities of EU law are constitutional in force, it is difficult, he notes, to argue that much of this law is constitutional in terms of its substantive qualities. He thus argues that the primacy of EU law should be confined to those EU laws, notably Treaty provisions, which have those qualities with states free to derogate from other EU laws (see also Grimm 2015). Chalmers has argued elsewhere that, if procedures were put in place which would allow states to override EU law in defined circumstances which would both limit free-riding and allow the citizens of other member states to express their views on national choices that would affect them, this would allow the Union to be more generally responsive, more tailored to local choices, and would better secure the position of national parliaments within the European Union (Chalmers 2013).

The final theme within this volume is that of relationality, namely, how EU law and government relate to domestic institutions, processes and symbols. Once again, the presence of such a relationship is not in doubt. However, it is dominated by too much hierarchy (EU law over national law) and mistrust (dependence on national administrations to secure EU goals). This leads to an under-valorisation of these domestic phenomena, particularly as the Union has no substitutes for them. Joerges points, therefore, both to the ubiquity of social conflicts, and to the fact that they are embedded in domestic social processes which do not allow the 'economic' or the 'political' to be easily disentangled from these processes. In the light of this, EU law has a number of roles. It must acknowledge which conflicts can simply not be resolved by law. It can allocate conflicts to be decided by particular institutions, such as parliaments, be these European or national. Finally, it can require resolution of these conflicts to be done in an open manner which fully take account of interests not represented within the territory. In similar vein, Chalmers notes how the crisis transformed domestic constitutional settlements. It subjected these to two forms of logics. A regulatory one required the constitutional settlement to be instrumentalised and aligned to securing a public good, be it a balanced economy or budget. The other logic was that of the bond, which set out an (imagined) ethical imperative for the constitutional settlement to repay a debt which restored an imaginary status quo. These two logics had such powerful effects on domestic notions of sovereignty, parliamentary powers and citizenship that it has led, he notes, to a Europeanised resistance by both national parliaments and constitutional courts. Rooted in domestic settlements but responding to European events and with an eye to the actions of counterparts in other states, this resistance is establishing a new language, albeit inchoate and disorganised, of parliamentary contestation and citizenship.

References

Bickerton, C., Hodson, D., and Puetter, U. (eds) (2015) *The New Intergovernmentalism: States and Supranational Actors in the Post-Maastricht Era*, Oxford: Oxford University Press.

Borghetto, E., and Mäder, L. (2014) 'EU Law Revisions and Legislative Drift', *European Union Politics*, 15(2), 171–91.

Börzel, T. A. (2005) 'Mind the Gap! European Integration between Level and Scope', *Journal of European Public Policy*, 12(2), 217–36.

Buiter, W., and Rahbari, E. (2012), 'The European Central Bank as Lender of Last Resort for Sovereigns in the Eurozone', *Journal of Common Market Studies*, 50(S2), 6–35.

Chalmers, D. (2012), 'The European Redistributive State and a European Law of Struggle', *European Law Journal*, 18(5), 667–93.

(2013), *Democratic Self-Government in Europe*, London: Policy Network.

Chalmers, D., and Chaves, M. (2014) 'EU Law-Making and the State of European Democratic Agency', in O. Cramme and S. Hobolt (eds), *Democratic Politics in a European Union under Stress*, Oxford: Oxford University Press, 155–80.

Chiti, C., and Texeira, P. (2013) 'The Constitutional Implications of the European Responses to the Financial and Public Debt Crisis', *Common Market Law Review*, 50(3), 683–708.

Coser, L. (1956) *The Functions of Social Conflict: An Examination of the Concept of Social Conflict and its Use in Empirical Sociological Research*, New York: Free Press.

Dawson, M., and de Witte, F. (2013) 'Constitutional Balance in the EU after the Euro Crisis' *Modern Law Review*, 76(5), 817–44.

De Grauwe, P. (2013) *Design Failures in the Eurozone: Can they be Fixed?* London: London School of Economics and Political Science. http://eprints.lse.ac.uk/53191/.

Dehousse, R. (ed.) (2011) *The 'Community Method': Obstinate or Obsolete?* Basingstoke: Palgrave Macmillan.

Eichengreen, B. (2012) 'European Monetary Integration with Benefit of Hindsight', *Journal of Common Market Studies*, 50(S1), 123–36.

Esping-Andersen, G. (1990) *The Three Worlds of Welfare Capitalism*, Cambridge: Polity.

European Central Bank (2012) 'Technical Features of Outright Monetary Transactions', press release of 6 September 2012.

European Commission (2009) 'Impact Assessment Guidelines', SEC (2009) 92.

(2012a) 'A Roadmap towards a Banking Union', COM (2012) 510.

(2012b) 'A Blueprint for a Deep and Genuine Economic and Monetary Union Launching a European Debate', COM (2012) 777 final/23.

Falkner, G. (ed.) (2011) *The EU's Decision Traps: Comparing Policies*, Oxford: Oxford University Press.

Genschel, P., and Jachtenfuchs, M. (eds) (2014) *Beyond the Regulatory Polity? The European Integration of Core State Powers*, Oxford: Oxford University Press.

(2016) 'More Integration, Less Federation? The European Integration of Core State Powers', *Journal of European Public Policy* (forthcoming).

Grimm, D. (2015) 'The Democratic Costs of Constitutionalization: The European Case', *European Law Journal*, 21(4), 460–73.

Haas, E. (1964) 'Technocracy, Pluralism and the New Europe', in S. Graubard (ed.), *A New Europe?*, Boston: Houghton Mifflin, 62–88.

Habermas, J. (2015) 'Democracy in Europe: Why the Development of the EU into a Transnational Democracy is Necessary and How it is Possible, *European Law Journal*, 21(4), 546–57.

Hall, P. A. (2014) 'Varieties of Capitalism and the Euro Crisis', *West European Politics*, 37(6), 1223–43.

Hall, P. A., and Soskice, D. (eds) (2001) *Varieties Of Capitalism: The Institutional Foundations of Comparative Advantage*, Oxford: Oxford University Press.

Herdegen, M. (1998) 'Price Stability and Budgetary Restraints in the Economic and Monetary Union: The Law as Guardian of Economic Wisdom', *Common Market Law Review*, 35(1), 9–32.

Héritier, A., Mingers, S., and Knill, C. (1996) *Ringing the Changes in Europe: Regulatory Competition and the Transformation of the State – Britain, France, Germany*, Berlin and New York: de Gruyter.

Hix, S. (2007) 'The European Union as a Polity (I)', in K. E. Jørgensen, M. Pollack and B. Rosamond (eds), *Handbook of European Union Politics*, London: Sage, 141–58.

Hix, S., and Høyland, B. (2011) *The Political System of the European Union*, 5th edn, Basingstoke: Palgrave Macmillan.

Isin, E. (2013) 'Claiming European Citizenship', in E. Isin and M. Saward (eds), *Enacting European Citizenship*, Cambridge: Cambridge University Press, 19–46.

Iversen, T., and Soskice, D. (2013) '*A Structural-Institutional Explanation of the Eurozone Crisis*', Cambridge, MA: Harvard University, Department of Government.

Joerges, C. (2010) 'Integration through Conflicts Law: On the Defence of the European Project by Means of Alternative Conceptualisation of Legal Constitutionalisation', in R. Nickel (ed.), *Conflict of Laws and Laws of Conflict in Europe and Beyond: Patterns of Supranational and Transnational Juridification*, Antwerp: Intersentia, 377–400.

(2014a) 'Europe's Economic Constitution in Crisis and the Emergence of a New Constitutional Constellation', *German Law Journal*, 15(5), 985–1028.

(2014b) 'Brother, Can you Paradigm?', *International Journal of Constitutional Law*, 12(3), 769–85.

Keohane, R., and Nye, J. (1977) *Power and Interdependence: World Politics in Transition*, Boston: Little Brown & Co.

Kratochwil, F. (2010), 'How Il(liberal is the Liberal Theory of Law? Some Critical Remarks on Slaughter's Approach', *Comparative Sociology*, 9(1), 120–45.

Lavenex, S. (2014), 'The Power of Functionalist Extension: How EU Rules Travel', *Journal of European Public Policy*, 21(6), 885–903.

Lowi, T. (1972) 'Four Systems of Policy, Politics, and Choice', *Public Administration Review*, 32(4), 298–310.

Majone, G. (2005) *Dilemmas of European Integration: The Ambiguities and Pitfalls of Integration by Stealth*, Oxford: Oxford University Press.

(2014) *Rethinking the Union of Europe Post-Crisis: Has Integration Gone Too Far?* Cambridge: Cambridge University Press.

Moravcsik, A. (2002) 'In Defence of the "Democratic Deficit": Reassessing Legitimacy in the European Union', *Journal of Common Market Studies*, 40(4), 603–24.

Peers, S. (2013) 'Towards a New Form of EU Law? The Use of EU Institutions in Treaties between Member States', *European Constitutional Law Review*, 9(1), 37–72.

Polanyi, K. (1937) *Europe To-Day*, London: Worker's Educational Trade Union Committee.

Rodrik, D. (2011) *The Globalization Paradox: Democracy and the Future of the World Economy*, New York and London: Norton.

(2014) 'The Future of European Democracy', Princeton: Princeton Institute for Advanced Study. www.sss.ias.edu/files/pdfs/Rodrik/Commentary/Future-of-Democracy-in-Europe.pdf 1.

(2015) 'Reforming Greek Reform', *Social Europe Journal*, 16 February 2015. www.socialeurope.eu/2015/02/greek-reform/.

Scharpf, F. W. (1988) 'The Joint-decision Trap: Lessons from German Federalism and European Integration', *Public Administration*, 66(3), 239–87.

(1999) *Governing in Europe: Effective and Democratic?* Oxford: Oxford University Press.

(2015) 'Das Dilemma der supranationalen Demokratie in Europa' *Leviathan*, 43(1), 12–28.

Schelkle, W. (2014) 'Fiscal Integration by Default', in P. Genschel and M. Jachtenfuchs (eds), *Beyond the Regulatory Polity? The European Integration of Core State Powers*, Oxford: Oxford University Press, 105–23.

Schimmelfennig, F. (2014) 'European Integration in the Euro Crisis: The Limits of Postfunctionalism', *Journal of European Integration*, 36(3), 321–37.

Scott, J. (2014) 'Extraterritoriality and Territorial Extension in EU Law', *American Journal of Comparative Law*, 62(1), 87–126.

Tsebelis, G., and Garrett, G. (2001) 'The Institutional Foundations of Intergovernmentalism and Supranationalism in the European Union', *International Organization*, 55(2), 357–90.

Tuori, K., and Tuori, K. (2014) *The Eurozone Crisis: A Constitutional Analysis*, Cambridge: Cambridge University Press.

Wilkinson, M. (2015) 'Authoritarian Liberalism in the European Constitutional Imagination: Second Time as Farce?', *European Law Journal*, 21(3), 313–39.

Wilsher, D. (2013) 'Law and the Financial Crisis: Searching for Europe's New Gold Standard', *European Law Journal*, 20(2), 241–83.

2

The costs of non-disintegration: the case of the European Monetary Union

FRITZ W. SCHARPF

The efforts to rescue the euro have entered their fourth year without relieving market pressures on the sovereign debt of euro states. At the same time, the economic and social crises have deepened, and democratic processes have been suspended in some of the debtor states, whereas public resentment against the ever growing financial risks associated with the rescue programs is rising in creditor states. In fact, the public in Greece and Spain, and perhaps in Portugal and Ireland as well, is up in protest against retrenchment programs that are perceived as German 'dictates', while politicians and media in Germany are voicing their contempt for lazy southerners and their corrupt bureaucracies.

Remarkably, however, none of the protests and criticisms seems to demand the disintegration of the European Monetary Union (EMU). Instead, political debates focus either on limited modifications of the present rescue strategies or on solutions that would greatly deepen European integration, moving from the monetary to a fiscal union and, ultimately, to the political union of a United States of Europe. The idea that monetary integration might have gone too far, and that disintegration would be the best possible response to prevent economic and political crises, is not on the public let alone the political agenda anywhere in Europe (with the possible exception of the United Kingdom). Why that should be so might suggest three different, but not mutually incompatible, explanations:

(1) The monetary union is seen as an achievement of European integration that must be defended at all costs.
(2) In spite of its problems, the monetary union is still seen as an improvement over the previous conditions of the European political economy.
(3) Even if creating the monetary union should now be seen as a mistake, the potential costs of its disintegration are seen to outweigh the potential benefits.

The first of these arguments is derived from a fundamentally normative position according to which 'more Europe' must be lexicographically preferred to 'less Europe'. The second and the third arguments are open to empirical and theoretical challenges. Here, I will mainly challenge the second of these arguments, and I will also suggest an approach to discussions of the third argument.

What was lost: macroeconomic steering according to the Bundesbank model

After the Great Depression and the Second World War, and in competition with the central planning regimes of state socialism, liberal democracies had learned to protect themselves against the recurrent crises of capitalist economies through strategies of 'global steering' that avoided the need for state interventions in the market at the micro level. The international framework was provided by the Bretton-Woods regime which pegged national currencies to the gold-backed US dollar, which also became the main reserve currency of the world. At the national level, most Western industrial economies adopted Keynesian practices of managing aggregate demand through the coordinated use of monetary, fiscal and wage policies. And during the early post-war decades, they did succeed, by and large, in dampening booms and recessions and in avoiding the return of mass unemployment as well as rampant inflation. In the late 1960s, however, the Bretton-Woods regime was undermined by rising inflation when the USA expanded the world money supply by printing dollars to finance the Vietnam War. And it was replaced by floating exchange rates in 1972 when the USA ended its commitment to sell gold at a fixed dollar price.

In the Federal Republic of Germany, whose export-oriented industry had benefited from an undervalued Deutschmark during most of the Bretton-Woods period, Keynesian strategies were only introduced in 1966. They succeeded brilliantly in overcoming the first post-war recession through a 'concerted action' which combined expansionary fiscal policy, accommodating monetary policy and union wage restraint. But when inflationary pressures began to rise in the early 1970s, the Bundesbank ended its half-hearted commitment to Keynesian concertation which had required negotiated coordination between the bank, the government and the unions. In a bold move in the face of the first oil-price crisis, it committed itself to a quasi-monetarist strategy that asserted the priority of stability-oriented monetary policy. In game-theoretic terms, this would fundamentally transform macroeconomic coordination from a simultaneous cooperative game into a sequential non-cooperative game in which the bank would have first-mover advantages (Scharpf 1987).

The strategy succeeded through force and persuasion. While unemployment increased steeply, the extremely restrictive monetary policy of 1973/74 did indeed reverse the rise of inflation. But the bank also promised that, once rampant inflation was under control, it would annually pre-announce growth rates of the money supply that would correspond to the real growth potential of the West German economy. Hence, if public-sector budgets would be roughly balanced over the business cycle and if wage increases were guided by gains in productivity, its monetary policy would maximize inflation-free economic growth and employment. In other words, the Bundesbank model was monetarist in its insistence on price stability and its denial of a trade-off between inflation and unemployment. But it was also Keynesian in its belief that the macroeconomic management of aggregate demand has a responsibility for growth and employment (rather than relying on flexible wages and prices to clear all markets). As a consequence, macroeconomic coordination continued to matter – except that it was now to be conducted asymmetrically, with monetary policy assuming the leading role.

And since governments and unions had learned to respect both the Bundesbank's stability-oriented determination and the effectiveness of monetary restraint, the model worked reasonably well in Germany during the 1970s and 1980s – better at any rate than Keynesian strategies had worked in the United Kingdom and most European countries – or in the USA in the 1970s, and also better than the radical monetarism of Thatcher and Reagan was working during the 1980s. But, like Keynesian concertation, which had been defeated by the first oil-price crisis, the Bundesbank model was also vulnerable to the effects of increasing international capital mobility. Thus the bank's effective stability policy resulted in a steady rise of the floating Deutschmark – which eliminated the advantages of an undervalued currency that German industry had enjoyed under the Bretton-Woods regime. Worse yet, when the US Federal Reserve dramatically raised dollar interest rates to defeat US inflation after the second oil-price crisis, the Bundesbank could only avoid the inflationary effects of a massive devaluation by raising its own discount rate to a level that pushed the German economy into a recession (which spelled the end of Helmut Schmidt's chancellorship). By and large, however, Germany was doing reasonably well under the monetarist regime defined by the Bundesbank in comparison to how well its neighbors were doing.

The imperfect compromises of the EMS

But, as a consequence of successful stabilization, the Deutschmark was floating upwards whereas the exchange rates of other European currencies were falling – which was seen as a problem on both sides. Hence, when Helmut Schmidt and Giscard d'Estaing created the European Monetary System (EMS) in 1979, joining it was seen as an attractive opportunity for neighboring countries to 'borrow German stability'. In the EMS, currencies were pegged to the European Currency Unit (ECU), an artificial basket currency in which the Deutschmark had the greatest weight. National banks were obliged to use their policy instruments to maintain exchange rates within agreed-upon bandwidths. If lower or upper limits were approached, interventions in currency markets were expected. Beyond that, bandwidths could be adjusted or exchange rates modified by agreement.

On average, the EMS achieved its purpose of dampening exchange-rate fluctuations and increasing price stability in Western Europe. But not all governments and unions were equally able and willing to play the macroeconomic coordination game according to the rules the Bundesbank had defined for Germany. So inflation rates continued to differ; from time to time, some currencies had to be devalued; and the interest rates demanded by international credit markets reflected these national differences. Moreover, the Bundesbank seemed to ignore the obligations of hegemonic leadership by continuing its stability-oriented policy focused exclusively on the state of the German economy and by refusing requests to respond to problems of other currencies (Marsh 2011).

The Padoa-Schioppa report (1987) has (rightly) urged that coordination in the EMS should and could be improved. But that is not meant to suggest that there could be perfect solutions when exchange rates among economies with differing price and wage dynamics are to be stabilized under conditions of increasing international capital mobility. At the theoretical level, the basic problem is expressed by the famous 'Mundell-Fleming Trilemma' which asserts that open economies are only able to realize two of the following three policy options: capital mobility, fixed exchange rates or autonomous monetary policy. As the Bundesbank model assigns primary responsibility for the macroeconomic management of economies to monetary policy, the theoretical Trilemma suggests that coordination in the EMS confronts national central banks with a fundamental tension: as capital mobility increases, EMS central banks are expected to keep the exchange rate within the allowable bandwidth and to ensure inflation-free growth nationally. As long as exchange-rate movements have internal causes, both commitments are not in conflict. But when the central bank must respond to external factors, its exchange-rate-oriented policy may no longer fit the state of the domestic economy, and the Bundesbank model will no longer work effectively.

In the EMS, however, the Trilemma was not strictly in force. Capital mobility was not yet perfect; exchange rates were pegged, rather than fixed; and bandwidths were initially broad enough to leave some room for maneuver. Also, central banks might defend exchange rates by direct interventions in the currency markets, rather than by the use of monetary instruments. And, in the face of unsustainable imbalances, the EMS could still adjust bandwidths and, ultimately, exchange rates.

In short, the EMS regime was reasonably, but not perfectly, effective in stabilizing exchange rates. As a consequence, national central banks also did not completely lose the capacity to practice monetary policy with a view to the conditions and the growth potential of their national economies. And while coordination could and should have been improved, the EMS regime did represent a workable compromise between conflicting goals.

But instead of improving the EMS, as the Padoa-Schioppa Report had suggested, the Delors Commission (1989) proposed to replace it by a European Monetary Union. France and other EMS governments supported the project in order to escape from the hegemony of the Bundesbank and to avoid the political and financial disadvantages of periodic devaluations. And after 1989, when it needed international support for German unification, a reluctant German government agreed as well (Van Esch 2012). But it was still able to insist that the regime of the EMU should recreate the institutional conditions of the Bundesbank model – independence from political controls and a formal commitment to the priority of price stability and, as an afterthought, legal constraints on public-sector deficits (Delors 1989; McNamara 1998; Dyson and Featherstone 1999; Jones 2002; Heipertz and Verdun 2010; Vaubel 2010). In institutional terms, all these conditions were met in ways that even exceeded their realization in Germany. In economic terms, however, the macroeconomic steering functions the model had performed in Germany were not merely nullified but perverted at the European level.

The monetary union as a dysfunctional macroeconomic regime

In the monetary union, the 'Mundell-Fleming Trilemma' is at the same time reinforced and radically transformed, and its implications are more sinister.

On the one hand, a common currency goes beyond a commitment to fixed exchange rates by completely eliminating the possibility of exchange-rate fluctuations – which will also increase capital mobility by reducing transaction costs and avoiding interest-rate differentials that reflect exchange-rate risks. At the same time, the common currency eliminates the need to match trans-border payments by a transfer of gold or currency reserves from one central bank to another. By the same token, however, it also eliminates balance-of-payments deficits as a signal of external imbalances. Thus, tourist expenditures and imports may continue to exceed export revenues without forcing the central bank to intervene.

On the other hand, however, the monetary union also eliminates the possibility that a national central bank *could* intervene either against external imbalances or against internal booms or recessions. The instruments of monetary policy and exchange rate policies are removed from national control, and they are exercised by the European Central Bank (ECB) with a view to economic conditions in the Eurozone at large, rather than in the economies of individual member states. Given the structural heterogeneity of these economies, however, the Eurozone could not, and cannot, be considered an 'optimal currency area' (Mundell 1961; Eichengreen 1990; Feldstein 1998). As a consequence, uniform ECB monetary policy aiming at average conditions will be too tight for countries with below-average inflation and growth dynamics, and it will be excessively expansionary for countries with above-average rates of inflation and economic growth.

In other words, Europeanized monetary policy, which was meant to emulate the Bundesbank model, loses precisely the macroeconomic steering capacity on which the model's economic and political success had been based in Germany. Instead of ensuring inflation-free economic growth and preventing involuntary unemployment, it would amplify existing imbalances. And instead of relieving fiscal policy and wage policy of the difficult macroeconomic functions assigned to them under Keynesianism, ECB monetary policy would dramatically increase the economic and political challenges with which governments and unions had to cope.

The warnings of (primarily American) economists were ignored by European policy makers. They acted on the theory that the euro itself would transform member economies into an optimal currency area through the equalizing effect of market integration on interest rates, prices and wages throughout the Eurozone (Issing 2002). In part, these expectations were indeed fulfilled during the euro's first decade after 1999. Eventually, however, the world-wide financial crisis following the collapse of the Lehman bank revealed not only a lack of convergence, but extreme macroeconomic imbalances that had arisen under the monetary union (Scharpf 2011).

The immediate effect of the common currency had been a dramatic convergence of nominal interest rates. As the risk of devaluation was eliminated in the currency union and ECB refinancing was available at uniform rates, the rates of long-term government bonds in all member states fell to low German levels. Moreover, as inflation in former weak-currency economies continued to be higher than in Germany, real interest rates in countries like Greece, Ireland, Italy, Portugal and Spain (the 'GIIPS countries') were even lower, falling in fact below the zero level in some years. The immediate effect was a large boost to credit-financed consumer spending – which caused a rise to imports. Its effect on the domestic economy, however, differed between the tradable and non-tradable sectors.

Where structural conditions favored the demand-driven expansion of non-tradable goods and services, the sudden availability of cheap credit stimulated rapid domestic growth and rising employment as well as rising wages and prices. This was true in the housing and real estate sectors in Ireland, Spain and Greece where credit-financed demand ultimately generated real estate bubbles that greatly contributed to the subsequent crises. For reasons that are still poorly understood, falling interest rates caused little domestic growth in Portugal and Italy where additional consumer demand had mainly increased imports.

In the tradable sectors, by contrast, the rise of imports did in fact confirm expectations of converging prices – which spelt trouble for domestic producers. As they were operating under somewhat higher inflation rates and with higher unit labor costs to begin with, the monetary union intensified import competition in their home markets. The spillover effects of wage increases in the non-tradable sectors intensified the rise of unit labor costs and the loss of competitiveness in export markets. In the aggregate, therefore, the current account deficits of GIIPS economies increased continuously during the first decade of the monetary union.

During the same period, corresponding current account surpluses increased similarly in Germany and a few other EMU member states. Since Germany had joined the euro in a period of weak economic growth and with the lowest rate of inflation, uniform ECB interest rates were too high for its economy, and real interest rates were the highest in the Eurozone. As a consequence, investment and domestic demand were depressed, unemployment rose steeply, and between 2001 and 2005 Germany was the 'sick man of Europe'. But since import demand and wages stagnated, current account surpluses increased, and since export revenues were not consumed or invested at home, they were available for seemingly risk-free investment in countries with a high demand for credit.

In other words, the monetary union had created a vicious circle in which the ever increasing deficits of GIIPS economies were financed by the ever increasing surpluses of Germany and similar economies. At the same time, the international competitiveness of deficit economies was further depressed by an increasingly overvalued real exchange rate, whereas the exports of surplus countries were subsidized by correspondingly undervalued real exchange rates (Sinn et al. 2004; Enderlein 2004).

Thus, in 2007, the last year before the international financial crisis, German exports within the Eurozone benefited from a real effective exchange rate that was undervalued at 83 percent whereas exports were penalized by an overvaluation of 123 percent in Ireland, 114 percent in Spain, 109 percent in Portugal and 104 percent in Greece.[1] In the same year, the current account surplus in Germany had reached 7.5 percent of GDP, whereas deficits amounted to 14 percent in Greece, 10 percent in Spain and Portugal, and 5 percent in Ireland.[2] Correspondingly, Germany exported capital in the amount of 8.7 percent of GDP, whereas capital imports amounted to 12.4 percent of GDP in Greece, 9.6 percent in Spain, 8.5 percent in Portugal and 6.3 percent in Ireland.[3]

EMU institutions ignore rising imbalances

Before the onset of the international financial crisis, however, the macroeconomic divergence among its member states was of no concern for the governing institutions of the monetary union. The European Central Bank was rightly proud of its success in keeping average consumer price inflation in the Eurozone even below the level that the Bundesbank had achieved in Germany. Since the real estate bubbles in Ireland and Spain were defined as 'asset-price inflation', they did not matter as long as they did not affect the consumer price index of the euro area. And the imbalances of current accounts, capital accounts and real exchange rates were, of course, no part of the ECB's mandate (De Grauwe 2009).

1 Eurostat: real effective exchange rate (deflator: unit labor costs in the total economy – 16 trading partners – euro area); Index 1999 = 100.

2 Eurostat: current account in percentage of GDP, trading partners: all countries of the world.

3 Eurostat: financial account in percentage of GDP, trading partners: all countries of the world.

For the Commission in charge of the Stability Pact, the increasing indebtedness of GIIPS economies also did not matter as it consisted exclusively or predominantly of private debt. And public-sector debt, which had fluctuated at levels between 98 percent and 107 percent of GDP in Greece and had risen to 65 percent and 68 percent in Germany and Portugal, had actually fallen to 36 percent in Spain and 25 percent in Ireland by 2007.[4] Moreover, Irish budgets had been in surplus throughout the decade, Spanish budgets since 2005, and Germany, whose deficits had exceeded the 3 percent limit between 2001 and 2005, had also achieved a small surplus in 2007. Portugal was at the 3 percent line, and only Greek budget deficits had been significantly above the allowable limit ever since its accession to the monetary union in 2001.[5] In short, the Commission could and should have intervened against Greek deficits, whereas in the other GIIPS countries public-sector budgets and debts were either unproblematic or had been reduced far below the requirements of the Stability Pact (and the German level). In other words, the euro crisis was not caused by the fiscal irresponsibility of GIIPS government, and the presently dominant view in Germany and other creditor countries that financial mismanagement in GIIPS governments caused the crisis is simply wrong.

From macroeconomic imbalances to the euro crisis and its non-solution

What happened instead is that private debt was turned into public debt everywhere when governments had to rescue their 'system relevant' banks in the international financial crisis following the Lehman bankruptcy in the autumn of 2008. The increase was particularly steep in GIIPS countries whose credit-financed economies were thrown into deep recession by the international credit squeeze, and whose banks were deeply in trouble when international interbank lending dried up. In Ireland and Spain, moreover, the banking crisis was exacerbated when the real estate bubbles burst.

It was the steep rise of public debt that caused international investors also to respond to solvency risks. In the past they had treated the bonds of all EMU member states as equally risk free after the elimination of exchange-rate risks in the currency union. Considering current account deficits and the loss of international competitiveness, rating agencies began to doubt the capacity

4 Eurostat: government consolidated gross debt in percentage of GDP.

5 Eurostat: net lending/net borrowing under the Excessive Deficit Procedure (EDP) in percentage of GDP.

of GIIPS governments to service and eventually to repay their debts. Obviously, Greece became the first target as in late 2009 the incoming government had to admit that its predecessor had under-reported the deficit. But after the first rescue package for Greece had been adopted in May of 2010, the speculative downgrading of outstanding bonds and rising risk premia on new issues spread to Ireland, Portugal and Spain as well. Moreover, the solvency of Italy and even France has also been questioned by rating agencies. This unfortunate development may be attributed to the cognitive and normative constraints under which rescue operations have been proceeding.

On the cognitive side, it mattered that financial markets had first targeted their attacks on Greece – the one country where public-sector deficits had arguably contributed to the crisis. This provided the surface plausibility to a cognitive frame, which, by reference to the Stability Pact, defined deficits as the root cause of all euro problems, and the rapid reduction of deficits and total debt as the only effective solution to the crisis. Hence, while the rescue programs provided guarantees or subsidized credits to facilitate the refinancing of existing debt, the conditionalities under which they were granted imposed ever more rigorous fiscal retrenchment on recipient governments in order to eliminate the need for new credit as quickly as possible. Under conditions of deeply depressed economies, however, cutting public expenditures, pensions, social transfers and public-sector employment and wages reduced domestic demand and economic activity even further. Thus, rising unemployment and falling tax revenues tended to increase, rather than reduce, public-sector deficits – which predictably caused new challenges by rating agencies and capital markets.

Normatively, the responses of the 'rescuers' (i.e., the European governments, the ECB and the IMF) were shaped not only by the rules of the Stability Pact, but also by the no-bail-out clause of the Maastricht Treaty and its prohibition of monetary state financing. In practice, all of these rules were fudged under the pressure of necessity. But they still had the effect of delaying effective responses, of favoring half-hearted and ineffective compromises, of legitimating 'orthodox' opposition, and of preventing a comprehensive reappraisal of the hypotheses governing the Maastricht regime. Whereas a quick and clear-cut European guarantee for Greek government debts early in 2010 might have avoided further speculative attacks on other EMU member states, speculation was in fact encouraged by continuing political debates about the binding constraints of the no-bail-out clause that delayed the Greek rescue and that served to justify conditions that would deepen the crisis of the real economy.

In political terms, the main difficulty was that the succession of rescue funds – from the EFSM for Greece to the EFSF and now to the ESM – had the character of horizontal transfers from 'creditor' to 'debtor states'. They did require ever-increasing budgetary commitments by parliaments in fiscally sound states that were publicly justified by appeals to European solidarity, even if the recipients were much 'richer' in terms of GDP per capita than the donors (e.g., in the case of Ireland versus Slovakia). Inevitably, therefore, creating rescue funds of sufficient size to deter future challenges was politically divisive and prone to create mutual resentment among the populace on both sides.

These political repercussions might have been avoided if it had not been for the even stronger normative commitment to the Maastricht Treaty's prohibition of monetary state financing. Compared to states in the Eurozone, public sector indebtedness is as high or much higher in the USA or in Japan. Nevertheless, their solvency is not challenged by international capital markets because it is known that their central banks will act as 'lenders of last resort' not only for private banks but for the state as well. Thus, speculators betting on state insolvency could only lose their money. In the EMU, by contrast, the prohibition of state financing prevents the ECB from openly performing the same function for member states. In practice, again, the rule has been fudged a bit. So the ECB has compromised its commitment to price stability by flooding European financial markets with cheap and long-term money in the hope that banks may be enticed to buy the bonds of GIIPS states at highly profitable interest rates. Moreover, the ECB President's announcement that the bank will buy bonds of crisis-affected member states on the aftermarkets is a further indicator for the new practice of indirect (and hence more expensive) state financing channeled through the banking system. If, instead, the ECB would, within the framework of its stability-oriented monetary policy, allow governments to access central bank credit directly, speculation would become pointless and the burden of interest rates on national taxpayers would be reduced. At the same time, of course, the question of how much credit a particular state should be allowed to raise would have to be settled within the European rules established by the 'Excessive Deficit Procedure' and by the new 'Fiscal Pact'. In creditor states, moreover, European solidarity would no longer have to be invoked to justify budgetary commitments to rescue funds that only serve to ensure the security and prompt servicing of highly profitable private investments in state bonds.

The social costs of non-disintegration

If the monetary union is to be maintained, the Eurozone will be confronted with economic problems of the kind Germany had to deal with after the West German Deutschmark had been introduced in the GDR in the summer of 1990. Like East German industries, the GIIPS economies have lost their competitiveness under the unitary currency. Even after three years of a deep economic crisis, the gap between real effective exchange rates in 2011 still exceeded 20 percentage points – with Germany benefiting from an undervaluation at 89 per cent of parity, while the Greek and Irish economies suffered from an overvaluation of 112 per cent. If nominal devaluation is ruled out, the competitiveness of GIIPS economies can only be restored through a real devaluation that drastically reduces unit labor costs. In theory, that could be achieved through productivity-oriented investments. In practical terms, however, these cannot be undertaken without prospects of above-average profitability, requiring not only tax concessions but also a drastic reduction of nominal wages. And while governments may be able to impose wage cuts in the public sector and to reduce minimal wages, they have little influence on wage-setting in the traded sectors. At the same time, unions may be capable of practicing voluntary wage moderation, as was true in Germany during its recession after 2001, but they cannot be expected to agree to massive nominal wage cuts.

Hence, if real devaluation is to be achieved at all, it is likely to be the effect of market forces under the pressure of mass unemployment. This is, in fact, already happening, and the unit labor costs, current account deficits and real exchange rates of GIIPS economies have indeed come down over the last four years. But much more would be needed, and, before it is achieved, growth-oriented public investment and even subsidized private investment will not be able to stimulate sustained economic growth. Six decades of subsidizing the Italian Mezzogiorno and more than two decades of massive subsidies to East Germany have demonstrated the immense obstacles that would have to be overcome.

At the same time, however, in Greece and Spain unemployment has reached 25 percent, and youth unemployment has risen to 50 percent. As in East Germany after 1990, therefore, social catastrophes and political explosions can only be avoided through massive transfers from the more prosperous parts of the monetary union. They will have to stabilize the social-welfare and education systems of countries which, under the constraints of a unitary currency, are condemned to long periods of economic decline combined with the out-migration of their most skilled and mobile workforce. In other words, one should expect major social costs of non-disintegration. But a high price will also have to be paid in terms of the politico-economic effectiveness and legitimacy of economic governance.

Economic governance when macroeconomic policies are disabled

If the monetary union is to be maintained, its future system of economic governance ought to be able to prevent the return of the dynamic imbalances that uniform ECB monetary policy had generated before the crisis. In assessing the challenge, however, one should assume that the attempt to mold all European political economies on the German template will not succeed in the near future. In other words, the Eurozone will not soon become an 'optimal currency area'. This also implies that uniform ECB monetary policy must still respond to average Eurozone conditions, and that it will generate dysfunctional monetary impulses for economies with above-average and below-average rates of economic growth and inflation. In assessing the policy options that might work under these conditions, it seems useful to consider, historically or counterfactually, what Germany and the GIIPS countries did or could have done to deal with the imbalances arising in the first decade of the monetary union.

Germany: historical experiences

In the German recession in the years 2001 to 2005, the usual instruments for the macroeconomic management of aggregate demand were disabled. Monetary reflation was unavailable and fiscal reflation was ruled out by the Stability Pact, whose deficit ceiling was violated by the mere operation of 'automatic stabilizers' as unemployment was rising to 11 percent. Under these constraints, policy makers could only turn to supply-side strategies. German industrial unions practiced wage restraint to protect existing jobs in the export sectors. At the same time, the government reduced corporation taxes, liberalized employment-protection rules and reduced the reservation wages of unemployment insurance (Trampusch 2009; Hassel and Schiller 2010). As a consequence, the decline of domestic consumption was associated with rising export surpluses, and unemployment was reduced by the rapid expansion of low-wage, part-time and temporary employment. At the same time, however, social inequality increased more in Germany than in all OECD countries (OECD 2011).

GIIPS countries: counterfactual questions

Focusing on Spain as a paradigmatic case, what should the government have done if it had realized, perhaps in 2005, that the real exchange rate was overvalued and the current accounts deficit was deepening, that economic growth had come to depend on capital imports, and that the housing market was overheating? Assuming that these indicators had been perceived as a serious problem (even though inflation was moderate, and employment and real wages were increasing), monetary restraint would surely have been the preferred countermeasure. Instead, monetary reflation (resulting in real interest rates of zero percent) was so strong that it also overpowered the government's fiscal restraint (resulting in a balanced budget and rapidly falling public-sector debt). Moreover, any attempt to reduce the inflow of foreign capital or the rise of imports would have violated the internal market rules of the EU Treaty.

As had been true in Germany, therefore, the instruments of macroeconomic demand management were no longer available in Spain. Instead, it is now suggested that the Spanish government ought to have used regulations to reduce the attractiveness of credit-financed real estate purchases and housing construction. It could also have raised the value-added tax on traded goods to reduce imports, and it might have tried to impose statutory wage controls to impede the rise of unit labor costs in the traded sectors. With sufficiently imaginative hindsight, other measures could surely be suggested. What they all would have in common, however, is a radical turn in economic governance – away from the liberal paradigm of macroeconomic 'global steering' and toward *dirigiste* strategies of potentially very intrusive state interventions in market transactions at the micro or meso levels of the economy.

The need for interventionist economic governance

This conclusion can be generalized for both constellations: when monetary impulses become dysfunctional and other macroeconomic instruments are disabled, governments need to resort to micro- and meso-economic intervention. Leaving matters to the market would not be a useful response. If money is cheap, rational economic actors will go into debt and generate bubble economies; and if monetary impulses are excessively restrictive, rational actors will further reduce consumption and investment. Under both conditions, market responses will intensify, rather than correct imbalances. If the monetary union is to be maintained, in other words, economic governance must become considerably more active and interventionist at the micro and meso levels than had been envisaged in both the Keynesian and the Monetarist paradigms of macroeconomic steering of capitalist economies.

Political salience

In politico-economic terms, one should also expect a rise of political salience. The strategies of 'global steering' had achieved their effects by influencing the parameters of aggregate demand indirectly and with low political visibility. By contrast, the supply-side policies adopted to overcome the German recession had direct and highly visible impacts on the incomes, the jobs and the working conditions of millions of individuals. And the same would have been true if the Spanish government had tried to prevent the real estate boom, through regulations of housing credit, selective tax increases and wage controls. In Germany, Schröder's red-green government had to face mass protests and the rise of a leftwing opposition party – and it was defeated at the next election. In other words, the adoption and implementation of the micro and meso interventions that will be required by economic governance in the monetary union will have very high political salience, and they will be difficult to adopt and implement in liberal democracies.

The new European regime of economic governance

It is not obvious that European policy makers committed to rescuing the euro are fully aware of these implications. But they were indeed understood by the European Commission when it launched the 'Six Pack' regulations that were adopted – practically without public attention – by Council and Parliament at the end of 2011. Under the 'Regulation on the Prevention and Correction of Macroeconomic Imbalances' (EU 1176/2011), the Commission defines a 'Scoreboard' of ten potential indicators of imbalances, ranging from current account balances, effective exchange rates and unit labor costs to deflated house prices, private sector debts and unemployment rates. These statistical indicators are associated with upper and lower thresholds, which, if they are overstepped, will trigger more thorough economic analyses that may lead to the identification of 'excessive imbalances' that should be corrected. At that point, the Commission will issue 'recommendations' for corrective action which may employ a full range of national legislative and administrative competences. If these are not complied with by the governments addressed, the Commission will impose annual fines amounting to 0.1 percent of GDP (EU 1174/2011).

The new regime is remarkable for two reasons. It deals with macroeconomic imbalances, but there is no reference to the usual instruments of macroeconomic policy: monetary policy and fiscal policy at the European level are totally ignored, and national fiscal policy remains firmly constrained not only by the parallel tightening of the 'Excessive Deficit Procedure' but also by the new 'Fiscal Compact'. In other words, imbalances are to be prevented through the use of national, rather than European policy instruments, and member states will have no access to the usual instruments of macroeconomic policy. The Commission also realizes that practically all of the market imbalances listed on its 'Scoreboard' are not under the direct control of the state. And the text of the regulation does not even try to specify the policy instruments that governments are supposed to use in order to correct them. But once such imbalances have been identified by the Commission, the regulation does provide that:

> recommendations [...] should be addressed to the Member State concerned to provide guidance on appropriate policy responses. The policy response of the Member State should use all available policy instruments under the control of public authorities. (EU 1176/2011 at § 20)

In other words, the Commission will be free to specify any and all national measures which it may consider useful, without any regard to the constitutional allocation of European and national competences in the EU Treaty.

Formally, of course, these 'recommendations' have to be accepted, adopted and implemented by national governments. But the 'Excessive Imbalance Procedure', like the 'Excessive Deficit Procedure' or the 'Stability Pact' before it, will not trust national democratic governments to act in their economic self-interest. Thus, the recommendations will be backed by sanctions that are supposed to be severe enough to overcome political opposition at the national level. And the distrust of democratic politics extends to the European level as well. Recommendations and sanctions are formally treated as Council decisions, but they are proposed by the Commission and will become effective unless they are opposed by a qualified majority of the Council (in which the governments affected have no vote). And in the eyes of the European Parliament, even this minimal involvement of democratically accountable governments was too much: the European Parliament would have preferred the automatic effectiveness of Commission proposals.

The costs of over-integration, of non-disintegration and of disintegration

The monetary union has replaced workable national systems of macroeconomic governance that were coordinated in the EMS with a unitary currency and centralized monetary policy. Under conditions of a non-optimal currency area, centralized monetary impulses have been economically dysfunctional, generating dynamically increasing external imbalances among economies in the Eurozone. These imbalances have greatly increased the vulnerability of deficit countries to the international financial crisis of 2008 and its ensuing aftermath. As a consequence, GIIPS economies were particularly hard hit by the international credit squeeze – which caused a deep recession combined with a banking crisis that had the effect of transforming excessive private indebtedness into excessive public debt which then led international capital markets to challenge the solvency of debtor states.

The economic and social costs of economic over-integration

It is the last of these problems that so far has been addressed by the European 'rescue' operations – and it is being addressed in ways which are difficult for the donor states as well as for the recipient states. The former had to come up with politically controversial and financially costly budgetary commitments to create rescue funds whose size never seemed big enough to ensure the continuing availability of credit for recipient governments. But the less onerous option of enabling the ECB to act as a 'lender of last resort' for EMU member states was and still is ruled out by normative convictions.

For the recipient countries, a major problem was created by the asymmetry of the lender–borrower constellation in which they were not even treated as 'deserving poor'. Under the dominant frame defined by lender governments and publics, it was their excessive deficit spending (rather than the structural defects of the monetary union) that had caused a euro crisis, which in turn threatened all member states. Hence, if recipient countries were suffering from this harsh lender–borrower constellation, they had only themselves (or their previous governments) to blame. And if excessive deficits were the cause, the just punishment had to be tightly controlled requirements of fiscal retrenchment that could not be relaxed, even if such policy might deepen the economic misery. In short, the economic (and political) discourse around present rescue programs does not focus on European economic crises as induced by the imbalances created by the monetary union. Thus, the present rescue programs are in fact continuing to increase the economic and social costs of monetary integration.

The politico-economic costs of non-disintegration

At least the European Commission has in the meantime come to see not only public-sector deficits but also the rise of macroeconomic imbalances as proximate causes of the euro crisis. But instead of addressing the dysfunctional effects of a unitary currency and monetary centralization in a non-optimal currency area, present reforms attempt to impose centralized controls on the full range of national policies. The hope is that these might, in some way, counteract the destabilizing monetary impulses of the EMU regime. Whether these attempts have a chance of succeeding in economic terms is as yet uncertain. What is certain is that centralized European controls on national policies will have two structural impacts on the politico-economic regimes of economic governance.

On the one hand, macroeconomic regimes that did manipulate aggregate demand will be replaced with much more intrusive interventions at the micro and meso levels of market economies. Their targets must be wage-setting institutions, processes and outcomes as well as patterns of investment, consumption and private credit. As a consequence, the states must become much more heavily involved in the detailed operation of market economies – which might well appear as an extreme example of the 'pretense of knowledge' of economic policy makers that Hayek had ridiculed in his Nobel lecture (Von Hayek 1974).

On the other hand, interventions at the micro and meso levels of economies are likely to have high political salience. Such interventions are more likely to activate national publics than would be true of the macroeconomic policy choices they are supposed to replace. Thus, extremely restrictive Bundesbank policies never provoked public protests in Germany, while political mobilization against its 'Agenda 2010' caused the defeat of the red-green government in 2005. In other words, democratically responsive governments may lack the capacity to enact the supply-side and regulatory policies that the Commission considers necessary in order to correct and prevent macroeconomic imbalances. In the context of rescue operations, therefore, the 'memorandum of understanding' defined by the Commission and controlled by the 'Troika' had completely displaced political processes in the debtor states. And in the context of the 'Excessive Deficit' and 'Excessive Imbalance Procedures', policy choices are again to be determined by the European Commission, and national compliance is supposed to be ensured through a depoliticized sanctioning regime.

These European policy choices cannot be democratically legitimated. By their nature, they cannot be bound by general rules that might be defined by European legislation. They must be discretionary, contingent on highly variable conditions and dependent on non-verifiable interpretations and intuition as is true of most choices of national economic policy. In a democracy, their only base of legitimacy is that of a democratically accountable government willing to risk its political survival on its considered choices. That, definitely, is not the legitimacy base of the European Commission.

That is probably the reason why recommendations and sanctions are formally ascribed to the Council, even though reverse-qualified majority rules are supposed to disable political interventions. But that will not help. Governments in Council are democratically legitimated to speak and to accept obligations and general rules for their own state. But the chain linking their votes to their own constituencies does not legitimate governments to impose discretionary decisions on another member state that would intervene deeply in the institutional, social and economic fabric of its society.

In other words, if the euro is maintained, the economic governance regime needed to save it will entail three types of costs of 'non-disintegration': (1) macroeconomic policy will be replaced by a more intrusive regime of state intervention at the meso and micro levels of market economies; (2) the attempt of the European Commission to centralize control over these interventions will reduce their economic effectiveness; and (3) democratic legitimacy in Europe will be reduced as the policy choices of democratically accountable national governments are subjected to the directives of non-accountable bureaucrats whose claim to superior expertise must be discounted by their 'pretense of knowledge' regarding local conditions and effects.

The costs of disintegration

In present political discourses, these costs of non-disintegration are ignored – perhaps not out of sheer ignorance but because of the belief that the costs of disintegration would be quasi infinite in their magnitude.

The fear is that a retreat from the monetary union would not only trigger a world-wide financial and economic crisis, a collapse of the European banking system and a rise of the German exchange rate with catastrophic job losses in the export industries, but that it will also spell the end of European integration. If all that is believed, then defending the euro at all costs may indeed appear '*alternativlos*'. Thus any attempt to initiate a political debate about the costs of defending the euro would need to challenge the inchoate beliefs about the apocalyptic consequences of disintegration.

In such debates, it would probably not be enough to point to countries from Sweden to Canada, Australia, New Zealand or Japan that are not sacrificing their democratic legitimacy in order to cope with the challenges of globalized capitalism. It would also be necessary to present plausible scenarios of how the economic over-integration of the monetary union could be reduced, and national macroeconomic control could be restored without incurring prohibitive costs of disintegration.

Unfortunately, the unconditional political and ideological commitment to defending the euro has so far prevented the development of such scenarios or serious analyses of exit options. They also cannot be provided here, even though I consider them urgently needed. But I would suggest that the exit costs would be maximized by an uncontrolled unraveling of the monetary union, triggered perhaps by an economic or political collapse in Greece and with panic reactions spreading, domino style, to more and more of the member states. By contrast, an agreed-upon, well-planned and orderly return from the monetary union to an improved European Monetary System would probably not entail the catastrophic costs envisaged in the presently dominant beliefs. Future historians might come to see the unwillingness even to consider such scenarios as the main deficiency of present policy discussions.

References

De Grauwe, P. (2009) *Economics of Monetary Union*, 8th edn, Oxford: Oxford University Press.

Delors, J. (1989) *Report on Economic and Monetary Union in the European Community*, Brussels: European Council.

Dyson, K., and Featherstone, K. (1999) *The Road to Maastricht: Negotiating Economic and Monetary Union*, Oxford: Oxford University Press.

Eichengreen, B. (1990) 'Is Europe an Optimal Currency Area?', CEPR Discussion Paper, 478, London.

Enderlein, H. (2004) *Nationale Wirtschaftspolitik in der europäischen Währungsunion*, Frankfurt: Campus.

Feldstein, M. (1998) 'The Political Economy of the European Economic and Monetary Union: Political Sources of an Economic Liability', NBER Working Paper 6150, Cambridge, MA.

Hassel, A., and Schiller, C. (2010) *Der Fall Hartz IV: Wie es zur Agenda 2010 kam und wie es weitergeht*, Frankfurt: Campus.

Heipertz, M., and Verdun, A. (2010) *Ruling Europe: The Politics of the Stability and Growth Pact*, Cambridge: Cambridge University Press.

Issing, O. (2002) 'On Macroeconomic Policy Coordination in EMU', *Journal of Common Market Studies*, 40(2), 345–58.

Jones, E. (2002) *The Politics of Economic and Monetary Union: Integration and Idiosyncracy*, Lanham, MD: Rowman & Littlefield.

McNamara, K. (1998) *The Currency of Ideas: Monetary Politics in the European Union*, Ithaca, NY: Cornell University Press.

Marsh, D. (2011) *The Euro: The Battle for the New Global Currency*, 3rd edn, New Haven, CT: Yale University Press.

Mundell, R. (1961) 'A Theory of Optimal Currency Areas', *American Economic Review*, 51(4), 657–65.

OECD (2011) *An Overview of Growing Income Inequalities in OECD Countries: Main Findings*. www.oecd.org/dataoecd/40/12/49499779.pdf.

Padoa-Schioppa, T. (1987) *Efficiency, Stability and Equity: A Strategy for the Evolution of the Economic System of the European Community*. http://ec.europa.eu/economy_finance/emu_history/documentation/chapter12/19870410en149efficiencstabil_a.pdf.

Scharpf, F. (1987) *Sozialdemokratische Krisenpolitik in Europa*, Frankfurt: Campus.

(2011) 'Monetary Union, Fiscal Crisis and the Pre-emption of Democracy', *Zeitschrift für Staats- und Europawissenschaften*, 9(2), 163–98.

Sinn, H.-W., Widgrén, M., and Köthenbürger, M. (eds) (2004) *European Monetary Integration*, Cambridge, MA: MIT Press.

Trampusch, C. (2009) *Der erschöpfte Sozialstaat: Transformation eines Politikfeldes*, Frankfurt: Campus.

Van Esch, F. (2012) 'Why Germany Wanted EMU: The Role of Helmut Kohl's Belief System and the Fall of the Berlin Wall', *German Politics*, 21(1), 34–52.

Vaubel, R. (2010) 'The Euro and the German Veto', *Econ Journal Watch*, 7(1), 82–90.

Von Hayek, F. (1974) 'The Pretense of Knowledge', Prize Lecture. http://nobelprize.org/nobel_prizes/economics/laureates/1974/hayek-lectur0html.

3

Sharing the Eurocrats' dream: a demoicratic approach to EMU governance in the post-crisis era

KALYPSO NICOLAÏDIS AND MAX WATSON

Prologue: an iron cage in a bubble

We do not need to master the skills of *Inception's* hero, Leonardo DiCaprio, to understand the Eurocrats' dream. The dream involves flying over the plains, rivers and mountains of Europe on a constant mission to monitor and battle the dark shadows. In other words, to protect the European common good entrusted to them by the Treaties against the uncertainties of globalization, the selfishness of markets and the short-termism of politics. Europe's citizens often seem to be on the same wavelength, with their huge distrust of politicians, abandonment of political parties and worries about the fate of their children. Eurocrats are here to make Europeans' dreams of security and prosperity come true.

Why then should we remotely wish to tamper with the Eurocrats' dream? The reasons go back a long way indeed, we believe, to the foundational moment itself: our Eurocrats' rationalization of their desire to 'govern at a distance'. One could argue that the temptation to govern at a distance was a trope inherited from good old imperialism of yesteryear (Behr 2015, Nicolaïdis and Fisher Onar 2015). But in its post-war functionalist guise, such rationalization had much going for it. Weber had famously heralded organized bureaucratic hierarchies as the most efficient and rational way to organize human cooperation, maintain order, maximize efficiency and eliminate favoritism. Functionalists saw peace as only attainable by

The chapter has greatly benefited from discussions with the authors and editors of this volume as well as from participants in the 2013 Michaelmas Term seminar series of the Political Economy of Financial Markets Programme (PEFM) at the European Studies Centre in Oxford, especially Russell Kincaid and Francisco Torres.

restructuring transnational links between bureaucracies along functional lines and deliberately excluding nationalistic publics organized within state boundaries from this worthy project. Belief in bureaucratic expertise serving complex coordination and legal sophistication needs became the powerful underpinnings of the Eurocrats' ambition to govern at a distance under the broad messianic conviction that worthy ends can justify contestable means. And, indeed, the supranational version of functionalism with its many checks and balances against abuse of central power seemed to absolve it from its imperialist undertones. Monnet may not have called for 'democracies across Europe unite' but his 'central planners across Europe unite' seemed pretty convincing at the time.

Disenchantment did not wait for the euro crisis. After all, Weber himself had come to fear the unfettered bureaucratization of social life as a threat to individual freedom particularly in Western capitalist societies where individuals would become trapped in systems based purely on teleological efficiency, rational calculation and rule-based control. Would his 'iron cage,' 'the polar night of icy darkness' trap the European dream too? To be fair, the Eurocrats' dream did accommodate domestic politicians, but with a major caveat: domestic politicians without domestic politics. This involved a Faustian bargain: politicians commit to the European dead, Eurocrats tacitly accept to serve as scapegoat. The latter did not mind the blame given their messianic convictions and the former were generally neither able nor willing to resist co-optation in the functionalist governance logic. With time, they too would become Eurocrats, shielding the enterprise from mass domestic politics. In short, Europe has long been courting Weber's polar night, but with a technocratic logic once removed, an iron cage crafted in Brusssels' glass towers, an iron cage in a bubble.

Thankfully, the enterprise had seemed to step back from the brink over the last 20 years with the post-Maastricht wake-up call, the constitutional democratic angst and talk among Eurocrats of participatory and deliberative democracy, input legitimacy, local empowerment, and ownership. European citizens somehow were starting to try to break free. And Eurocrats seemed to be listening, tweaking their dream to stay in control.

The euro crisis taught us how fragile these timid developments were. Its management staged Eurocrats as the star *dramatis personae* on a stage they now shared under full limelight with national politicians and the beast they had been trying both to empower and control all along: the markets. But, this time around, the mission and the means it seemed to justify somehow got out of control. In a world where financial markets magnify manifold the many unavoidable follies, mistakes, or misdeeds of politicians, but where publics, especially vulnerable publics, pay for their mistakes, Eurocrats more than ever believe that they need to protect politicians against themselves. For some, they dramatically failed: 19 European leaders were sacrificed on the altar of euro-survival in the course of three years. But, for others, and above all Germany's iron lady, EMU has been reformed to be even truer to the Eurocrats' dream: rules now reign supreme. In the process, supranationalism seems to have truly lost its two redeeming features, namely symmetry, whereby big states refrain from bullying smaller ones at the center, and autonomy, whereby the center refrains from coercing the parts. Little wonder that citizens feel trapped in a Eurocrats' dream only outsiders can extract them from. Bring it on, Leonardo!

This chapter argues that Europe can do better. Indeed, the euro crisis should be treated as an opportunity for European citizens to appropriate the Eurocrats' dream and make it their own, even while embellishing and subverting it in the process. In other words, at least some parts of the euro-cracy seem to want to achieve *supranational entrenchment of creditor-designed 'governing at a distance'*. Instead, we hope and believe that a new EMU architecture can evolve away from crisis mode towards a steady state inspired by a different model: *supranational management of governing together but not as one.* In other words, we argue for a 'demoicratic' approach to EMU governance and believe that many, inside and outside EU institutions, actually support this vision.

The idea that Europeans ought to 'govern together but not as one' is associated with the belief that the EU's normative benchmark ought to be that of a 'demoicracy,' or a Union of peoples (Nicolaïdis 2013). Accordingly, the Eurocrats' dream may have been a necessary original sin as it is this dream that put the EU-to-be on such a demoicratic path. But that logic has run its course. The dream must be democratized, or, better, demoi-cratized. Today, we need to explore the translation in monetary and economic governance terms of a simple fact: that fifty years and more of European integration may have led to a steady strengthening of the European *cratos* according to the Eurocrats' dream, but that the demos has mainly remained domestically constituted (Cheneval and Schimmelfennig 2013; Crum 2013; Nicolaïdis 2004; Nicolaïdis 2013). As a result, the dramatic shift of competences to the supranational level as witnessed in the last five years while legitimation processes remains with national politics is bound to create a legitimacy crisis especially if social costs are so high: no amount of supposed democratization of EU-level decision-making will do the trick. Instead, it is desirable for the EU to design its institutions and rules in the spirit of demoicracy for reasons not only of political legitimacy but also of socio-economic rationality. The management of the Eurozone has yet to reckon fully with the deeply pluralist nature of the European project (Weiler 1999). Using the crisis simply as a fulcrum to embed centralizing and intrusive approaches, for application *en temps normal*, would be philosophically undesirable, politically unviable, and economically ineffective. Instead, the most EU-friendly response to the flaws of current EMU governance is to ask what are the least centralizing approaches that will nevertheless do the work.

The remainder of the chapter is organized as follows. Part I lays out the three governance deficits to be filled by EMU reform and the constraints for addressing them provided by the demoicratic referent. Part II discusses the political-economic diagnosis of the euro-area crisis – exploring where errors of analysis, and pressures of political convenience, have led to ill-advised approaches, and how the circumstances of the crisis have threatened to derail the EU from its demoicratic path in part because it has made possible the merger between two hitherto separate logics, namely that of conditionality and that of polity-building. Part III asks what the crisis suggests should be a stable pattern of EMU governance if one believes that the demoicratic character of the EU should not be betrayed. We seek to disentangle where insights gained during the crisis truly do call for a permanent strengthening of central institutions and/or a heightened role for markets – and where by contrast the longer run imperative is to internalize more deeply the nature of interdependencies at the national level.

I Governance deficits and the demoicratic lens

Critical analysis requires normative benchmarks. Along with the other authors in this volume, we believe that the euro crisis has amplified existing failures in the integration process. We highlight three kinds of governance deficits brought to the fore by the euro crisis that EMU reform has failed to mitigate and indeed sometimes magnified when assessed against the benchmark of a sustainable demoicratic polity.

The compliance deficit

If a first core question raised by the EU in general and EMU in particular is how to ensure compliance with shared international obligations in the absence of coercive state-like structures, what are the options available? If compliance is predicated on the *legitimate* enforcement of shared rules, then the most universal response is well known: reciprocity. Reciprocity is one of the most deeply entrenched social norms. But in the international realm as elsewhere it can come in many shapes and forms. It can be symmetric (e.g., reciprocal right to resort to trade barriers) or asymmetric (aid in exchange for conditions having to do with domestic policies); proportionate or disproportionate; legal or political; unilateral or multilateral in decisions over (mutual) punishment and rewards. Moreover, and most importantly, reciprocity can range from the most specific to the most diffuse reciprocity (across time and partners). When the granting of rights is a function of simple membership in a club (as with the most-favored-nation treatment under GATT, or, indeed, membership in the EU), we are dealing with very diffuse reciprocity. To be sure, even then, enforcement can end up relying on specific reciprocity methods against free-riding behavior (e.g., sanctions). Conditionality is a form of specific reciprocity, requiring deeds in exchange for cash, for instance.

The EU has traditionally been a creature of diffuse reciprocity. It gave up at birth the option of resorting to specific reciprocity among its member states as a way to ensure compliance with its rules: competition law instead of antidumping; single-market rules instead of retaliatory trade barriers in case of breach. To make up for banning reciprocity as an enforcement mechanism, and in the absence of state-like enforcement capacities, common disciplines were to be grounded on the force of law as both an object and an agent of integration (Joerges and Zurn 2005; Joerges in this volume). In practice, infringement action by the European Court of Justice (ECJ) was to be supplemented by supranational or peer pressure as well as, rarely, notional fines.

There has been much debate on the sources of legitimacy of the law when it carries so much onus in upholding social order. At a minimum, on the output side, its authority stems from the character of the law itself, the perception that it be non-arbitrary or serving particularistic interests. On the input side, it must be seen as emanating from representative government which Fritz Scharpf calls in the EU context 'legitimacy intermediation' by member state governments (Scharpf 2013). In a polity-building project, cooperation and its rewards are a public good underpinned either by the common social contract of a demos or a contract among demoi.

A deficit in the realm of *legitimate enforcement of shared rules* – which we refer to in short as a *compliance deficit* – results when polity-building through law ceases to be sufficiently legitimate while classic reciprocity is not part of the toolkit. The gap is best closed by addressing the former: bolstering the demoicratic ethos of individual member states and the demoicratic character of its shared institutions. But if this does not happen, the temptation is great to rediscover the latter, the kind of specific reciprocity that had been eschewed by the EU from the start: conditionality as a mode of external governance, or governing at a distance, by parts of the Union over other parts. This is indeed what has happened with EMU as the policies aimed at the euro crisis eroded the perception of impartiality attached to EU law and therefore its effectiveness. The demoicratic ethos has been tested to its limits in part, we argue, because of the logic of conditionality that has come to pervade EU policies, merging with that of polity-building.

The stabilization deficit

Even if the legitimacy deficit could be addressed, structural asymmetries remain between states, as well as regions and cities. The second governance deficit in managing a common currency without a state therefore has to do with the mechanisms that serve to ensure stabilization in the face of these asymmetries. What happens with economic cycles and the fact that periods of expansion and recessions are not synchronized between states? What to do with the fact that states or regions can be subject to asymmetric shocks – through, for instance, different levels of vulnerability to external shocks? The EU is never likely to benefit from the kind of share of GDP (25 percent in the USA) which allows the federal level to provide the kind of automatic stabilizers making the adoption of a common currency among heterogeneous economies possible (even if in the USA the stabilization function is also provided by financial markets, a point to which we will come back). Even were a common EU budget to jump from 1 percent to 5 percent we would still be far from the mark. So the question remains: how can the EU's political economy be stabilized over time? And at which level of governance?

The justice deficit

There are various options for addressing the two deficits above. But underlying these questions is a third and last justice deficit which acknowledges that no technical approach can fully do justice to the distributional issues at stake in addressing crisis (Kochenov et al. 2015; Sangiovanni 2013). In other words, how should the costs of adjustment and the risks associated with them be distributed not only among countries but also among different social and economic actors within a transnational polity like the EU? This has to do above all with what philosophers discuss as 'duties of fairness,' which always arise between the winners and losers of integration in a steady state, but which are magnified under crisis. Simply put, polities are sustainable when they distribute and redistribute the bads as well as goods of integration fairly, including the distribution of risk in the EU context (Beck 2009).

Fairness in the EMU context is about the distribution of economic and social risks, and the redistribution of the gains and losses stemming from mis-distribution of these risks in the first place. Even if this was not considered an EU-level matter (say through cross national transfers), EMU has a crucial impact on how member states themselves are able to provide core tasks of government, including those that determine the state's capacity to comply with requirements of distributive justice, such as welfare policies and the provision of public goods (for a discussion, see Viehoff and Nicolaïdis 2015). How then should the justice deficit be addressed? It has long been clear that national macroeconomic policy can no longer shield labor-market institutions and social-protection arrangements from the need to adjust to international competition – but adjustment does not need to mean destruction (Hemerijck and Ferrera 2004; Menéndez in this volume). EMU winners have obligations to EMU losers, especially if the latter cannot be compensated through purely intra-national logics. If monetary union restricts member states' ability to implement redistributive principles of social justice, what balance ought to be struck between restoring this capacity at the national level and delivering on duties of fairness at the EU level?

A demoicratic lens

Adopting a demoicratic lens means coming to terms with the fact that these deficits cannot be addressed through classic federal remedies: there are no 'feds' to enforce common law, no EU central budget can be big enough to serve as automatic stabilizer, and no EU federal welfare system can compensate losers permanently across national lines. In response, the demoicratic ideal refuses the presumed binary choice between constructing an ever-closer fiscal union to approximate these solutions or, alternatively, entrenching more deeply the primacy of the sovereign state. To be sure, we accept that both sides in this debate have a point. As per the latter, stable governance architecture for EMU must include strong elements of national responsibility – internalizing the disciplines of monetary union. At the same time, some elements of centralization, or at least 'soft' coordination among governments, may also be needed to preserve stability and foster growth.

But in contrast with the classic representation of the EU as an 'in-between,' the idea that the EU is a 'demoicracy in the making' represents a third way against both these alternatives each of which equates democracy with a single demos – national or European. What is special about peoples engaged in a demoicratic project is that if they are to retain a high degree of political autonomy while managing their interdependence in acceptable and sustainable ways they better be greatly open to each other and set up institutions that help them do so. This implies a system of multiple but connected national politics where the notion of shared responsibilities is fundamental: the system depends on states taking responsibility for the ways in which they deal with their own externalities. Eurocrats should help make it happen, not supplant it.

Demoicratization theory is a theory of correspondence between shifts in power and the democratic anchoring of such powers, emphasizing the disconnection between the locus of managerial authority (the combination of shifting competences and institutional roles) and the locus of political life in Europe. The management of the euro crisis has been based on the assumption that if the euro suffers from being a currency *without* a state it must acquire one. Instead, we argue that it must evolve from a currency *without* a state to a currency *among* states. The EU as demoicracy is not a political waiting room for fuller union, or an economic emergency ward for nations experiencing financial stress, but the normative frame to inform long-term EMU governance architecture.

More specifically, a demoicratic frame of analysis takes European diversity seriously not simply by accepting it as a constraint we must overcome through the right kind of pedagogy or the right kind of incentives for convergence at all costs. Instead we must acknowledge the fact that each member state is an arena for different social bargains, state–society relationships as well as different debates which echo across borders but are also grounded in different constitutional languages. The role of the EU should be to engineer their permanent compatibility and horizontal contagion, not their homogeneity.

This is not the place to discuss specific blueprints on how to translate such a broad ethos into policy (Cheneval, Lavenex, and Schimmelfennig 2015; Nicolaïdis 2015). Suffice to say that if EMU is to be managed qua *demoicracy* without crossing the Rubicon to a classical federal form of governance, the three deficits laid out above must be addressed while respecting the integrity of *national* democracies, enhancing *transnational* democracy, or the demoi commitment to their common 'cratos,' and constraining the *supranational* locus of democracy through genuine politics.

II Demoicracy at risk: the political economy of the euro-area crisis

There is clearly no dearth of diagnoses for the euro crisis and ours concurs with the widespread acknowledgement that the management of the crisis to date has demonstrated what everyone should have known in the first place: one cannot manage a currency shared among nations without some kind of stable agreement on how to share the bounty and risks of the system. The messianic mantra that *the euro cannot fail even if it cannot succeed* has meant that bounty and risks have been distributed according to power relations and in the shadow of implosion. And moral hazard, an initially sound principle to guard against skewed incentives, has been invoked to legitimize what we referred to as the *supranational entrenchment of creditor-designed 'governing at a distance'* along four broad questions.

Who to blame?

As is well known, there are two competing diagnoses concerning the sources of the euro-area crisis (see, inter alia, Schmidt 2014): the 'creditor discourse,' embraced by euro-area states that were running current account surpluses as the crisis developed is essentially a discourse of blame. The roots of the crisis are held to lie in lax fiscal policies and inadequate structural reforms, with Greece cited as the archetypal crisis country. In this view, the policy requirements for living in a non-optimal currency area need no re-examination in light of the crisis. The instability resulted, it is held, from poor observance and enforcement of the rules, not from the scope and substance of the rulebook. In this world, conditionality will be needed to make sure that taxpayers of creditor countries 'get their money back.'

The alternative diagnosis, which can be termed the 'debtor discourse,' comprises three main counter-arguments: (1) It takes two to tango: the crisis involved undisciplined lenders and complacent supervisors in the surplus countries of the euro area, as well as undisciplined borrowers in the deficit countries – so the blame for imprudent lending is shared. (2) Prior to the crisis, Spain and Ireland were running fiscal surpluses; had low public debts; and, in the case of Ireland, had a flexible and highly reformed economy – yet both fell into deep crises: this was not a problem of flaunting top-down fiscal rules. (3) The dynamics of the crisis in fact took all parties by surprise, including the surplus countries and the euro-area elite, due to flawed analyses, whether from the European

Commission, the IMF, or academic experts who failed to foresee the crucial feedback effects between the financial sector, the real economy, and public finances (Kincaid and Watson 2013). The implication of this second – 'debtor' – point of view is that the crisis reflected a systemic malfunctioning of adjustment incentives and mechanisms in the euro area, encompassing both creditors and debtors, public and private sectors, as well as wage-price mechanisms and risk premia.

We are still far from any synthesis of these two views – and, more generally, between neo-liberal and neo-Keynesian readings of the crisis. Logically and empirically, some key aspects of the case made in the 'debtor discourse' seem hard to refute, even if the creditors' concern with moral hazard cannot be dismissed. But the genesis of the crisis is complex, and, more prosaically, 'he who pays the piper calls the tune'. Thus the crisis solutions, and the politics surrounding them, remain heavily determined by the surplus countries and their dominant narrative enhancing a sense of unfairness in debtor countries and a sense of self-righteousness in creditor countries when taking the EU down the road of permanent conditionality schemes to address the deficit as they see it.

Who should adjust?

Episodes of systemic instability, including the euro-area crisis, are typically treated as liquidity crises – at least initially. Debt reduction is ruled out. Provided debtors adjust, it is claimed that there is no threat to the integrity of bank lenders. The reason for this is pragmatic rather than analytic. Creditor countries (such as Germany and France in this case) need time to recapitalize their banks and run down the banks' risky exposures through transfer of claims from banks to the public sector, and, if feasible, to jointly owned institutions such as the IMF or the ECB, which dilutes the national fiscal cost and shifts claims (perhaps at par) to a preferred creditor entity. The Latin American debt crisis of the 1980s is, on all points, the *locus classicus* of the incentives for creditor countries to frame policy in these ways.

The euro-area crisis has proved no exception. The initial focus has been on fiscal adjustment to 'restore' the solvency of the debtor, and liquidity provision to buy time for this adjustment and for a recapitalization of creditor country banks. The burden of adjustment – as is typical – has been viewed by creditors in a very asymmetrical manner. The underlying fiscal adjustment implemented between 2009 and 2012 amounted to 15 percent of GDP in Greece, 4 percent in Ireland, 5 percent in Portugal and 4 percent in Spain, accompanied by vast levels of unemployment and declining output. Only at the end of 2013 did Germany and the other EU creditor countries start to accept implicitly some responsibility for adjusting their economies away from structural surpluses through modest wage increases, while the period of fiscal consolidation in Germany was probably coming to an end. Overall, the nature and symmetry of private sector imbalances, the role of creditor bank indiscipline, and the impact of systemic creditor surpluses were camouflaged.

The difficulty of overcoming asymmetries in the burden of adjustment, where surplus countries escape discipline, has been a feature of debates since Keynes's advocacy of a more balanced system at Bretton Woods. In the euro-area context, however, this asymmetry became systemically dangerous for the living standards of all of the parties leading both to generalized deflationary bias and then to placing countries in an oscillating cycle of insufficient and then excessive competitiveness, excessive to the extent that demand will have been overly depressed in the process (Allsopp and Vines 2008). Nevertheless, it was entrenched in the EU's new rulebook, thus failing adequately to address the stabilization deficit.

Who should pay?

But what happens when adjustment is too slow and insufficient? Who, if anyone, should be bailed out, and by whom? EMU had ruled out fiscal transfers between member states based on three assumptions which were to prove optimistic, to say the least. First, national fiscal deficits were to be limited by EU law, as embedded in the Stability and Growth Pact; second, national *private sector* deficits were declared to have been abolished as Eurostat ceased to publish balance of payments statistics for euro-area members on the grounds that, with the advent of monetary union, their national balance of payments had ceased to exist. However, given the existence of predominantly national budgets, labor markets, and bank resolution systems, this assessment defied economic gravity and the hubris of dismissing this risk came home to roost; third was the failure to perceive the scale on which liabilities might migrate from private to public balance sheets in a crisis. When all three of these hazardous premises crumbled the question of who should pay for the failure of different actors involved in the crisis – for example, governments, banks, firms – came back with a vengeance.

If the question of who should pay started with who *can* pay, the answer could rest on prior capacity to pay – asymmetric wealth – but more importantly, on capacity added by the crisis itself. Before we reach arguments regarding duties of assistance on various grounds of commonality or humanity, the justice deficit stems from the fact that asymmetric benefits fail to be acknowledged by creditors as grounds for fair distribution claims. Indeed, at least until 2015, surplus countries have benefited disproportionately not only from monetary union but also from the crisis itself (Sergio 2013). They may have taken a risk in further lending to bail-out countries but they have avoided major bank losses in connection with poor lending decisions within the euro area; they are seeking to avoid losses on inter-government loans, so, if the strategy works, their support loans and associated interest are good investments; their economies and exports continue to boom because membership of the euro holds down their implicit exchange rates; they have benefited from very low real interest rates as a result of the 'flight to quality'– indeed, since the peak of the crisis, Germany has even experienced negative interest rates; and as a result, they have benefited from the spread between the cost of capital for them and the lending rates to the debtor countries. Yet the case that debtor countries and their citizens must pay for most of the legacy costs of a systemic failure remains the predominant discourse.

The eventual setting up of the European Stability Mechanism (ESM) in 2012 did help address temporarily the need for stabilization, especially when coupled with the ECB's commitment to 'do whatever it takes' by buying government bonds on the secondary market through the so-called Outright Monetary Transactions (OMTs) in order to contain the increasing rise in debtor country spreads. In essence, the fabric of economic and financial connections between members of the euro area had turned out to feature much greater degrees of interdependence than the architects of EMU had dreamed. Support for addressing a systemic failing in this network had to be rooted directly in national rather than supranational responsibility, unsurprisingly involving veto power; and even then the process required an external ring-holder (the IMF) as regards adjustment design and financing.

Unsurprisingly, EMU governments ruled out holding in common bad debts resulting from bad national approaches to banking stability. Hence the agreement that the ECB should centralize and carry out the supervision of major euro-area banks. We are thus left with the question of how and to what extent should the EU provide a central backstop for public and private debt (for example) and insurance or last-resort for raising capital or guaranteeing loans. For all the talk of a banking union, the taste for committing unlimited amounts of government money to support banks headquartered in other countries simply seems to be lacking. This leaves the euro area in the strange position of having the ECB doing supervision centrally, but member states (mainly) paying for its errors. In this sense, supranational intermediation has also been first and foremost a multilateralization of the orthodox creditor stance.

Who should set the rules?

Critically, a monetary union requires rules. The question remains, whose rules? This is not the place to describe how the orthodox narrative sketched above led to the supranational entrenchment of creditor-designed reformed EMU (see, inter alia, Pisani-Ferry 2014). Suffice to say that that Eurocrats and political leaders in tandem have progressively operationalized the new 'Six Pack' and 'Two Pack' legislation flanked by the ESM agreement and the Fiscal Compact through a new system of macroeconomic policy coordination. This is carried through the 'European Semester,' a process lasting almost half the year whereby the Commission with the input of the member states produces a hierarchy of EMU members: all members are subject to broad 'preventive' surveillance (generic country recommendations); most countries at different times fall under various degrees of 'corrective' measures (e.g., 'excessive deficit procedures'); and so-called programme countries are subject to macroeconomic adjustment programmes (memoranda of understanding administered by the Troika). The rationale is clear. The extent and effect of surveillance is a function of the risks which each member state's economic policy creates for others. On what grounds can we question the Eurocrats' architecture designed to deal with a world of externalities and moral hazard?

At a most general level, we can grasp the dramatic increase in Eurocrats' authority to 'govern at a distance' by noting the implied shifts between two notional boundaries which define the intensity and scope of EU involvement in internal member state affairs. The first notional boundary is between what national systemic capacity is assumed as a matter of course (a capacity to comply with European values and norms and which warrants mutual trust; see von Bogdandy and Ioannidis 2014) and what cannot be assumed in such ways and will therefore be subject to explicit rules. The second notional boundary is within this second realm, the boundary between what we could call national 'commitments,' whereby states explicitly commit (through primary or secondary law or political declarations) to uphold a number of shared policy ends translating these values through nationally designed means and common 'disciplines' whereby not only ends but means are specified in a top-down manner. We argue that EMU governance reform has shrunk the space where national capacity can simply be assumed, while at the same time widening the space of disciplines at the expense of commitments, thereby deepening the penetration of EU 'law' in national contexts. To be sure, the shift is obviously most dramatic for countries falling under loan conditionality, the most extreme case of expansion of the 'disciplines' logic.

Is this simply the natural consequences of the EU political bodies having to become players in an IMF-type world? No. In fact, it would be wrong to assume that the EMU reform saga has simply followed IMF operating procedures. For the last 20 years, and drawing lessons from the Argentinian debacle, the IMF has been seeking to coral undue bilateral influence (from, say, the USA) among the different creditors vying seniority in repayment. As its officials say they see it, because the bilateral official creditors have a biased interest in the outcome, defining the boundaries between their interest (which inspires strict disciplines) and common interest is a difficult exercise, in particular when it is clear that debt restructuring ought to happen early on. But these lessons were selectively applied in the EU context as the Troika refused to contemplate debt restructuring at the outset given the 'orthodox narrative' discussed above. When a haircut had to be accepted for Greece in 2012, its magnitude was not enough to do away with the structure of a situation whereby Greece (and possibly other debtors in the Eurozone) would continue to be subject to external governance in the foreseeable future, with debt write-offs big enough to keep it afloat but small enough to keep it dependent or in a 'bond relationship' bypassing extant notions of citizenship as analyzed by Damian Chalmers in this volume. But the bond narrative has progressively blended into the risk regulation (see also Chalmers 2013).

Bail-out programmes may be outliers in the new EU governance system but the difference is in degree rather than in nature. First, because *fiscal determinism* has underpinned the drive to govern at a distance in the whole Eurozone. Admittedly, the main preoccupation that has informed responses to the crisis has been to prevent member states of the Eurozone from falling into Troika-ESM territory – thus subjecting them to disciplines short of credit conditions. As if the 2012 Fiscal Compact compelling member states to introduce requirements of fiscal balance in their own constitutional arrangements was not to be trusted, EMU governance has orchestrated the dramatic curbing of the political discretion of all EMU governments not only when it comes to deficits *per se* (a legitimate concern) but on the entire set of choices that may lead directly or indirectly to such deficits. To make this possible, the *modus operandi* of EMU governance stems from overriding the disjunction between short-term recommendations regarding fiscal policy (the old Stability and Growth Pact) and long-term structural policy embedded in the Lisbon strategy and the Open Method of Coordination (OMC) – two processes which before the crisis belonged to different worlds of governance. While scholars have disputed for the last 15 years their relative merits, this key innovation has blurred the distinction between rules-based and coordination-based governance in the EU in fascinating ways (Armstrong 2013).

This may have been a good thing: in an evolving demoicracy, the consensual development of recommendations corresponded to the search for more legitimate forms of governance as the EU started to interfere with core state powers (Borrás and Radaelli 2014). There had been attempts to strengthen the preventive arm of the Stability and Growth Pact much before the beginning of the crisis, and the idea of synchronizing fiscal and structural assessments corresponds to a sense that there is a realm of post-legislative governance that can only be implemented through hybrid forms of governance. But, as Armstrong points out, this has happened with a twist: the OMC has been hardened through the community method, with a preponderant role for the Commission in the interpretation, monitoring and enforcement of rules. In other words, the management of the euro crisis has allowed the wolf of supranational conditionality to penetrate the EU den in OMC sheep's clothing. Witness the European Semester's Macroeconomic Imbalance Procedure (MIP) under which countries can in principle be subject to fines for the failure to take structural measures assumed to help reduce their imbalances in the long run.

Second, and relatedly, governing at a distance has been justified in the Eurocrats' world view by a profound suspicion of agonistic politics throughout the Eurozone, in other words the idea that politics is about open conflicts resolved through democratic competition. The member states should be able collectively and the Commission concurrently to suggest ways of making shared membership in EMU sustainable. But the question is whether in doing so they can assume one 'right approach' to macroeconomic policy and to the handling of redistributive trade-offs made through national budget deals. Technocracy often relies on this (ordoliberal) belief. Unsurprisingly, we have witnessed a great deal of resistance since 2011 to the idea that the Commission can decide how pension reform or wage de-indexation can increase a given country's competitiveness. In some cases, say Malta and Belgium on de-indexation, it even had to backtrack. At the time of writing, there are signs that the new 2014 Commission has started to show marginally more flexibility.

In the end, the shrinkage of political space under EMU takes us back to asymmetric supranationalization, subject to creditor countries' dominance. The very definition and status of 'law' has changed with crisis management and the reconfiguration of sovereignty it has involved. How and to what extent do the conditions contained in the Troika's memorandum correspond to classic understandings of 'law'? They are indeed approved by the Eurogroup and the process has been sanctioned by Treaty, but the traditional EU checks and balances, including parliamentary involvement, are absent. This is true, albeit to a lesser extent, regarding the European Semester process.

Let us assume even that, subject to improvements in design and execution, such departures from previous euro-area practices could be defended as dealing with legacy costs in countries which exploited the structural flaws of the euro to borrow above their means in EMU's first decade after having accumulated deficits for much longer. But can we imagine these practices as part of the longer run design of economic surveillance under EMU?

The political drama acted out across debtor countries of the Eurozone between 2010 and 2015, with politicians one after the other sacrificed on the altar of euro-survival, clearly speak to the unsustainability of an approach which channeled the opprobrium of European publics – and not only in the south – against a new kind of supranational democracy pre-emption. To pursue rule surveillance and enforcement along these lines during normal times would simply continue to erode Brussel's legitimacy. The conditionality mindset sees the EU as an instrument to bring governments into line rather than to develop shared notions of proper division of labor between levels of government and proper incentive structures to go along with it. Is it in the interest of Eurocrats to give 'Brussels' the look-and-feel of the IMF but to do so 'in the name' of a common polity – not an ad hoc, temporary outside institution like the IMF? Their strategy has partially backfired as the attempt to borrow from the EU's political legitimacy to make the new conditionalities more effective was turned on its head with symbolic borrowing the other way around: the EU has become the scapegoat for the most unpopular set of policies experienced in Europe since the Second World War, while the political and economic wisdom of these policies came to be questioned by the IMF itself (International Monetary Fund 2013). Indeed, it seems that at times all clarity and transparency was lost as to what 'Brussels' meant – as the distinct and respective roles of the Commission, the Eurogroup, the Council, the ECB and individual creditor governments became impenetrable to outsiders.

In sum, today's EMU governance approach is far from an optimal steady state, except to the extent that EU decision-makers may succeed in extirpating member states from the crisis, albeit at prohibitive social costs. Yet this merger between the conditionality and polity-building logics seeks to make permanent some elements of conditionality that were forged in the heat of the moment as technocratic rather than political solutions to EMUs woes. Hard cases make bad law, unless great care is taken; and the stress of crisis resolution is not an easy setting in which to shape a new permanent architecture for EMU. To be sure, the short-run dictates of conditionality are hard to disentangle from the enduring requirements in a steady state. But conditionality implies an intrusiveness – and fosters a divisiveness – that do not belong in the operating process of a successful European polity over the long run. Ultimately, governing at a distance will spell the end of common rules.

III Demoicracy recovered: a non-federal EMU governance

What kind of a paradigm shift – both analytical and political – is required in order for the economic governance of EMU to evolve to a viable, steady state? If measures designed in 'emergency mode' to deal with the flawed structure inherited from the original EMU design become the blueprint for long-term EMU governance then all three deficits – compliance, stabilization, and justice – are likely to remain.

Instead, and under a demoicratic paradigm, EMU's continued governance reform ought to navigate a third way between unity in the name of the euro and fragmentation because of it. First, because political leaders must allay public resentment of intrusive centralization, or indeed the perceptions of hegemony within the EU by surplus countries which necessarily accompanies enforcement-through-conditionality. Second, because EMU governance reform needs to be framed much more systematically in terms of the political architecture, not just of the euro area, but of the wider EU. Some call for the EU to become a 'club of clubs', with the supranational level mainly responsible for monitoring competition and cooperation among different territorial and/or functional clubs (Majone 2014; Majone in this volume). But, in our view, our key collective concern ought to be sustainable integration in the overall Union to hold together the ins and the outs of monetary union, whose relationships ought to vary in intensity but not in nature.

In the spirit of the demoicratic approach, therefore, we argue that the goals of EMU governance over the long run be thought through in three interconnected realms of responsibility:

(1) markets: we need to understand key interdependencies and externalities involved and the extent to which these can be addressed by market-based mechanisms, including through better financial integration;
(2) governments: we need to prove fiscal disciplinarians wrong by strengthening the incentives for national governments to conduct and coordinate policies on a more forward-looking basis, taking account of spillovers and externalities to determine national responsibilities;
(3) union: we need to engineer the minimum centralized financial support mechanisms needed to allay public fear of euro-area or banking disintegration.

These, to be clear, are indeed 'elements,' not sequential steps. The qualities of a unique EU system will be to a significant degree emergent. Constructing a demoicratic governance of EMU is to be seen as an exploration, not an entelechy.

The role of markets and financial integration in an EMU context

The stabilization deficit is due to EMU's nature as a closed system with high interdependencies. In a non-optimal currency area that is subject to economic 'shocks' (external and internal) where members are affected in different ways, economies will at times converge and at time diverge. But, provided they do not overshoot, these swings are natural and needed to help bring economies back to balance under the common monetary policy rather than long-run gains or losses of 'competitiveness' in the deep structural sense of relative skills, labor-market efficiency, and technology, which matter for medium-term growth. Each adjustment process carries risks. Current account deficits within EMU emerge and widen over quite long periods, as relative competitiveness changes; low or negative real interest rates may make credit and asset price booms more likely (as occurred in Ireland and Spain); or spending may increase during the boom in the presence of these low interest rates (as was the case in Greece and Portugal); but people do not move easily enough to compensate for these swings. There will always be adjustment crisis but the question is how to prevent them from becoming full-blown economic and financial crises.

Two market-based mechanisms can in principle stop this process becoming dynamically unstable. First and foremost, Europe needs to unlock the benign potential of financial integration. To be sure, the highly integrated financial market system in the pre-crisis euro area facilitated the financing of destabilizing trends, thereby potentially increasing the scale of risks involved (Jones 2013). But financial integration can also offer private-sector mechanisms to help absorb country-specific economic shocks. When referring to financial integration, we mean three things: the spider's web of cross-border financial flows; the spreading out of a network of bank branches and subsidiaries; and the web of cross-holdings of companies across borders. The last two of these processes (if well structured) can particularly act as buffers to national shocks, as agents – including firms – borrow across borders and as their incomes are 'smoothed' by their holdings in other states that are unaffected by a shock. Thus, the integration of financial markets under EMU along these lines can mitigate the need for either fiscal transfers between member states or a sizable federal government to play a role in cushioning shocks and spreading economic risks. This phenomenon prevails in the USA and was emerging in the euro area before the crisis (Asdrubali, Sorensen, and Yosha 1996; Artis and Hoffman 2008). In short, financial integration, as it deepens over time (assuming current developments are progressively reversed), offers a private sector channel for risk-sharing which we believe is more congruent with a demoicratic polity than full-blown fiscal integration. But, of course, this diagnosis is predicated on the assumption that such financial market integration would not again lead to heavy over-borrowing, which in turn calls for more restrictive regulatory constraints – a topic beyond the scope of this chapter.

Second, markets respond to loss of competitiveness through the slowdown of a booming economy, bringing it back in line with euro-area interest rates. If this does not happen enough, the current account deficit gets troublingly wide, and banks or governments start to over-extend themselves, risk premia should rise in a gradual fashion and start to constrain borrowers. For these mechanisms to work, however, consumers, wage-setters, and financial market participants all need to behave in a forward-looking manner. If not, the unchecked imbalances may get dangerously wide, and the correction processes can exhibit destabilizing lags. This means in particular that defaulting on debt needs to remain an option and need not imply exit from the euro area (for a forceful argument in this regard, see, inter alia, Mody 2014). But allowing governments to default will not appear a credible option unless the sovereign-bank link is broken, since the default of a sovereign would be likely to trigger a run on its banks. Thus a full banking union, with mutual fiscal support for banks, is a sine qua non for introducing default as a credible option to strengthen national incentives under EMU (see below).

More broadly, we know from experience during the run-up to the euro-area crisis that these market-based mechanisms did not work early and fast enough to prevent a 'sudden stop' in lending to some countries (Kincaid and Watson 2013). There had been far too great a complacency about the efficiency of unbridled financial markets. Interdependencies occur in the European monetary areas but not in the same way as they would in an integrated national space. The markets can help manage these interdependencies but only if individual member states are in a position to play a central role, an issue to which we now turn.

National discretion, capacity, and incentives: proving fiscal disciplinarians wrong

We are therefore back to the role of states individually and collectively in addressing our governance deficits. Certainly, strong public finances are part of the bedrock on which an economy's resilience is built. But can we prove the disciplinarian focus on public deficits and centralized rules wrong? How can we constrain democracies democratically in the EU?

Our preferred approach can be summed up as moving from the spirit of top-down EU disciplines to bottom-up national commitments. These commitments can of course be formalized as EU rules or at least guidelines. But the cardinal mindset here is that supranational governance is supposed to be deployed to limit the arbitrariness of its constituent actors' policies rather than their capacity to decide among meaningful alternatives – choices which may need to be constrained when it comes to the free riding on neighbors or on future generations, but meaningful choices nevertheless. When it comes to structural reforms in particular, only domestic politics, with all its flaws, can make them democratically sustainable.

Three dimensions need to be considered, namely national discretion, capacity, and incentives.

For one, while EU-led policy prescriptions may in part be valid, if the experience of the crisis has taught us anything, it is that when national economies in the euro area undergo huge swings in the financial sector – affecting credit, asset prices, and capital flows together – avoiding dangerous instability requires *more* not *less* national discretionary leeway on the fiscal front. Thus, the first priority in the crisis context was not to strengthen central fiscal rules but to lay a clearer basis for internalizing the risk of boom–bust cycles at the national level. Addressing destabilizing competitiveness swings requires a discretionary and proactive use of fiscal policy which need not conflict with the kind of prudent rules embodied in the Stability and Growth Pact, particularly when a surplus is being built. And when fiscal risks arise from private- and not only public-sector imbalances, as we saw with the tripling of the (initially low) public debt in Ireland and Spain, an approach dominated by top-down fiscal discipline misses the point.

This leads us to the second critical ingredient of the national equation, namely the importance of national capacity. In a nutshell, the MIP uses concurrent and lagging indicators, so that the eventual impact as the procedure moves through its stages could be so delayed as to end up being pro-cyclical. Indeed, it can be questioned whether pre-emptive action through national fiscal and macroprudential policies can realistically be managed centrally in this way, except as a back-up process in the case of national failure to take responsible steps. The interpretation of leading indicators and of detailed fiscal data of the kind needed to act in time on private sector imbalances in the absence of an independent monetary policy is something for which national governments need to assume responsibility. Forward-looking analysis of financial stability trends depends heavily on country-specific analysis at the national level, and has a large interpretative content. It can better be performed in real time, based on a painstaking review of fiscal and cyclical indicators at the national level, departing substantially from the simple lines of standard processes agreed at the EU level (Martinez-Mongay, Luis Angel Maza Lasierra, and Yaniz Igal 2007). To feed such a preventive fiscal policy, much more attention is needed at the national level to the analysis of economic shocks and their impact on the economy as an interdependent part of the euro area. And national governments are obviously better placed to assess the socio-economic fundamentals that will allow them to implement effective policies. Coordination is much more likely to deliver than centralization.

This suggests a need to strengthen domestic institutions so that both systemic stability risks and externalities – including those arising from interdependency under EMU – are better internalized. The Fiscal Compact, for instance, already requires member states to enact a domestic 'implementation law' establishing a self-correcting mechanism guided by the monthly surveillance of a *governmentally independent fiscal advisory council*. Member states need to build on this commitment to establish Financial Stability Councils with a mandate both to engage in forward-looking analyses and to monitor the domestic implications of euro-area monetary conditions. But such councils must work in tandem with the political process to assess which branches of policy (and which institutional actors) are relevant to forestalling the identified risks. And when it comes to distributing risk the ultimate authority must be democratic accountable actors and transparently engaged.

A third, key, question, however, is how incentives are to be strengthened for behavior that internalizes the interdependencies of EMU, if this is not to be done by an intrusive, top-down approach along the lines of conditionality. For a demoicratic approach to EMU governance to prove viable, the private sector needs to face losses if banks engage in imprudent lending. Governments need to internalize the challenge to national fiscal and macro-prudential policies posed by country-specific shocks under the common monetary policy. For one, stabilization requires more symmetry in the Eurozone. The Macroeconomic Imbalances Procedure may be the first international procedure to seek to discipline large and protracted imbalances in surplus countries but remains asymmetrical as between current account surplus and deficit countries (trigger levels of 6 percent versus 4 percent). A most valuable role could well be as an aid to policy cooperation among member states in the long run rather than a disciplinary arm in the short run. And in this respect the Commission can affect incentives by sharing analysis with systemic risk experts at the ECB and the European Systemic Risk Board (ESRB) and above all national settings. And publics in surplus countries should be exposed to the counter-intuitive idea that their surpluses are risk-creating.

On the other hand, while the risk of falling under Troika conditionality procedures does represent a deterrent for deficit countries, some would argue that a genuine fear of default is needed to change the incentives facing both governments and those who lend to them. But it can be questioned whether greater default risk is a proximate enough concern to change incentives for governments at the stage when destabilizing financial trends in the economy are starting to emerge and pre-emptive action is needed. Overall default risk is a blunt instrument, a nuclear option, which all actors will want to avoid. Alternatively, the name of the game ought to be to create the conditions under which default is least likely, through both the strengthening of domestic institutions as discussed above and minimal centralized features to which we turn.

Spelling out why and when some centralized functions and backstops are indispensable

While centrally enforced fiscal disciplines should progressively become less necessary on the rule compliance front in the steady state, we still need to ask to what extent they may be necessary on the stabilization and justice front, to restore and sustain growth and a fair distribution of risks in the wake of the euro-area crisis. In this respect, EMU's longer-run architecture needs to address three areas introduced in Part II, which are distinct but ultimately interconnected. In each case we need to discuss what is the minimal degree of centralization deemed necessary for sustainable integration.

First, soft fiscal coordination may be needed if national budgetary actions are not to impart a deflationary bias to adjustment across the euro area as countries try to restore their fiscal situation simultaneously after a shock, rather than this effort being limited initially to countries experiencing and causing systemic risk. Coordination then must address overall deficiency of demand at the EMU level, made worse by ill-coordinated fiscal tightening.

Second, there is a need for insurance on sovereign debt short of a 'transfer union' which would involve systemic funding of some countries by others – a topic which has been the object of much contention since the beginning of the crisis. As discussed above, this starts by allowing for national bankruptcy simply by pre-emptively dealing with spillover effects. But in light of the Greek restructuring, and market fears about countries leaving the euro area as a result, it seems necessary to have some form of long-run bail-out mechanism *in exceptional circumstances*. Creditors may continue to insist on consensus decision-making; and the associated conditionality may need to be intrusive, if domestic vested interests in a crisis-affected economy are jeopardizing recovery: but it needs to come as a last not first resort after all domestic-grounded policies have been allowed to enfold.

In this respect, we would not argue against the broad shape of the ESM/OMT system as it has evolved with four caveats. First, provided that it is held in reserve for this exceptional role. Second, with a recognition that it fulfills the essential backstop needs for medium-sized and small members but that the tax base of the euro area is not large enough to sustain the rescue of an economy as large as Italy which would have to be a G7 or even G20 affair. Third, the EU should consider outsourcing conditionality to the IMF in these cases, thus institutionally delinking the kind of conditionality and polity-building that has been so detrimental to EU legitimacy. Last, but not least, provided that the kind of 'humanitarian' support advocated in some of the southern countries to support the most vulnerable segments of the population affected by debt-repayment measures be considered independently from financial incentive considerations. Restoring a sense of fair distribution of pain among European citizenry does not need to entail the kind of structurally entrenched transfer union dreaded by Germany.

Third, policy frameworks need to be in place in order to unlock the favorable potential of financial integration discussed above and prevent its potential destabilizing effects. This includes more effective and intrusive microprudential supervision, while diminishing the scope for regulatory capture and for 'group-think' in national financial communities – hence the role attributed to the ECB in supervising big banks. But, of course, macroeconomic imbalances financed by debt-creating private flows also affect the benign (or not) character of financial integration.

Finally, the role of the ECB in a demoicratic polity demands special attention. A central bank for a currency without a state presumably has an even greater role to play than traditional central banks. In the EMU context, the ECB can help foster long-run solutions that are politically sustainable, including by creating policy space to cope with the tensions of transition. The commitment of essential fiscal resources as a backstop to market stability (with troubled area-wide banks too large for one government to handle) seems a very favourable trade-off in order to secure the gains of financial integration jeopardized by renewed fragmentation. This in turn calls for a central supervisory function at the ECB both to avoid moral hazard as regards the availability of mutual funds for banking support (and in this connection it is also logical to leave some portion of banking losses at the national level, where much of the responsibility for dealing with imbalances and preserving financial stability still lies) and to encourage countries to show reciprocity in avoiding actions by their banks that could jeopardize macroprudential restraint in another, booming, euro-area member.

Two aspects of the ECB's current role prompt concerns in that regard. First, in spite of the ECB's role as supervisor of large euro-area banks, the mutual loss-bearing share will remain small. Second, its buying of bonds on the secondary market through the OMT is dependent on compliance with a Troika programme, a very surprising thing for a central bank to be doing, more akin to the IMF's traditional role, and only understandable as a way of buying political space for more durable policies to be put in place with democratic support. Indeed, and at the time of writing the reference by the German *Bundesverfassungsgericht* to the ECJ on OMT could well result in a delinking from Troika conditionality and a quantitative limitation in scale or time.

Conclusion: from top-down disciplines to mutual commitments

The current discussions on the governance of EMU can be seen as an extreme and skewed version of the wider, long-standing debate about the political architecture of Europe. In this chapter, we argue that EU politics are at their best when avoiding to cross the Rubicon to a federal state while engineering the kind of mutual responsibilities befitting a polity still grounded on the sovereign autonomy of its *demoi*. EU demoicracy may have been stretched to its limits by the kind of dependencies and governance requirements associated with EMU. It may even be argued that monetary union is not soluble in demoicracy. We have argued otherwise. We cannot wish away 20 years of integrative fits and starts. This does not mean that we must turn to the most centralizing variants under consideration of so-called fiscal, banking, or political union.

We have discussed the evolving debate on the governance of EMU in its own terms to suggest that it is possible to conceive of EMU governance not as consisting in a set of deep fiscal disciplines and transnational transfers, but rather as embedded in domestic politics accountable to the peoples of Europe. Dealing with crisis may have required the kind of emergency steps taken by European leadership in so-called bail-out countries although not the national democratic disempowerment that accompanied them. The 'conditionality capture' witnessed there has come to permeate the Eurozone as a whole. If some countries, small or with pegged currencies, are accustomed to being archetypal 'price-takers' in world markets we cannot expect most EU populations passively to accept being governed at a distance, not only regarding the fact of austerity but its form, content, and timing. Nor will structural reforms work when implemented under duress. The EU has allowed the growth within itself of a logic of governing at a distance which goes much beyond traditional (ad hoc and temporary) conditionality in the international system through organizations like the IMF. This alien logic should not be left slowly to invade its host, leaving it a very different creature than its former self.

Instead, the steady state needs to be envisioned in a positive manner as a discovery of the promise that interdependence holds and conditional on the responsibilities that it entails. Getting to such a steady state EMU will not be easy. The presence of legacy costs meant that it was always bound to be difficult to move to a new incentive system associated with a new regime. The state of public opinion in surplus countries has made it inconceivable to 'jump' straight to a long-run solution. A more balanced and constructive narrative in both debtor and surplus countries will need to take hold.

The hallmarks of a governance system for EMU that is true to the idea of demoicracy would be to minimize both the disciplinarian nature of relations between the Union and its member states and the extent of centralized mechanisms put in place to hold the union together. Markets can help – through financial integration that can mitigate the need for 'federal' transfers – but cannot do the trick by themselves. The onus is on national governments to internalize the implications of interdependence as they frame fiscal and macroprudential policies. And it is on coordination among states to ensure that externalities and spillovers are adequately addressed on both the micro-prudential and macro-prudential fronts.

In the end, there are at least two visions for a steady state in EMU governance. One is a centralized economic and monetary union in which the political and policy discretion of individual member states has been drastically curbed; the other consists in trying to stay faithful to the idea of demoicracy grounded in the autonomy and interdependence of its individual peoples even while attempting to manage a non-optimal currency area. The latter is a tall order. But one well worth aiming for if the euro is to remain the currency of a democratically sustainable union.

References

Allsopp, C., and Vines, F. (2008) 'Fiscal Policy, Inter-Country Adjustment, and the Real Exchange Rate', DG-ECFIN, Economic Papers No. 344.

Armstrong, K. (2013) 'The New Governance of EU Fiscal Discipline', *European Law Review*, 38(5), 601–17.

Artis, M., and Hoffman, M. (2008) 'Declining Home Bias and the Increase in International Risk Sharing: Lessons from European Integration', in L. Jonung, C. Walkner and M. Watson (eds), *Building the Financial Foundations of the Euro*, London: Routledge.

Asdrubali, P., Sorensen, B., and Yosha, O. (1996), 'Channels of Interstate Risk-sharing: United States 1963–90', *Quarterly Journal of Economics*, 111(4), 1081–100.

Beck, U. (2009) *World at Risk*. Cambridge: Polity Press.

Behr, H. (2015) '"Empire", "Governing from the Distance", and the "Mitigation of Violence"', in H. Behr and I. Stivachtis (eds), *Revisiting the European Union as an Empire*, Routledge: London.

Borrás, S., and Radaelli, C. M. (2014) 'Open Method of Coordination for Demoicracy? Standards and Purposes', *Journal of European Public Policy*, 21(1), 21.

Chalmers, D. (2013) 'European Restatements of Sovereignty', LSE Law Department Working Paper 10/201.

Cheneval, F., and Schimmelfennig, F. (2013) 'The Case for Demoicracy in the European Union', *Journal of Common Market Studies*, 51(2), 334–50.

Cheneval, F., Lavenex, S., and Schimmelfennig, F. (2015) 'Demoi-cracy in the European Union: Principles, Institutions, Policies', *Journal of European Public Policy*, 22(1), 1–18.

Crum, B. (2013), 'Saving the Euro at the Cost of Democracy?', *Journal of Common Market Studies*, 51(4), 614–30.

European Commission (2006), 'Adjustment Dynamics in the Euro Area – Experiences and Challenges', Brussels.

Hemerijck, A., and Ferrera, M. (2004) 'Welfare Reform in the Shadow of EMU', in A. Martin and G. Ross (eds), *Euros and the Europeans: Monetary Integration and the European Model of Society*, Cambridge: Cambridge University Press.

International Monetary Fund (2013), 'Greece: Ex Post Evaluation of Exceptional Access under the 2010 Stand-By Arrangement', Washington, DC: IMF.

Joerges, C., and Zurn, M. (eds) (2005) *Law and Governance in Postnational Europe: Compliance Beyond the Nation-State*, Cambridge: Cambridge University Press.

Jones, E. (2013), 'European Financial Integration and the Sovereign Debt Crisis', Lecture at Sala del Capitolo, Badia Fiesolana.

Kincaid, R., and Watson, M. (2013), 'Avoiding New Crises in the Euro Area: Public and Private Imbalances, Capital Flows and National Policy Responses', Discussion draft, Chatham House/Konrad Adenauer Stiftung.

Kochenov, D., de Búrca, G., and Williams, A. (eds) (2015) *Europe's Justice Deficit*, Oxford: Hart Publishing.

Lindseth, P. (2010) *Power and Legitimacy: Reconciling Europe and the Nation-state*, Oxford: Oxford University Press.

Majone, G. (2014) *Rethinking the European Union Post-Crisis: Has Integration Gone too Far?*, Cambridge: Cambridge University Press.

Martinez-Mongay, C., Luis Angel Maza Lasierra, L., and Yaniz Igal, J. (2007) 'Asset Booms and Tax Receipts: The Case of Spain, 1995–2006', European Commission Occasional Paper 293.

Mody, A. (2014) *A Schuman Compact for the Euro Area*, Brussels: Bruegel.

Nicolaïdis, K. (2004) 'We, the Peoples of Europe …' *Foreign Affairs* (November/December), 97–110.

(2013) 'European Demoicracy and its Crisis,' *Journal of Common Market Studies*, 51(2), 351–69.

(2015), 'Demoicratic Theory and Europe's Institutional Architecture in Times of Crisis', in S. Piattoni (ed.), *The European Union: Democratic Principles and Institutional Architectures in Times of Crisis*, Oxford: Oxford University Press.

Nicolaïdis, K., and Nora Fisher, O. (2015) 'Europe's Post-Imperial Condition', in H. Behr and I. Stivachtis (eds), *Revisiting the European Union as an Empire*, London: Routledge.

Pisani-Ferry, J. (2014) *The Euro-Crisis and its Aftermath*, Oxford: Oxford University Press.

Sangiovanni, A. (2013) 'Solidarity in the European Union', *Oxford Journal of Legal Studies*, 33(2), 213–41.

Scharpf, F. (2013) Political Legitimacy in a Non-optimal Currency Area, MPIfG Discussion Paper 13/15.

Schmidt, V. (2014) 'Speaking to the Markets or to the People? A Discursive Institutionalist Analysis of the EU's Sovereign Debt Crisis', *British Journal of Politics and International Relations*, 16(1), 188–209.

Sergio, A. (2013) 'Is Germany Paying for Southern Europe?', *Open Democracy*, 6 July.

Viehoff, J., and Nicolaïdis, K. (2015) 'Social Justice in the European Union: The Puzzles of Solidarity, Reciprocity and Choice', in D. Kochenov, G. de Búrca, and A. Williams (eds), *Europe's Justice Deficit*, Oxford: Hart Publishing.

von Bogdandy A., and Ioannidis, M. (2014) 'Systemic Deficiency in the Rule of Law', *Common Market Law Review*, 51(1), 59–96.

Weiler, J. (1999) *The Constitution of Europe*, Cambridge: Cambridge University Press.

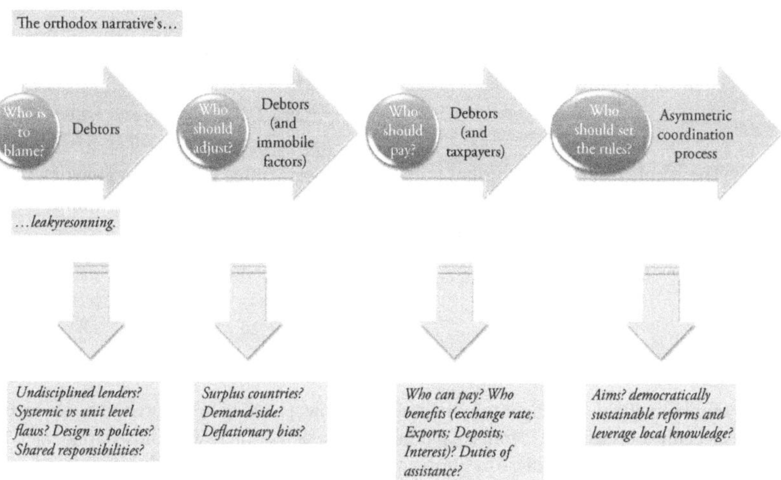

4

Neumark vindicated: the three patterns of Europeanisation of national tax systems and the future of the social and democratic *Rechtsstaat*

AGUSTÍN JOSÉ MENÉNDEZ

To Juanma Barquero: Thou shouldst be living at this hour.

> Conversely, however, the cause of European integration would be retarded if monetary integration were to be pursued but the attempt were to fail. The potential dangers of monetary integration stem from the loss of power of altering the national exchange rate; such a loss could threaten the more stable countries with excessive inflation and/or the more inflationary countries with a loss of prosperity that would be the more intractable because it would be manifest as a regional problem rather than a balance of payments problem. This danger is particularly acute in the European context because different national traditions and institutions could give rise to inconsistent trends in unit costs in different national 'regions'. This development would be so disastrous, if released, that it would inevitably lead to the destruction of monetary union.
>
> Altiero Spinelli, *The European Adventure*

> The whole legal establishment of the office of the judge advocate was magnificent. Every state on the brink of total, political, economic and moral collapse has an establishment like this.
>
> Jaroslav Hašek, *The Good Soldier Švejk*

Many thanks to all the participants in the research project leading to the present book, and very especially to its leaders, Damian Chalmers, Mark Jachtenfuchs and Christian Joerges. I would also like to thank Professors Tuori and Losada (both at Helsinki University) and Professor Rasmussen (at Copenhagen University) for being so kind as to arrange the seminars in which previous drafts of this chapter were discussed. Special thanks to Andrés Boix, Jeremy Leaman, Francisco Rubio Llorente, Sergio Ramírez Pedro Teixeira and Klaus Tuori.

Introduction

This chapter aims at tackling two closely related questions:

- What role did the set of European norms governing national tax laws play in the gathering of the European crises?
- What changes should be made into the European framework of taxation to overcome the crises?

The first question tends not to be posed because taxation is regularly depicted as one of the last trenches behind which national sovereigns resist the incoming European tide (but see Genschel and Jachtenfuchs 2010; Menéndez 2005; a comparative perspective on transformation of tax systems in Steinmo 1993). This assumption is simply wrong. National tax systems have in fact been deeply and thoroughly Europeanised since the very moment the European Communities were established (Section I). The persistent myth of the untrammelled national sovereign is largely the result of an optical illusion. Resulting from the (wrong) reduction of the power to tax to the power to collect taxes (when the power of shaping these taxes at the constitutional and legislative levels is also a key part of that power) and from the belief that the abandonment of the original pattern of Europeanisation of national tax systems in the early 1980s. Actually, as I show in Section II, the end of harmonisation was not the end of the Europeanisation of national tax systems; on the contrary, Europeanisation became deeper and faster, only it proceeded *by very different means*. National taxes were homogenised by the pressure exerted by economic actors making use of their revamped economic freedoms to challenge, one after the other, national tax laws that were said to create obstacles to the exercise of economic freedoms. This shift fostered the financial, fiscal and macroeconomic weaknesses that became open crises in 2007.

The present European crises and the way in which they have been governed have resulted in the radicalisation of the pattern of Europeanisation of national tax laws. The absorption by exchequers of massive amounts of financial risks (a good deal of which were the direct result of asymmetric monetary union) has made many member states of the Eurozone *indebted states*. These states have been required by European Union law to place their tax systems at the service of repaying principal and interests of massive piles of debts, so as to protect the interests of creditors, even if at the cost of abandoning the constitutional commitments of the *social and democratic Rechtsstaat*.

In Sections III and IV I argue that if integration through fiscal consolidation gets entrenched, Europeans will be forced to choose between *this form of* European integration and the social and democratic *Rechtsstaat*. This is why we need a very different Europe, and indeed a very different tax Europe. In particular, we do not need *more Europe*, i.e., the transferring of tax collecting powers to the European Union, but a *radically different Europe*, i.e., a Europe that becomes (again) the servant of the *social and democratic Rechtsstaat* by means of rescuing the capacity of member states to make autonomous and democratic use of their tax powers.

I The original tax paradigm of European integration: integration through tax harmonisation

Establishing 'an internal market in the form of a common market' (Art. 2 TEC) implied redrawing and redefining economic borders. Taxes were (and remain) a fundamental instrument in the creation of economic borders. Consequently, European integration could not but entail the transformation of national tax systems.

The national constitutions which authorised and mandated European integration as well as the founding Treaties (which should be interpreted in the light of the former, Fossum and Menéndez 2011) required tax integration aimed at the simultaneous realisation of three goals.

First, national tax systems had to be made integration friendly. Economic borders had to be made porous to the goods and economic actors from all member states. This involved four main things:

- Substituting national by European customs duties, or, what is the same, removing customs duties inside the Communities, enacting a European customs code and transferring the power to collect duties at the external borders of the Communities to the supranational level (Art. 3(a) and 3(9) EC).
- Redesigning national consumption taxes – including turnover taxes and excise duties (Art. 99 EC in light of Art. 95 EC) so that they would not become customs duties by other means; this required assigning the power of legislative design of consumption taxes to the Communities (Art. 99 EC).
- Harmonising other tax figures when that would be required in view of the stage of economic integration reached (Art. 100 EC).
- Coordinating the use of taxes as macroeconomic levers (Arts 103 and 105 EC).

Secondly, the Europeanisation of national tax systems should shelter, not undermine, the social and democratic tax state. If post-war constitutions mandated integration, this was not for the sake of integration itself, but as a means to realise the normative ideals of the social and democratic *Rechtsstaat*. The tax system was expected to discharge three functions, closely related to each of the pillars of the social and democratic *Rechtsstaat* (Musgrave et al. 1945; Musgrave 1959; Neumark 1974; Barquero Estevan 2002). The Rechtsstaat ideal required the provision of revenue with which to pay for public goods and services. A key operationalisation of the democratic state was the use of taxes as macroeconomic pulls and levers with which to steer the economy, so as to ensure that the democratically forged will was effectively implemented and not hampered by the structural power of market actors.[1] Finally, the social state required that the kind of taxes to be collected and the pattern of distribution of the tax burden not only generated revenue with which to fund public goods and services (aimed at ensuring material, and not only formal, equality) but at the same time taxes contributed to the redistribution of income, so as to keep inequality in check.

This required in particular that:

- The harmonisation of national taxes (and even more so the assignment of tax collecting powers to the European Communities) had to be the result of political decisions with strong democratic legitimacy. Thus the requirement of unanimous agreement within the Council (Art. 100 EC) and of a quasi-constitutional decision to assign tax collecting powers to the Communities (Art. 201 EC *in finem*).
- The autonomy of national tax legislators should be preserved (Von der Groeben 1968). The design of the tax system, the tax mix (the different taxes to be collected), the design of each tax, the objectives to be realised through each tax were questions that had to be tackled in a highly contextual fashion. The socio-economic and political context, but also the history and culture of each country had a role to play (European Commission 1962: 98–100). This was clearly established in 1953 when the High Authority affirmed that restitution of turnover taxes at the border did not constitute price discrimination (European Commission 1953: 109), but actually was necessary to ensure that member states

1 But it should be kept in mind that ordoliberals, German and non-German, contested the wisdom of any form of active interventionism and limited steering to 'stabilisation' (Röpke 1963: chap. 8; Einaudi 2012).

remained capable of determining the level of turnover taxation to be applied in their territory (Haas 1958: 60 et seq.; Regul 1966: 88–97). The reconciliation of integration and national tax autonomy was also reflected in the understanding of free movement of goods and the other economic freedoms as operationalisations of the right to non-discrimination on the basis of nationality. The goal of creating a common market did not by itself predetermine the substantive content of national regulations, very especially those aimed at realising socio-economic goals, but only that nationals and goods from other member states would be treated as nationals were treated.
- The use of national taxes as macroeconomic levers should be coordinated; indeed, the further integration proceeded, the stronger was the case for coordination, as the effects of national steering policies would likely be felt in the common market as a whole, not only within single states.

Thirdly, an autonomous supranational power to tax should be developed. In the short and mid runs, the Communities needed a minimum set of tax collecting powers to fund the running costs of the Communities (Art. 172 ECSC and Art. 201 EC). In the mid and long runs, the size of the supranational tax collecting powers had to be proportional to the policies and tasks of the Communities (Art. 201 EC, analogically). Explicit mention was made to financial assistance to member states experiencing a balance of payments crisis (Art. 108(2) EC).

The constitutional philosophy of *integration through tax harmonisation* was perhaps most clearly articulated in the Neumark Report of 1962. The report was penned by leading public finance experts, both European and non European (for a collection of related papers, see Shoup 1967). Its chairman Fritz Neumark cut a remarkable figure. He was born and educated in the turbulent interwar Germany. He was then forced into exile in Turkey from 1933 to 1952, to return then to Frankfurt and become the *doyen* of German and indeed European public finance (Fuentes Quintana 1970). Extremely well read in the (then leading) US public finance literature, deeply knowledgeable about the post-war transformation of European national tax systems, active participant in the recasting of the tax system of Turkey (Andic and Andic 1981; Andic and Reisman 2007), Neumark exerted a decisive influence in the Committee, and contributed to the normative articulation of the implications of the social and democratic tax state for European integration (compare European Commission 1962 with European Commission 1967).

Significant pieces of harmonising legislation were passed in the first two decades of the common market. A common customs code was in force by 1 July 1968.[2] The key principles of a common system of turnover taxation, in particular of Value Added Taxation (VAT) were agreed upon in 1967[3] (as we will see, the VAT tax base would be further harmonised in 1977). The Directive concerning indirect taxes on the raising of capital was approved in 1969.[4] Despite the spectacular clash in 1965 between the Commission and the French Republic over the assignment of tax collecting powers to the Communities to fund the common agricultural policy (European Commission 1965), a modest set of tax collecting powers were transferred to the Communities in 1970 on the understanding that they would make the Communities financially autonomous.

At the same time, the Court of Justice played a relevant but thoroughly supporting role. The Court acted as enforcer of the Treaty provisions that established the concrete tax steps to be taken to create the common market, including standstill clauses on customs duties[5] and, crucially, the provision prohibiting the introduction of measures equivalent to quantitative restrictions.[6] From 1968, the Court started to review the validity of national tax norms by reference to the now directly effective right to free movement of goods.[7] The Court was keen to go beyond a formal analysis of the way in which national legislators taxed goods, and engage in an analysis of whether formal equality cloaked discrimination in material, economic terms.[8] However, the Luxembourg judges restrained themselves from both reviewing the validity of tax norms that had not been yet harmonised (thus staying clear of all personal taxes) and from quashing national tax norms that affected the exercise of economic freedoms but did not discriminate against economic actors or goods from other member states.

2 Regulation 950/68 on the common customs tariff, OJ 1968, L 172/1. The original Treaty established a complex division of labour between intergovernmental and Community decisions on the matter. Tariffs were harmonised in 1968, but customs law as such was only harmonised much later, through the 1992 Customs Code.

3 Directive 67/227/EEC on the harmonisation of legislation of member states concerning turnover taxes, OJ 1967, L71/1301; Directive 67/228/EEC on the harmonisation of legislation of member states concerning turnover taxes, structure and procedures for application of the common system of value added tax, OJ 1967, L 71/1303.

4 Directive 69/335/EEC concerning indirect taxes on the raising of capital, OJ 1969, L 249/25.

5 *Van Gend en Loos*, EU:C:1963:1.

6 *Fink Frucht*, EU:C:1968:22.

7 *Rewe*, EU:C:1976:22.

8 *Commission* v. *France*, EU:C:1980:51.

Table 4.1 *Tax revenue, 1965–1971, European Communities*

	1965	1968	1971
Germany	31.6	32.2	32.0
France	33.6	33.8	33.1
Belgium	30.6	34.2	34.4
Netherlands	30.9	33.8	34.9
Italy	24.7	26.1	25.5
Luxembourg	26.4	25.9	24.4

Source: OECD.

This slow and politically mediated process of harmonisation of taxes was clearly compatible with the consolidation of the social and democratic *Rechtsstaat*, and, in particular, of the welfare state. While both public spending and taxation were largely stable in relative terms (the latter despite the programmed decline of customs duties, eliminated for intra-EC trade, and lowered for international trade, see Table 4.1), sustained and high economic growth meant a steady increase in actual resources. And indeed the weight of social expenditure over total public expenditure tended to grow in a context of very low unemployment (Table 4.2).

Parallel to the supranationally induced harmonisation (as was the case with consumption taxes), there were signs of a process of slow convergence of national tax systems (through what now may be fashionable to refer as a process of mutual learning). The key four (personal income tax, corporate income tax, social security contributions, general consumption taxes) became even more so the pillars of national tax systems. Idiosyncratic tax formulae (as the Belgian personal tax applied to both corporations and physical persons) tended to be repealed. And, by the late 1960s, a new German government was experimenting with a modest set of tax measures to steer the economy (Leaman 1998). All this goes some way to account for the fact that when the newly democratised Greece, Spain and Portugal had to think about what shape to give to their tax systems, the template to be found in the Neumark report was the obvious one to consider.[9]

9 This was outstandingly clear in the Spanish case (Comín 2007).

Table 4.2 *Social spending, selected European countries*

	1950	1954	1958	1962	1966	1970	1974	1978
Germany	16.63	17.18	20.51	20.70	22.49	23.55	28.67	30.89
Belgium	12.57	13.55	15.90	19.27	22.55	25.10	28.70	37.27
Italy	9.39	12.23	15.25	17.36	20.17	21.11	23.53	26.54
Spain	4.07	3.18	3.90	3.98	5.06	9.98	12.05	16.68
Portugal	3.21	3.78	4.33	4.67	4.79	6.08	8.60	11.90

Source: Espuelas 2012.

II From integration through tax harmonisation to integration through the removal of tax obstacles

The monetary and economic crises that hit Europe in the early 1970s pushed the process of European integration off balance. Economic integration had proceeded quite a long way, but national socio-economic structures were still rather different. Consequently, the crises had different impacts in different member states. Moreover, the Communities lacked sufficient institutional, structural and financial means with which to give a coordinated response to the crises. So the very different impact of the crises was further compounded by the uncoordinated national policies applied to contain and overcome them (Scharpf 1991). Under such conditions, it was only a matter of time before the background conditions that had made it possible to reconcile integration with the consolidation of the social and democratic *Rechtsstaat* would start to deteriorate. By the end of the 1970s, it would be the very socio-economic consensus around the social and democratic *Rechtsstaat* that will be seriously challenged. Ordoliberal ideas were ascendant in Germany, and the apparent success of the Bundesbank in the fight against inflation was seen by many as turning the German socio-economic constitution (as understood by ordoliberals) into a model (Leaman 2000). Even more decisively, the British socio-economic constitution underwent a radical mutation after the electoral victory of Thatcher in 1979 (Gamble 1988; Fry 2008; but see Rogers 2013). Neo-liberalism had come to stay.

It was against this background that a fundamental shift in the means and goals of integration came to happen. The very fact that integration was politically mediated (and decisions subject consequently to unanimous consent within the Council of Ministers and the European Council) came to be seen as a key part of the problem. This created the conditions under which the DG Common Market persuaded the ECJ that it was time a new understanding of free movement of goods was endorsed (Grin 2004). In *Cassis de Dijon* the ECJ widened quite drastically the bite of free movement of goods by establishing that it will be ready to quash national laws that placed obstacles to the exercise of that freedom, even if those obstacles were *not* discriminatory.[10] This was interpreted by the Commission as opening up a new *path* of integration alternative to that mediated by politics, i.e., integration through mutual recognition of national legal standards (European Commission 1980).[11] On the face of it, this seemed a radically pluralistic option. As a matter of fact, mutual recognition implied empowering economic actors to foster the homogenisation of national laws by means of challenging their validity on the basis of their economic freedoms. This new approach, with its sharpest corners somehow cut, underpinned the policy programme of the European Commission from the mid-1980s (European Commission 1985). The goal of establishing an internal market was no longer defined by reference to the regulatory ideal of the common market, but by reference to that of the single market. And still, *l'Europe par le marché* was conceived as a 'neutral' goal which could be appealing to otherwise increasingly antagonistic socio-economic visions (Jabko 2009; Van Apeldoorn, 2002). This paradigmatic shift in the goals and vision of European integration led to a transformation of the European framework governing national tax laws.

No more tax harmonisation

1970s: tax harmonisation stalls

During the 1970s, the élan of integration through tax harmonisation was still strong enough so as to lead to the approbation of some important pieces of legislation. First, a much tighter common definition of the tax base of VAT was introduced in 1977, making it possible to make a fraction of VAT a European tax from 1979.[12] Secondly, the institutional and economic means to provide financial assistance to countries experiencing

10 *Cassis de Dijon*, EU:C:1979:42.

11 Communication from the Commission concerning the consequences of the judgment given by the Court of Justice on 20 February 1979 in Case 120/78 ('*Cassis de Dijon*'), OJ 1980, C 256/2.

12 Directive 77/388/EEC on the harmonisation of the laws relating to turnover taxes, OJ 1977, L 145/1.

balance of payments problems were created.[13] Italy (in 1974) and Italy and Ireland (in 1976) were recipients of that assistance. Thirdly, member states agreed to introduce changes in their national tax legislation so as to make it technically possible to coordinate tax increases or decreases as a means of coordinated macroeconomic steering.[14] Fourthly, arrangements to exchange data between national tax administrations were put in place in 1977, as a means of counteracting the growing extent to which the most mobile forms of capital income and wealth were disappearing from the radar of national tax authorities.[15] Fifthly, mechanisms of assistance in the cross-border collection of taxes were created.[16]

Still, with the single exception of the VAT directive, these decisions either did not have a lasting impact or remained simply without any real effect. Moreover, many other tax proposals gathered dust. Including, in particular, Commission proposals concerning the harmonisation of corporate income taxation, which failed to be seriously considered by the Council of Ministers.[17]

1980s: tax harmonisation is abandoned for good

The systematic failure to broker the required unanimous agreement in the Council, coupled with growing divergence of views about the point of European tax norms, led to the Commission renouncing the ambition of enacting a comprehensive set of European laws ensuring the harmonious interaction of national tax laws.[18]

13 Decision 143/71/EEC setting up the machinery for medium-term financial assistance, OJ 1971, L 73/13; Regulation 397/75/EEC concerning Community loans, OJ 1975, L 461.

14 Directive 74/121/EEC on stability, growth and full employment in the Community, OJ 1974, L 63/19, especially Articles 5 and 8.

15 Directive 77/799/EEC concerning mutual assistance by the competent authorities of the member states in the field of direct taxation, OJ 1977, L 336/15. Article 3 provided for automatic exchange of information, but Article 8(1) provided a waiver when a member state was 'prevented by its laws or administrative practices from carrying out these enquiries or from collecting or using this information for its own purposes'.

16 Directive 76/308/EEC on mutual assistance for the recovery of claims resulting from operations forming part of the system of financing the European Agricultural Guidance and Guarantee Fund, and of the agricultural levies and customs duties, OJ 1976, L 73/18.

17 European Commission, 'Proposal for a Directive of the Council concerning the Harmonisation of System of Company Taxation and of Withholding Taxes on Dividends', COM (75) 392.

18 Abandonment of tax harmonisation was already in the making by 1980 (European Commission 1980). The conclusions are telling: ibid.: 64 et seq. The Commission highlights the difficulties and renounces the fixing of a schedule.

Indeed, the choice for the single market led to a radical new understanding of the relationship between integration and the power to tax. The Commission came to expect that the convergence of national tax systems would not be the result of political agreements, but of the unilateral adaptation of national laws to the dynamics of market integration. This new approach would come to be labelled in the mid-1980s 'tax coordination' or 'tax cooperation' (European Commission 1997a). This was to a large extent the tax equivalent of the single market.

Although regulations and directives were still needed, the Commission will now put forward minimalistic proposals, tackling rather narrowly the tax distortions unlikely to be wiped out by 'market-led' integration. This was the spirit in which the Parent Subsidiary Directive[19] and the Merger Directive[20] proposals (finally approved in 1990) were drafted. And this was the vision underlying the Ruding report on corporate income taxation (European Commission 1990). Moreover, when possible, mechanisms of social integration other than law were to be preferred to coordinate tax systems. Instead of a directive on transfer pricing, the Commission ended up proposing an arbitration convention.[21] And instead of a directive on corporate income taxation, a 'code of conduct' and a rather informal procedure (the first instance of what later came to be known as the open method of coordination) were tried.[22]

Tax cooperation was expected to result in leaner and narrower secondary norms. It was hoped the minimalistic character of these regulations and directives would make it easier to approve them. This was not the case. Few and far between tax proposals ended up in the *Official Journal*.

19 Directive 90/435/EEC on the common system of taxation applicable in the case of parent companies and subsidiaries of different member states, OJ L 1990, L 225/6.

20 Directive 90/434/EEC on the common system of taxation applicable to mergers, divisions, transfers of assets and exchanges of shares concerning companies of different member states, OJ 1990, L 225/1.

21 Convention on the elimination of double taxation in connection with the adjustment of profits of associated enterprises, OJ 1990, L 225/10.

22 See European Commission 1997a. The Conclusions of the ECOFIN Council of 1 December 1997 concerning tax policy contain a code of conduct identifying harmful tax practices. See OJ 1997, C 2/1. The Code of Conduct was fleshed out by the so-called Primarolo Group, Code of Conduct Group (Business Taxation), SN 4901/99, of 23 November 1999. On this as a precedent for the open method of coordination see Radaelli 2003.

Turning private actors (largely multinationals) into enforcers of integration through the removal of tax obstacles

The 1980s and early 1990s: widening the set of national tax laws the validity of which was reviewed by the ECJ

The new understanding of economic freedoms as operationalisations of a substantive conception of private property and freedom of enterprise, first fleshed out in *Cassis de Dijon*, had a double impact on the review of the European constitutionality of national tax laws.

First, the Court became willing to review the validity of *all national tax laws* and not only national laws concerning taxes that had been previously harmonised. The leading cases were *Avoir Fiscal*[23] and *Schumacker*.[24] They entailed a massive increase in the breadth and depth of the Europeanisation of national tax systems because Europeanisation became *fully autonomous* from political decision-making. Whether the relevant tax had been harmonised or not, the European validity of national tax laws could now be reviewed.

Secondly, and simultaneously, the ECJ was careful to calibrate the impact that the vast expansion of tax laws susceptible of being challenged on the basis of eventual breaches of economic freedoms had. The ECJ introduced limits to the scope of economic freedoms by acknowledging the extent to which the coherent functioning of the tax system was a fundamental collective interest. In *Daily Mail*, the ECJ affirmed that the freedom of establishment did not entail the right to reincorporate in another state to avoid paying the taxes due on capital gains not realised at the time of the transfer.[25] This reflected the premise, made explicit in the case by Advocate General Darmon, that freedom of establishment only extended to activities with a genuine economic link, and not to activities aimed at avoiding the full application of laws. In *Bachmann*,[26] the ECJ showed its readiness to limit the freedom to provide services so as to protect the *coherence* of the Belgian tax system. Even if the ruling left largely unspecified what was exactly meant by *coherence of the tax system*, the decision had the potential of reorienting the case law of the Court, and make it more sensitive to the relational and redistributive character of the tax system (Menéndez 2009: 201 et seq.).

23 *Avoir Fiscal*, EU:C:1986:37.
24 *Schumacker*, EU:C:1995:31.
25 *Daily Mail*, EU:C:1988:456.
26 *Bachmann*, EU:C:1992:35.

The late 1990s and early 2000s: taxes as obstacles to economic freedoms

The final step in the transformation of the pattern of Europeanisation of national tax systems was triggered by two decisions of constitutional importance: the reconfiguration of free movement of capital as a full-blown economic freedom and the launch of an idiosyncratic and asymmetric economic and monetary union.

- Directive 88/361 liberalised all capital movements, particularly movements of a purely financial nature, unrelated with the exercise of any other economic freedom. In its turn, the Treaty of Maastricht expanded the freedom to movements of capital to and from third countries. The purpose of this massive extension of the breadth of the freedom to move capital was to maximise the chances that financial markets operated as a disciplining force on national fiscal policies within EMU (Dyson and Featherstone 1999).
- Asymmetric economic and monetary union came hand in hand with not only free movement of capital but also with rules disciplining fiscal policy, and, indirectly, public spending and taxation. The Protocol attached to the Maastricht Treaty on the excessive deficit procedure established ceilings of 3 per cent GDP for the deficit and 60 per cent GDP for public debt.[27] Thresholds that were reiterated and procedurally fleshed out in the Stability and Growth Pact.

It was after these two transformations were in place that the Court of Justice took a further step and started to regard all tax laws, whether or not discriminatory, as potential obstacles to the exercise of economic freedoms. The cases where the Court first shifted its approach were *Futura*[28] and *Verkooijen*.[29] This multiplied the possibilities for challenging national laws taxing capital income by means of rearranging all investments and corporate structures as cross-border ones. At the same time, the Court restricted the extent to which the collective interest in the efficiency of the tax system would justify the infringement of an economic freedom. If *Bachmann* opened the door to understanding cohesion as a property of the tax system as a whole, and thus related to the relational and redistributive character of the tax system, coherence was soon reduced to a property of the relationship between the tax system and each individual taxpayer;

27 Protocol 12 TFEU.
28 *Futura*, EU:C:1997:239.
29 *Verkooijen*, EU:C:2000:294.

what mattered was the coherent treatment of each taxpayer, which left out the relational and redistributive character of the tax system. The leading cases in that regard were *Wielockx*[30] and, perhaps even more clearly, *Svensson and Gustaffson*,[31] with *Verkooijen*[32] closing the argumentative turnaround.

This led to a maximalist interpretation of economic freedoms that the Court itself (partially) rectified. This came via a combination of the private law notion of 'abuse of rights' (of economic freedoms) and of the affirmation of 'tax sovereignty' as an overriding interest that might justify the restriction of economic freedoms, as in *Marks and Spencer*,[33] *Cadbury*[34] or *Thin Group Litigation*.[35] Still, the Court remained reluctant to overcome its formalistic approach to the tax implications of the 'obstacle' conception of economic freedoms. Indeed, the creation and recreation of legal structures for the purpose of not paying taxes would only constitute an 'abuse' of economic freedoms under rather exceptional circumstances. It is worth quoting at length from *Cadbury*:

> It follows that, in order for a restriction on the freedom of establishment to be justified on the ground of prevention of abusive practices, the specific objective of such a restriction must be to prevent conduct involving the creation of *wholly artificial arrangements* which do not reflect economic reality, with a view to escaping the tax normally due on the profits generated by activities carried out on national territory.[36]

Or, what is the same, partially artificial arrangements did not constitute an abuse of economic rights. The 'genuine economic link' required by Advocate General Darmon in *Daily Mail* was no longer required.

Abandoning plans to transfer taxing powers to the EU

Diluting the 1970 decision to transfer tax collecting powers to the EU

The long labours of transferring tax collecting powers to the European Communities were rather quickly lost.

In 1984, the British 'cheque' was agreed, reintroducing the logic of member states, not individual taxpayers, as the main units of contribution to the

30 *Wielockx*, EU:C:1995:271.
31 *Svensson and Gustaffson*, EU:C:1995:379.
32 *Verkooijen*, EU:C:2000:294.
33 *Marks and Spencer*, EU:C:2005:763, paras. 39 and 49.
34 *Cadbury*, EU:C:2006:544, paras. 55 and 56.
35 *Thin Cap Group Litigation*, EU:C:2007:161, para. 75.
36 *Cadbury*, EU:C:2006:544, para. 55 (my italics).

European budget.[37] This trend was further confirmed in 1988. In that year the size of the European budget was increased, but at the price of diminishing the relative weight of European taxes as a source of revenue. National contributions relative to GDP were to become a key component of the European budget, as they are still now. Finally, in 1993, the European rate of VAT was capped at one penny in the pound (and then halved in 2000).[38]

Plans to transfer tax collecting powers to the EU abandoned for good

Blueprints for monetary union and studies on the future shape of European public finances had made invariable reference to monetary union coming hand in hand with a sizeable increase in the tax collecting powers of the European Communities (most clearly, European Commission 1977).

However, when monetary union was agreed in 1992, no new tax collecting powers were transferred to the European Union. In the run up to monetary union, there was a (formally) temporal increase in the monies spent in structural and cohesion funds, a decision (politically) linked to that of launching monetary union. But that was the only decision that was taken.

The decision not to grant new taxing powers and new resources to the supranational level was especially surprising given the fact that the degree of economic heterogeneity among the states that finally made up the Eurozone was very considerable. Standard economic knowledge regarding optimal currency areas (Mundell 1961; Kaldor 1978) was left aside. Instead, the implicit assumption was that the *economic and financial dynamics* that monetary integration will unleash will by themselves ensure that the Eurozone would become an increasingly optimal currency area (Rose 2000; presciently against Gustavsson 2002).

Implications

From taxing according to the ability to pay to taxing according to the ability to evade taxes

Capital unbound entailed the erosion of tax bases and a dynamics of competition between tax systems The unleashing of capital after the

37 Conclusions of the Presidency of the European Council, 25–26 June 1984.

38 Decision 88/376/EEC, Euratom on the system of the Communities' own resources, OJ 1988, L 185/ 24. The Inter-institutional Agreement of 29 October 1993 on budgetary discipline and improvement of the budgetary procedure, OJ 1993, C 331/1, contained the financial perspective from 1993 onwards.

monetary and economic crises of the early 1970s challenged the capacity of states to track capital income and wealth flows (see Table 4.3; Helleiner 1994). This created not only new structural opportunities to evade taxes, but also many novel opportunities to play out one tax system against the other, triggering dynamics of tax competition (Avi Yonah 2000).

When in 1979 the United Kingdom liberalised capital movements, other member states came under enormous pressure to follow suit (especially because they were increasingly reliant on debt to fill the gap between taxation and expenditure, as we will see). Directive 88/361 and the Treaty of Maastricht resulted in the full liberalisation of capital movements. At that point, states entered into a race to attract capital by means of offering

Table 4.3 *Size of shadow economies, selected countries*

	Currency demand (percentage of official GNP)					Model approach (percentage of official GNP)	
Country	1960	1970	1980	1990	1994	1960	1978
Austria	0.4	3.9	5.0	7.2	8.32[1]	4.6	8.9
Belgium	7.8[4]	10.4	16.4	19.6	21.4	4.7	12.1
Canada	n.a.	5.8/7.2[2]	10.1/11.2	n.a.	14.6	5.1	8.7
Denmark	3.8/4.8	5.3/7.4	6.9/10.2	9.0/13.4	17.6	3.7	11.8
Germany	2.0/2.1	2.7/3.0	10.3/11.2	11.4/13.1	14.5[1]	3.7	8.6
Finland	n.a.	n.a.	n.a.	n.a.	n.a.	3.1	7.6
France	n.a.	3.9	6.9	9.4	14.3	5.9	9.4
Ireland	n.a.	4.3	8.0	11.7	15.3	1.7	7.2
Italy	8.4[4]	10.7	16.7	23.4	25.8	4.4	11.4
Japan	n.a.	n.a.	n.a.	n.a.	n.a.	2.0	4.1
Netherlands	n.a.	4.8	9.1	13.9	13.6	5.6	9.6
Norway	1.3/1.7	6.2/6.9	10.2/10.9	14.5/16.0	17.9	4.4	9.2
Spain	n.a.	n.a.	18.0[3]	21	n.a.	2.6	6.5
Sweden	1.5/1.8	6.8/7.8	11.9/12.4	15.8/16.7	18.3	5.4	13.2
Switzerland	1.2	4.1	6.5	6.9	7.5[1]	1.1	4.3
United Kingdom	n.a.	2.0	8.4	10.2	n.a.	4.6	8.0
USA	2.6/4.1	2.6/4.6	3.9/6.1	5.1/8.6	9.4	4.6	8.3

Source: Schneider 1997.

[1]1996.

[2]1975.

[3]1978.

[4]1965.

non-residents a zero rate on their returns.[39] In the absence of proper tax cooperation among European states, non-residents could reap a zero-tax at destination, and avoid reporting the capital income at the state of their residence (Lodin 2000). Unsurprisingly, it became part of the financial game that British banks advertised in German newspapers, and German banks advertised in British newspapers, offering attractive investment opportunities with an 'advantageous' tax treatment (Mohamed 2000: n. 57). Similarly, the combined effect of the radical interpretation of freedom of establishment and free movement of capital was to reorganise multinational corporate structures so as to maximise the chances of reducing tax liabilities (Bartelsman and Beetsma 2000; Murphy 2013).

The dynamics of tax competition became so evident that the Commission was forced into putting forward proposals to deal with it. Quite interestingly, the result was not a re-evaluation of the new pattern of Europeanisation of national tax systems but the development of a peculiar distinction between 'good' and 'bad' tax competition, the latter being relabelled 'harmful tax competition' (see European Commission 1997a; European Commission 1997b). So, quite paradoxically, the acknowledgment of the effects of unleashing capital over tax systems resulted in the further entrenchment of the assumption that the proper relationship between national tax systems should be one of *competition*.

How tax revenue could keep on going up despite the erosion of tax bases Despite the growing opportunities to evade taxes, the revenue collected through taxes did not go down, but kept on growing (even if at rates insufficient to cover expenditure) (Table 4.4). How could that be?

The revenue-yielding capacity of the tax system was preserved by means of shifting the criteria of allocation of the tax burden. The tax sacrifice demanded from taxpayers came to be graduated not only by reference to their ability to pay but also by reference to their capacity to avoid taxes. In practice, that meant that the tax burden imposed upon the less mobile tax bases (employed labour through income tax, social security contributions

39 It is instructive to note that the 10 per cent withholding tax on savings in Germany introduced after Directive 88/361 was quashed by the German Constitutional Court on the basis that compliance was bound to be extremely asymmetrical. The tax was repealed, and a new one at 30 per cent was introduced, only this time non-residents were explicitly exempted from the tax, 2 BvR 1493/89 *Withholding Tax*, Judgment of 27 June 1991.

Table 4.4 *Total tax revenue as percentage of GDP, 1970–1991, selected European countries*

	1970	1973	1976	1979	1982	1985	1988	1991	1970/1991
Germany	31.5	35	34.3	36.4	35.5	36.1	36.0	35	+3.5
France	34.1	33.5	36.7	38.1	40.3	41.9	41.2	41.3	+6.8
Italy	24.8	23.1	25.4	25.3	31.9	32.5	34.6	36.8	+8.0
United Kingdom	35.3	30	33.5	30.7	37.1	35.8	34.8	32.7	−2.6
Netherlands	33.5	37	38.2	40.1	40.2	39.9	42.8	42.4	+8.9
Spain	15.5	17.2	17.9	21.4	23.5	26.8	30.1	31.9	+16.4
Portugal	17.6	16.7	20.5	19.9	23.7	24.1	25.6	27.5	+9.9
Greece	19.1	17.3	20.2	21.2	23.5	24.4	23.5	25	+5.9
Ireland	27.6	27.6	31	27.6	32.6	33.7	35.7	32.4	+4.8

and fees for the use of public services) went up.[40] At the same time, taxes on more mobile tax bases were reduced. Paradigmatic in that regard was the splitting of the personal income tax base and the creation of schedular taxes on capital gains (at a lower and flat rate) (Sørensen 1994).[41] Both the marginal rates and the number of brackets of personal income taxes were reduced (with the revenue effect partially compensated by reducing deductions and tax credits, with rather asymmetric distributive effects) (OECD 2006). The revenue-yielding capacity of corporate income taxes stagnated or declined, despite the fact that the capital share in national income grew constantly.

Revenue was maximised, but only at the price of compromising the structural coherence of each tax and of national tax systems as a whole (Williams 1997: 10). This dynamic was hard to stop once set in motion, because integration through the removal of tax obstacles resulted in the impotence of both European and national legislators to rebalance tax systems. In most cases, the European legislator could not intervene, either because no unanimity within the Council could be obtained (as was, for

40 By 1996, the Commission claimed that there had been a clear shift in the distribution of the tax burden. Taxes burdening labour had gone up from 34.7 per cent to 40.5 per cent, while taxes on other factors of production had gone down from 44.1 per cent to 35.2 per cent of the total tax yield (European Commission 1996).

41 This was justified as a means to make more probable that at a least a fraction of the tax was paid. If the rate was low enough as to be lower than the 'price' that should be put on the risk of the taxpayer being discovered by the tax authorities, taxpayers will choose to pay *even if they could avoid the tax.*

example, the case with the tax treatment of cross-border dividends), or because there would not be a unanimous majority in the Council to amend the existing regulation or directive (as was the case with VAT). National legislative interventions ran the high risk of being challenged again before the ECJ.

The (partial) return of the debt state

Tax revenues were maximised, but total tax revenue lagged behind public expenditure.

This was already the case in the 1970s. However, it did not lead automatically to the growth of public debt. High levels of inflation, plus resort to the monetisation of debt by central banks, curbed the growth of debt. Inflation reduced the weight of the stock of debt, while central bank intervention kept down the costs of financing deficits.

The tax gap became a real problem once deflationary policies were applied to kill inflation.[42] On the one hand, the growth of the structural levels of unemployment reduced the yield of social security contributions while increasing social expenditure. On the other hand, it was decided that the state should only borrow at 'market' conditions. Indeed, the prohibition of the monetising of debt via the central bank and/or the acquisition of debt by the central bank was understood to be a precondition for joining the immediate precedent of EMU, the Exchange Rate Mechanism (Bagnai 2012) Finally, the end of inflation was also the end of the constant erosion of the stock of public debt (Table 4.5).

Private debt as booster of tax revenue

Private debt grew in most European states at unsustainable levels in the 1990s and early 2000s. This was hardly an exclusively European development, even less a pattern only registered within the Eurozone. It was in fact a general trend of 'Western' economies (Wade 2008).

The growth of private debt was to a rather large extent the flip side of the repression of wages through which inflation was curbed (as reflected in a constantly declining labour income share since the late 1970s) (European Commission 2007: chap. 5; Bagnai 2014: 213 ff.) and of the erosion of the capacity of states to tax effectively.

42 Indeed, public debt levels started to grow much earlier in Germany, where the autonomous Bundesbank applied anti-inflationary monetary policies since very early on (Streeck 2014).

Table 4.5 *Total government spending, 1970–1999, selected European countries*

	1970	1973	1976	1979	1982	1985	1988	1991
Germany	38.5	41.6	48.3	46.5	47.5	45.2	45.0	46.3
France				44.9	49.9	51.9	50.1	50.7
Italy	32.7	35.1	38.4	40.6	46.7	49.8	50.4	54.0
United Kingdom	41.7	43.2	48.9	44.8	50.4	48.4	40.0	42.5
Netherlands	43.2	44.6	50.8	53.7	59.1	57.3	56.4	54.9
Spain	22.5					42.7		
Portugal				30.8	35.7	37.5	36.1	41.3

Sources: www.cesifo-group.de/ifoHome/facts/DICE/Public-Sector/Public-Finance/Public-Expenditures.html (Germany, United Kingdom, Netherlands), Italia, Raggioneria dello Stato.

More profits and fewer taxes resulted in more capital in private hands, which in turn had to seek for investment opportunities (Harvey 2014; Bagnai 2014). This fostered three critical developments:

- First, resort to private debt as a means of compensating the loss of available income resulting from the repression of wages and over-taxation. Private individuals started to engage in debt not to pay for long-term investments but to pay for consumption. At the same time, the growth of private debt counteracted the deflationary effect of wage repression, in fact, resulting in a peculiar form of 'private' Keynesianism, in a 'private' substitute of expansionary fiscal policy (Crouch 2011; Streeck 2014; Bagnai 2014).
- Secondly, unsustainable growth of economic activities which offered high returns in the short run. The paradigmatic example was real estate bubbles, where unsustainable non-financial and financial growth met (Taub 2014).
- Thirdly, the constant exponential growth of financial assets, with a series of financial bubbles facilitated when not triggered by accommodating monetary policy (Coggan 2011; Lapavitsas 2013).

The specific pattern of growth of private debt within the Eurozone was very much shaped by the economic and financial dynamics of asymmetric economic and monetary union. The decision of German governments to aim at a reduction of the unit labour costs through the repression of wage growth far below the growth of productivity aggravated the structural shortcomings of a far from optimal currency area which lacked institutional and financial means to redress imbalances (Bagnai 2012; Flassbeck and Lapavitsas 2015). Germany and the states that followed German wage policy (such as Finland) cumulated growing trade surpluses thanks to low labour unit costs, while other states cumulated deficits. With fixed parities, adjustment via the exchange rate could not happen. The structural consequences of this development were postponed thanks to massive capital flows moving in the opposite direction of trade. This was reflected in the symmetric current account positions of, on the one hand, Germany and the Netherlands, and, on the other hand, Greece, Spain, Ireland and Portugal. In the short run, this resulted in the mirage that asymmetric economic and monetary union could by itself foster convergence and turn the European Union, by the *spontaneous* action of market forces, into an optimal currency area (Rose 2000). Massive capital flows were interpreted as proving that if capital was liberated it would seek the best investment opportunities, and, in the process, level off income and wealth levels within the Eurozone. Indeed, the countries at the receiving end of capital flows seemed to be doing better (with Portugal being the odd exception) than those exporting capital (Germany being for a long period regarded as the *sick man* of Europe; cf. *The Economist* 2004) (see Table 4.6).

Table 4.6 *Current account deficits, 1997–2013, selected Eurozone countries*

	Year								
Country	1997	1999	2001	2003	2005	2007	2009	2011	2013
Germany	−0.44	−1.31	−0.01	1.9	5.1	7.4	5.9	6.8	7.5
Netherlands	6.22	3.67	2.45	5.27	7.4	6.7	5.2	9.1	10.4
Austria	−2.42	−1.64	−0.80	1.7	2.2	3.5	2.7	1.6	2.7
Spain	−0.09	−2.85	−3.85	−3.5	−7.4	−10	−4.8	−3.7	0.8
Greece	−3.84	−3.41	−6.7	−6.5	−7.6	−14.6	−11.2	−9.9	0.7
Italy	2.72	0.66	−0.06	−0.8	−0.3	−1.3	−1.9	−3.0	1
Ireland	2.35	0.28	−0.64	0	−3.5	−5.3	−2.3	1.2	6.6
Portugal	−5.78	−8.60	−10.23	−6.4	−10.3	−10.1	−10.9	−7	0.5
Eurozone as a whole	n.d	n.d	n.d	0.3	0.1	0.1	−0.1	0.1	2.4

Sources: OECD, Eurostat.

From a tax perspective, the growth of private debt, and, in particular, the specific pattern of growth of private debt within the Eurozone, resulted in the development of various strategies to develop *alternative tax bases* with which to fill the tax gap *without the need of resorting to public debt.*

- Some states fostered the growth of unsustainable economic activities that in the short run seemed to contribute to high growth and to result in massive tax yields. The real estate bubbles in Spain and Ireland are paradigmatic examples in that regard (McCabe 2011; Naredo and Álvarez 2011). In Greece and Portugal, the economic and fiscal stimulus resulted from the growth of private consumption.
- In other states, the rapid growth of private debt *in other countries* allowed the constant growth of exports, which yielded taxes through personal and corporate income taxation. By 2010, 50 per cent of German GDP was exported. This reflected changes in the way the chain of production was reorganized (most trade remains in Europe and elsewhere *intra-firm* trade, Pellegrin 2001), but also the extent to which the German economic and tax model became dependent on external demand.[43]
- Finally, some states have facilitated, through a mixture of an odd form of active neglect and active participation, the development of the legal and economic activities which make possible the artificial circulation of money through their financial institutions, or the establishment of 'shell' corporate structures within their territory, with the aim of avoiding the payment of taxes (Palan 2002; Shaxson 2011; Brooks 2014). This does not only undermine the tax collecting capacity of other states, but also allows the countries from which the providers of this legal and economic services operate to tap the tax revenue that results from the location in that jurisdiction of highly paid lawyers and economists specialising in 'tax management'. The three Benelux countries, Ireland and the United Kingdom have a considerable share of the tax evasion industry.[44]

43 According to World Bank figures, export of goods and services stood for 27.1 per cent of German GDP in 1999, and for 45.6 per cent in 2013. Although the relative weight of exports was constant, the key turning point was 2004. In 2003, exports were still at 32.6 per cent. By 2006, they were at 41.2 per cent. It is hard to miss the relation between the Harz reforms and this acceleration of exports. This high level of dependence on the external sector makes the German economy very exposed to the evolution of international trade. In 2009, exports fell by 5.7 per cent of GDP, and this accounts for most of the very sharp contraction of GDP in Germany.

44 For the Netherlands, see Van Dijk, Weyzig and Murphy 2007. See the reports on each of the mentioned EU states in the Financial Secrecy Index compiled by the Tax Justice Network. www.financialsecrecyindex.com/.

As is well-known, the Lux Leaks investigation has revealed the extent to which the Luxembourgeois government participated actively in corporate schemes to avoid taxes.[45] By 2010, the financial and tax evasion industries had substituted the iron industry in its role as driver of the national economy (Shaxson 2011).

Integration through the removal of tax obstacles and the gathering of the crises

Integration through the removal of tax obstacles played a role in fostering the financial, fiscal and macroeconomic structural weaknesses of the European Union, which will become open crises when the subprime crisis would hit Europe in 2007.

First, integration through the removal of tax obstacles contributed to the growth of the structural gap between the levels of public expenditure and tax revenue. It also created some of the means through which the tax gap could be dissimulated, such as the different strategies to turn the growth of private debt into sources of tax revenue. The obvious problem was that the tax gap was structural, while the dissimulation strategies were not only bound to be unsustainable, but came with massive hidden costs to the taxpayer (so more than filling the tax gap, they delayed the moment in which the gap materialised). As a result, it can be said that integration through the removal of tax obstacles played a very important role in fostering enormous fiscal weaknesses, which would play a major role in the unfolding of the European crises. The rapid deterioration of the fiscal position of countries such as Ireland or Spain was indeed due to the arrears of tax dissimulation strategies becoming suddenly due. By facilitating the growth of finance to get taxes today, states had ensured massive losses for tomorrow (Shaxson and Christiensen 2014).

Secondly, integration through the removal of tax obstacles was far from being unrelated to the accumulation of structural financial weaknesses. For one, the unleashing of capital from controls led not only to growth of massive opportunities to evade taxes, but also to the progressive adjustment of the pattern of taxation to the ability to evade of taxpayers. The net result was that the tax system absorbed less of the income accruing to capital owners. And what capital owners saved in taxes further fed the growth of financial assets and the process of financialisation of both economic and

45 www.icij.org/project/luxembourg-leaks.

social activities. For two, the flip side of the coin was constituted by those taxpayers who saw their tax burden grow to compensate the revenue lost due to the erosion of the capacity to tax mobile capital income and wealth. Because most of these taxpayers were private or public employees, they were affected at the same time by stagnant wages resulting from the structural decline of the wage share since the 1980s. These two trends fostered the growth of private debt, including borrowing to pay taxes. For three, the growing tax gap opened up the way to the financialisation of public finances. The tax gap was only partially filled through the adjustment of the tax system to the ability to evade taxes. A good deal of the gap was filled through public debt first, and through the tax proceedings of economic activities sustained by the growth of public debt later. In both cases the means to make possible state functions came to depend directly or indirectly on financial actors and institutions. As Streeck has highlighted, this had major political implications (Streeck 2014: 79 et seq.). But by itself it further contributed to the growth of financial activities.

Thirdly, integration through the removal of tax obstacles led to making tax systems ineffective tools of macroeconomic steering. For one, the less that tax authorities know about income and wealth flows, the more difficult it is to estimate the impact of tax changes, and, consequently the riskier it is to engage in active intervention through tax policy. For two, over-taxation of 'honest' taxpayers and under-taxation of 'mobile' taxpayers reduces the margin of manoeuvre for macroeconomic steering. When some taxes are pushed to a level close to those at which they would become simply unbearable for those paying them, and other taxes have to be kept artificially low to preserve the incentive of mobile taxpayers to pay them, macroeconomic steering through taxes becomes close to impossible. For three, the fiscal rules at the core of the Stability and Growth Pact further dented the possibility of macroeconomic steering through taxes. The original rules of 3 per cent deficit and 60 per cent debt were not only rather arbitrary, but prevented proper steering when that would require breaching fiscal rules, while leaving states full discretion to implement pro-cyclical policies as long as they stayed within the fiscal rules.

The long-term tax implications of the massive pile of widow risks

The massive current account imbalances to which I have referred were the result of the rapid growth of cross-border lending and borrowing. Financial integration was led and propelled by cross-border flows of capital. This was not only well received, but regarded as evidence of a well-functioning monetary union. However, it is important to keep in mind that no steps were taken to create either coordinated or supranational structures of supervision of cross-border financial activity or mechanisms either to allocate responsibility for the ensuing cross-border financial risks or to share such risks (Teixeira 2011).[46] In a rather similar way to monetary union proceeding without fiscal union, the integration of financial markets proceeded without banking union.

This had massive tax implications. A community of risks was created by stealth, through the individual decisions of private financial institutions. But no community of insurance was established. A massive pile of 'widow' risks culminated. The (wrong) belief that the new techniques of pricing of risks could do away with risks (Tett 2009; Derban 2011) made European institutions proclaim once and again that widow risks were quasi-hypothetical risks. In the remote event that such risks became losses, markets will absorb them.

III Integration through fiscal consolidation: taxes in the indebted state

General but asymmetric fiscal crises, 2007–2010

The immediate public finance implications of the crises

The economic crisis pushed almost all member states into deficit positions. However, the fiscal impact of the crises was asymmetric. The degree of deterioration of public finances largely depended on two factors. One was the financial losses that each state absorbed. The other was the degree to which tax revenue had come to depend on economic activities propelled by the constant growth of private debt during the previous decade.

First, the rapid transformation of the financial crisis into an economic crisis led to a rather automatic deterioration of the public finances of all member states of the European Union (Table 4.7). The economic slowdown made tax revenue decline, while employment-assistance (as in Germany) or unemployment insurance (as in Spain) pushed social expenditure up.

46 Some preparations were made for that eventuality. *Memorandum of Understanding on High-Level Principles of Cooperation between the Banking Supervisors and Central Banks of the European Union in Crisis Management Situations*, 10 March 2003; *Memorandum of Understanding and Co-Operative between the Banking Supervisors, Central Banks and Finance Ministries of the European Union in Financial Crisis Situations*, 18 May 2005. See also Schnasi and Teixeira 2006.

Table 4.7 *Deficits, 2007–2011, selected Eurozone countries*

	2007	2008	2009	2010	2011	2012
Germany	0.3	0	−3.0	−4.1	−0.9	0.1
Netherlands	0.2	0.2	−5.5	−5.0	−4.3	−4.0
France	−2.5	−3.2	−7.2	−6.8	−5.1	−4.9
Italy	−1.5	−2.7	−5.3	−4.2	−3.5	−3.0
Spain	2.0	−4.4	−11.0	−9.4	−9.4	−10.3
Portugal	−3.0	−3.8	−9.8	−11.2	−7.4	−5.5
Greece	−6.7	−9.9	−15.2	−11.1	−10.1	−8.6
Ireland	0.2	−7.0	−13.9	−32.4	−12.6	−8.0

Some states (but far from all) engaged in significant discretionary fiscal spending. Temporary tax rebates played an important role.[47]

Secondly, national exchequers absorbed a rather considerable amount of the financial risks that had been created through the exponential growth of financial assets in the years preceding the crises. The non-rescue of Lehman Brothers was widely believed to have unleashed a global financial crisis, and to have proven that it was *absolutely necessary* that states intervened to avoid the collapse of any other major financial institution (no 'systemically relevant' bank should be allowed to fail: the *too big to fail* doctrine). Banks should be underwritten by exchequers, relieved of their troubled assets by the state, or have their capital basis improved by injections of public money (European Council 2008). The fact that this entailed *protecting* the interests of capital holders, despite the fact that they may have been reckless, was regarded as beside the point. The bail-out of banks, and the consequent full protection of its shareholders, was the lesser evil (Geithner 2014).

This was bound to have massive tax implications, as the costs of bailing out the banks will end up being paid by the taxpayer. However, it was constantly argued that this was not really the case. The crisis of European financial institutions had not much to do with the state of those financial institutions, but was merely a crisis of *confidence* resulting from the panic imported from the USA after the near meltdown of the US financial system (Trichet 2009). When intervening to bail out financial institutions,

47 A summary is available at https://www.cesifo-group.de/ifoHome/facts/DICE/Public-Sector/Public-Finance/Taxes/over-tax-measur-crisis/fileBinary/over-tax-measur-crisis.pdf.

states were assuming purely *contingent* financial risks that once the panic was overcome would report *profits* to states.

The financial crisis made it impossible to keep on assuming that widow risks were purely hypothetical risks. The solution finally applied in 2010/11 was now preconfigured by two key decisions:

- For one, the fundamental decision *not to* create a community of insurance against financial risks created by cross-border activities. The then incumbent French presidency proposed the creation of a €300 billion fund to deal with banking crises (*The Economist* 2004). This was summarily rejected by the German Chancellor of the Exchequer. Attempts at ad hoc coordination of bail-outs (Dexia and Fortis) revealed the limits of the contingency plans elaborated before the crisis (for Dexia, see Van de Woestyne and Van Caloen 2008).
- For two, states took unilateral decisions to support *their* financial institutions. The obvious conflicts that this entailed with European norms on state aid were first ignored, and then avoided by means of a rather retroactive and very lax construction of state aid norms by the European Commission.[48] A race to the top concerning deposit guarantees, initiated by Ireland, was cloaked as a common decision to increase the guarantee ceilings in the relevant Directive.[49]

Thirdly, the enormous fragility of some of the tax compensatory strategies used to dissimulate the tax gap was suddenly revealed (Table 4.8). As the real estate bubbles burst, tax revenue collapsed in Spain (from 38 per cent of GDP in 2007 to 31.6 per cent of GDP in 2009) and took a plunge in Ireland (for the same years, 32.8 per cent GDP to 29.7 per cent GDP). The United Kingdom also experienced an important decline of its tax revenue. To the difficulties of the very tax significant real estate market, there were added the crisis in the massively oversized financial sector. The contribution of the City to total British revenue declined from 17 per cent GDP in 2007 to only slightly more than 12 per cent GPD in 2009 (Table 4.9).

Two momentous fiscal decisions that will become decisive later on

The Irish financial sector was not only extremely leveraged, but also extremely exposed. Even if one bank in particular (the Anglo Bank) was

48 Presidency Conclusions, European Council, 15 and 16 October 2008. Three Commission Communications followed. OJ 2008, C 270/8; OJ 2009, C 102/ 2; OJ 2009, C 72/1.

49 Directive 2009/14, OJ 2009, L 68/3.

Table 4.8 *Public debt, 2007–2011, selected Eurozone countries*

	2007	2008	2009	2010	2011	2012	2013
Germany	63.5	64.9 (+1.4)	72.4 (+7.5)	80.3 (+8.1)	77.6 (−2.7)	79.0 (+1.4)	76.9 (−2.1)
Netherlands	42.7	54.8 (+12.1)	56.5 (+0.7)	59.0 (+2.5)	61.3 (+2.3)	66.5 (+5.3)	68.6 (+2.1)
France	64.2	67.8 (+3.6)	78.8 (+11)	81.5 (+2.7)	85.0 (+3.5)	89.2 (+4.2)	87.2 (−2)
Italy	99.7	102.3 (+2.5)	112.5 (+10.2)	115.3 (+2.8)	116.4 (+1.1)	122.2 (+5.8)	127.9 (+5.7)
Spain	35.5	39.4 (+3.9)	52.7 (+13.6)	60.1 (+7.4)	69.2 (+9.1)	84.4 (+15.2)	92.1 (+7.9)
Greece	103.1	109.3 (+6.2)	126.8 (+17.5)	146.0 (+19.2)	171.3 (+25.3)	156.9 (−14.4)	174.9 (+18)
Ireland	24.0	42.6 (+18.6)	62.2 (19.6)	87.4 (+25.2)	111.1 (+27.7)	121.7 (+10.6)	123.3 (+1.6)
Portugal	68.4	71.7 (+3.3)	83.6 (+11.9)	96.2 (+12.6)	111.1 (+14.9)	124.8 (+13.7)	123.3 (1.5)

Table 4.9 *Tax revenue, 2007–2011, selected Eurozone countries*

	2007	2008	2009	2010	2011
Germany	38.7	38.9	39.4	38.0	38.5
Netherlands	38.7	39.2	38.2	38.9	38.6
Austria	41.7	42.7	42.4	42.1	42.2
France	43.4	43.2	42.1	42.5	43.7
Italy	42.7	42.7	42.9	42.5	43.7
Spain	37.1	32.9	30.7	32.2	31.8
Greece	32.5	32.1	30.5	31.7	32.4
Ireland	31.5	29.5	28.1	28.0	28.2
Portugal	32.8	32.8	31.0	31.5	33.2
United Kingdom	35.7	37.1	34.3	35.0	35.8

especially troubled, all Irish banks had come to depend on the massive inflows of capital from other Eurozone states, which now suddenly dried up. The Irish government proposed, and the Irish Parliament ratified, the extension of a blanket guarantee to all Irish financial institutions for two years.[50] It is important to notice that the blanket guarantee implied that Ireland as state of incorporation of the debtor financial institution would absorb in full all the financial risks generated by the flows of capital incoming to Ireland during the first ten years of EMU.

The cost of underwriting financial institutions had a major long-term effect. The €500 billion plan to support its financial institutions was presented by the incumbent German government as both absolutely necessary (Connolly 2008) and as further proof of the need to introduce a debt brake in the German Fundamental Law. The debt brake proposal pre-dated the crises and was prompted by the chronic fiscal problems of some *länder*, which forced the federal state to assist them again and again. To put it differently, up to 2008 the debt brake was seen as a German answer to a German problem. But the potential costs of underwriting German banks started to alter the way in which constitutional fiscal rules were seen (see Deutsche Bank 2011; Hamker 2012; for a critical analysis, see Hein and Truger 2014). As we will see, the European fiscal crises of 2010 and 2011 will turn the debt brake into a German answer to a European (but now allegedly non-German) problem.

50 Credit Institutions (Financial Support) Bill, of 30 September 2008, available at www.oireachtas.ie/documents/bills28/bills/2008/4508/b4508d.pdf; Credit Institutions (Financial Support) Act, 2 October 2008. www.oireachtas.ie/documents/bills28/acts/2008/a1808.pdf.

No changes to either European tax policy or in the case law of the ECJ

Despite the fact that the crises had an obvious and immediate financial impact, there was no major change in European tax policy. The Commission engaged in a new exercise of relabelling. After tax cooperation, now it was the turn of good (even robust) governance on tax matters (European Commission 2009). There was no substantive change and, indeed, no major policy initiative was launched.

Rather similarly, the crises did not seem to have an impact on the case law of the ECJ. The rebalancing of its case law, through reference to the tax sovereignty of member states, pre-dated the crises, and was not significantly affected by it (Pantazatou 2013).

From asymmetrical fiscal crisis to integration through fiscal consolidation: 2011 onwards

The time gained in 2007 and 2008 by underwriting financial risks was soon up. By late 2009, the Greek state was on the verge of fiscal collapse. By the fall of 2010, it would be the turn of the Irish state. Portugal, Cyprus and Spain would follow. The mix of causes of the fiscal crises of these states was not exactly the same. But in all cases the massive inflows of capital from other Eurozone states had played a major role in the gathering of the crises. And, in all cases, the way in which the 'widow' risks were finally assigned and dealt with played a decisive role in how the crises were solved.

Forging the consolidating tax state through 'financial assistance'

It was already noticed that the crises hit most rapidly and deeply the Eurozone states that had been net importers of capital during the first decade of monetary union. In the sequence characteristic of external debt crises, the sudden stop of capital flows revealed the fragility of public and private finances. Financial institutions were pushed off balance and had to be underwritten by states. The Treasuries saw the interest rates they had to pay to issue debt grow. Eurozone states were especially vulnerable, because they had lacked since the beginning of EMU the means of last resort to deal with a fiscal crisis, i.e., issue new currency to pay principal and interest on their debt. This is why member states experiencing similar problems but not members of the Eurozone did not experience a fiscal crisis (De Grauwe 2012; Wolf 2013). It is important to keep in mind that there is no debtor without a creditor. The eventual non-payment of the public and private debt of the Eurozone states nearing fiscal asphyxia would have inflicted a major blow to the financial institutions of the Eurozone through which capital had been exported during the first ten years of EMU. In particular, German, Dutch and French banks ran the risk of suffering major losses. The German, Dutch and French states were insurers and guarantors of last resort of those banks. So, if losses in proportion to the risks incurred would have been inflicted upon those banks, massive burdens would have resulted for those states (see Table 4.10).

Starting in late 2009, Greece, Ireland, Portugal, Cyprus and Spain came more or less close to fiscal collapse. The causes of the fiscal crises were many, and varied from one country to the other. It could fairly be said that all of them had been weak tax states (although the patterns of transformation had been different) and were especially vulnerable to financial crisis because of their traditional dependence on foreign capital.[51] What made the crises really explosive was the rapid growth of their external indebtment since the launch of EMU and the fact that EMU implied that these states lacked any policy lever with which to face a fiscal crisis.

Four key decisions were taken to deal with the fiscal crises of these states.

First, the fiscal and the financial crises were exchequered, or, what is the same, financial risks were absorbed by exchequers (and ultimately made to bear on taxpayers).

- States were prevented from defaulting. Even if there was no Treaty provision foreclosing default, European institutions, and very especially the ECB, prevented the Greek government from even considering default. IMF involvement would have required partial Greek default, and indeed some of the IMF board members insisted on that happening (see IMF 2010). Their opposition was overrun and the IMF Articles of Agreement were changed on the hoof to reconcile IMF massive involvement with Greece not defaulting (see Bagnai et al. 2015). Once Greece did not default, the precedent was set (Bini Smaghi 2011a).
- States were required to underwrite in full their banks, so financial institutions would not default either. We already saw how the Irish state was strongly required to underwrite its banks in 2008. In 2010, pressure was exerted so that Ireland would stand by the blanket guarantee, even if that made it unavoidable that Ireland asked for financial assistance from

51 Indeed, these were the states for which special provisions were foreseen when free movement of capital was liberalized through Directive 88/361.

other Eurozone states (O'Brien 2011a; O'Brien 2011b; Collins 2012; Honohan 2014).

Secondly, the costs of nationalising financial risks were to be borne exclusively by the exchequer of the states at the receiving end of capital flows. The costs of non-defaulting and of underwriting financial institutions were to be borne by the 'debtor' states. The responsibility that stemmed from the miscalculation of the risk they were incurring when lending to 'debtor' states or to the financial institutions of 'debtors' states was simply set aside. This of course implied the relieving of any responsibility of the states where these financial institutions were established as insurers and guarantors of last resort of these institutions.

Thirdly, *taxpayers of the Eurozone as a whole* were to underwrite the debt of debtor states. Given that the states which were required to bear all financial risks were already bordering fiscal collapse, further additional debt required underwriting by a third party. Most of this came in the form of financial assistance from the Eurozone as a whole (with the support of the IMF). Formally, this assistance was structured either through 'coordinated bilateral' loans (the first Greek programme in 2010)[52] or through the various variants of a European Monetary Fund that followed (plus IMF assistance).[53] But relief was also provided by means of the ECB buying sovereign bonds in secondary markets.[54] In practice, this meant that the taxpayers of debtors states were required to collect the bill for absorbing financial risks, but the taxpayers of the Eurozone as a whole were required to underwrite the taxpayers of debtor states.

Fourthly, the underwriting was given under the condition of creditors dictating the economic and fiscal policy to be applied by debtor states (this is what the so-called 'conditionality' implied). Debtor states were forced to undergo an internal devaluation (which meant a devaluation of labour instead of the impossible currency devaluation) and to engage in fiscal policies fitting into the so-called growth through austerity paradigm (Alesina and Ardagna 1998; very decisively Alesina 2010): or, what is the same, massive cuts to public expenditure (very especially social expenditure, which was in some cases strictly capped by reference to specific figures) combined with a redistribution of the tax burden, by means of a further

52 See Economic Adjustment Programme for Greece, European Commission, May 2010.

53 Press release on the extraordinary ECOFIN of 9 May and 10 May 2010; Regulation 407/2010 establishing a European financial stabilisation mechanism, OJ 2011, L 118/1.

54 Decision 2010/281 establishing a securities market programme, OJ 2010, L 124/8.

Table 4.10 *Exposure to debtor states of financial institutions, 3rd quarter 2010*

Greece

	Public sector	Banks	Non-bank private	Unallocated sector	Foreign claims	Other exposures	Total exposures	Percentage of total exposures ($277.9 million)
Germany	26.3	3.9	10.1	0	40.3	29.2	69.4	24.97
France	19.8	1.4	42.1	0	63.3	28.7	92.0	33.19
Italy	2.6	0.3	1.9	0	4.7	1.7	6.4	2.30
Spain	0.6	0	0.5	0	1.1	0.4	1.5	0.54
United Kingdom	3.2	4.3	7.5	0	15.1	5.3	20.4	7.34
USA	1.8	0.5	4.7	0	6.9	36.2	43.1	15.50
Japan	0.5	0.5	0.9	0	1.9	0.1	2.0	0.71

Source: Bank of International Settlements. www.bis.org/publ/qtrpdf/r_qt1103b.pdf.

Ireland

	Public sector	Banks	Non-bank private	Unallocated sector	Foreign claims	Other exposures	Total exposures	Percentage of total exposures ($813.7 million)
Germany	3.4	57.8	92.8	0	154.1	54.3	208.3	25.59
France	6.6	16.83	21.2	0	44.7	33.4	78.1	9.59
Italy	0.8	3.3	10.9	0.3	15.3	9.1	24.4	2.99
Spain	0.3	3.3	9.4	0	13.0	4.5	17.5	2.15
United Kingdom	6.6	37.4	116.1	0	160.2	64.4	224.6	27.60
USA	1.5	17.9	40.3	0	59.7	54.3	113.9	13.99
Japan	1.5	1.8	17.7	0	21.0	1.5	22.5	2.76

Source: Bank of International Settlements. www.bis.org/publ/qtrpdf/r_qt1103b.pdf.

Portugal

	Public sector	Banks	Non-bank private	Unallocated sector	Foreign claims	Other exposures	Total exposures	Percentage of total exposures ($321.8 bn)
Germany	8.4	18.1	13.6	0	40.0	8.5	48.5	15.07
France	16.1	6.5	14.8	0	37.4	8.1	45.6	14.17
Italy	0.9	2.3	1.5	0	4.7	3.2	7.9	2.45
Spain	8.8	6.1	70.3	0	85.2	23.4	108.6	33.74
United Kingdom	2.6	6.2	16.5	0	25.4	8.5	33.7	10.47
USA	1.6	1.4	1.5	0	4.5	43.6	47.1	14.63
Japan	1.3	0.3	0.8	0	2.4	0.4	2.8	0.87

Source: Bank of International Settlements. www.bis.org/publ/qtrpdf/r_qt1103b.pdf.

Spain

	Public sector	Banks	Non-bank private	Unallocated sector	Foreign claims	Other exposures	Total exposures	Percentage of total exposures ($1,098 bn)
Germany	29.5	85.8	85.7	0	200.9	41.4	242.4	22.07
France	46.0	55.8	81.3	0	183.1	41.6	224.7	20.46
Italy	3.3	9.0	16.2	0.2	28.7	13.1	41.8	3.80
Spain	–	–	–	–	–	–	–	–
United Kingdom	10.0	34.0	72.4	0	116.3	36.1	152.4	13.87
USA	4.7	20.6	26.3	0	51.6	136	187.5	17.07
Japan	9.7	4.5	10.2	0	24.4	4.8	29.2	2.65

Source: Bank of International Settlements. www.bis.org/publ/qtrpdf/r_qt1103b.pdf.

shift of the tax burden from capital to labour (with the typical mix being an increase of the standard VAT rate, suppression of concessionary VAT rates for essential goods, the increase or introduction of fees for the use of public services; while taxes on capital income were expected to be, if anything, lowered) and the rather rapid sale of public property (Bini Smaghi 2011b). The rationale was that shock economic therapy will result in the rapid reduction of labour costs and lead to strong trade surpluses. These surpluses would be able to pay external debt and trigger private investment.

These decisions were presented as the operationalisation of European 'solidarity' with the debtor states. However, the loans did not support the debtor states as such. Most (when not all) the monies were not spent by the states recipient of financial assistance, but merely transited through them, quickly ending in the hands of the financial institutions that had lent to the debtor states or to the financial institutions of the debtor states (ATTAC Austria 2013). To label this as solidarity is deeply problematic. Solidarity means literally to bear risks together. Eurozone taxpayers were not being so much solidaristic towards the citizens of debtor states as solidaristic with the financial institutions that loaned capital to debtor states and the financial institutions of debtor states. It is indeed telling that in all assisted countries public debt levels experienced a drastic increase after being recipients of 'solidarity'. This reveals the extent to which 'solidarity' with debtor countries was as a matter of fact solidarity with the financial institutions exposed to debtor countries. The rhetoric of solidarity could be abused because it was not understood that the conflict of interest between capital holders and debtors was transformed through 'financial assistance' into a conflict of interest between the taxpayers of debtor and creditor countries. This did not only relieve lenders of any financial responsibility but also created the false impression that the fiscal crises were caused by the fiscal profligacy of debtor states. This diagnosis failed to consider the structural forces at play in the massive cross-border capital flows during the first decade of EMU, and the role played by financial institutions in the gathering of the crises.

Internal devaluation plus growth through austerity had a massive impact on the configuration of debtor states. Debtor states were transformed into indebted states. As such, these states were required to make their tax system a key element in the process of transformation of its socio-economic structure into a *more competitive* one. Taxes were to regain redistributive and economic steering functions. Only the pattern of redistribution was now aimed at increasing the capital at the disposal of capital owners, and steering consisted in fiscal *dirigisme* aimed at micromanaging economic policy (Scharpf 2014) so as to facilitate internal devaluation and ensure automatic corrections in the fiscal position to ensure that the principal and interest of the debt were honoured.[55]

Constitutional and legal entrenchment of the consolidating tax state

The blueprint of the consolidating tax state was first forged and developed during the fiscal crises of 2011 and 2012. That this was not intended as a temporary, 'crisis management', expedient became very clear during 2012 and 2013, as the changes in the primary and secondary law of the European Union, as well as idiosyncratic quasi-constitutional norms, were approved through formal international treaties codifying the legal basis of the tax consolidating state.

At the constitutional or quasi-constitutional level, it is important to stress the significance of the obligation imposed to patriate and enshrine in the constitution (or norms of constitutional nature) 'debt brakes'.[56] The ECJ was given the formal power of reviewing the national constitutional or quasi-constitutional norms adopted to comply with this obligation.[57] While many member states have still to introduce the reforms, some followed the 'German' debt brake model and reformed their constitutions accordingly (Spain, Italy and Slovenia). The Spanish constitutional reform of September 2011 is especially relevant. The procedure followed was at the very least peculiar, avoiding all the consultations needed to approve even an ordinary law (García Gestoso 2012: 79–81). The amended text did not only include a debt brake, but, more transcendentally, a clause giving preference to the payment of principal and interest of public debt over any other public expenditure (including, quite obviously, social expenditure).[58]

The tax consolidating state was given concrete shape by the new fiscal rules at the basis of the revamped Stability and Growth Pact. The 'old' fiscal rule regarding public deficit was tightened. Public accounts should be in surplus or close to surplus, meaning at most a 1 per cent deficit, and for those states with a far from unblemished fiscal record, the threshold

55 It is very important to keep in mind that the memoranda of understanding are an odd mix of soft form (subject to change every quarter, when creditors revise the degree of compliance with the programme) and extremely hard coercion mechanisms (the constant threat of the next payment of the assistance not being disimbursed unless the assisted state does not comply in full with the evolving terms of the memorandum).

56 Article 3(2) TSCG.

57 Article 8 TSCG.

58 See amended text of Article 135 of the Spanish Constitution.

was −0.5 per cent.[59] Moreover, new rules establishing deficit and debt-reduction trajectories were introduced. The latter rule is of enormous importance. It foresees that all states exceeding the 60 per cent debt ceiling should reduce their debt levels, year in and year out, by 5 per cent of the amount in which they exceed 60 per cent.[60] In practice, this implies the obligation for many states to run constant massive primary surpluses. What the memoranda of understanding obliged countries provided with financial assistance to do, this rule requires of states which had not been subject to such discipline, such as Italy (or Spain, receiver of financial assistance in its 'light touch' version) (Giacché 2012 argues, quite convincingly, that the decision to impose the debt-reduction trajectory had a major causal role in the 2011 fiscal crisis in Spain and Italy). Moreover, Eurozone states are obliged to introduce automatic correction mechanisms, so that either expenditure goes down or taxation goes up when the yearly fiscal objectives become clearly imperilled by the way in which the economy and public finances evolve.[61] Finally, the assignment to the supranational level of the power to supervise the macroeconomic balance of each national economy is bound to result in a further limitation of the space to take autonomous fiscal decisions (Scharpf 2013).

The bite of these new sets of fiscal rules has been largely trusted to the new procedures of fiscal coordination and supervision within the Eurozone. The sequence of the so-called European Semester implies a radical empowerment of supranational institutions. For one, national budgetary processes are subject to much closer monitoring, to the point that the draft budget is submitted to the Commission before it is submitted to the national parliament. For two, national budgetary procedures are required to become structured not around the yearly budget but around the five-yearly fiscal perspectives, something which drastically reduces not only the margin for discretionary fiscal policy but also for change in fiscal policy resulting from a new democratic majority being elected in a Eurozone state.[62] For three, decisions concerning the monitoring and supervision of

59 Regulation 1466/97 on the strengthening of the surveillance of budgetary positions and the surveillance and coordination of economic policies, OJ 1997, L 209/1, as amended by Regulation 1175/2011, OJ 2011, L 306/12, Article 2(2)(a). Further tightened by Articles 3(1)(a) and (b) TSCG to 0.5 per cent GDP, except for countries with debt levels significantly below 60 per cent and clearly 'sustainable' public finances, Article 3(1)(d) TSCG.

60 Article 4 TSCG.

61 Article 3(1)(e) TSCG.

62 Directive 2011/85 on requirements for budgetary frameworks of the member states, OJ 2011, L 306/41.

fiscal policy are now taken when a qualified minority of Eurozone states supports Commission's proposals.[63] This largely entails giving de facto power to the creditor states over the debtor states (on the extent to which creditor states have shaped the government of the crises, see Dyson 2014).

The counterpoint: automatic exchange of information?

At the very same time that the pattern of tax integration through fiscal consolidation got entrenched, the fiscal crises have led to legislative initiatives and actual Directives that may point to the recovery of the old integration through tax harmonisation paradigm and, in particular, the reintroduction of dynamics of cooperation between tax administrations.

In 2010, a new Directive on cooperation on the recovery of tax claims (of debts owed to tax authorities) was introduced, drastically widening the scope of the old 1976 Directive and improving the mechanics of cooperation.[64] In 2011, the 1977 Directive on administrative tax cooperation was superseded by a new Directive aiming at automatic exchange of information between member states.[65] The Directive was rendered operative by a first implementing regulation in 2012,[66] and even more clearly so by a second one in 2014.[67] This new framework for tax cooperation came hand in hand with the amendment of the savings income directive, closing a good deal of its loopholes.[68]

To be noticed also is the fact that in 2011 the Commission put forward a Directive proposal aiming at the harmonisation of the tax base of the corporate income tax,[69] which revives the understanding that harmonisation

63 Article 7 TSCG.

64 Directive 2010/24 concerning mutual assistance for the recovery of claims relating to taxes, duties and other measures, OJ 2010, L 84/1.

65 Directive 2011/16 on administrative cooperation in the field of taxation and repealing Directive 77/799/EEC, OJ 2011, L 64.

66 Commission Regulation 1156/2012 laying down detailed rules for implementing certain provisions of Directive 2011/16 on administrative cooperation in the field of taxation, OJ 2012, L 335/42.

67 Commission Regulation 1353/2014 amending implementing Regulation1156/2012 laying down detailed rules for implementing certain provisions of Directive 2011/16 on administrative cooperation in the field of taxation, OJ 2014, L 365/70.

68 Directive 2014/48 amending Directive 2003/48 on taxation of savings in the form of interest payments, OJ L 2014, L 111/50.

69 European Commission, 'Proposal for a Council Directive on a Common Consolidated Corporate Tax Base (CCCTB)', COM (2011) 121/4.

going beyond the correction of the failures of homogenisation through tax competition is needed.

IV Reconciling (again) integration and the social and democratic tax state

This book aims not only at increasing the understanding of how the present European crises came about, but also at considering what should be done to contain and overcome the crises. A concrete tax policy agenda cannot but be shaped in the 'in-between' that is the political sphere. Consequently, it is a political and not a scholarly task. What can be done here is to sketch five general observations which are perhaps stronger on *what should not be done* than on what *should be done*.

First, the degree of Europeanisation of national tax systems is so high that any meaningful reform proposals have to factor that into account. Any tax policy proposal needs to spell out what changes would be required both at the supranational and the national levels, what obstacles to change result from the present configuration of supranational and national constitutional law, and what consequences reform would have at both the European and the national levels.

Secondly, it is quite obvious that one possible alternative is to dismantle in full the European framework constraining and disciplining national tax systems. But two things should be kept in mind. For one, such a dismantlement would only be coherent (and indeed stand a chance of being functional) if it came hand in hand with the redefinition of the overall relationship between the national and the European socio-economic constitutions. As was shown in this chapter, national tax systems have been deeply Europeanised, but not only and not so much as a result of European tax regulations and directives, but mainly through the influence that the present understanding of economic freedoms as operationalisations of the right to private property and freedom of enterprise has structurally exerted over the tax system (plus the structural constraints stemming from the 'new economic governance' of the Eurozone in the process of becoming consolidated). Simply opting out from European tax legislation would not recreate national tax autonomy. For two, a complete retreat into national sovereignty (through a radical exit from any form of European cooperation) may not do either. The European framework of national tax law has become a straitjacket due to its structural bias in favour of the *consolidating tax state*. There is no guarantee, however, that outside of the framework of European integration the structural power of capital would not end up limiting tax choices. This should not be constructed, however, as a plea in favour of the status quo. The status quo (including EMU very especially, but not exclusively, as has come to be shaped in the aftermath of the crisis) is part of the problem, not of the solution (Flassbeck and Lapavitsas 2015; Streeck 2014; Bagnai 2014). But the original paradigm of taxation through tax harmonisation is a powerful reminder of the possibility of making European integration and the consolidation of the social and democratic *Rechtsstaat* mutually reinforce each other.

Thirdly, the cases put forward to transfer tax collecting powers to the European Union since the crises began are hardly convincing. These proposals are the wrong proposals, for the wrong reasons and at the wrong time. Most of these proposals regard European taxes as the source of the financial means with which to postpone (again) the payment of debt (Trichet 2011; Poiares Maduro 2012). But it is high time we either pay debt, or declare it will not be paid. The case for a European power to tax is also based on wrong reasons. The advocates of European taxes present such taxes as a *functional means* to solve the crises. But taxes are not a mere expedient to collect revenue, but a key institution in the functioning of democracy. This is indeed the key blind spot in the proposals. Advocates of introducing European taxes to pay for fiscal assistance are rather vague regarding the democratic procedure that will be followed to empower the Union and actually to approve the regulations creating the taxes. Trichet simply avoids the issue, and pretends that a European Treasury could issue debt without collecting taxes (which defies the law of gravity of public finance). Poiares Maduro appeals to the need of avoiding transfers between states, because the latter will undermine the European 'we feeling'. The alternative is to collect revenue directly from those profiting most from European integration. But leaving aside whether it is wise to fund financial assistance, the need of which will be pro-cyclical, with taxes which are bound to be pro-cyclical (as profits, whether to those profiting from integration or not, are cyclical), it is obvious that no matter how progressive a tax, it should be democratically approved. Poiares Maduro also avoids that key issue. Finally, the proposals come at the wrong time. The way in which the crises have been governed, and, very especially, the way in which the pile of widow risks stemming from cross-border capital flows have been dealt with has strengthened (and recreated) national cleavages. In such a context, European taxes could only be forced upon Europeans in an authoritarian fashion. This would not only be unacceptable, it is likely to result in an outcome opposite to that apparently wished for by the advocates of new European taxes now, as the non-democratic imposition or dissimulation of such taxes is likely to feed disintegration.

Fourthly, European tax norms could play a major role in *rescuing* the power of member states to take autonomous decisions. Instead of European law hollowing national tax autonomy, European law should be an instrument at the service of recreating the political space for democratic national tax choices. To achieve that three things could be done.

- For one, the institutional and procedural means should be created to make tax authorities capable of identifying and quantifying all income, wealth and consumption flows. This requires mutual, automatic and complete exchange of tax information among the member states of the European Union. All relevant tax data should be shared (Zucman 2013: 74 ff.). The new framework of automatic exchange recently adopted is a much better starting point than previous legislation. This is the only way of stopping some states (at present including some member states) literally selling their sovereignty in exchange for a fraction of the proceedings of tax evasion on the side of multinational corporations and wealthy individuals (Palan 2002; Palan, Murphy and Chavagneux 2009). Moreover, the European Union should make use of its collective bargaining power and subject free movement of capital and goods to uncooperative third countries to the said countries accepting in full automatic exchange of tax data (Zucman 2013: 87 ff.).
- For two, economic freedoms should be recalibrated. The recreation of the effective capacity to tax requires recharacterising economic freedoms as the operationalisation of the principle of non-discrimination when it comes to tax matters (and not only). The social and democratic tax state was fiercely opposed in the name of the right to private property and to freedom of enterprise. Its consolidation implied a recharacterisation of both rights, a recharacterisation which was very much at the core of the identity of post-war constitutions. It is high time we stand by what is still the deep constitutional identity of most European constitutions. The ECJ should reorient its case law and return to a less abrasive understanding of economic freedoms when coming into conflict with national laws, especially national tax laws (Menéndez 2011).
- For three, some key national tax laws should be harmonised. The objective should not be to homogenise national tax laws but, on the contrary, to create the conditions under which *different* political choices could be possible. The VAT template could be of use. Wide harmonisation of the definition of the tax base (with room for specific national rules) could be combined with the widest possible latitude in the setting of tax rates.

Fifthly, when, and only when, European law would have proven useful in the recreation of the autonomous power to tax of member states, the time would have come to discuss granting the European Union further collecting tax powers. I have argued that we should distinguish two rather different cases for granting such collecting powers to the European Union (Menéndez 2004). For one, there is a very strong case to act upon the decision taken in 1970 to fund the current European budget through taxes, not state contributions. At present, less than 15 per cent of the European budget is funded from genuine European taxes, and less than a quarter comes from that and the European share of VAT. Paying for Europe via taxes is indispensable if we want finally to foster democratic debate about what Europe does and what it should be doing (and not doing). Secondly, there is a very good case for having European taxes capable of redistributing revenue across Europe and of serving as a supranational macroeconomic lever. But these very good reasons should be validated *democratically*, not imposed in an authoritarian manner as *faits accomplis* (Majone 2014). In the present political, economic and legal context the assignment of new tax collecting powers to the European Union cannot but be damaging to democracy.

Conclusions

The long arc of transformation of the European framework of taxation can thus be seen as vindicating Fritz Neumark. The rejection of the active fiscal interventionism characteristic of the Social and Democratic Tax did not result in a liberated market economy, but has ended up condemning Europeans to the fiscal *dirigisme* of the *consolidating tax state*. (On the crucial distinction between interventionism and *dirigisme*, see Neumark 1964 in dialogue with Ludwig Erhard.) Self-stabilising capitalism does not result in economic freedom, but in authoritarian liberalism (Polanyi 1944; Heller 2015).

This economic and monetary union will not last. The European Union may collapse as a result. Or, far worse, it may slowly keep on transforming itself into the liberal authoritarian direction that underpins the consolidating tax state. We need a very different Europe. It would be ludicrous to claim that this different Europe can be engineered through a collection of tax policies only; or, for that matter, a combination of tax and expenditure policies. The problems of Europe are deep and structural and require decisions concerning not only the stock of debt but also the generation of income and wealth; not only redistribution but also changes in production and distribution (Berman 2006; Wade 2014; Piketty 2015). But changes in the European framework of taxation could play its role. In this chapter

I have made a case *against* the transfer of tax collecting powers to the European Union *as part* of the government of the crises. That would be the wrong prescription for the wrong reasons at the wrong time. The assignment of new taxing powers to the European Union *in this political context* is a democratic non-starter. We do not need more Europe when it comes to taxes, but a very different Europe. What can and should be achieved through action at the European level is the *rescue* of the capacity of member states to tax the income, expenditure and wealth of their citizens and of those economically active in their territory, by means of drastically reducing the chances of evading the tax net.

The European rescue of the social and democratic tax state is an ambitious task, but it is one that, contrary to the transfer of tax collecting powers to the supranational level of government to postpone the day of the reckoning, has a realistic chance of recreating the cohesion between European citizens without which the European Union is bound to become the nemesis of the *social and democratic Rechtsstaat*.

References

Alesina, A. (2010) 'Fiscal Adjustments: Lessons from Recent History', prepared for the Ecofin Meeting, Madrid, 15 April. http://scholar.harvard.edu/alesina/publications/fiscal-adjustments-lessons-recent-history.

Alesina, A., and Ardagna, S. (1998) 'Tales of Fiscal Adjustment', *Economic Policy*, 27(13), 498–545.

Andic, F., and Andic, S. (1981) 'Fritz Neumark, Teacher and Reformer: A Turkish View', *FinanzArchiv*, 39(1), 11–19.

Andic, F., and Reisman, A. (2007) 'Migration and Transfer of Knowledge: Refugees from Nazism and Turkish Legal Reform', *Forum historiae iuris*. www.forhistiur.de/zitat/0707andic_reisman.htm.

ATTAC Austria (2013) 'Irish "Rescue": 67.5 bn of Bail-out Loans, 89.5 bn to Banks', 27 December.

Avi Yonah, R. (2000) 'Globalization, Tax Competition and the Fiscal Crisis of the Welfare State', *Harvard Law Review*, 113(7), 1573–675.

Bagnai, A. (2012) *Il Tramonto dell'Euro*, Reggio Emilia: Imprimatur.

(2014) *L'Italia può farcela*, Milan: Saggiatore.

Bagnai, A. et al. (2015), 'The Economic Consequences of Greece', Project Syndicate, 24 February. www.project-syndicate.org.

Barquero Estevan, J. (2002) *La Function Del Tributo En El Estado Social y Democratico De Derecho*, Madrid: Centro de Estudios Constitucionales.

Bartelsman, E., and Beetsma, R. (2000) 'Why Pay More? Corporate Tax Avoidance through Transfer Pricing in OECD Countries', CesIFO, Working Paper 324.

Berman, S. (2006) *The Primacy of Politics*, Cambridge: Cambridge University Press.

Bini Smaghi, L. (2011a) 'Whither Europe after the Crisis?', speech, 11 March 2011.

(2011b) 'Private Sector Involvement: From (Good) Theory to (Bad) Practice', speech, 6 June 2011.

Brooks, R. (2014) *The Great Tax Robbery*, London: Oneworld.

Coggan, J. (2011) *Paper Promises, Money, Debt and the New World Order*, Harmondsworth: Penguin.

Collins, S. (2012) 'Lenihan Told No Way Out but Bailout', *Irish Times*, 1 September.

Comín, F. (2007) 'Reaching a Political Consensus for Tax Reform in Spain: The Moncloa Pacts, Joining the European Union and The Rest of the Journey', in J. Martínez Vázquez and J. Félix Sanz (eds), *Fiscal Reform in Spain: Accomplishments and Challenges*, Cheltenham: Edward Elgar, 8–57.

Connolly, K. (2008) 'Banking Crisis: Germany Earmarks €500bn for Rescue Package', *Guardian*, 13 October.

Crouch, C. (2011) *The Strange Non-death of Neoliberalism*, Cambridge: Polity.

De Grauwe, P. (2012) 'The Governance of a Fragile Eurozone', *Australian Economic Review*, 43(3), 255–68.

Derban, E. (2011) *Models Behaving Badly*, London: Wiley.

Deutsche Bundesbank (2011) 'The Debt Brake in Germany: Key Aspects and Implementation'. www.bundesbank.de/Redaktion/EN/Downloads/Publications/Monthly_Report_Articles/2011/2011_10_debt_brake_germany.pdf?__blob=publicationFile.

Dyson, K. (2014), *States, Debt and Power*, Oxford: Oxford University Press.

Dyson, K., and Featherstone, K. (1999) *The Road to Maastricht: Negotiating Economic and Monetary Union*, Oxford: Oxford University Press.

The Economist (2004) *The World in 2005*.

(2008) 'Lifelines', 11 October.

Einaudi, L. (2012) *Quello di Keynes non e il mio piano*, Soveria Mannelli: Rubbettino.

Espuelas, S. (2012) 'Are Dictatorships Less Redistributive? A Comparative Analysis of Social Spending in Europe, 1950–1980', *European Review of Economic History*, 16(2), 211–32.

European Commission (1953) 'Rapport sur les problems poses par les taxes sur le chiffre d'affaires dans le marché commun établi par la commission d'experts institituée para la Haute Autorité'.

(1962) 'Commission EEC Reports Tax Harmonisation (including the "Neumark Report")', Brussels.

(1965) 'Financing the Common Agricultural Policy', COM (65) 150 final.

(1967) 'Tax Harmonisation Programme: Programme for the Harmonisation of Direct Taxes'.

(1977) 'Report of the Study Group on the Role of Public Finances in European Integration ("Mc Dougall Report")', Brussels.

(1980) 'Report on the Scope for Convergence of Tax Systems in the Community', COM (80) 139 final.

(1985) 'Completing the Internal Market', COM (85) 310 final.

(1990) 'Conclusions and Recommendations of the Committee of Independent Experts on Company Taxation, Luxembourg'.

(1996) 'Taxation in the European Union', COM (96) 546 final.

(1997a) 'Towards Tax Coordination in the European Union', COM (97) 495 final.

(1997b) 'A Package to Tackle Harmful Tax Competition', COM (97) 564 final.

(2007) *Employment in Europe*, 19th edn, Luxembourg: OOPEC.

(2009) 'Promoting Good Governance in Tax Matters', COM (2009) 201 final.

European Council (2008) 'Declaration of 12 October on an Action Plan in the Euro Zone States'.

Flassbeck, H., and Lapavitsas, C. (2015), *Against the Troika*, London: Verso.

Fossum, J. E., and Menéndez, A. (2011) *The Constitution's Gift*, Lanham, MD: Rowman & Littlefield.

Fry, G. (2008) *The Politics of the Thatcher Revolution*, London: Palgrave Macmillan.

Fuentes Quintana, E. (1970), Introduction, in F. Neumark, *Principios de la Imposición*, Madrid: Instituto de Estudios Fiscales.

Gamble, A. (1988), *The Free Economy and the Strong State*, Basingstoke: Macmillan.

García Gestoso N. (2012), 'La respuesta constitucional a la crisis económica en el marco de la Unión Europea: ¿remedio efectivo o devaluación constitucional?', *Anuario da Facultade de Dereito da Universidade da Coruña*, 16, 57–94.

Geithner, T. (2014) *Stress Test*, New York: Crown.

Genschel, P., and Jachtenfuchs, M. (2010), 'The Fiscal Anatomy of a Regulatory Polity: Tax Policy and Multilevel Governance in the EU', Bremen Transtate Working Paper 114.

Giacché, V. (2012) *Titanic Europa*, Reggio Emilia: Aliberti.

Grin, G. (2004) *The Battle of the Single Market*, London: Kegan and Paul.

Gustavsson, S. (2002) 'What Makes a European Monetary and Economic Union Politically Sustainable', in S. Dosenrode (ed.), *Political Aspects of Economic and Monetary Union: The European Challenge*, Aldershot: Ashgate, 87–120.

Haas, E. (1958) *The Uniting of Europe*, Stanford, CA: Stanford University Press.

Hamker, J. (2012) 'Implementing Germany's New Constitutional Fiscal Rules', in *Rules and Institutions for Sound Fiscal Policy after the Crisis*, Rome: Banca d'Italia, 301–20.

Harvey, D. (2014) *Seventeen Contradictions and the End of Capitalism*, Oxford: Oxford University Press.

Hein, E., and Truger, A. (2014), 'Fiscal Policy and Rebalancing in the Euro Area: A Critique of the German Debt Brake from a Keynesian Perspective', *Panoeconomicus*, 1(1), 21–38.

Helleiner, E. (1994) *States and the Reemergence of Global Finance*, Ithaca, NY: Cornell University Press.

Heller, H. (2015) 'Authoritarian Liberalism?', *European Law Journal*, 21(3), 295–301.

Honohan, P. (2014). 'Brian Lenihan and the Nation's Finances', in B. Murphy, M. O'Rourke and N. Whelan (eds), *Brian Lenihan: In Calm and Crisis*, Merrion: Dublin.

International Monetary Fund (2010), Board Meeting Notes of 9 May 2010.

Jabko, N. (2009) *L'Europe par le marché. Histoire d'une strategie improbable*, Paris: Presses universitaires de France.

Kaldor, N. (1978) 'The Dynamic Effects of the Common Market', in *Further Essays on Applied Economics*, New York: Holmes & Meier, 187–220.

Lapavitsas, C. (2013), *Profiting without Producing*, London: Verso.

Leaman, J. (1998), *The Political Economy of West Germany, 1945–1985*, London: Macmillan.

(2000) *The Bundesbank Myth: Towards a Critique of Central Bank Independence*, London: Macmillan.

Lodin, S. (2000) 'What Ought to be Taxed and What Can be Taxed', *Bulletin for International Fiscal Documentation*, 54, 210–17.

McCabe, C. (2011) *The Sins of the Father, Tracing the Decisions that Shaped the Irish Economy*, London: History Press.

Majone, G. (2014) *Rethinking the European Union Post-Crisis*, Cambridge: Cambridge University Press.

Menéndez, A. (2004) 'Taxing Europe', *Columbia Journal of European Law*, 10(2), 297–338.

(2005) 'The Purse of the Polity', in E. Eriksen (ed.), *Making the European Polity: Reflexive Integration in the EU*, London: Routledge, 187–213.

(2009) 'The Unencumbered European Taxpayer as the Product of the Transformation of Personal Taxes by the Judicial Empowerment of Market Forces', in R. Letelier and A. Menéndez (eds), *The Sinews of Peace*, Oslo: Arena Report 7/2009, 157–268.

(2011) 'A Very Proportionate Constitution? Economic Freedom, Substantive Constitutional Choices and *Dérapages* in European Union Law', in Rául Letelier and Agustín José Menéndez (eds), *Hope, Reluctance and Fear*, ARENA: University of Oslo, 167–252.

Mohamed, S. (2000) *European Community Law on the Free Movement of Capital and the EMU*, Dordrecht and Stockholm: Kluwer/Norstedts Juridik.

Mundell, R. (1961) 'Theory of Optimum Currency Areas', *American Economic Review*, 51(4), 657–65.

Murphy, R. (2013) *Over Here and Undertaxed*, London: Vintage Digital.
Musgrave, R. (1959) *The Theory of Public Finance*, New York: McGraw Hill.
Musgrave, R. et al. (1945) *Public Finance and Full Employment*, Washington, DC: Federal Reserve.
Naredo, J., and Álvarez, A. (2011) *El modelo inmobiliario español*, Madrid: Icaria.
Neumark, F. (1964) 'Política Fiscal Intervencionista y Dirigista', in *Problemas Económicos y Financieros del Estado Intervencionista*, Madrid: Editorial Revista de Derecho Privado.
(1974) *Principios de la Imposición*, Madrid: Instituto de Estudios Fiscales.
O'Brien, D. (2011a), 'Ireland was Forced by ECB to Take Bailout, says Lenihan', *Irish Times*, 23 April 2011.
(2011b) 'Bailout Boys Go to Dublin', BBC Radio 4.
OECD (2006) *Fundamental Reform of Personal Income Tax*, Paris.
Palan, R. (2002) 'Tax Havens and the Commercialisation of Sovereignty', *International Organization*, 56(1), 151–76.
Palan, R., Murphy, R., and Chavagneux, C. (2009) *Tax Havens: How Globalization Really Works*, Ithaca, NY: Cornell University Press.
Pantazatou, K. (2013) 'Economic and Political Considerations in the Court's Case Law Post Crisis: An Example from the Internal Market', *Croatian Yearbook of European Law*, 9, 77–118.
Pellegrin, Julie (2001) *The Political Economy of Competitiveness in an Enlarged Europe*, Basingstoke: Palgrave Macmillan.
Piketty, T. (2015) 'Putting Distribution Back at the Center of Economics: Reflections on Capital in the Twenty-First Century', *Journal of Economic Perspectives*, 29(1), 67–88.
Poiares Maduro, M. (2012) 'A New Governance for the European Union and the Euro: Democracy and Justice', Robert Schuman Centre Working Papers, 2012/11.
Polanyi, K. (1944) *The Great Transformation*, Boston: Beacon.
Radaelli, C. (2003) 'The Code of Conduct against Harmful Tax Competition: Open Method of Coordination in Disguise?', *Public Administration*, 81(3), 513–31.
Rasmussen, M., and Davies, B. (2014) 'From International Law to a European Rechtsgemeinschaft: Towards a New History of European Law, 1950–1979', in J. Laursen (ed.), *Institutions and Dynamics of the European Community, 1973–83*, Baden Baden and London: Nomos/Bloomsbury.
Regul, W. (1966) *Finances and Taxes in European Integration*, Amsterdam: International Bureau of Fiscal Documentation.
Rogers, C. (2013) *The IMF and European Economies: Crisis and Conditionality*, London: Palgrave Macmillan.
Röpke, W. (1963) *Economics of the Free Society*, Chicago: Henry Regnery.

Rose, A. (2000) 'One Money, One Market: The Effect of Common Currencies on Trade', *Economic Policy*, 30(1), 9–45.

Scharpf, F. (1991) *Crisis and Choice in European Social Democracy*, Ithaca, NY: Cornell University Press.

(2013) 'Political Legitimacy in a Non-optimal Currency Area', MPIfG Discussion Paper 13/15.

(2014) 'No Exit from the Euro-Rescuing Trap?', MPIfG Discussion Paper 14/4.

Schnasi, G., and Teixeira, P. (2006) 'The Lender of Last Resort in the Single Financial Market', IMF Working Paper 06/127.

Schneider, F. (1997) 'Empirical Results for the Size of the Shadow Economy of Western European Countries over Time', Working Paper of the Department of Economics of the University of Linz.

Shaxson, N. (2011) *Treasure Islands*, London: Palgrave Macmillan.

Shaxson, N., and Christiensen, J. (2014) *The Finance Curse*, London: Commonwealth Publishing.

Shoup, C. (ed.) (1967) *Fiscal Harmonisation in Common Markets*, New York and London: Columbia University Press.

Sørensen, P. (1994) 'From the Global Income Tax to the Dual Income Tax: Recent Tax Reforms in the Nordic Countries', *International Tax and Public Finance*, 1(1), 57–80.

Steinmo, S. (1993) *Taxation and Democracy*, New Haven, CT: Yale University Press.

Streeck, W. (2014) *Buying Time*, London: Verso.

Taub, J. (2014) *Other People's Houses*, New Haven, CT: Yale University Press.

Teixeira, P, (2011) 'The Regulation of the Financial Market after the Crisis', in P. della Posta and S. Talani (eds), *Europe and the Financial Crisis*, Basingstoke: Palgrave Macmillan, 9–27.

Tett, G. (2009) *Fool's Gold*, London: Little, Brown.

Trichet, J.-C. (2009) 'The Financial Crisis and the Response of the ECB', speech of 12 June.

(2011) 'Construire l'Europe, bâtir ses institutions', speech of 2 June 2011.

Van Apeldoorn, B. (2002) *Transnational Capitalism and the Struggle over European Integration*, London: Routledge.

Van de Woestyne, F., and Van Caloen A. (2008) 'Comment Sarkozy a mangé tout crus les p'tits Belges', *Courier International*, 11 December.

Van Dijk, Michiel, Weyzig, Francis, and Murphy, Richard (2007) *The Netherlands: A Tax Haven*, Amsterdam: Somo.

Von der Groeben, Hans (1968) 'Harmonizing Taxes: A Step to European Integration', Brussels: European Community Information Service.

Wade, R. (2008) 'The First-World Debt Crisis of 2007–2010 in Global Perspective', *Challenge*, 51(4), 23–54.

(2014) 'The Piketty Phenomenon: Why Has Capital Become a Publishing Sensation?', *International Affairs*, 90(5), 1069–83.

Williams, D. (1997) 'Asscher: The European Court and the Power to Destroy', *EC Tax Review*, 6(1), 4–10.

Wolf, M. (2013) 'Exchange Rate Arrangements: The Strange Case of Spain and the UK', paper presented at the Rethinking Macro Policy II: First Steps and Early Lessons Conference, Washington, DC, 16–17 April.

Zucman, Gabriel (2013) *La Richesse cachée des nations*, Paris: Seuil.

5

What Europe does to citizenship

CATHERINE COLLIOT-THÉLÈNE

Introduction

The democratic deficit in Europe is by no means a new topic, but it is now timelier than ever before. This is visible not only in the distrust of many Europeans in the EU policies set in Brussels, but also in the relationship of citizens with politics in general, on both national and European scales. Declining voter turnout, the fickleness of voters – due to the fact that their votes more often indicate a disavowal of current leaders than support for their opponents' programmes, the rise of a pure protest vote – all these are symptoms of a crisis in citizenship that cannot be resolved by merely making a few changes to EU institutions. Knowledge of these institutions is reserved to small circles of specialists. What ordinary citizens perceive of Europe is the impact of its policies on their daily lives. For many, this impact now looks mainly negative. As the possibility of exerting influence on the bodies that decide these policies is extremely limited, citizens show their discontent at national level. But, by overtly curbing the room for action of national political leaders, notably on social policy, the European Union affects how democracy works and what it means within the member states. Offering no real choices, with no relatively consistent alternatives, democracy tends to be just a media spectacle with political clans mainly focused on taking power. The democratic weaknesses of the *structures* of the European Union fuel a generalised feeling that politics is powerless, which, in turn, undermines the conditions of democratic *citizenship* in all European countries.

In this chapter, I will investigate the current state of democracy in Europe from the angle of citizenship. It is often observed that, as a

English translation by Christopher Mobley.

political entity, the European Union is hard to characterise, and political philosophy has difficulties adapting its conceptual corpus, built around the nation state, to this new entity. The most frequent approach is to consider Europe to be a virtual nation state, a federal state in the process of coming into being, and thus to measure how democratic it is by comparing it to the structures of a modern nation state, considered to be an approximation – albeit an imperfect one – of community life organised democratically. This kind of approach focuses on 'political' institutions, in the narrow sense of the term, covering only how the legislative and executive powers are constituted, organised and controlled. Here, I will adopt a different standpoint. In my view, the democratic nature of modern democratic regimes does not result solely from the organisation of political power, no matter how important this may be, but also, and more fundamentally, from the kind of political subjectivity that developed as these regimes were established and consolidated over the past two centuries.

The modern political subject is a citizen who no longer is, or no longer considers himself to be, a subject (*subditus*), but who understands himself to be a rightful political actor. The legally codified participation of each citizen in the formation and control of power (via the vote) is one way for the citizen to act. But this participation, formally laid out, in principle, in the declarations of rights in the revolutionary period, is not the sole expression of modern citizenship. The extension of voting rights, first to all adult men through universal suffrage, then to women, was won through fights that, even when not achieved through legal means, played an essential role in the progress of democracy. Civil and political rights were used to make very divergent claims, leading to the institution of new rights, including labour rights in the past, and environmental rights today. All these rights, insofar as they were claimed in the name of equality, as asserted in the declarations of the rights of man, are ingredients of what democracy has become. Citizenship cannot be reduced to what constitutional and legislative texts say it is; instead, it covers all the dispositions, practices and expectations that individuals have developed over the past two centuries while becoming actors in political life.

However, in contrast with the classical texts of ancient philosophy, which are the source of our concept of citizen, modern citizenship appears to go beyond the boundaries of politics. Today, we speak of social citizenship, a notion that is unheard of in classical texts. Social citizenship is, indeed, related to two distinctions that appeared in the nineteenth century, between society and the state, and between the bourgeoisie and the citizen. These distinctions are a sign of a specific difficulty of modern societies, noted back in the second decade of the nineteenth century by various authors, from Benjamin Constant to Hegel. Constant is remembered for presenting the liberty of the ancient world to be in opposition with that of the modern one, as expressed through the title of his famous 1819 speech, 'The Liberty of Ancients Compared with that of Moderns'. However, it is often forgotten that, at the end of this text, he called for these two kinds of liberty to be combined. While he asked the legislator not to intervene in the private affairs of citizens, he also wanted institutions to 'achieve the moral education of the citizens' in order to 'consecrate their influence over public affairs'. This speech was a manifesto for a representative regime which would enable citizens to exercise, control and monitor power. At the same period, Hegel was also confronting the difficulty in reconciling the individualism of modern societies with the demands of citizenship. Yet his solution was quite different. I will go into more detail later on, but, to simplify, Hegel argued that political citizenship, in modern societies, must be grounded in primary forms of socialisation that develop an individual's sense of the 'universal'. What we call social citizenship today is a series of forms of solidarity (granted, different from the forms considered by Hegel) that are created within society. These forms of solidarity can be described as horizontal in comparison with the vertical relationship between individuals and the bodies of political power. How can these two levels of socialisation – social and political – be combined? This is the central problem of modern politics. Modern citizenship is not a *purely political* concept, but it would lose all precise meaning if it were not at all political. Horizontal forms of solidarity do not take the place of citizenship, and they are constitutive of citizenship only insofar as they help determine the relationship between members of a community with the 'universal' that political powers are supposed to represent and uphold.

The first part of this chapter proposes a broad concept of the institution, which I believe is necessary to understand the conditions for modern citizenship. To do this, I rely on Hegel (1967) and Durkheim (1982; 1984; 2003), and, laterally, on Marx's *Critique of Hegel's Philosophy of Right* (Marx 1970). The second part will show how the democratisation of modern Western societies reshaped these conditions. Lastly, in the third part, I will look at Europe today. The hypotheses put forward in the first two parts should enable us to understand why it is currently impossible to develop genuine European citizenship. However, as already implied in these introductory remarks, I will not place the state of European citizenship in opposition with that of national citizenship. Citizenship in general is affected by how Europe functions. Not only has the European Union failed to enrich national citizenship by enlarging it, as some observers hoped it would when the status of European citizen was introduced, but it has also unsettled the meaning of citizenship within member states. The future of European democracy is no longer at stake only during European elections, but also during any national election in any EU member state.

The institutional conditions of modern citizenship

As I have suggested, addressing the EU democratic deficit from the perspective of citizenship implies not judging it in terms of its political structures alone, from the weight and competencies of the European Parliament compared to the executive, and the relationship between the Commission and intergovernmental organisations. Yet, far from wishing to oppose the institutional viewpoint, on the one hand, and citizens' subjective perceptions, on the other, I would argue for a broad concept of the institution of citizenship, a sociological or even anthropological concept, rather than a juridico-political one, even though it also encompasses these last two aspects. This concept can only be vague, compared with the precision of legal definitions.[1] Indeed, it encompasses all the social dimensions of human existence: close relationships within a family or otherwise, economic relationships, law and political structures. Some might object that extending the concept to this degree nearly makes it indeterminate. However, this broad concept of the institution has a twofold advantage. First, it lets us avoid the dualism of the individual and the collective, i.e., to understand from the outset that individuals' subjective dispositions are steeped in social aspects, and vice versa, that these dispositions are the foundations that support the existence and solidity of the institutions of society. Secondly, it avoids the excessive compartmentalisation of the individual's spheres of activity, between private and public, economic and political, etc. This is because the distinction between these spheres, which sociologists rightly consider to be a characteristic feature of modern societies, does not correlate to a fragmentation of the individual into multiple different and unrelated entities. What we call politics is just one of the dimensions

1 Thus, for example, Durkheim 1982: 45: 'One may term an *institution* all the beliefs and modes of behaviour instituted by the collectivity'. This concept is the inspiration behind Vincent Descombes's excellent *Les Institutions du sens* (1996). Note that, while very far removed from Hegel, he nevertheless rehabilitates the notion of 'objective spirit'. The need for such a concept of the institution has also been defended by some legal scholars. Thus, Maurice Hauriou, *Aux sources du droit: le pouvoir, l'ordre et la liberté* (1986 [1925]), notably book II, chap. 1: 'La théorie de l'institution et de la fondation (Essai de vitalisme social)'.

of collective life, and the relationship that individuals maintain with this dimension (interest or indifference, trust or distrust) is not solely determined by the structure of political institutions.

Only this broad concept of the institution can enable us to grasp citizenship in the totality of its conditions. From the juridico-political standpoint, citizenship is only a status, granted by official texts to certain individuals, connected to a determined set of rights and duties. From the social standpoint, citizenship is what Greek philosophy called an *ethos*, i.e., a set of mental dispositions that determines the relationship between the individual and the collective. The structures of modern societies are admittedly very different from those of the ancient *polis*. But the ethical connotations that we attach to the notion of being a citizen make it clear that this meaning of citizenship has not been forgotten. Granting a status is a formal act that is not sufficient *per se* to transform subjectivities. It generates an *ethos* only insofar as the individuals concerned appropriate it: in other words, if they perceive and use the rights conveyed by this status as possibilities for action. The political rights tied to national citizenship were effectively perceived and used in this way. So far, this has not been the case for the rights tied to European citizenship, and we must ask ourselves why.[2]

Before returning to this question, I would like to take a moment to look at the implications of an extensive conception of the institution, relying on Hegel's political philosophy. Hegel's works are probably not the best place to look for the means to understand the conditions of modern *democratic* citizenship. We know that he virulently rejected the notion of sovereignty of the people, as well as most of the institutional arrangements that are supposed to allow such sovereignty to be expressed.[3] Nor do we find in his *Philosophy of Right* a detailed theorisation of the role of the public sphere in the functioning of modern political regimes.[4] However, to understand the conditions of modern citizenship in general (and not democratic citizenship), this text is still quite relevant. Its strength lies in the fact that Hegel thought simultaneously about the consequences of both revolutions – economic and political – that gave rise to modern societies. Interested in the new political economy, he was the first philosopher

2 It is no surprise that EU citizens have made very little use of the European Citizen's Initiative, introduced by the Treaty of Lisbon, considering how this right is 'straitjacketed'. On this topic, see Vauchez 2014: 28–29.

3 See the remark at para. 273 of Hegel 1967 along with the remark at para. 308 on representation.

4 Some elements of such a theory can be found in Hegel 1967: 314–19. I will return to this point later on.

to acknowledge the break in the processes of socialisation brought about by the spread of the market economy. A fervent admirer of the French Revolution, he considered the recognition of individual liberty to be the foundation for rational right without abandoning the ethical ideal of citizenship. Thus, he was the first to address the typically modern opposition between *homo economicus* and *homo politicus*. Before Marx, and well before early twentieth-century sociology, Hegel observed that the structures of the modern economy favoured the development of individualism, sapping the meaning of the collective and voiding the ancient notion of purely political citizenship. The revolutions of the late eighteenth century, even while referring to models of Antiquity, profoundly transformed citizenship by removing its character of a status reserved to a narrow fringe of the population, whose liberty was based on the subjugation of others (women, servants and slaves), bound by the limits of the *oikos*, restricted to the activities of 'simply living'. By proclaiming liberty for all human beings, the declarations of the rights of man also asserted, at least in principle, that everyone had a right to citizenship. Yet this extension meant that politics could no longer take up most of the social activity of citizens. If any aspect of the *ethos* of political citizenship could be saved, it could only be saved if it were reconciled with the non-political activities that most members of modern society must carry out, and, chiefly, their economic activity. This reconciliation is made difficult not just by the lack of free time (or *otium*), but also, and more fundamentally, by the contradiction between the subjective dispositions that the modern economy fosters in individuals and those that the ideal citizen apparently requires.

What the complex construction of *Philosophy of Right* endeavours to show is that the individualisation resulting from new forms of production and trade does not definitively condemn citizenship, but that it must be rebuilt on new foundations. The 'universal' is no longer opposed to the individual, as in ancient societies. Instead, the universal now envelops the individual, penetrating it throughout, and the universal is only real and stable insofar as individuals are convinced that collective institutions are the conditions and guarantees of their individual liberties. Political citizenship, which Hegel called '*politische Gesinnung*',[5] is nothing more than the final and culminating point of a process whereby the individual learns the meaning of the collective, a process aided by all the types of relationships that a

5 See Hegel 1967 at para. 268.

particular individual can form within civil society.[6] Using terms that seem esoteric to us today, such as 'ethical objectivity' and 'ethical life' (*Sittlichkeit*), Hegel conceives of the same thing that twentieth-century sociology and anthropology target through the broadened notion of 'institution', i.e., the secret nucleus of all sociality in general, which lies in individuals' (more or less conscious) internalisation of the constraints and demands of collective existence, according to forms specific to the place and era in which they live.

Liberals and Marxists alike have misunderstood this essential dimension of Hegel's political philosophy. We must read, or reread, Marx's *Critique of Hegel's Political Right* to see what Marx owes to the reading of *Philosophy of Right* in his famous analyses of the egoism of civil society and the opposition between the 'burgher' and the citizen, and also to measure how much this reading is truncated.[7] I mean 'truncated' in the literal sense of the term, for Marx's commentary covers only paragraphs 261–313 of Hegel's work, i.e., the third part ('The State') of the third section ('Ethical Life'). Marx's reading is also truncated in its substance. Indeed, Marx endeavours to show that all the mediations that Hegel claims to establish between civil society and the state are failures, and that this cannot be otherwise, because, from the outset, Hegel constructs civil society and the state as two hostile armies. Yet Marx can uphold this thesis only because, by limiting his remarks to the section on the state, he ignores what forms the basis for these mediations, namely, the social dispositions that the individual already develops within the various institutions of civil society. Beginning with *Critique of Hegel's Philosophy of Right*, Marx reduces the notion of civil society to the 'system of needs', which, for Hegel, is only the first moment, namely, the ties of interdependence that men form with one another via labour and trade, in short, those

6 On this topic, see Jean-François Kervégan's particularly enlightening analyses (Kervégan 2013: 91–92). 'In the modern, post-revolutionary State, the particularity of the social state of the "bourgeois" is the mediation between the objective political constitution and the subjective disposition of citizens. This is why Hegel can assert that "patriotism" (*politische Gesinnung*) is fuelled and even made possible by particularist subjective dispositions generated by institutions of *civil society*.'

7 As a reminder, *Philosophy of Right* is divided into three sections: Abstract Right, Morality and Ethical Life (*Sittlichkeit*). In turn, this third section, Ethical Life, is divided into three sub-parts, dedicated to the family, civil society and the state, in that order. The part on the state begins with para. 257. We can assume that Marx's commentary (1970), the first pages of which have been lost, started with this paragraph. Moreover, this commentary is incomplete, as it stops a few paragraphs before the end of Hegel's analyses of the constitution of the state, and therefore does not address the paragraphs on international law (under the title 'Sovereignty vis-à-vis Foreign States') and world history.

ties that are the object of economics.[8] At this level, the individual's motives appear to be purely personal, and his action is social only in its unintentional effects. Here, society is none other than the 'complex interdependence of each on all', which results in 'subjective self-seeking [turning] into a contribution to the satisfaction of the needs of everyone else' (Hegel 1967: 199). But Hegel's civil society also includes the 'Administration of Justice', 'Police' and 'Corporations', all institutions that structure civil society politically and whereby the individual is educated in the 'universal'. If Hegel can assert that the corporation is, alongside the family, an 'ethical root of the State' (255), this is because it is a sphere for partial socialisation wherein the individual develops dispositions that are no longer selfish. Political citizenship would not be possible if it were not prepared by these narrower spheres of socialisation that are more immediately tied to the economic activities that occupy most of the individual's time. A few decades later, Durkheim would defend the same idea, and it would inspire his untimely proposal (in 1890s France) of forming new kinds of corporations. As Durkheim's language is no doubt easier for contemporary readers to understand than Hegel's, I will quote a passage from the preface to the second edition of *The Division of Labor in Society*, which casts light on 'ethical life' according to Hegel:

> A society made up of a mass of extremely unorganised individuals, which an overgrown State attempts to limit and restrain, constitutes a veritable sociological monstrosity [...] The State is too remote from individuals, its connections with them too superficial and irregular, to be able to penetrate the depths of their consciousness and socialise them from within [...] A nation cannot be maintained unless, between the State and individuals, a whole range of secondary groups are interposed. These must be close enough to the individual to attract him strongly to their activities, and in so doing, to absorb him into the mainstream of social life. (Durkheim 1984: 54)

But isn't the corporation a definitively anachronistic institution? We could definitely assert that Hegel's corporations are not those of the Ancien Régime, and that Durkheim (1984) was perfectly aware that the 'secondary groups' he deemed necessary for the proper functioning of society would vary in structure according to the era. However, this is not what is important. A corporatist organisation of society, apart from the fact that this suggests fascism to us today and is therefore discredited, is incompatible with the

8 Hegel cites Smith, Say and Ricardo. On Hegel's knowledge of economists, see notably Dickey 1987: 186–204. Marx's reduction of Hegel's civil society to its first moment is explicit in the preface to Marx 1970.

contingence and instability of the occupations of individuals in modern societies. Marx also noted this point in his remarks on Hegel's *Philosophy of Right*, and we must agree with him. One's occupation no longer defines an 'estate', as in past societies. While the occupation may have an impact on an individual's identity, it is still a relatively 'external' determination, no longer forming an 'objective communal being organised according to firm laws and related firmly to [the individual]' (Marx 1970: 136).[9] Thus, it is not the corporatist idea per se that warrants our attention, but rather the intuition that inspired it. Hegel, and Durkheim later on, understood that, the economic structures of modern societies being what they are, political citizenship must be shaped around pre-political forms of solidarity (Hegel 1967; Durkheim 1984).

The democratisation of citizenship

We would need to go through a somewhat detailed social history of the past two centuries up to the present to show that citizenship has always been supported by partial forms of socialisation, albeit with structures that are very different from what Hegel and Durkheim hoped for. Modern societies have never been as atomised as is assumed by economic theory or deplored by a certain type of social criticism. Solidarity has never been lacking, and forms of solidarity have nourished and continue to nourish the formation of various kinds of groups, more or less formally or sustainably, including labour unions, political parties, activist groups, consumer associations, NGOs, today's social networks, etc. Through participation in these kinds of groups, citizenship becomes social, thus becoming an *ethos*, linked to the feeling of belonging to a community. In other words, these groups have, in their own way, carried out the mediating function that Hegel and Durkheim attributed to corporations. However, as they are based on free association, their development has come hand in hand with a new transformation of political citizenship itself, thereby becoming democratic.

For Hegel (1967) and for Durkheim (1984), citizenship should be manifested essentially through the *trust* of citizens in the rationality of institutions and the competence of governing bodies. While both Hegel and Durkheim held a place for public opinion in the functioning of modern political regimes, the function they attributed to it was unilateral. In their view,

9 Marx (1970) deems that the transformation of political Estates (*Stände*) of the Middle Ages into social Estates depoliticised the social by privatising it. This thesis is obviously linked to the extreme representation that he makes of individualism in civil society.

public opinion was chiefly a means for educating the population by communicating the reasons for the decisions of governing bodies. Thus, Hegel was in favour of making parliamentary debates public, expecting this to cause the public 'to respect the work, abilities, virtues, and dexterity of ministers and officials' (Hegel 1967: 315). However, he did not wish for the public to use this as a means to influence governing bodies. His characterisation of public opinion, which he says 'deserves to be as much respected as despised' (318), is ambiguous only in appearance. Despisal, or contempt, seems to have the upper hand over respect, for Hegel says it should be despised for its concrete expression and concrete consciousness, and respected solely for its essential basis, which political leaders and their administration alone are able to see. For Hegel, the term 'opinion' encompasses virtually indistinctly slander and libel, on the one hand, and criticism and popular protest of laws and the government, on the other.[10] The dialectal unity of the universal and the particular finds its limits here: particularity and subjectivity are entirely on the side of those being ruled (the 'multitude'), while the meaning and knowledge of the universal are on the side of rulers and government officials ('the universal class' – *der allgemeine Stand*). Durkheim's view is hardly different.[11] Unlike Hegel, Durkheim calls the modern political regime 'democracy'. However, he has a very particular representation of democracy, which he carefully distinguishes from the Rousseau-inspired conceptions whereby the 'thought of the governing parties' should be identical and intermingled with 'the thought and wills of those being governed' (Durkheim 1984: 125). For relations between the population (which he sometimes designates as the 'mass' or 'crowd') and the governing bodies, at first glance, he appears to have a more balanced conception than Hegel's. Communication between the population and the governing bodies should, in his view, operate in both directions. Yet dissymmetry remains clear in the opposition between the two types of collective conscious: 'diffused', 'unreflective' and 'obscure' in the population, 'elaborate', 'organised' and 'reflective' in the government. Granted, governing bodies must be informed of what is happening within the population, and it is even recommended that they consult the population occasionally, but they should determine the

10 See Hegel 1967: para. 319: 'But the substance of the matter is and remains that traducing the honour of anyone, slander, abuse, the contemptuous caricature of government, its ministers, officials, and in particular the person of the monarch, defiance of the laws, incitement to rebellion, &c., &c., are all crimes or misdemeanours in one or other of their numerous gradations.'

11 Here, I am relying on the three chapters dedicated to democracy in Durkheim 2003: 110–41.

questions. By virtue of the knowledge that these governing bodies hold (Durkheim mentions statistical and administrative information) and their supposedly superior ability to judge, it is admitted that they know better than the population what is good for it: 'To know what is useful, [the government] is better placed than the crowd; thus, the former must see things differently from the latter' (Durkheim 1984: 125).

The idea that politics can be essentially conflictual, that it can consist of a continuous challenge to the foundations of the law, of power and of social relations,[12] was profoundly foreign to Hegel and Durkheim. As concerned as they were to establish mediations between ordinary citizens and the state, they held the view of political leaders whose main preoccupation is public order. Hegel assimilates protest to 'contemptuous caricature', and Durkheim was worried about an excessive development of 'critical spirit' that, no longer held back in modern societies by the ties of tradition, saps the stability of governments.[13] Here, we understand the link between the two authors' restrictive conception of public opinion and the corporatist project. For political citizenship not to remain a simple status with no impact on the mental dispositions of individuals, it requires a social anchoring. But the political dispositions required of simple citizens are limited to trusting that law and government policies are just. We are still far from the citizen as a political actor. At the very best, we expect him to show a lower degree of passivity: democracy, 'because it is a regime of reflection [...] allows the citizen to accept the laws of his country with more intelligence, going out with less passivity' (Durkheim 2003: 125).

However, Hegel saw the weak point of the mediations that he attempted to build between social and political life, and this point would prove decisive for later history. While he believed it was possible to reconcile the citizen's *ethos* with the structures of the market economy, despite the 'selfishness' that these structures tend to produce, the same cannot be said of the massive inequalities resulting from the uncontrolled development of this economy. In this respect, certain passages of *Philosophy of Right* seem to anticipate Marx's later analyses. Hegel notes that economic growth goes hand in hand with the accumulation of fortunes and a correlative 'dependence and distress' of individuals tied to labour with such limited

12 Here, I borrow a formulation from Lefort 2007: 563.
13 Durkheim 2003: 127: 'Society is missing solid ground. There is no longer anything settled. And as critical spirit is then well developed, and each has his own way of thinking, the disarray is amplified even more by all these individual diversities. Hence the chaotic aspect shown by some democracies, their perpetual mobility and instability'.

perspectives, or even their degradation below a standard of living considered necessary for a decent life in a given society. This material degradation can lead to a 'loss of the sense of right and wrong, of honesty and the self-respect which makes a man insist on maintaining himself by his own work and effort' (Hegel 1967: 244). Hegel could naturally only postulate what would become the 'social question' twenty years later, and his few proposals to remedy poverty do not go very far. Yet it is remarkable that he saw the phenomenon that threatened the conditions for the citizen's *ethos* not in market utilitarianism per se, but rather in the polarisation between extreme wealth and poverty (Hegel 1967: 243).

There is no need to recall here the role that this polarisation played in the history and transformations of European political regimes in the following decades, and well into the twentieth century. 'Class warfare', in its revolutionary and reformist forms, marked the political debut of these masses to whom the bourgeois revolutions had granted equal civil rights, before also having, under duress, to grant political rights and, much later, social rights. It is of little importance whether these rights were attained forcibly from political leaders or granted freely by them. In any case, this 'generosity' was motivated by the fear of the masses, by virtue of the principle laid out notably by Gustav Schmoller, whereby 'revolution can always be avoided by opportune reform'.[14] But if the masses of the poor could spark fear (rather than pity, which inspires charity), it is because they organised labour unions and political parties. From the standpoint of radical revolutionism, the institutionalisation of such organisations and their involvement in the normal political process may appear to be a means to domesticate them. They nevertheless reshaped the political field, making dissensus one of its structural characteristics. The democratisation of modern political regimes came hand in hand with increased conflict in ordinary politics whereby all citizens – rich and poor, mighty or powerless – could view themselves as political agents, not as simple political subjects. From this perspective, the fact that social protection was built as a *right* goes well beyond its simply legal and administrative form.

The threat and spectre of revolution has long been an obstacle to acknowledging this conflictual dimension of modern democratic regimes. Yet some authors, without challenging the civil and political liberties guaranteed by these democracies, have validated this. Hence, Claude Lefort, who defended liberal democracy and counted free enterprise as a basic

14 Rosanvallon 2011: 241. Regarding the reforms of Napoleon III and especially Bismarck in the late nineteenth century, Rosanvallon also speaks of a 'reformism of fear' (ibid.: 240).

liberty, observed that modern democracy has legitimised social divisions by institutionalising conflict.[15] Must we understand that trust, which Hegel or Durkheim expected from the citizen, has given way to distrust? Pierre Rosanvallon, who, in a recent book, catalogued the various practices (control, prevention, judiciarisation) that the citizens of Western democracies use in an attempt to act on legitimately elected powers, does indeed speak of the politics of distrust.[16] However, we must note that this distrust is aimed chiefly at political leaders, be they legislative or executive, but not at the general organisation of institutions. The purely political procedures of the constitution of powers are no longer enough to ensure the trust of citizens in their leaders. In turn, politicians have had to adapt to critical public opinion, manifested not only through speech or writing, but also in protest practices (strikes and demonstrations, for the most classic forms) that are a legitimate part of democratic life. By making room for dissensus within the public sphere, however, democracy saved overall trust in its institutions. Here I will follow Vincent Descombes, who rightly notes that, while elections and negotiations may express disagreement, they are nevertheless based on 'common representations', namely, 'instituted significations that are not only political, but also social' (Descombes 1996: 294).[17] If democracy has unanimous support today,[18] this is because, by incorporating conflict, it built a bridge between the free associations of civil society and the bodies of political power.

Citizenship in the European era

How do these debates of the past affect Europe today? The construction of the European Union cannot avoid reopening the question of the interconnection between social solidarity and political citizenship. The engineers

15 Lefort 2007: 562–63. He went even further by stating that 'modern democracy irreversibly asserts the legitimacy of debate over the distinction between legitimate and illegitimate' (ibid.).

16 The subtitle is 'La Politique à l'âge de la défiance', politics in the age of distrust. In my view, the main title ('Counter-Democracy') does not reflect the author's thesis that these various signs of distrust and attempts to control the action of political leaders do indeed fit with 'democratic activity', which 'largely goes beyond the framework of elective and representative institutions' (Rosanvallon 2011: 253).

17 Descombes 1996: 294: 'Disagreement itself, conflict of opinions, in order to be handled as disagreement or conflict during a negotiation or vote, requires that participants have the same representation of what they are doing (negotiating, voting).'

18 Unlike in the 1920s and 1930s, democracy as such is not challenged. Divergences involve the interpretation of its meaning and implications.

of the European Union wagered that it could be built based on the economy. We will not go into this history in detail here, as it was not a straightforward programme conceived from the beginning.[19] Between 1951 (the Treaty of Paris, establishing the European Coal and Steel Community) and 2007 (the Treaty of Lisbon, a substitute for the Constitution that had been rejected by the referendums in France and the Netherlands), the construction of the European Union faced several successive moments of choice that could have given it an entirely different shape to what it is today. Since approximately the late 1980s, this economic construction has been explicitly driven by the dogmas of what is regarded as 'neo-liberalism',[20] whose key themes are competition and growth. At present, this policy in Europe is leading to growing inequality in the distribution of wealth, in the share of revenues for labour and capital, and among the different categories of workers.[21] I will leave it to economists to debate whether this phenomenon is temporary or lasting. The focus of the political debate on jobs and unemployment covers up and stifles the necessary debate on inequality, suggesting that the only thing of importance is that everyone has access to work. We do not even ask whether workers' wages allow them to live decently. The 'value' of work is tending to become a moral category, insofar as it is no longer seen as a means for propertyless individuals to take part in a fair distribution of society's wealth.

In 2007, the European Commission implemented a programme on European citizenship for the period until 2013. Another such programme is set to follow for the period 2014 to 2020 (European Commission 2007). These texts give some indications on how the EU bodies in Brussels understand citizenship. The stated objective of 'bringing Europe closer to its citizens' is proof, in itself, of the democratic deficit. To achieve this objective, the Commission relies on educational means aimed at developing 'a sense of belonging to common European ideals', encouraging the democratic and civic participation of citizens at EU level, and fostering their social and intercultural involvement. Concrete proposals are few and far between, or

19 Salais 2013 presents a detailed and nuanced analysis of the various stages of this construction.
20 The genesis and unity of the fundamental orientations of current economic politicise are widely debated. See, notably, Audier 2012. However, detailing these debates here would take me too far from my central message.
21 This phenomenon is not unique to Europe. See Piketty 2013. Regarding Europe, this rise in inequality is observed even within the wealthiest EU member states; see Wehler 2013, which casts doubt on whether growth will enable inequality to be resolved. Given the current form of this growth, it appears to be the cause rather than the solution.

simply inappropriate. The 'involvement' expected from citizens appears to refer to horizontal solidarity, or even volunteering activities, to be extended to the EU level. It is hard to object to these good intentions, but these forms of social solidarity, no matter how desirable they might be, can only create citizenship if they can exert influence on political decisions. Yet the educational perspective that these texts inspire implicitly excludes such influence. While they intend to promote an 'active European citizenship', this is apparently limited to better knowledge of European institutions and reasons for EU policies. European leaders' idea of the public democratic space appears quite close to the conception of Hegel or Durkheim. They appear to identify themselves readily with this 'universal class – *der allgemeine Stand*' to which Hegel reserved knowledge of the substantial interests of society, or the governing bodies that Durkheim considered to hold 'social consciousness'.

The 2007 agenda was more concrete. Unlike more recent texts, it noted rising inequality within Europe, among regions, urban and rural areas, member states, along with the polarisation of the labour market and some categories of the population being stuck in unqualified jobs (thus with low pay) with no possibilities to move ahead. However, all these inequalities were treated as 'risks', the flip side of the 'new opportunities' opened by 'more innovative knowledge societies'. This phrasing suggests that poverty and exclusion are due solely to the insufficiencies of individuals, to their failure to avail themselves of the new opportunities open to everyone. To promote citizenship, this text called for EU nationals to develop the skills and flexibility that would enable them to adapt better, on an individual basis, to the demands of 'globalisation', this 'one-size-fits-all' notion of contemporary political language that, by confusing scientific, technological and economic development, gives the appearance of being a natural, and thus inevitable, necessity of the structures of contemporary capitalism. Moreover, the authors of this text showed a disconcerting frankness when they noted that promoting this form of citizenship would offer the advantage of being a good financial investment.[22]

22 Proof can be found in this quotation: 'A well-functioning, confident and buoyant society which invests in its human capital and creates opportunities for individuals to move on throughout their life cycle is essential to sustain economic growth, labour market participation, living standards and combat social exclusion. This is also a sound financial investment: tackling social problems at their source reduces the risk that the welfare system will have to pick up the bill for social dysfunctions and lack of economic opportunities at a later stage.'

These texts provide a good illustration of the characteristics that are, according to some contemporary critical analyses, those of neo-liberal governmentality.[23] They reveal to what extent European political leaders have lost all understanding of the political meaning of citizenship. Yet we must not overestimate their influence. Most citizens see the reality of Europe through the policies implemented in its name, rather than through the discourse that political leaders use in an attempt to make such policies acceptable. At nation state level, the 'acculturation' of citizenship, i.e., transforming the status of citizen into an *ethos*, mainly took place (more or less effectively depending on the country) via practices wherein the population appropriated this status. They became genuine political actors through the use of the rights conferred by citizenship and while fighting for new rights. If it is true that this understanding of citizenship goes hand in hand with a conception of politics that includes dissensus as one of its essential dimensions, then we cannot expect political leaders to acquiesce explicitly to such a conception. Regardless of the representations that political leaders make of citizenship, it is unlikely that these representations are the decisive cause of the current problems with European citizenship.

The pedagogical efforts of European bodies, be they focused on citizenship or on trying to explain the reasons for current economic policies, will have great difficulty convincing the people who continue to suffer the devastating effects of such policies. Furthermore, one need not be an expert in economics to understand the overarching rationale of a company relocating to another country (be it within or outside the EU) where labour costs are lower, nor need to read *Les Echos* (or the *Wall Street Journal*) to understand what is meant by the euphemism 'structural reform'. European political leaders are either very naive or intentionally blind to imagine that the rise in economic and social inequality in Europe and the stark contrast between growing precariousness, on the one hand, and the 'secession of the rich', on the other, will not dent the overall trust of citizens in their institutions. The democratic crisis in Europe is not visible only during elections (through abstention or protest votes), but also in the surge in suicides in

23 I am alluding here to the analyses inspired by Foucault's lectures at the Collège de France in 1978–79 (Foucault 2004), analyses notably echoed (via an article by Thomas Lemke) by Brown (2003). She gives thought-provoking analyses of the USA during the presidency of George W. Bush. These texts have set a matrix for neo-liberalism and the governance of contemporary liberal states, casting light on some aspects, but not respecting the chronology and often used dogmatically. For a critique of this 'neo-Foucauldian' matrix, see Audier 2012.

Greece, the increasing difficulty in accessing healthcare in some countries for the unemployed, working poor or pensioners,[24] or the forced exodus of young people seeking work. By levying accusations against the 'welfare state', a certain form of liberalism forgets that public services and social 'protections' are rights that were instituted in the march towards equality. By interpreting these protections in terms of 'welfare', we obscure two centuries of history that shaped citizenship in modern democratic states.[25] Far from fostering the development of solidarity among European workers, current economic policies divide them by forcing them to compete against one another in a *race to the bottom*. Asking each person to acquire the skills to be among the winners of the new economy does nothing to dispel the fact that there will necessarily be losers as long as this economy's main imperative remains to lower labour costs while considering labour rights to be an obstacle to optimal markets.[26]

The capitalism of the early twenty-first century is no longer that of the nineteenth century. Nevertheless, the need for social anchoring of citizenship is still timely. The corporations of Hegel's or Durkheim's time are a thing of the past, as we have said. For more than 200 years, free and dynamic forms of solidarity provided the necessary mediation between social and political life. Contrary to a widely accepted view of individualism in contemporary societies, these forms of solidarity still exist today. Yet the current power structures in Europe prevent such solidarity from being converted into political power at European level.[27] In my view, it would be a serious error to interpret the lack of a wide-scale social response to the gradual degradation of the social state as a sign of resigned, if not enthusiastic, acceptance. For the main reason for this lack of a response is that the conditions for building a public democratic space, allowing room for protest and negotiation, are currently inexistent at European level. By making the formation of such a space practically impossible, the European Union condemns itself to remain an abstract Universal, unable to integrate the particular spheres of sociality.

24 See *Le Monde* 2013. Also Stuckler and Basu 2013.

25 Certain administrative methods are what transform these rights into 'welfare'. On this topic, see Rosanvallon 2011: 287.

26 It is well known that CJEU jurisprudence treats the rights conferred under the European Social Charter as second-category rights, subordinate to economic liberties. See Salais 2013: 369.

27 The main obstacle lies in the independence of the main bodies of power that determine European policies. See Antoine Vauchez's reflections (2014) on the 'independent bodies': Court of Justice of the European Union, European Commission, European Central Bank.

Unfortunately, it is entirely understandable that social protest seeks refuge in more concrete collective forms. Rekindled nationalism is fuelled by these structural deficiencies of Europe, as are all tendencies to withdraw into separate communities, identities or even xenophobia, now the source of the rise in populism.[28]

Conclusion

Europe's democratic deficit is often attributed to the absence of unity or even the inexistence of a European people. Indeed, a democracy requires a people, doesn't it? Some well-intentioned minds think that they can overcome this lack by developing, notably through education, an awareness of common values that all the peoples of Europe are supposed to share. The idealism of this analysis hides a certain degree of hypocrisy. For what the European people is lacking is mainly a political consistency, and the main reason for this lack is the bureaucratic way in which Europe was built from its very beginnings. Divergences, when they existed, were discussed in cenacles of experts. Thus, a sphere for public debate never emerged or developed, whereas the history of modern Western states shows that such a sphere is indispensable to forming a democratic people. This bureaucratic construction enjoyed a certain degree of indifferent tolerance from citizens for so long as European policies were barely perceptible or could be viewed positively. But the situation becomes intolerable once these policies essentially call for austerity and sacrifice. The European political people does not exist because the designers and engineers of Europe have, until now, intentionally or not, made its formation impossible. If we wish to prove wrong the Cassandras predicting that Europe will break up in the short or medium term, we must urgently work on forming a veritable European citizenship. All the citizens of Europe are responsible for this task, but chiefly the political leaders, who must break with the dogma of economic rationality sheltered by principle from public debate. For only through such debate can the citizenship granted as a status become this shared *ethos* that makes the (conflictual) unity of a democratic collectivity.

28 We should be wary of the current inflated use of the word 'populism', which is tending to be a 'one-size-fits-all' term for any signs of criticism of Europe. I would refer to my own article: 'Quel est le peuple du populisme?'. In Colliot-Thélène and Guénard 2014.

References

Audier, S. (2012) *Néolibéralisme(s). Une archéologie intellectuelle*, Paris: Grasset and Fasquelle.

Brown, W. (2003) 'Neo-liberalism and the End of Liberal Democracy', *Theory and Event*, 7(1).

Colliot-Thélène, C., and Guénard, F. (2014) *Peuples et populisme*, Paris: Presses universitaires de France.

Descombes, V. (1996) *Les Institutions du sens*, Paris: Éditions de Minuit.

Dickey, L. (1987) *Hegel: Religion, Economics and the Politics of Spirit, 1770–1807*, Cambridge: Cambridge University Press.

Durkheim, E. (1982) *Rules of Sociological Method*, New York: Free Press.

(1984) *The Division of Labor in Society*, New York: Free Press.

(2003) *Leçons de sociologie*, Paris: Presses universitaires de France.

European Commission (2007) 'Opportunities, Access and Solidarity: Towards a New Social Vision for 21st Century Europe', COM (2007) 726 final.

Foucault, M. (2004) Naissance de la biopolitique: Cours au Collège de France (1978–1979), Paris: Gallimard/Seuil.

Hauriou, M. (1986) *Aux sources du droit: le pouvoir, l'ordre et la liberté*, Bibliothèque de philosophie politique et juridique, Textes et documents, Caen: Centre de philosophie politique et juridique, University of Caen.

Hegel, G. (1967) *Hegel's Philosophy of Right*, trans. T. M. Knox, Oxford: Oxford University Press.

Kervégan, J. (1986) Introduction to his translation of Hegel's *Grundlinien der Philosophie des Rechts (Principes de la philosophie du droit)*, Paris: Presses universitaires de France.

Lefort, C. (2007) 'La Dissolution des repères et l'enjeu démocratique', in *Le Temps présent. Écrits, 1945–2005*, Paris: Belin.

Marx, K. (1970) *A Contribution to the Critique of Political Economy*, ed. Maurice Dobb, New York: International Publishers.

Le Monde, 19 April 2013.

Piketty, T. (2013) *Le Capital au XXIe siècl[e]*, Paris: Seuil.

Rosanvallon, P. (2011) *La Société des égaux*, Paris: Seuil.

Salais, R. (2013) *Le Viol d'Europe. Enquête sur la disparition d'une idée*, Paris: Presses universitaires de France.

Stuckler, D., and Basu, S. (2013) *The Body Economic: Why Austerity Kills*, New York: Basic Books.

Vauchez, A. (2014) *Démocratiser l'Europe*, Paris: Seuil.

Wehler, H.U. (2013) *Die neue Umverteilung. Soziale Ungleichheit in Deutschland*, Munich: C. H. Beck.

6

Silencing the Eurocrats in public crisis politics

PIETER DE WILDE

Introduction

Although the euro crisis is particularly pronounced and prolonged, crises in the EU are certainly not a new phenomenon. In fact, the political process of European integration since the end of the Second World War in which states increasingly share sovereignty has been driven forward by a variety of crises, from the onslaught of the Second World War itself to Suez in 1956 and the oil crises of the 1970s. It is therefore interesting to find that crises play little role in European integration theories. On the one hand, liberal intergovernmentalist theory emphasizes the big moments of Treaty change in which national executive actors play the key role in shaping the integration process, based on domestic economic interests (Milward 2000; Moravcsik 1993; Moravcsik 1998). On the other hand, neo-functionalists stress the gradual process of spillover leading to ever more integration, further stimulated by supranational entrepreneurs like the European Commission and the European Court of Justice (Burley and Mattli 1993; Haas 2004; Schmitter 1970). Neither of these grand theories, however, allows an explicit role for crises to explain European integration. Only recently, driven by the long-term legitimacy crisis of the European Union and – particularly – the ongoing euro crisis, have theorists started to address the question of how crises affect European integration (Jachtenfuchs and Genschel in this volume; Schimmelfennig 2014; Tosun et al. 2014; Vilpisauskas 2014). To add to this agenda, this contribution focuses on the public politics of crisis. It thus asks: how are crises discussed in public debates? Who features in these debates and what determines the success of their arguments? And, ultimately, how do the public politics of crises affect European integration?

European integration and crises

Crises have often seemed to threaten the continued existence of the European integration project and member states' immediate responses have tended towards a nationalist reflex. This is in line with crisis management theory, which predicts that successful crisis management is not conducive to policy reform (Boin and 't Hart 2003; Van Hooren et al. 2014). But, more often than not, crises presented an opportunity for further integration. It might take some time for EU leaders to respond, but the answer they provide to crises has been, by and large, more integration. The euro crisis is no exception (Schimmelfennig 2014). Yet, to understand why and how crises have fostered integration and whether this is likely to occur in the future too, we need to bring crises and their effects more systematically into European integration theory. While Markus Jachtenfuchs and Philipp Genschel apply an institutionalist perspective to this task in this volume, the present contribution applies a sociological approach with a public sphere perspective (cf. Koopmans and Statham 2010; Risse 2015; Trenz 2005; Van de Steeg 2006) leading to different expectations, especially in the long term.

To further the aim of bringing crises into European integration theory, this contribution first attempts to conceptualize crises before applying its various components to European integration. In doing so, it is argued that crises provide opportunities for integration as pro-integration political entrepreneurs successfully convince key stakeholders and decision-makers that these external shocks signify a failure of the Westphalian system of independent sovereign nation states to provide a variety of necessary public goods. However, as integration has resulted in an ever more authoritative Union with extensive powers in many policy fields, the opportunities for anti-European entrepreneurs to shape our understanding of crises and their solutions have increased. Their numbers have also increased as a series of enlargements have brought in more 'reluctant partners' into the European family of member states (Wallace 2002). What is more, politicization has brought European politics into 'daylight' (White 2010) as media cover EU issues, political parties campaign on them and citizens are more aware and concerned about what is happening in Brussels (Hooghe and Marks 2009; De Wilde 2011b; De Wilde and Zürn 2012; Statham and Trenz 2013b; Hutter and Grande 2014). Key decision-makers, like Commissioners, can exploit politicization to advance their agenda, depending on the constellation of powers in the issue at hand (Rauh 2012). European integration is no longer the prerogative of member state governments, EU institutions and privileged interest groups (Schmitter 1970; Moravcsik 1993; Haas 2004). Instead, the major political decisions now have to be articulated and defended in the public sphere, making society at large a factor in influencing the future trajectory of integration. The debates in the public sphere make it increasingly clear that democracy forms a major source of contention, feeding Euroscepticism (De Wilde et al. 2014). With the transfer of EU politics from secretive settings behind closed doors to the wider public sphere, the benchmark against which to evaluate further steps has changed from improving functional efficiency and effectiveness of public good deliverance to upholding and improving democratic legitimacy (Eriksen and Fossum 2000; Kohler-Koch and Rittberger 2007; Eriksen 2009). Anti-European entrepreneurs now have both the foundational material (powerful EU institutions with low democratic legitimacy) and the platform (the wider public sphere) to advance their agenda, in contrast to earlier crises. Taking advantage of these opportunities, such anti-European entrepreneurs are becoming ever more successful at exploiting crises by arguing that it is the EU itself, rather than nation states, that fail in the supply of public goods. This conceptualization points to the open-ended outcome of the current euro crisis and to the importance of the many possible ways in which it can be interpreted. Through this conceptualization, it becomes clear that a shock to the system does not explain itself, nor does it automatically lead to a new equilibrium. Instead, the interpretation of what went wrong and how to solve it is an essential part of crisis politics. Hence, Colin Hay argues:

> Crises are representations and hence 'constructions' of failure. A given constellation of contradictions and failures within the institutions of the state can sustain a multiplicity of conflicting narratives of crisis. Such narratives compete in terms of their ability to find resonance with individuals' and groups' direct, lived experiences, and not in terms of their 'scientific' adequacy as explanations for the condition they diagnose. (Hay 1996: 255)

This 'interpretation' or 'representation' is conducted by competing political elites in the public sphere, trying to push various revisionist and status quo agendas. In advancing their agendas, elites see themselves increasingly compelled to take the public detour and to relate their agenda to improving democracy in Europe. In that sense, crisis management in Europe comes to resemble crisis management in the state. This will illustrate how both the build-up of the EU system and the widening of the audience play into the hands of anti-European entrepreneurs. In other words, the very success of European integration in the past, the increasingly public profile of EU politics and the rising potency of 'democracy' as legitimating principle provide anti-European entrepreneurs with ammunition, the higher ground and an easy target.

Unpacking the definition of crisis advanced here, the first component is a fundamental shock to the system with the widespread subjective conviction that a political order is malfunctioning in one way or another, to the point of imminent threat to its survival, with accompanying sense of urgency and time pressure. The second component is a process of interpretation, with various entrepreneurs trying to advance their views on what the crisis is, which institutions failed to prevent it from happening and how to solve or absorb the shock. In pushing their various agendas, these entrepreneurs use whatever means available to amplify and disseminate their line of reasoning. The third component is a particular essential public good that is considered to be jeopardized by the shock in question. The main manifestation of a crisis – from an empirical sociological perspective – is thus a broadly observable frenzied social outcry targeting a particular political regime or institution as culprit for failing to safeguard a key public good, in a dramatic way.

System and shock

A political crisis has been defined as 'an abrupt and brutal challenge to the survival of a political regime' (Dogan and Higley 1998: 6–7). Hence, there is something imminent and uncertain inherent in every crisis. A crisis shakes a political system to its core. In threatening its survival, it puts high pressure on political elites to act immediately in order to avert the collapse of the system. This needs to happen under uncertain circumstances as to the exact cause and solution to address the crisis.

What exactly the political regime is threatened by in its survival is by no means given. I will return to the importance of interpretation in the next section. But, interpretation is not free of bounds. The nature, severity and spread of the shock present a framework and direction for such interpretation. Geopolitical shocks, whether major devastations of war and loss of human life or merely the threat thereof, inherently point to the failure of (military) security systems. The devastation of the Second World War indicated to many the failure of the Westphalian system of sovereign nation states to safeguard human life. The old geopolitical system of Realpolitik and checks and balances between coalitions of great powers had failed to prevent all-out war and mass killings. This conviction was widespread by 1945, if not in 1918 already. Half-hearted attempts to supersede the Westphalian system with the overarching institutions of the League of Nations had failed (Northedge 1986). The massive shock of the Second World War thus presented a survival challenge to fundamental world political order, including its most powerful component: the sovereign nation state (Milward 2000). Smaller shocks have a more limited impact in terms of the system or regime threatened. The Suez crisis of 1956, for example, demonstrated the bankruptcy of European imperial and colonial politics and the capacity of even the biggest European powers to conduct effective foreign policy independently. From the first oil crisis in 1973 to the current Ukrainian–Russian conflict, a range of crises demonstrate the high vulnerability of the energy markets of European states, both in terms of supply and in terms of price (Molle 2001: chap. 11). Financial crises such as the attack on several European currencies – most notably the British Pound – in 1992 convinced many of the increasing failure of state currencies to support a stable domestic financial market and economic prosperity.

What we see in consequence is the attempt to supersede the old system of independent nation states, each with their own foreign policies, energy policies and their currencies. The widespread conviction of the failure of the old system provides impetus for radical policy changes. Having witnessed nation states fail to provide security and economic prosperity, European elites embark on the adventure of creating a new system of European Union, including a Common Foreign and Security Policy, an energy policy and the euro. In the wake of these various crises, complementing systems at European level have been built up. The creation of the European Coal and Steel Community – aimed at communalizing the key industries of warmongering – cannot be understood without the immediate background of the Second World War shock. The gradual build-up of what is now Europe's Common Foreign and Security Policy cannot be understood without the history of failures of individual European countries to maintain their Great Power status and colonial empires, as exemplified by the Suez crisis (Dinan 1999: 30). The build-up of a common energy market – from Euratom to the liberalization of electricity markets – cannot be understood without the effects of such external shocks as the oil crises of the 1970s (Molle 2001: chap. 11). The Russian–Ukrainian conflicts of the new millennium are likely to provide renewed momentum to the integration of energy markets. Finally, economic and monetary union is directly stimulated by volatility of currency markets and attacks on individual currencies, such as the upheavals of 1992–93 (Marsh 2009: 133).

Of course, there are many more smaller and bigger crises I could mention with direct effects on European integration. Rather than providing a comprehensive and encompassing overview, these examples above merely serve to illustrate the argument that the nature, severity and scope of shocks threaten the continued survival of various systems as these are considered to fail in delivering key public goods. The nature of the shock – whether geopolitical, economic, financial or otherwise – tends to pinpoint the system at fault as security, economic or currency related. The severity of the shock affects its reach on the system. So, the Suez crisis may have demonstrated the bankruptcy of French Great Power politics but was not severe enough to endanger the entire French state. For such an engrained and encompassing system to be threatened, a much more severe shock is needed, such as the Second World War. Finally, the scope of a shock also points to the system at fault. As the various oil and gas crises affect multiple if not all European countries simultaneously, it is hard to blame a specific national energy policy within Europe.

The build-up of a European political system has, so far, not replaced but complemented the pre-existing nation states. Both the European and the national system currently exist in some form of uneasy symbiosis. What this means is that it has become much harder to identify the system that is shocked by the next crisis. Furthermore, European integration has not prevented new shocks from happing. Throughout history since 1945, shocks have continued to hit Europe despite increasingly powerful EU institutions and policies. The replacement of national currencies with the euro under supervision of both European and national central banks with European interest rate and national fiscal policies, has not prevented what is probably the biggest economic crisis Europe has experienced since the 1930s (Baldwin and Wyplosz cited in Tosun et al. 2014: 197). What we know is that 'the system' failed to safeguard economic prosperity in the face of the financial and sovereign debt shocks of 2007 to 2009. The nature of the shock is both financial and fiscal, the severity is intense but highly uneven throughout Europe and the scope affects many Eurozone countries, specifically Greece, Portugal, Spain and Ireland, but also countries outside the euro, like Iceland and the United Kingdom. Yet it is not clear whether the system at fault is the common currency, or national fiscal policies, or global capitalism for that matter. To answer this question, we need interpretation which political entrepreneurs operating in the public sphere supply in abundance. This will be addressed in the next section.

Players and stage

During politics in normal times, a possibly infinite number of potential conflicts vie for attention. Yet, in practice, some core conflicts crowd others out. Repeated conflicts and rituals solidify the landscape of actual conflict into a few dividing lines. These tend to become institutionalized, as political parties or other organizations come to represent opposing camps on a more or less permanent basis, each representing a different societal group and value set. As a result, cleavages are born (Lipset and Rokkan 1967; Mair 2005), which tend to be long-lived as both organizational sides develop an interest in maintaining the conflict. As long as their conflict remains central in political life, other potentially cross-cutting conflicts that could split the opposing camps remain limited. These cross-cutting conflicts simultaneously provide the biggest threat. In the words of Schattschneider:

> The greatest hazard in the development of any conflict is not a frontal attack by the opposition but a flank attack by bigger collateral, inconsistent and irrelevant competitors for the attention and loyalty of the public. (Schattschneider 1957: 939)

Compromise or equilibrium reached by the main opposing camps settles the polity on a certain course after which minor or gradual changes are possible, but few landslides will occur. In this way, stable cleavages account for much of the stability and continuity in politics and policy of Europe in the twentieth century. Often, only fundamental changes in society can upheave a cleavage system once it has become ingrained in society, leading to Bartolini and Mair's 'frozen cleavage' hypothesis (Bartolini and Mair 1990). Besides major gradual societal changes, the alternative source of change is crisis.

Elites frequently stand at the genesis of a crisis (Dogan and Higley 1998), with some faction allegedly responsible for the cause and impact of the shock and another jumping on it to spread the notion of crisis among the wider population in hopes of benefits in power. If this second faction is successful, the resulting public outcry provides opportunities to all those with revisionist agendas. That is, once a shock has become a crisis through the successful dissemination of the perception that the system is facing an imminent threat to its survival, political entrepreneurs who want to change the political status quo gain a window of opportunity to push their agendas (Kingdon 1984). It means that crises do not 'just happen', but form a tool in political struggles.

> Those who are able to define what the crisis is all about also hold the key to defining the appropriate strategies for resolution. Conversely, for those who seek to instigate change, it is of vital importance to be able to aggravate the sense of societal crisis so as to foster a psychological and political climate receptive to non-incremental change. ('t Hart 1993: 41)

Hence, a crisis will not only feature a broad public outcry but also an intense competition among political entrepreneurs to define it by identifying the particular order that is failing and the particular public good it fails to deliver, followed by a championed solution for changing the order. By providing both a clear failure of the status quo system and by putting decision-making under high time pressure, an external shock may provide an opportunity for substantial change, either by tipping the balance between opposing cleavage coalitions or by blowing wind in the sails of a new group upheaving previously existing cleavage conflicts.

When we apply the notion of interpretation conflicts by agents as the key process that turns a shock to a system into a crisis to the history of European integration, the following picture emerges. The mother of all crises in Europe – the Second World War – was successfully interpreted by a coalition of pro-European entrepreneurs as signifying a failure of the Westphalian political order in Europe of independent sovereign nation states. Destruction had swept across Europe to such an extent and the existing political order was close enough to the Westphalian ideal type that this interpretation gained powerful resonance among the wider population. At least, the campaign of these pro-European entrepreneurs was successful to a sufficient extent among the population and key decision-makers of the six founding fathers of the Treaty of Paris to allow them to engage in the first steps of European integration. The importance of the shock of the Second World War furthering the cause of European federalists cannot be underestimated. Jean Monnet tried to create a proto-European federal state including at least the United Kingdom and France during the interwar period, but failed. Without the opportunity to 'ride the wave' of systemic shock provided by a crisis, he was unable to muster the necessary support for his project. Bolstered with new allies after 1945, and playing into the consternation and desire for new order in Europe's most devastated countries, Monnet succeeded after the Second World War where he failed before it. What was subsequently created was a political system which is neither a classic international organization nor a federal state, but has characteristics of both. As a consequence of this ambiguous state of the EU, both pro-European federalists and anti-European sovereigntists have a revisionist agenda. The first group wants to change the EU into a truly federal United States of Europe, while the second group wants to change it to a loose Free Trade Area, or abolish it all together. Subsequent lesser crises rekindled the conflict between pro-European and anti-European entrepreneurs time and again with both seeing the time ripe to change the political order towards their ideal, even if it was only in limited policy areas. Most of the time, the pro-Europeans succeeded in arguing the remains of the Westphalian system were the culprit of the crisis and that 'more Europe' was the solution. Their victory is evidenced in the progressing steps in integration taken since the Treaty of Paris (Urwin 1997). However, as the political system of the EU gains more and more powers at the partial expense of the nation state, the foundational basis is created to blame the EU for the next crisis, rather than the nation state. As the EU decides more and more, yet fails to prevent crises from happening, it becomes easier to argue that the EU is part of the problem rather than part of the solution. In this sense, the rising authority of the EU provides the material for anti-European political entrepreneurs to contest the Union (De Wilde and Zürn 2012; Zürn et al. 2012).

Yet, over time, the binary conflict between pro-Europeans and anti-Europeans is complicated by other conflicts. As the EU affects an increasing range of policy areas, the respective interests have mobilized to affect the course of integration and the direction of EU policy (Berkhout and Lowery 2010). Growing evidence shows that the issue of integration is increasingly folded into a more encompassing globalization-induced cleavage that includes other 'border-crossing' issues, particularly immigration and economic liberalism (Kriesi et al. 2007). However, this only applies – at least at citizen level – to those holding supportive normative value systems (Teney et al. 2014). Pro Europeans could be in favour of market regulation or market deregulation, for example, and the same applies to anti-Europeans. We find this reflected in rather different conflict patterns surrounding European issues, depending on which specific issue is at stake and how it is framed (Helbling et al. 2010). The result is a plurality of groups providing 'flank attacks' to the pro-integration versus anti-integration scheme making it harder for either one of them to push through their agenda. Thus, there is increasing pluralism in societal conflict over European integration, brought about by the mobilization of new players responding to the increasing influence of the EU on their lives and that of their constituencies. While this complicates both the agendas of pro- and anti-European entrepreneurs, it makes the 'one-solution-fits-all' agenda of European federalists especially problematic.

The debate between these various entrepreneurs and cleavage coalitions has always taken place in the confines of elite politics, but increasingly also in the wider public sphere constituted by mass media, parliaments, street protests and political campaigning. As Europe features rising *politicization* since the early 1990s, the growing awareness, mobilization and polarization have shifted the playing field of crisis politics (Hooghe and Marks 2009; De Wilde 2011b; De Wilde and Zürn 2012; Statham and Trenz 2013b; Hutter and Grande 2014). I thus draw attention to the public sphere as the main locus of crisis politics where the battle between political entrepreneurs to define the crisis and advocate solutions unfolds (for a similar argument, see Statham and Trenz 2015). It is through such crisis politics in the public sphere that the foundations of the crisis are interpreted and 'sold' to the wider audience. The implication is that, in the words of Paul 't Hart: 'The most important instrument of crisis management is language' ('t Hart 1993: 41).

When reading the pages of *Frankfurter Allgemeine Zeitung*, *Le Monde* or the *Guardian* during the euro crisis, a grand Europeanized debate comes to the fore. These newspapers reflect on politics at home and in other member states. They provide a platform for domestic politicians, economists and other experts, civil society organizations, EU institutions and foreigners. National executive actors continue to dominate public debates on European issues (Koopmans and Statham 2010; Kriesi et al. 2007), but the opportunity for alternative entrepreneurs – including Eurosceptic challenger parties – to shape the public debate about European integration and thereby delimit the range of acceptable policy alternatives increases as Europe becomes more debated (De Wilde 2011a). The Yellow press especially provides a platform for anti-European actors and actively campaigns themselves against Europe through editorials (Kleinen-von Königslöw 2012). The British and Austrian yellow press – especially the *Daily Mail* and *Kronenzeitung* – stand out as openly anti-European political entrepreneurs (Daddow 2012; De Wilde et al. 2013: chap. 4).

Like before, the current euro crisis features a conflict between pro-European and anti-European entrepreneurs. In debates on the euro crisis in the Italian news, Mazzoni and Barbieri (2014) identify two main narratives (see also Nicolaïdis and Watson in this volume). First, there is the narrative that assigns blame to the governments and societies of southern member states for corruption, overspending and laziness. While the north might be willing to help out by extending loans, these are conditional on structural reforms and austerity and will have to be paid back. The alternative narrative assigns blame to the international system of capital and the run-wild financial banking system in particular. While such narratives may appear at odds, they are, however, reconcilable. In both cases, the EU is part of the problem of 'international interconnectedness'. The EU should not have led the southern member states to spend more than they earn and it should not have let the financial markets go unregulated. Without the EU, the north would not have to foot the southern bill and the south could decide for itself if and how it wants to be involved in international capitalism. Overviewing such various public narratives, Trenz (2012) therefore concludes that 'Public debates in response to [the euro] crisis are driven by new re-nationalising dynamics of contestation'. The balance of power has shifted towards anti-EU entrepreneurs as conflict about Europe has become 'socialized' (Schattschneider 1960: 142), bringing in more players beyond executive elites. Part of this multiplication of agency is the changing of the stage. Where crisis politics used to unfold behind closed doors among a limited group of political elites, they now unfold in the wider public sphere, including mass media coverage and protest on the streets. The ranks of the anti-Europeans have thereby grown more – with the likes of the *Daily Mail* and *Kronenzeitung*, for example – than those of the pro-Europeans.

How a shock affects the system, in terms of which policy innovations or other solutions are brought about, thus depends on the successful interpretation of shocks by entrepreneurs. We first need to become convinced that there is a crisis, what has caused the crisis and what should be done about it before the societal acceptance of solutions grows to sufficient proportion to support and sustain changes. These entrepreneurs operate in conflictual settings, facing each other in opposing coalitions. Successful European integration in terms of widening and deepening have brought more and more players into the field, which has partially complicated the situation by diversifying conflict and partially reinforced the anti-European camp. Diversification further complicates the Federalist agenda especially, since they advocate a more unitary solution than the anti-Europeans do. Moreover, the pro-Europeans are challenged by increasing politicization which has shifted the stage of crisis politics from narrow elite publics to the wider public sphere, empowering citizens and Eurosceptic mass media to present further restraint on successful pro-integrationist interpretation of shocks to the system.

The public good

To identify a crisis in the context of European integration correctly and investigate its implications for the EU we need to be more inclusive than only looking at the shock, the system, the players and the stage. For a regime's survival to be at stake, a central pillar under its legitimacy must be perceived to be challenged. That is, for a political climate to be characterized as 'crisis', the widespread public perception that a specific political order fails to supply one or more necessary public goods must be present. In my sociological perspective, a crisis is located in the eye of the beholder. Many beholders may play a role in crisis politics as passive observers and stakeholders, but the most important beholders in today's Europe are citizens. Their empowerment dovetails with the growing monopoly 'democracy' has as legitimate form of rule in Europe. With historical modernization, self-expression has taken an increasingly important place in our social value system, supporting democracy as the only legitimate game in town: 'No longer content to be disciplined troops, the public has become increasingly autonomous and elite-challenging' (Inglehart and Welzel 2005: 44).

The task faced by political entrepreneurs aiming to exploit an external shock by spreading the notion of crisis, identifying a particular system or institution as the culprit and advancing a championed solution is thus to convince the public of their particular interpretation and agenda. In 'going public' (Kriesi et al. 2007) to reach the citizenry, entrepreneurs frame their interpretation, articulating a particular public good that citizens care about that is considered in jeopardy as a result of the shock. Such persuasion strategy then tends to portray the entrepreneurs themselves as the possible saviours just waiting to be empowered by public support (Boin et al. 2009; Diez Medrano 2003; Helbling et al. 2010; Semetko and Valkenburg 2000).

The current financial and sovereign debt crisis features a now familiar contest between political entrepreneurs. With the currently existing EU in limbo between a fully federal United States of Europe and a loose *Europe des Patries*, both the federalist agenda of pro-Europeans and the sovereigntist agenda of anti-Europeans are revisionist. In fact, it is of notable interest how few actors are willing to defend the current political status quo (cf. De Wilde et al. 2014). Some have argued that the EU – and the Eurozone in particular – are not federal enough. According to such voices, the powers of the European Central Bank need to be strengthened and the EU needs a much more substantial budget to deal with asymmetric economic shocks (see, for an academic contribution to this interpretation, De Grauwe 2010). In terms of crisis concepts, such entrepreneurs identify the incomplete state of European integration in which member state governments retain too much power as the political system that fails to deliver economic prosperity. Others agree that economic prosperity is the public good that is not delivered, but identify the EU – i.e., too much integration – as the system at fault (see, for an academic contribution to this interpretation, Scharpf 2011). In this interpretation, the Eurozone is impossible to maintain. Countries may have to leave the common currency and/or a substantial renationalization of macroeconomic policy is required. Beyond the economic institutional set-up of the union, there are those blaming the democratic deficit of the crisis (see, for an academic contribution to this interpretation, Weiler 2012). Such entrepreneurs identify the lack of public control over macroeconomic policy and governance in general as the main culprit of the crisis. The EU, in this line of reasoning, is the political system at fault, but it is not so much economic prosperity as public control and political equality that remain undelivered. Several contributions in this volume identify an incomplete or malfunctioning European legal order as the problem and rule of law as the necessary public good that remains undelivered in the current crisis. In short, there are ample political entrepreneurs and scholarly visions on the current European crisis with widely differing views on which necessary public good is not delivered and which political system is to blame for it.

Whilst economic concerns of growth, employment and prosperity have long taken a role as key public goods for both European nation states and the EU to deliver, concerns about the legitimacy of the EU, the participation of citizens in decision-making and the accountability of elites to the public are comparatively recent (Eriksen, 2009; Kohler-Koch and Rittberger 2007; Lord 1998; Weiler 1999). As the EU has gained in power and citizens have become increasingly aware of the impact it has on their lives while feeling deprived of ways to influence its operation, the perceived democratic deficit of the EU has become a major source of contention and fueled Euroscepticism (De Wilde et al. 2014). To some extent, the conflict between pro-European and anti-European entrepreneurs is sidelined by an increasingly pronounced conflict between citizens and elites (Aarts and Van der Kolk 2006; De Wilde et al. 2014; Wessels 1995). Partially, this conflict sidelines the one between pro- and anti-European elites and to some extent it gets co-opted, with Eurosceptic elites somewhere in the middle and parliaments taking up an uneasy balance between voicing public protest and taking responsibility for European and national governance (Puntscher Riekmann and Wydra 2013). The current crisis demonstrates this very well as citizen outrage over the euro crisis is not just targeted at EU institutions but at national governments as well, many of which have been voted out of office since its beginning.

The increasing prominence of 'democracy' as the public good not delivered, means that interpretations of crises that identify the lack of voice citizens have as a problem and advocate increased mechanisms of democracy as solution gain traction. With democracy still understood by most citizens to be confined inherently to the nation state and impossible in the EU, this tends to play into the hands of the anti-Europeans. We see resonance of this in recent internet discussions on European topics, where those articulating 'democracy' as their primary concern overwhelmingly tend to criticize the institutions of the EU and/or directly advocate renationalization of competencies (De Wilde et al. 2014). Even at the height of the euro crisis, Greek citizens commenting online complained more about the lack of voice they had in EU decisions of the Troika and Germany than about a loss of jobs or economic livelihood (Michailidou et al. 2014: 117).

Modern European politics equals democratic politics placing citizens in the ultimate position of granting or withholding support for various political agendas, including the revisionist agendas of pro-European and anti-European entrepreneurs in crisis politics. As key 'beholders', citizens ultimately decide which interpretation of crisis gains most traction and thus which policy course is endowed with the needed support to enable it. The logics of European integration may have sidelined the public in this role for a long time, but the increasing politicization of European integration makes this no longer the case. Like in domestic politics, policy entrepreneurs now need to go public to convince citizens of their agenda and, to do this successfully, must articulate a public good that citizens can relate to that is considered in jeopardy because of the crisis, and championed by the entrepreneur in question. The dominant public goods advocated by pro-European elites: 'safety' and 'economic prosperity' are still important, but the resonance of 'democracy' as public good has gained much traction in recent years. Arguing that the EU is undemocratic and that citizens need to be empowered, primarily through renationalization, tends to resonate well with vast numbers of European citizens. Recent developments in the public good component of crisis politics thus tend to empower anti-European entrepreneurs, just as do recent developments in the system itself, the constellation of players and the stage.

Conclusion

This contribution sets out to theorize the role of crises in the process of European integration and its changing effects over time. A crisis is defined as a broadly observable frenzied social outcry targeting a particular political regime or institution as culprit for failing to safeguard a key public good, in a dramatic way. This definition contains the perceived failure of a political system to deliver a necessary public good in a situation of uncertainty as to causes and consequences and with the complication of time pressure to find a solution. Although there is a foundational basis for each crisis, the complexity of modern society and the time pressure create room for interpretation as to what the political system is that has failed and which public good it has failed to deliver. In developing such an understanding of crises, I focus on the crucial role of political entrepreneurs in interpreting the crisis and championing a certain understanding of which political system fails to deliver which necessary public good. European integration can then be understood as a sequence of crises, starting with the Second World War, where pro-European entrepreneurs have successfully convinced significant parts of Europe's population that the political system that failed was the Westphalian system of independent nation states, while the public good undelivered varies from security in the Second World War to economic prosperity and democratic legitimacy in the current euro crisis. But as the EU has become increasingly powerful and influential in the daily lives of EU citizens, the foundational material available to anti-European entrepreneurs for advocating their interpretation of the crisis has increased. In other words, now that the EU is a powerful political system in itself, it has also become easier to blame for a failure in deliverance of public goods. The euro crisis has rekindled the conflict between pro-European and anti-European political entrepreneurs, each side trying to convince the wider population of their interpretation and solution. But, over time, the players of crisis politics in European integration have increased beyond a narrow circle of executive elites to a much broader engagement of society. Most of the newcomers have joined the anti-European camp. In particular, rising Eurosceptic challenger parties are backed by campaigning Eurosceptic yellow press. With the politicization of Europe, citizens have become more aware of how the EU impacts their lives and EU politics now play out more and more in the wider public sphere. It has shown – in public debates – that a major bone of contention feeding Euroscepticism is the perceived democratic deficit of the EU. Entrepreneurs wanting to portray crisis in Europe as one of democratic legitimacy will find it easier now to get their message across than before. By and large, anti-European entrepreneurs succeed in claiming themselves to be the rightful champions of the democratic cause.

In three important ways, therefore, have crisis politics developed in a direction that will probably inhibit European integration in the future. First, the system has changed, with a powerful EU now characterizing the system besides nation states. As the EU has proven incapable of preventing crises from happening, it has become part of the problem. Second, the number of players in crisis politics contributing to the interpretation of what went wrong and how to solve it has increased, tipping the balance in favour of anti-European entrepreneurs. As the stage of crisis politics shifts from closed elite circles to mass politics facilitated by mass media organizations, anti-European entrepreneurs are not only becoming more numerous but also gain strongly conducive channels for selling their message to the public. Thirdly, increasingly widespread concern with democratic legitimacy in Europe tends to strengthen the arguments of anti-European entrepreneurs who play on the fears of citizens feeling deprived of influence and ultimate control over their own livelihoods.

References

Aarts, K., and Van der Kolk, H. (2006) 'Understanding the Dutch "No": The Euro, the East, and the Elite', *PS: Political Science and Politics*, 39(2), 243–46.

Bartolini, S., and Mair, P. (1990) *Identity, Competition and Electoral Availability: The Stabilisation of European Electorates, 1885–1985*, New York and Cambridge: Cambridge University Press.

Berkhout, J., and Lowery, D. (2010) 'The Changing Demography of the EU Interest System since 1990', *European Union Politics*, 11(3), 447–61.

Boin, A., and 't Hart, P. (2003) 'Public Leadership in Times of Crisis: Mission Impossible?' *Public Administration Review*, 63(5), 544–53.

Boin, A., 't Hart, P., and McConnell, A. (2009) 'Crisis Exploitation: Political and Policy Impacts of Framing Contests', *Journal of European Public Policy*, 16(1), 81–106.

Burley, A.-M., and Mattli, W. (1993) 'Europe before the Court: A Political Theory of Legal Integration', *International Organization*, 47(1), 41–76.

Daddow, O. (2012) 'The UK Media and "Europe": From Permissive Consensus to Destructive Dissent', *International Affairs*, 88(6), 1219–36.

De Grauwe, P. (2010) 'Crisis in the Eurozone and How to Deal with It', CEPS Policy Brief 204, Centre for European Policy Studies, Brussels.

De Wilde, P. (2011a) 'No Effect, Weapon of the Weak, or Reinforcing Executive Dominance? How Media Coverage Affects National Parliaments' Involvement in EU Policy Formulation' *Comparative European Politics*, 9(1), 123–44.

(2011b) 'No Polity for Old Politics? A Framework for Analyzing the Politicization of European Integration', *Journal of European Integration*, 33(5), 559–75.

De Wilde, P., and Zürn, M. (2012) 'Can the Politicization of European Integration be Reversed?', *Journal of Common Market Studies*, 50(1), 137–53.

De Wilde, P., Michailidou, A., and Trenz, H.-J. (2013) *Contesting Europe: Exploring Euroscepticism in Online Media Coverage*, Colchester: ECPR Press.

(2014) 'Converging on Euroscepticism: Online Polity Contestation during European Parliament Elections', *European Journal of Political Research*, 53(4), 766–83.

Diez Medrano, J. (2003) *Framing Europe: Attitudes to European Integration in Germany, Spain, and the United Kingdom*, Princeton, NJ: Princeton University Press.

Dinan, D. (1999) *Ever Closer Union. An Introduction to European Integration*, Basingstoke: Palgrave Macmillan.

Dogan, M., and Higley, J. (1998) 'Elites, Crises, and Regimes in Comparative Analysis', in M. Dogan and J. Higley (eds), *Elites, Crises, and the Origins of Regimes*, Lanham, MD: Rowman & Littlefield.

Eriksen, E. (2009) *The Unfinished Democratization of Europe*, New York: Oxford University Press.

Eriksen, E., and Fossum, J.-E. (eds) (2000) *Democracy in the European Union: Integration through Deliberation?*, London: Routledge.

Haas, E. (2004) *The Uniting of Europe: Political, Social, and Economic Forces, 1950–1957*, Notre Dame, IN: University of Notre Dame Press.

Hay, C. (1996) 'Narrating Crisis: The Discursive Construction of the "Winter of Discontent"', *Sociology*, 30(2), 253–77.

Helbling, M., Hoeglinger, D., and Wueest, B. (2010) 'How Political Parties Frame European Integration', *European Journal of Political Research*, 49(4), 496–521.

Hooghe, L., and Marks, G. (2009) 'A Postfunctionalist Theory of European Integration: From Permissive Consensus to Constraining Dissensus', *British Journal of Political Science*, 39(1), 1–23.

Hutter, S., and Grande, E. (2014) 'Politicizing Europe in the National Electoral Arena: A Comparative Analysis of Five West European Countries, 1970–2010', *Journal of Common Market Studies*, 52(5), 1002–18.

Inglehart, R., and Welzel, C. (2005) *Modernization, Cultural Change and Democracy*, Cambridge: Cambridge University Press.

Kingdon, J. (1984) *Agendas, Alternatives and Public Policy*, Boston: Little Bown.

Kleinen-von Königslöw, K. (2012) 'Europe in Crisis? Testing the Stability and Explanatory Factors of the Europeanization of National Public Spheres', *International Communication Gazette*, 74(5), 443–63.

Kohler-Koch, B., and Rittberger, B. (eds) (2007) *Debating the Democratic Legitimacy of the European Union*, Plymouth: Rowman & Littlefield.

Koopmans, R., and Statham, P. (eds) (2010) *The Making of a European Public Sphere: Media Discourse and Political Contention*, Cambridge: Cambridge University Press.

Kriesi, H., Grande, E., Lachat, R., et al. (2008) *West European Politics in the Age of Globalization*, Cambridge: Cambridge University Press.

Kriesi, H., Tresch, A., and Jochum, M. (2007) 'Going Public in the European Union: Action Repertoires of Western European Collective Political Actors', *Comparative Political Studies*, 40(1), 48–73.

Lipset, S., and Rokkan, S. (1967) 'Cleavage Structures, Party Systems, and Voter Alignments: An Introduction', in S. Lipset and S. Rokkan (eds), *Party Systems and Voter Alignments*, New York: Free Press.

Lord, C. (1998) *Democracy in the European Union*, Sheffield: Sheffield Academic Press.

Mair, P. (2005) 'Cleavages', in R. Katz (ed.), *Handbook of Party Politics*, London: Sage.

Marsh, D. (2009) *The Euro: The Politics of the New Global Currency*, New Haven, CT: Yale University Press.

Mazzoni, M., and Barbieri, G. (2014) 'Grasshoppers against Ants or Malfunctions of Capitalism? The Representation of the European Economic Crisis in the Main Italian Newspapers', *Perspectives on European Politics and Society*, 15(2), 238–53.

Michailidou, A., Trenz, H.-J., and de Wilde, P. (2014) *The Internet and European Integration: Pro- and Anti-EU Debates in Online News Media*, Opladen: Barbara Budrich Publishers.

Milward, A. (2000) *The European Rescue of the Nation-State*, London: Routledge.

Molle, W. (2001) *The Economics of European Integration: Theory, Practice, Policy*, Aldershot: Ashgate.

Moravcsik, A. (1993) 'Preferences and Power in the European Community: A Liberal Intergovernmentalist Approach', *Journal of Common Market Studies*, 31(4), 473–524.

(1998) *The Choice for Europe: Social Purpose and State Power from Messina to Maastricht*, Ithaca, NY: Cornell University Press.

Northedge, F. (1986) *The League of Nations: Its Life and Times, 1920–1946*, Leicester: Leicester University Press.

Puntscher Riekmann, S., and Wydra, D. (2013) 'Representation in the European State of Emergency: Parliaments against Governments', *Journal of European Integration*, 35(4), 565–82.

Rauh, C. (2012) 'Politicisation, Issue Salience, and Consumer Policies of the European Commission', PhD dissertation, Free University Berlin.

Risse, T. (2015) *European Public Spheres: Politics is Back*, Cambridge: Cambridge University Press.

Scharpf, F. (2011) 'Monetary Union, Fiscal Crisis and the Preemption of Democracy', LSE 'Europe in Question' Discussion Paper 36/2011.

Schattschneider, E. (1957) 'Intensity, Visibility, Direction and Scope', *American Political Science Review*, 51(4), 933–42.

(1960) *The Semisovereign People: A Realist's View of Democracy in America*, New York: Holt, Rinegart & Winston.

Schimmelfennig, F. (2014) 'European Integration in the Euro Crisis: The Limits of Postfunctionalism', *Journal of European Integration*, 36(3), 321–37.

Schmitter, P. (1970) 'A Revised Theory of Regional Integration', *International Organization*, 24(4), 836–68.

Semetko, H., and Valkenburg, P. (2000) 'Framing European Politics: A Content Analysis of Press and Television News', *Journal of Communication*, 50(1), 93–109.

Statham, P., and Trenz, H.-J. (2013a) 'How European Union Politicization can Emerge through Contestation: The Constitution Case', *Journal of Common Market Studies*, 51(5), 965–80.

(2013b) *The Politicization of Europe: Contesting the Constitution in the Mass Media*, Abingdon: Routledge.

(2015) 'Understanding the Mechanisms of EU Politicization: Lessons from the Eurozone Crisis', *Comparative European Politics*, 13(2), 287–306.

Teney, C., Lacewell, O., and de Wilde, P. (2014) 'Winners and Losers of Globalization in Europe: Attitudes and Ideologies', *European Political Science Review*, 6(4) 575–95.

't Hart, P. (1993) 'Symbols, Rituals and Power: The Lost Dimensions of Crisis Management', *Journal of Contingencies and Crisis Management*, 1(1), 36–50.

Tosun, J. Wetzel, A., and Zapryanova, G. (2014) 'The EU in Crisis: Advancing the Debate', *Journal of European Integration*, 36(3), 195–211.

Trenz, H.-J. (2005) *Europa in den Medien. Die europäische Integration im Spiegel nationaler Öffentlichkeit*, Frankfurt and New York: Campus Verlag.

(2012) 'The European Public Sphere in Times of Crisis: Disentangling the Debate. Introductory Remarks', *Romanian Journal of Communication and Public Relations*, 14(1), 7–9.

Urwin, D. W. (1997) *A Political History of Western Europe Since 1945*, London: Longman.

Van de Steeg, M. (2006) 'Does a Public Sphere Exist in the European Union? An Analysis of the Content of the Debate on the Haider Case', *European Journal of Political Research*, 45(4), 609–34.

Van Hooren, F., Kaasch, A., and Starke, P. (2014) 'The Shock Routine: Economic Crisis and the Nature of Social Policy Responses', *Journal of European Public Policy*, 21(4), 605–23.

Vilpisauskas, R. (2014) 'Eurozone Crisis and European Integration: Functional Spillover, Political Spillback?', *Journal of European Integration*, 35(3), 361–73.

Wallace, H. (2002) 'Enlarging the European Union: Reflections on the Challange of Analysis', *Journal of European Public Policy*, 9(4), 658–65.

Weiler, J. (1999) *The Constitution of Europe: 'Do the New Clothes Have an Emperor?' and Other Essays on European Integration*, Cambridge: Cambridge University Press.

(2012) 'In the Face of the Crisis: Input Legitimacy, Output Legitimacy and the Political Messianism of European Integration', *Journal of European Integration*, 34(7), 825–41.

Wessels, B. (1995) 'Evaluations of the EC: Élite or Mass-Driven?', in O. Niedermayer and R. Sinnott (eds), *Public Opinion and Internationalized Governance*, New York and Oxford: Oxford University Press.

White, J. (2010) European Integration by Daylight, *Comparative European Politics*, 8(1), 55–73.

Zürn, M., Binder, M., and Ecker-Ehrhardt, M. (2012) 'International Authority and Its Politicization', *International Theory*, 4(1), 69–106.

7

Conflict-minimising integration: how the EU achieves massive integration despite massive protest

PHILIPP GENSCHEL AND MARKUS JACHTENFUCHS

Introduction

The new 'postfunctionalist' conventional wisdom of political science theories of European integration argues that EU politics was dominated by constraining dissensus (Hooghe and Marks 2009). Postfunctionalism argues that political parties and mass publics are increasingly responding to the perceived positive or negative effects of European integration. In a nutshell, the more they see the EU and its policies as negative, the more they are likely to resist further integration.

This is a highly plausible argument. Its effects should become most clearly visible during the euro crisis which is without doubt the most severe crisis in the EU's history and which has had a huge negative impact on most if not all member states. Paradoxically, however, the constraining dissensus does not seem to constrain governments very much. Far from constituting a break in integration, it has led to a veritable boost. Within a few years only, the EU has created new institutions (most notably the European Stability Mechanism (ESM)), massively extended the mandate of others (the ECB assuming a quasi-fiscal role and taking over banking supervision) and adopted an impressive number of far-reaching and highly intrusive rules for fiscal policy and banking that were unimaginable before (most notably Treaty changes, the Fiscal Compact treaty, the 'Six

We are grateful to Paula Kift for outstanding research assistance and to the contributors to this volume for extremely thoughtful and constructive comments. We are also thankful for comments received at the Annual Meeting of the European Political Science Association in Barcelona in 2013.

Pack' and 'Two Pack' regulations as well as the banking union legislation). Despite the formation and increasing strength of populist EU-critical parties, massively declining rates of trust in the EU, and the ousting of many incumbent governments, the overall response to this integration-induced crisis is more integration, not stalemate or disintegration. Why?

We argue that the EU reacts to increasingly critical mass publics in its usual mode of joint-decision-making (Falkner 2011), which it has continued in highly unusual times. More specifically, it has reacted to the crisis by conflict-minimising decision procedures of incomplete contracts, delegation to independent institutions and integration by regulation. As a result, the EU perpetuates its highly peculiar structure of regulating, but not assuming, core state powers (Caporaso et al. 2015). This peculiar decision-making pattern allows it to increase integration (of a particular type), despite massive protests, by insulating it from the constraining dissensus. At the same time, it perpetuates this decision-making pattern and its pathologies.

Joint-decision-making and the avoidance of intergovernmental conflict

The joint-decision trap as an alternative explanation of integration

A crucial and essentially still unresolved puzzle for theories of European integration is to explain the dynamics and trajectories of centralisation and decentralisation in the EU – in other words, the strengthening of the European versus the member state level. Neofunctionalism, intergovernmentalism and also postfunctionalism attempt to explain this dynamics with the preferences and powers of specific actors which differ between theories. For instance, supranational actors, such as the European Commission or the ECJ, can use their powers to achieve more centralisation, supported by transnational business and domestic political elites. EU-critical publics in turn would lead to a more decentralised EU or at least to a weakening of centralising tendencies.

In this longstanding debate, Fritz Scharpf introduced a new explanatory pattern. He started from the observation that the EU had reached a strange equilibrium: 'frustration without disintegration and resilience without progress' (Scharpf 1988: 239) and argued that the EU would neither progress towards a more federal union nor decline into an intergovernmental organisation, but remain in a stable intermediary state. This was the 'joint-decision trap' (see Scharpf 2006 for an ex-post evaluation of his own theory). This innovative explanation was not actor-based but institutional. The joint-decision trap is characterised by two features: member state governments are directly involved in taking decisions at the higher level, and these decisions are taken by unanimity or quasi-unanimity. This peculiar set-up is typical for the EU and for German federalism but not for other federations such as the USA. As this is an institutional configuration, it is largely insensitive to actor preferences on specific policy issues. Instead, member state governments which take part in European-level decision-making are reluctant to take steps towards an ever closer union because of their institutional self-interests. To give an example: while states may strongly desire an increased military role for the EU and may be strongly aware of their own limits in this respect, they refrain from creating a European military capacity because they do not want to give away a crucial aspect of their existence, the control over military power. The result is that states neither keep their military forces solely for themselves nor create European military structures which are solidly financed and organisationally autonomous.

More specifically, the joint-decision trap is the cause of two distinct pathologies: a *blockade effect*, which makes agreement on common EU policies difficult as long as a minority of member states prefers uncoordinated national solutions, and a *ratchet effect*, which makes a return to uncoordinated national policies difficult as long as a minority of member states profit from common EU policies once agreed upon. In other words, integration is difficult and resisted even if most participants would prefer it for functional reasons, but disintegration from levels once achieved is also difficult.

Although the concept of the joint-decision trap has been frequently applied to the EU (see Falkner 2011 for a recent assessment), most attention was devoted to analysing the blockade effect – hardly surprising given the experiences of marathon negotiations in the EU Council and the widespread feeling of stalemate from the early 1960s until the 1980s. During this period, not only Treaty changes and enlargement decisions, but even the overwhelming part of ordinary legislation had to be adopted by unanimity. The national veto and the resulting blockades seemed to be the EU's curse.

Since the mid-1990s, however, the integration process gained momentum again. The internal market was completed, and, despite successive rounds of enlargement, the EU did not become completely paralysed but on the contrary entered into ever more policy fields. The EU had learned to overcome the joint-decision trap by two means. The first was the relaxing of the unanimity requirement for decision-making in the Council and the increasing delegitimisation of the national veto. As a result, the joint-decision trap became weaker and blocking minorities less important.

The constant roll-back of the unanimity requirement over the last 25 years is part of the standard account of EU history. With few exceptions, most EU laws can now be passed with a qualified majority in the Council (and an absolute majority in the European Parliament). Although Treaty changes are still subject to unanimous approval in the European Council and ratification by all member states including referendums in some, the Lisbon Treaty introduced a 'simplified revision procedure' (Art. 48, paras. 6 and 7 TEU), which 'only' requires unanimity in the European Council but no ratification by national parliaments for changes to part 3 of the TFEU. During the euro crisis, it was used for changing Article 136 TFEU on reinforced budgetary discipline.

However, the significance of relaxing the unanimity requirement should not be overestimated. The Council still does not use simple majority voting in the legislative procedure but a 'double majority' of 55 per cent of the member states representing 65 per cent of the EU's population. In addition, the possibility of majority voting did not involve major changes in the practice of consensual decision-making in the Council. Votes happen, but member states try to avoid them (Hayes-Renshaw 2006).

While the Council has indeed slowly moved away from strictly unanimous decision-making, the European Council has increased in significance. This has not only been the case with emergency decision-making during the euro crisis but is a long-term trend of a 'new intergovernmentalism', which according to some authors characterises the last two decades of the EU (Bickerton et al. 2014; Puetter 2014). The European Council still decides by unanimity most of the time.

Thus, despite a considerable relaxation of the unanimity requirement in the last three decades, the EU's decision-making architecture is still not neutral in terms of outcomes but biased in favour of the status quo. Even compared to the USA, which puts a high premium on preventing unhampered central government decisions, the EU has substantially more veto players and possibilities for blocking decisions (Moravcsik 2002). In areas relating to the euro crisis, the two conditions for the joint-decision trap – direct member state participation in central decision-making and quasi-unanimous decisions – still largely apply.

The use of conflict-minimising strategies

The second way of dealing with the joint-decision trap is to accommodate its underlying intergovernmental conflicts with conflict-minimising integration strategies. As these are less prominently discussed in the literature than the relaxation of unanimity, we will discuss three such strategies more extensively here: delegation to non-majoritarian actors, incomplete contracts and integration by regulation. These strategies emerged incrementally as a reaction to past decision-making blockades (Falkner 2011; Héritier 1999) and are highly relevant for explaining the EU's reaction to the euro crisis.

Delegation to non-majoritarian actors. The significance of the European Commission or the ECJ as supranational 'engines of integration' (Pollack 2003) is well known and works in several respects. Supranational agenda-setting and hierarchical decisions from supranational actors are a way out of the joint-decision trap because they can resort to hierarchical-unilateral decisions instead of being bound by unanimity requirements (Scharpf 2006). Thus, the Commission can use its agenda-setting function for proposing pro-integrationist and conflict-minimising legislation. In its role as an independent regulator (for instance, in competition policy) it can exercise its powers against member state resistance. Most notably, the Commission can use its role as a guardian of the Treaties for breaking out of decision-making blockades in the Council with the strategic use of infringement procedures (Schmidt 2011). This makes it possible for the ECJ to overcome political blockades by judicial politics. Corporate taxation is a case in point: for many years, member states were unable to agree on a common system of corporate tax legislation. But by drawing far-reaching conclusions from the primary law of the four freedoms, which the member states had never imagined, the ECJ was able to create a set of rulings which incrementally draw corporate taxation under the umbrella of European law (Genschel et al. 2011). Ironically, the potential of integration through judge-made law is particularly high if the potential for agreement in the Council is low because this prevents the Council from changing ECJ rulings by legislation or Treaty change (Alter 2006; Tsebelis and Garrett 2001). As we will argue in the next section, the ECB took over as a supranational engine of integration in situations of intergovernmental decision-making blockade.

Incomplete contracts. In this case, intergovernmental conflicts are either obscured by vague wordings or postponed to a later stage by limiting the agreement to uncontroversial general principles and long-term goals which are in need of specification in order to be applicable (Cooley and Spruyt 2009; Héritier 2014). Incomplete contracts are not only widespread in EU legislation but also characteristic for the decisions of the European Council, which has often limited its decisions to the setting of general goals ('completion of the internal market') and symbolic dates ('1992'). Whereas international relations theory tends to regard contracts with a low precision as rather ineffective in shaping state behaviour (Abbott et al. 2000), the situation is different in the EU. Here, incomplete contracts open a window of opportunity for non-majoritarian actors such as the Commission to advance integration by adopting much more specific implementing decisions. For the ECJ, incomplete contracts are a welcome opportunity to adopt highly specific integration-friendly rulings, as in the case of corporate taxation discussed above (Stone Sweet 2004: 24). The European Semester may be the prime example of such an approach.

Integration by regulation. There are two fundamentally different instruments of integration (Genschel and Jachtenfuchs 2014). The EU can either regulate how member states use their national capacities for policy-making (integration by *regulation*) or it can create such resources for itself and use them in addition to those of the member states (integration by *capacity building*). Historically, western states developed and consolidated through capacity building: by creating national security forces (police and military), a national tax-financed budget and a comprehensive public administration (Skowronek 1982; Tilly 1990). The EU lacks precisely those capacities of a sovereign state: it has no army or police of its own, no large administrative infrastructure, no tax income of its own and a rather limited budget compared to its GDP, and there is no indication that it could soon acquire such capacities. Instead, it governs by regulation. But our understanding of the EU as an essentially regulatory polity goes beyond the original formulation by Majone (1996), according to which the EU integrates the internal market by harmonising and replacing market regulations by the member states with European regulations. Beyond this, however, it also subjects policies which are remotely or not at all related to the internal market to European regulation, including core state powers such as security, budgets and public administration. A comparison with the USA illustrates the difference: in the USA, the federal government receives substantially more tax income than the states but is in turn hardly involved in taxing and spending policies of the states. In the EU, taxation remains an exclusive prerogative of the member states and the EU's budget is negligible if compared to the combined budgets of the member states. In turn, however, the EU regulates national taxation and budgets to a degree that is unimaginable in the USA (Genschel and Jachtenfuchs 2011; Hallerberg 2014). This difference is significant for our understanding of the euro-polity and its reaction to the euro crisis.

For at least two reasons, integration by regulation is less vulnerable to decision-making blockades than integration by capacity building. First, it leaves the formal responsibility of the member states for carrying out their tasks intact. Member governments, responsible to democratically elected national parliaments, remain responsible for taxes, infrastructure, social welfare or other priorities, and arrest criminals and carry out military missions. Only the specific modalities of how these tasks are carried out is subject to common European regulation (Hodson 2009; Kemmerling and Seils 2009). On first sight, therefore, integration by regulation does not change the vertical division of powers in the EU but keeps the old division of labour intact, according to which the EU is essentially responsible for Pareto-improving technical regulation whereas the member states are responsible for highly salient, politically controversial and deeply intrusive policies (Hix 2007: 143–44; Moravcsik 2005). The facade of statehood remains intact and reduces the pressure for justification of member states towards their domestic publics – member states can claim that they control the EU and the exercise of their core powers. In addition, most regulatory policy measures are not immediately effective, particularly in the case of directives which usually include a generous period for national implementation. The costs of implementation may not be immediately visible, may fall on the next government and may also be watered down after adoption, as the Stability and Growth Pact illustrates (Hallerberg 2014; Heipertz and Verdun 2010).

Creating European capacities, however, visibly changes the vertical division of power between the EU and the member states in favour of the former, as the EU acquires resources for action which it did not possess before. This increases the audience costs (Lohmann 2003) of member state governments because it makes a fundamental difference whether, for instance, they give the EU the right to tax or merely allow it to regulate member state taxes in order to improve the functioning of the internal market.

The second reason is that integration by regulation obscures the redistributive consequences of European policies because at least nominally all member states are subject to the same rules. For example, the Stability and Growth Pact requires all member states to keep their public debt below 60 per cent of GDP even though it is much more difficult for some member states to comply with the rule than for others. Although it is well known from the literature that regulation also has redistributive effects, and that these effects may be really strong, it is politically important that this horizontal redistribution is not directly visible. Creating common capacities instead immediately leads to the question of who pays and who profits how much. EU budget negotiations and most notably the negotiation of the medium-term financial perspectives nicely illustrate the salience of easily visible redistributive effects, as does the history of the European Stability Mechanism (ESM) and its predecessor, the European Financial Stability Facility (EFSF), analysed in the next section.

To summarise our argument: the blockade effect of the joint-decision trap has not brought integration to a standstill but merely to an increasing reliance on conflict-preventing mechanisms. This constant attempt to avoid the joint-decision trap gives the EU reaction to the crisis its specific institutional form, which is characterised by delegation to independent institutions, incomplete contracts and a strong preference for integration by regulation. These mechanisms have made it possible to increase the level and the scope of integration (Börzel 2005; Lindberg and Scheingold 1971) despite a massive increase of membership and the constant threat of decision-making stalemate. The ratchet effect makes incremental and orderly disintegration difficult.

The conflict-minimising mechanisms by which member states tried to escape the joint-decision trap also loosened the grip of the constraining dissensus on member state governments. As far as possible, capacity creation was avoided. If capacity was created (for instance, in the case of the ESM), it was constructed in an intergovernmental way. For many measures taken, important elements were left open due to incomplete contracts. Others were delegated to non-majoritarian institutions, which are by definition not subject to direct majoritarian control. The consequences of others were not visible at the time of their adoption due to their regulatory nature. These are no dysfunctional side-effects of intergovernmental conflict-avoidance but the very core of it and the main reasons why the EU could overcome the joint-decision trap and escape the constraining dissensus. We will now show how these mechanisms worked during the euro crisis.

The anatomy of the crisis

The relation between monetary and fiscal policy has been a key problem of European Monetary Union from the very start. Functionally, both policies are closely related (e.g., Sims 2012: 217–23). Most monetary policy actions have fiscal implications because, for instance, a rise of the interest rate increases the costs of government debt. Fiscal policy actions, in turn, feed back on key monetary variables like the inflation rate. In the run up to monetary union, it was therefore a contested issue therefore whether one could have a European monetary policy without a European fiscal policy. Indeed, many academic commentators argued that this was not possible and was known from the outset (Eichengreen 2012).

Politically, however, it was inconceivable to endow EU institutions with the fiscal capacities of a federal government, i.e., with independent taxing power, budgetary autonomy and the right to issue debt. The implied loss of national sovereignty would have been so obvious and great, and the required level of transnational solidarity so demanding, that the option of a European fiscal federation was never truly considered. Over time, and despite a rhetoric of 'own resources', the EU's budget became more, not less intergovernmental, with the lion's share consisting of explicit national contributions. The domestic opposition to 'true' fiscal federalism was huge. Take the example of Germany: the largest government party, the Christian-Democrats, had traditionally championed a strongly euro-federalist approach to integration (Jachtenfuchs 2002). In principle, it should have been supportive of the idea of European fiscal capacity building. In practice, however, it had to cope with a vocal opposition from the Bavarian Christian Socialist Union, the central bank, the federal constitutional court, and large segments of the media who saw European fiscal empowerment as a threat to national sovereignty and German fiscal interests. Fiscal integration by capacity building was not an option – but neither was monetary integration without any fiscal backing.

Integration by regulation and incomplete contract

The conflict-minimising way out of the dilemma was a purely regulatory integration of fiscal policy on the basis of incomplete contracts. The core of this regulatory solution is encapsulated in three provisions of the Maastricht Treaty: Article 126 TFEU on the avoidance of 'excessive government deficits', the 'no bail-out' clause of Article 125 TFEU, and Article 123 TFEU's prohibition of debt monetization by the ECB. The purpose of these provisions was to make European monetary policy compatible with national fiscal policy by strictly separating the two – squaring the circle. How exactly they would achieve this purpose was left intentionally open at Maastricht. The treaty provisions were vague and incomplete in order not to upset the fragile Franco-German compromise on monetary union (Jabko 2014).

The Stability and Growth Pact closed some of the remaining regulatory gaps but failed to allay doubts about the incentive compatibility and effectiveness of the regulatory approach to fiscal integration (e.g., Sims 1999: 415–36). For instance, what incentive should the Council of ministers ever have to impose fines on an over-indebted member state in accordance with Article 126 (para. 11) TFEU and thereby add to that state's fiscal problems and inability to comply with European fiscal rules?

Budgetary surveillance

The lack of incentive compatibility of the Stability and Growth Pact became quickly apparent after the start of monetary union in 1999. While the European Commission tried to infuse a certain rigour into the excessive deficit procedure, the attitude of the member states was more relaxed. France and Germany repeatedly ignored Commission advice to get their budget deficits below 3 per cent of GDP, and received de facto backing from the Council against the Commission's recommendations on sanctions. Other member states had a similarly bad record of compliance. By 2005, half of the EMU member states were in excessive deficit (Hallerberg 2014). This hardly mattered, however, because the financial markets ignored the deficit procedure anyway: countries in excessive deficit were not punished by higher interest rates. To the contrary, interest rates converged on the low German level throughout the Eurozone. Inflation rates were generally low. In this setting, the fiscal regulation of the Stability and Growth Pact was redundant.

This changed with the onset of the Greek crisis in 2010: market fears of an impending national insolvency increased the rate spreads between the Eurozone member states again and revealed the ineffectiveness of the EU's fiscal regulation. The markets did not grant any bonus to countries that had always complied with the Stability and Growth Pact in the past such as Ireland and Spain. Rather, these countries were punished by steeply increasing interest rates, as investors flocked to countries like Germany and the Netherlands, which were considered save euro-havens even though they had a record of breaking the Stability and Growth Pact.

The Greek crisis showed that the potential insolvency of a Eurozone member state was not a national affair, as the no-bail-out clause might suggest, but a problem of the Eurozone as a whole. In contrast to the USA, where the impending insolvency of a single federal state (such as Massachusetts in the 1990s) hardly matters for other federal states or the stability of the US dollar because the fiscal fall-out is largely absorbed by the large federal budget, this is not the case in the EU. Given the EU's lack of fiscal capacity, the failure of even a small member state such as Greece (2 per cent of Eurozone GDP) has immediate knock-on effects on other member states that can undermine the euro and push the EU into existential crisis (Hallerberg 2014).

While the EU reacted to the crisis also by creating some limited fiscal capacity (see next section), its main response consisted in intensive regulatory activity. In several steps, a whole series of far-reaching measures was adopted. In March 2011, the euro-Plus Pact was adopted by the European Council, in July, the first 'European Semester' was concluded, and in December of the same year, the 'Six Pack', five regulations and one directive intended to strengthen the Stability and Growth Pact entered into force. In January 2013, the 'Treaty on Stability, Coordination and Governance' (TSCG, the Fiscal Compact) followed, and, in May 2013, two regulations on increased budgetary surveillance (the 'Two Pack') followed. It is not easy to understand the complex system of standard EU legislation, intergovernmental Treaties, declarations, programmes, national action plans etc., accompanied by increasing differentiation of membership which is now summarised under the general label of 'EU economic governance'.[1] As most of the rules are still rather new, it is too early to judge whether they will be effectively implemented – the past history of the Stability and Growth Pact is a history of breaking initial commitments.

Still, the scope and the intrusiveness of the measures are impressive. The overall purpose is also clear: the convergence of macroeconomic cycles and budgetary policies in the member states is to be achieved by increasingly tighter regulation. The rules are deeply intrusive: the Fiscal Compact demands from signatory states to add a balanced budget rule to their national constitutions and to establish independent fiscal institutions. The European Semester requires governments to send draft budgets to the European Commission for scrutiny even before they are sent to national parliaments (for an assessment of the European Semester, see Hallerberg et al. 2012).

The rules also strengthen the European Commission, mainly because they transform it into the central supervisory and enforcement agency for member states' macroeconomic performance and for their budgetary policies. The Commission produces a number of economic indicators (e.g., the 'scoreboard' of the macroeconomic imbalance procedure) and receives macroeconomic and budgetary information from the member states. In

1 http://ec.europa.eu/economy_finance/economic_governance/index_en.htm (accessed 23 November 2015) provides a descriptive up-to-date overview.

using these indicators, it has a considerable amount of discretion. More importantly, it can issue binding orders to member states which it finds to be in violation of the rules of the European semester (for instance, the 'Country-specific recommendations'). If a member state does not follow these 'recommendations', a process starts which can ultimately lead to financial sanctions. While these sanctions are not automatic, they are to be adopted by reverse qualified majority (i.e., a qualified majority in the Council is needed to reject the Commission proposal), which amounts to a major strengthening of the Commission's role (Cisotta 2013: 6–7).

The purpose of the entire set of regulations is clearly to bring member states' macroeconomic performance and budgetary policies in line with the help of a dense and detailed set of indicators, targets as well as procedural rules. While a lot of emphasis is placed on the initial phases of the policy cycle by monitoring developments with increased reporting (e.g., the Annual Growth Survey and the Alert Mechanism Report) and a long set of indicators and by trying to prevent imbalances with a whole arsenal of medium-term objectives, national reform programmes, country-specific recommendations and so on, there is also an increased emphasis on sanctioning rule violations in the 'correction' phase, with the Excessive Deficit Procedure and the Excessive Imbalance procedure.

At the same time, these rules very much resemble the Open Method of Coordination (OMC), initially introduced by the 2000 Lisbon Strategy in order to coordinate policies for which the EU does not have an explicit mandate, such as employment and growth policies (Dawson 2011; Trubek and Trubek 2005). The 'open' part of the OMC implies relying on incomplete contracts. Only general targets are set (such as a balanced budget or the avoidance of macroeconomic imbalances). The essence of the European Semester, however, is a process of mutual observation and adaptation. The difference to the classical OMC is that it is at least in part accompanied with the possibility of massive sanctions which makes it less an exercise of mutual learning but more one of hierarchical enforcement.

By adopting these complex and far-reaching regulations, the EU has largely avoided the creation of a strong fiscal capacity at the European level. It has also escaped the constraining dissensus by several means. Resorting largely to ordinary legislation meant adoption by QMV instead of unanimity, which would have been necessary in the European Council. Resorting to directly binding regulations avoided the need for national implementation and the risks of delayed and incomplete implementation. Differentiated integration both in the 'Six Pack' regulations as well as in the Fiscal Compact and in the euro-Plus Pact allowed to leave out dissenting states. Finally, the framing of the entire set of rules as measures for improving convergence and applicable to all member states keeps the facade of statehood intact. The member states alone remain formally responsible for taxing and spending, and national parliaments do not lose their 'crown jewels' (as the President of the German Bundestag, Norbert Lammert, has called them), the right to pass the budget. The procedures are in many respects similar to the OMC but with much executive discretion for the Commission and a weakened formal possibility for the Council to block binding Commission recommendations because of the reverse QMV requirement. The rules adopted apply to all member states, although they are much easier to achieve for some than for others. A key difference is, however, their visibility. As is well known from the literature, policies which are directly redistributive (i.e., which shift resources or power from one actor to another) are sensitive to high levels of conflict. The EU's budget negotiations are a well-known illustration of such policies and conflict levels, as are debates about changing voting rights in the EU Council or the size of national groups in the European Parliament. Regulatory policies may also have massive redistributive implications but they are often not clearly visible during the adoption of the decision (Jachtenfuchs 2007). In sum, the regulatory mode of 'EU economic governance' avoids the building of a strong EU fiscal capacity, conceals its redistributive consequences and the far-reaching changes to the EU's institutional architecture which strongly strengthens the executive at the expense of the Community method (Dawson and de Witte 2013), and achieves this to a large degree through an intergovernmental treaty (the Fiscal Compact) without an explicit process of Treaty change (Peers 2013: 37–38).

Banking supervision

In parallel to the strengthened supervision of national budgeting processes, it became increasingly clear that the 'euro crisis' was not only a crisis of public finances but also of private banks. In theory, the case for regulating banks on the EU-level is clear as European regulation is a much more credible commitment and can much better deal with negative externalities than national supervision. Politically, however, states had a massive interest in keeping banks under national supervision because banks are an important source of tax income (in some member states in particular), and because they are important indirect instruments of economic policy. However, member states became increasingly aware of the 'sovereign-bank nexus', a vicious circle during which crises of public finances and of the banking sector mutually reinforce each other. In its 'roadmap towards a banking union', the Commission estimates that more than 4.5 trillion euro of taxpayers' money had been used to rescue banks in the EU (COM (2012) 510, p. 3). Estimates vary, but member states were clearly aware of the enormous sums involved and of the impossibility of insulating themselves against bank crises occurring elsewhere.

If banking crises in the internal market were to be prevented, the appropriate territorial scope of remedial action should not be limited to the Eurozone but would have to cover (at least) the entire EU. However, the United Kingdom in particular did not agree to a European supervision of its banking sector, in part because it was faced with an increasingly successful protest party (UKIP) and a very sceptical public opinion towards further transfers of sovereignty to the EU. The conflict-minimising means to adopt the complex set of rules which figured under the umbrella term 'banking union' was a conscious choice of the legal base. The 'Banking Recovery and Resolution Directive' (BRRD) 2014/59, Regulation 806/2014 on the 'Single Resolution Mechanism' (SRM) and a number of supplementary rules were adopted according to Article 114 TFEU on the approximation of laws in the internal market allowing for qualified majority voting. Regulation 1024/2014 on the 'Single Supervisory Mechanism' (SSM) was adopted by unanimity but by the Eurozone member states only, and merely with consultation of the European Parliament according to Article 127(6) TFEU. Key elements of the 'Single Resolution Fund' were adopted by intergovernmental agreement among 26 member states but without Sweden and the United Kingdom. It was thus possible to reduce the influence of vocal opposition from some member states.

Although the length of a legislative measure is only a very crude measure of its potential intrusiveness, the banking union is impressive in this respect: 90 pages for the SRM regulation 806/2014, 159 pages for the EBBD directive 59/2014 and 337 pages for the capital requirements regulation 575/2013 are well above the EU's normal standards. But the importance of the banking union set of rules does not only reside in its enormous degree of detail but also in its strong delegation to independent institutions, mainly the ECB. Since November 2014, the ECB assumes a completely new set of tasks not foreseen in the EU Treaties, namely the role of the European banking supervisor. The powers of the resolution authority to dissolve banks have been described as 'near dictatorial' (Ferran 2014: 14). Further delegation, mainly in the field of prudential regulation and supervision, has conferred powers to a whole system of regulatory agencies forming the European System of Financial Supervision which consists of the

European Banking Authority (EBA, now located in London), the European Securities and Markets Authorities (ESMA), the European Insurance and Occupational Pensions Authority (EIOPA) and the European Systemic Risk Board (ESRB). The Joint Committee of the European Supervisory Authorities is a forum for cooperation between the EBA, the ESMA and EIOPA as well as for exchange with the ESRB. There is clearly no shortage of regulatory bodies for European financial supervision!

At the same time, the structure and substance of European banking regulation is an almost classical example for the arcane complexity of regulatory policies, which makes distributive and power implications less visible. Even for specialists it is difficult to understand the exact tasks of more than half a dozen agencies and coordinating bodies created in a short period of time. Public debate about the pros and cons of such a system hardly emerged. Most public discussions focused on a single element of the system, the Single Resolution fund, which is an instance of capacity creation and will be discussed in the next section.

Capacity building by conflict-minimising means

To cope with this crisis, the EU had to create some of the fiscal capacities ex post that the member states had always been wary of granting to EU institutions ex ante. The more the sovereign-bank nexus became important, a backup for bank resolution seemed imperative. This is a showcase of functional spillover: in defiance of the original intentions of the member states, the integration of one policy field (monetary policy) creates problems in other policy fields (fiscal policy and banking supervision) that trigger its further integration.

Fiscal capacity

In the wake of the Greek crisis, the EU began building up fiscal capacity in three steps (Schelkle 2014): in March 2010, the European Council passed the first rescue package for Greece; in May 2010, the ECOFIN Council agreed on the contours of a provisional European Financial Stabilization Facility (EFSF); and in December 2010, the European Council agreed on a more permanent crisis resolution mechanism, the European Stability Mechanism (ESM). Each step was highly contested within and between member states. One issue was why the vertical distribution of power should be changed in favour of European institutions at a moment of manifest European failure. Another, even more contentious issue concerned the distributive consequences of European fiscal capacity building: who foots the bill? Especially in Germany, Finland and the Netherlands there was little enthusiasm for guaranteeing financial risks, which, in public perception, were caused by the reckless policies and moral degradation of individual 'PIIGS' countries (i.e., Portugal, Italy, Ireland, Greece and Spain), and not by the common fault of entering into monetary union without sufficient fiscal backup. Creating a 'transfer union' became a political taboo in Germany. The conflict-minimising advantage of a purely regulatory integration, to keep fiscal policy a purely national responsibility, became the cause of new conflicts as European publics began to blame each other for the common problems: lazy Greeks, domineering Nazi-Germans, etc. The villain in these conflicts was not primarily EU institutions but other member states.

The constraining dissensus at home aggravated intergovernmental conflicts in Brussels. Yet, the mechanisms of conflict-minimising integration allowed for the build-up of considerable fiscal capacity nevertheless. These mechanisms included, first, incomplete contracts. Numerous weekend summit meetings in 2010 ended with early hour agreements, the content of which was already controversial the next morning. This allowed the heads of government to present politically convenient readings of the agreement at home, while civil servants in Brussels hammered out the details of the deal.

Second, European fiscal capacity building was limited to a bare minimum (Schelkle 2014). At each step of the process – the first rescue package for Greece, the EFSF and the ESM – the relevant actors were careful to avoid any semblance of a comprehensive fiscal empowerment of the EU. The role model was the International Monetary Fund, not the fiscal order of a federal state. Functionally, the newly created European capacities were strictly limited to the provision of liquidity support. The member states refused to assume joint liability for the funds but limited their national guarantees, as far as possible, to the national share in the funds' capital. Also, the decision-making procedures were strictly intergovernmental, and introduced weighted voting according to capital shares rather than the voting weights established by the Lisbon Treaty.

Third, European fiscal capacity building was accompanied by additional fiscal regulation. On the one hand, the general provisions of the Stability and Growth Pact were supplemented by a complex set of new macroeconomic regulations including the 'Six Pack', the 'Two Pack' and the Fiscal Compact. The promise was that these additional regulations would provide the regulatory effectiveness that the Stability and Growth Pact obviously lacked. On the other hand, the financial support of the EFSF and the ESM was made contingent on certain conditions to be fulfilled by the recipient country ('conditionality'). In the case of Portugal, this included not only general fiscal requirements, but also rather detailed plans for the reform of labour market legislation, the health sector, public education, and the judiciary (Portugal 2013). It is not entirely obvious if and how this conditionality helped to improve Portugal's access to capital markets. The purpose was mostly political: to demonstrate to the publics in surplus countries that Portugal did not receive its aid free of charge.

Fourth, non-majoritarian actors, especially the ECB, moved centre stage. In principle, the ECB can make quick and effective fiscal aid to troubled Eurozone countries by directly or indirectly buying their public debt. While this fiscal assistance 'through the monetary backdoor' (Schelkle 2014) conflicts with the prohibition of debt monetisation (Art. 123 TFEU), the ECB repeatedly used it during 2010 and 2011 to compensate for delays and set-backs in the intergovernmental creation of fiscal capacity and further generalized it later with the announcement of the OMT programme. Because the governments were unable or unwilling to calm the markets by unlimited collective guarantees, the ECB picked up the slack. For many observers, Mario Draghi's announcement: 'ECB is ready to do whatever it takes to preserve the euro. And believe me, it will be enough' (Draghi 2012) was the decisive turn in the euro crisis. The justification given was, of course, monetary: the disruption of the monetary transmission mechanism. The effect was to unburden the Council of conflictive decisions on intergovernmental fiscal capacity building.

As the ECB is an independent supranational institution, criticism from member states or from academics (Sinn and Wollmershaeuser 2011) could be ignored. The result of these conflict-minimising integration strategies is ambiguous. On the one hand, they allowed for the build-up of considerable fiscal capacity in a context of a vocal constraining dissensus. On the other hand, they hardly contributed to calming down the dissensus but, to the contrary, fuelled it. The Eurozone governments paid a high price for their crisis management. Twelve out of 17 were voted out of office between 2010 and 2012. As Jean-Claude Juncker once remarked: 'We all know what to do but we just don't know how to get re-elected once we have done it' (quoted in Hix and Høyland 2011: 271). The rest had to cope with a massive wave of Euroscepticism. In Germany, Eurosceptics seized upon the constitutional court to reign in the government. Issues concerned the control rights of the federal parliament (Kinski 2012), the admissibility of the EFSF and the ESM under the German constitution and the lawfulness of the ECB's purchase programmes for government bonds (Schmidt 2013). Both the constitutional court and the parliament have seen their positions as veto players in European affairs strengthened in the process.

Banking resolution

In the framework of the 'banking union', both administrative and financial capacity has been created. With its takeover of a substantial part of banking supervision, the ECB had to build up a substantive additional administrative capacity. The new structure has substantial powers in banking supervision and banking resolution. Still, it is not a centralised system as it exists for instance in the USA but a multilevel system bringing European and national supervisors together. In a special report, the European Court of Auditors criticises that before the ECB took over its leading role in November 2014 the EBA had a limited legal mandate and limited staff for conducting effective banking supervision and resolving disputes between national legislators. Also, and despite the enormous length of the legislation creating the banking union, the exact division of tasks between the various supervisory bodies on the European level and most notably between the ECB and the national regulators is not yet settled (European Court of Auditors 2014). Most notably, there is a dispute whether the ECB is responsible for all European banks with only a secondary role for national supervisors, or whether there is a division of tasks with the ECB supervising the largest banks and the national regulators the others. Thus, the crucial question of the vertical division of powers between the European and the national level is still governed by an incomplete contract, as can be expected in a situation of joint decision-making.

The Single Resolution Fund which is a part of the Single Resolution Mechanism for the ordered dissolution of banks is another substantial aspect of capacity creation at the EU level. Once fully operational, it is expected to amount to more than €50 billion from bank contributions. Like the ESM, the Single Resolution Fund starts with 'national compartments' in order to avoid that contributors from one country pay for bank resolutions in another country, at least as long as contributions from the latter are sufficient to cover the losses. Over the years, an increasing mutualisation is foreseen. This may sound as a major step forward towards the building up of a true European financial capacity instead of segmented national compartments. One can speculate that agreement on this principle was possible because the Single Resolution Fund consists of bank contributions but not of public funds. The more serious issue is, however, that the fund is widely believed to be sufficient only for the resolution of a medium-sized bank. It is insufficient in the case of a failure of a large European bank or of a systemic crisis. Instead of attempting to solve the problem of bank failures in an integrated market, the Single Resolution Fund as well as the entire banking resolution procedure may rather be 'meant as placebos to avert political protest against a regime in which the financial industry has blackmailed taxpayers into providing support, for fear that otherwise things might get much worse' (Hellwig 2014: 16). In the case of large bank failures, the taxpayer will have to step in again, and the Council has only been able to agree that it will deal with this issue at a later stage while the Single Resolution Fund is slowly becoming operational.[2]

The European dilemma

The joint-decision trap has two effects, a blockading effect and a ratchet effect. The blockading effect makes the integration process prone to crises, the ratchet effect makes it difficult to solve such crises by orderly disintegration. As a result, the EU structurally prefers to react to crises of integration with more integration rather than with less.

The blockade effect of the joint-decision trap makes integration prone to crises because of its tendency to favour conflict-minimizing integration strategies such as delegation to non-majoritarian actors, incomplete contracts and regulatory integration. This has allowed progress in integration in terms of scope and depth despite increasing membership and heterogeneity. But it has also led to an increasing estrangement between governments and electorates in the same member state as well as between governments and electorates of different member states. This development creates a latent Euroscepticism, which transforms into a manifest dissensus as soon as integration produces negative consequences. When output legitimacy decreases, the lack of input legitimacy becomes a problem for the EU.

The ratchet effect prevents disintegration as a means to cope with a crisis. In principle, there are three options for reacting to crises of integration: not doing anything, disintegration and further integration. The first is a non-option because it changes neither output nor input deficits. The second option offers the potential to increase input legitimacy by increasing the democratic accountability within member states. But there are high hurdles to overcome before this option can be realised. Independently of whether disintegration is pursued radically by the exit of several states from the Eurozone or incrementally by lowering the level of integration, it needs to pass high majority requirements or unanimity, unless some states decide to leave the EU unilaterally.

2 www.eurozone.europa.eu/media/502738/20131218-SRM-backstop-statement.pdf (accessed 23 December 2015).

The possibilities to use conflict-minimising strategies in order to undermine the ratchet effect for disintegrative strategies are limited. All three major European non-majoritarian actors (the Commission, the ECJ and the ECB) are strongly pro-integrationist. Suggesting that the Commission should sue the ECB in front of the ECJ for its breach of Treaty law by entering into the monetary financing of public debt (Vaubel 2013: 18) is at odds with their self-definition. Using national non-majoritarian institutions such as the German *Bundesverfassungsgericht* as an agent of disintegration has also not worked until now. Despite numerous reserves and caveats in the past decades, the *Bundesverfassungsgericht* has until now resisted openly disintegrative rulings (Schmidt 2013). It is also not easy to obtain incomplete contracts on disintegration, as David Cameron is currently experiencing. Instead, the British announcement of its intention to leave certain policy areas has increased differentiated integration – rather than giving the UK leverage for renegotiation with formal Treaty changes, the other member states prefer to continue with further integration via territorial differentiation by adopting measures for the Eurozone countries alone, by concluding intergovernmental treaties of the willing or by substantively vague procedural solutions such as the European semester.

The EU thus chooses the last and well-known option of solving crises of integration with incremental increases of integration (Marsh 2013). In the short term, this buys time and might help to alleviate the immediate symptoms of the crisis, to conceal the huge redistributive implications of the crisis and thus to keep constraining dissensus at bay. In a medium- to long-term perspective, however, this does not improve input legitimacy but rather risks to decrease it and increase constraining dissensus. It also further exacerbates the negative effects of the crisis politics of the last years: a massive strengthening of the executive and of non-majoritarian actors at the expense of parliamentary accountability and a massive intervention of the EU in core state powers with massive redistributive effects. Normatively, this is not very attractive, and, politically, this state of affairs may overstretch the legitimacy of EU institutions.

References

Abbott, K., Keohane, R., Moravcsik, A., et al. (2000) 'The Concept of Legalization', *International Organization*, 54(3), 401–19.

Alter, K. (2006) 'Delegation to International Courts and the Limits of Re-contracting Political Power', in D. Hawkins, D. Nielson and D. Tierney (eds), *Delegation and Agency in International Organizations*, Cambridge: Cambridge University Press, 312–38.

Bickerton, C., Hodson, D., and Puetter, U. (2014) 'The New Intergovernmentalism: European Integration in the Post-Maastricht Era', *Journal of Common Market Studies* (Early View), 1–20.

Börzel, T. (2005) 'Mind the Gap! European Integration between Level and Scope', *Journal of European Public Policy*, 12(2), 217–36.

Caporaso, J. A., Kim, M., Durrett, W. N., and Wesley, R. B. (2015) 'Still a Regulatory State? The European Union and the Financial Crisis', *Journal of European Public Policy*, 22 (7), 889–907.

Cisotta, R. (2013) 'What Role for the European Commission in the New Governance of the Economic and Monetary Union?', IAI Working Papers 1324, Istituto Affari Internazionali, Rome.

Cooley, A., and Spruyt, H. (2009) *Contracting States. Sovereign Transfers in International Relations*, Princeton, NJ: Princeton University Press.

Dawson, M. (2011) *New Governance and the Transformation of European Law. Coordinating EU Social Law and Policy*, Cambridge: Cambridge University Press.

Dawson, M., and de Witte, F. (2013) 'Constitutional Balance in the EU after the Euro Crisis' *Modern Law Review*, 76 (5), 817–44.

Draghi, M. (2012) Speech by Mario Draghi, President of the European Central Bank at the Global Investment Conference in London, 26 July 2012. www.ecb .europa.eu/press/key/date/2012/html/sp120726.en.html.

Eichengreen, B. (2012) 'European Monetary Integration with Benefit of Hindsight', *Journal of Common Market Studies*, 50(S1), 123–36.

European Court of Auditors (2014) 'European Banking Supervision Taking Shape – EBA and its Changing Context', Luxembourg: Publications Office of the European Union.

Falkner, G. (ed.) (2011) *The EU's Decision Traps: Comparing EU Policies*, Oxford: Oxford University Press.

Ferran, E. (2014) 'European Banking Union: Imperfect, But It Can Work', University of Cambridge Legal Studies Research Paper Series 30.

Genschel, P., and Jachtenfuchs, M. (2011) 'How the European Union Constrains the State: Multilevel Governance of Taxation', *European Journal of Political Research*, 50(3), 293–314.

(2014) 'Beyond Market Regulation: Analyzing the European Integration of Core State Powers', in P. Genschel and M. Jachtenfuchs (eds), *Beyond the Regulatory Polity? The European Integration of Core State Powers*, Oxford: Oxford University Press, 1–23.

Genschel, P., Kemmerling, A., and Seils, E. (2011) 'Accelerating Downhill: How the EU Shapes Corporate Tax Competition in the Single Market', *Journal of Common Market Studies*, 49(3), 585–606.

Hallerberg, M. (2014) 'Why is there Fiscal Capacity but Little Regulation in the US, but Regulation and Little Fiscal Capacity in Europe? The Global Financial

Crisis as a Test Case', in P. Genschel and M. Jachtenfuchs (eds), *Beyond the Regulatory Polity? The European Integration of Core State Powers*, Oxford: Oxford University Press, 87–104.

Hallerberg, M., Marzinotto, B., and Wolff, G. (2012) 'An Assessment of the European Semester', IP/A/ECON/ST/2010-24. European Parliament, Brussels.

Hayes-Renshaw, F. (2006) 'When and Why the EU Council of Ministers Votes Explicitly', *Journal of Common Market Studies*, 44(1), 161–94.

Heipertz, M., and Verdun, A. (2010) *Ruling Europe: The Politics of the Stability and Growth Pact*, Cambridge: Cambridge University Press.

Hellwig, M. (2014) 'Yes Virginia, There is a European Banking Union! But it May Not Make Your Wishes Come True'. http://ssrn.com/abstract=2487757.

Héritier, A. (1999) *Policy-making and Diversity in Europe: Escaping Deadlock*, Cambridge: Cambridge University Press.

(2014) 'Covert Integration of Core State Powers: Renegotiating Incomplete Contracts', in P. Genschel and M. Jachtenfuchs (eds), *Beyond the Regulatory Polity? The European Integration of Core State Powers*, Oxford: Oxford University Press.

Hix, S. (2007) *The European Union as a Polity (I). Handbook of European Union Politics*, London: Sage, 141–58.

Hix, S., and Høyland, B. (2011) *The Political System of the European Union*, 5th edn, Basingstoke: Palgrave Macmillan.

Hodson, D. (2009) 'EMU and Political Union. What, if Anything, Have We Learned from the Euro's First Decade?', *Journal of European Public Policy*, 16(4), 508–26.

Hooghe, L., and Marks, G. (2009) 'A Postfunctionalist Theory of European Integration: From Permissive Consensus to Constraining Dissensus', *British Journal of Political Science*, 39(1), 1–23.

Jabko, N. (2014) 'The Divided Sovereignty of the Eurozone', in P. Genschel and M. Jachtenfuchs (eds), *Beyond the Regulatory Polity? The European Integration of Core State Powers*, Oxford: Oxford University Press.

Jachtenfuchs, M. (2002) *Die Konstruktion Europas: Verfassungsideen und institutionelle Entwicklung*, Baden-Baden: Nomos.

(2007) 'The European Union as a Polity (II)', in K. Jørgensen, M. Pollack and B. Rosamond (eds), *Handbook of European Union Politics*, London: Sage, 159–73.

Kemmerling, A., and Seils, E. (2009) 'The Regulation of Redistribution: Managing Conflict in Corporate Tax Competition', *West European Politics*, 32(4), 756–73.

Kinski, L. (2012) 'The European Debt Crisis and the Functional Logic of the Parliamentary System: A Case Study of the German Bundestag, Berlin', Hertie School of Governance, Student Paper Series, HSSPS 03/2012.

Lindberg, L., and Scheingold, S. (eds) (1971) *Regional Integration: Theory and Research*, Cambridge, MA: Harvard University Press.

Lohmann, S. (2003) 'Why Do Institutions Matter? An Audience-Cost Theory of Institutional Commitment', *Governance*, 16(1), 95–110.

Majone, G. (1996) 'The European Community as a Regulatory State', *Collected Courses of the Academy of European Law*, 5, 321–419.

Marsh, D. (2013) *Europe's Deadlock: How the Euro Crisis Could Be Solved – and Why it Won't Happen*, New Haven, CT: Yale University Press.

Moravcsik, A. (2002) 'In Defense of the "Democratic Deficit": Reassessing Legitimacy in the European Union', *Journal of Common Market Studies*, 40(4), 603–24.

(2005) 'The European Constitutional Compromise and the Neofunctionalist Legacy', *Journal of European Public Policy*, 12(2), 349–86.

Peers, S. (2013) 'Towards a New Form of EU Law? The Use of EU Institutions outside the EU Legal Framework', *European Constitutional Law Review*, 9(1), 37–72.

Pollack, M. (2003) *The Engines of European Integration: Delegation, Agency, and Agenda-Setting in the EU*, Oxford: Oxford University Press.

Portugal (2013) Memorandum of Understanding on Specific Economic Policy Conditionality, 17 May 2011.

Puetter, U. (2014) *The European Council and the Council: New Intergovernmentalism and Institutional Change*, Oxford: Oxford University Press.

Scharpf, F. (1988) 'The Joint-decision Trap: Lessons from German Federalism and European Integration', *Public Administration*, 66(3), 239–87.

(2006) 'The Joint-decision Trap Revisited', *Journal of Common Market Studies*, 44(4), 845–64.

Schelkle, W. (2014) 'Fiscal Integration by Default', in P. Genschel and M. Jachtenfuchs (eds), *Beyond the Regulatory Polity? The European Integration of Core State Powers*, Oxford: Oxford University Press, 105–23.

Schmidt, S. (2011) 'Overcoming the Joint-Decision Trap in Single-Market Legislation: The Interplay between Judicial and Legislative Politics', in G. Falkner (ed.), *The EU's Decision Traps. Comparing EU Policies*, Oxford: Oxford University Press, 38–53.

(2013) 'A Sense of Déjà Vu? The FCC's Preliminary European Stability Mechanism Verdict', *German Law Journal*, 14(1), 1–20.

Sims, C. (1999) 'The Precarious Fiscal Foundations of EMU', *De Economist*, 147(4), 415–36.

(2012) 'Gaps in the Institutional Structure of the Euro Area', *Banque de France, Financial Stability Review*, 16, 217–23.

Sinn, H.-W., and Wollmershaeuser, T. (2011) 'Target Loans, Current Account Balances and Capital Flows. The ECB's Rescue Facility', NBER Working Paper 17626, November 2011.

Skowronek, S. (1982) *Building a New American State: The Expansion of National Administrative Capacities, 1877–1920*, Cambridge: Cambridge University Press.

Stone Sweet, A. (2004) *The Judicial Construction of Europe*, Oxford: Oxford University Press.

Tilly, C. (1990) *Coercion, Capital, and European States, AD 990–1992*, Cambridge, MA: Blackwell.

Trubek, D., and Trubek, L. (2005) 'Hard and Soft Law in the Construction of Social Europe: The Role of the Open Method of Co-ordination', *European Law Journal*, 11(3), 343–64.

Tsebelis, G., and Garrett. G. (2001) 'The Institutional Foundations of Intergovernmentalism and Supranationalism in the European Union', *International Organization*, 55(2), 357–90.

Vaubel, R. (2013) 'Der Gerichtshof als Agent der Zentralisierung', *Frankfurter Allgemeine Zeitung*, 14 January, 18.

8

An unholy trinity of EU Presidents?: Political accountability of EU executive power

MARK BOVENS AND DEIRDRE CURTIN

A trinity of EU 'Presidents': out of control?

As the dust settles after years of acute crisis decision-making in the EU and the euro area, the contours of a new and powerful trio of EU 'Presidents' have become visible. Herman van Rompuy, President of the European Council, turned out to be a key mover and shaker, who was able to steer the highest-level EU decision-makers on salient political and economic questions confronting the EU and its member states (e.g., banking union). The European Commission in recent years acquired the power effectively to force national governments to adapt their draft budgets to meet EU criteria before they are sent to their national parliaments for final approval (European Semester). The main actor in this regard for the past years was Olli Rehn, Commissioner for Economic and Monetary Affairs and the euro (hereafter: the euro Commissioner). As one of six Vice-Presidents of the Commission he had an increasingly visible and even seemingly autonomous role in the area of economic governance – hence his nickname, the 'budget tsar'.[1] And, thirdly, Mario Draghi, President of the European Central Bank (ECB), took decisive action to keep the euro stable and monetary policy healthy, directly affecting citizens in creditor and debtor states alike.

We are grateful to Alex Crespo van de Kooij, who was of great help in collecting and analyzing the minutes of Plenary and Committee meetings of the European Parliament, and to Tatevik Manucharyan, who provided useful research assistance on the European Central Bank.

1 'Europe Close to Creating "Budget Tsar"', *Financial Times*, 9 November 2011.

Behind each of these three (Vice-) Presidents is a powerful institution whose role and tasks are changing and expanding incrementally in economic governance. These new powers and practices fit within a broader picture of expanding executive power of the European Union (Curtin 2009). Executive 'dominance' is more clearly delineated than was previously the case (Curtin 2014). The economic crisis resulted in an acceleration of decision-taking by supranational and national executives at the European level, often with a very profound and wide-reaching national impact (Scharpf 2011; Habermas 2012). Executive dominance by EU institutions and by (some) national actors at the European level has now reached into such sensitive policy fields as national budgets, monetary policy, and macroeconomic decisions (Chalmers 2012; Fossum 2014).

None of these 'EU Presidents' (and their respective institutions) is directly accountable to citizens. They are not elected and none of them can be removed when the electorate considers him to be a rascal. Yet their decisions have enormous consequences for the economies of the member states and for the welfare of citizens. There is also a growing asymmetry in the effects and reach of the adopted measures between Eurozone and non-Eurozone countries. This institutional complexity and lack of transparency across the EU as a whole complicates efforts to address issues of accountability across the trinity (and 'their' institutions) in a uniform fashion.

The salience of the political control of these powerful EU executives by national parliaments or by the European Parliament is obvious but also complicated. This chapter necessarily constitutes a first cut at this crucial issue. To what extent can we observe emerging political accountability relations between these three executive actors – and the institutions they 'represent' – and parliamentary forums at the different governance levels? Given the constitutional provisions and parliamentary practices in the member states, one would expect more extensive political accountability processes in place for the President of the European Council and for the Vice-President of the Commission. Their roles resemble the political executives in the member states, which are subjected to extensive political scrutiny. Central bank presidents, on the other hand, usually operate at arm's length of parliaments and one would expect the same at the EU level.

Secondly, we are interested in how the roles and practices (as well as internal working methods) of these accountability forums evolved and adapted in recent years. What conclusions can be drawn in terms of the overall levels of political accountability that are being exercised in practice over this increasingly visible trinity of EU level Presidents and can – and should – change be envisaged?

Executive political accountability: a framework for analysis[2]

The rise of EU executive power after the various crises raises important issues of executive accountability. Has the rise been accompanied by an equal increase in formal and informal accountability relations? In order to establish this, we need to elaborate on the concept of accountability. In its *White Paper on Governance* and in several consecutive documents, the European Commission (2001; 2003) uses 'accountability' rather loosely. It serves not only as a synonym for 'clarity', 'transparency', and 'responsibility', but it is also equated with much broader concepts such as 'involvement, 'deliberation', and 'participation'. This lack of clarity is not surprising, as it mirrors the existence of different schools of thought in the wider literature (Bovens 2010).

One school treats it as a normative concept, as a set of standards for the evaluation of the behaviour of public actors. Accountability or, more precisely, 'being accountable', is seen as a *virtue* of organizations or officials. Hence, some accountability studies focus on normative issues, on the assessment of the actual and active behaviour of public agents (Dubnick 2002; Koppell 2005). Another school of thought conceptualizes accountability as a social *mechanism*: as an institutional relation in which an actor can be held to account by a forum (Day and Klein 1987; Scott 2000; Mulgan 2003; Pollitt 2003; Bovens, 't Hart and Schillemans 2008; Schillemans 2008; Meijer and Schillemans 2009). The locus of analysis in such studies is not the behaviour of public agents per se, but the way in which these institutional relations operate; and their focus is not whether the agents have acted in an accountable way, but whether they are or can be held accountable ex post facto by accountability forums.

This chapter fits within this latter tradition. We leave the broader, deontological discussions about accountability and EU governance to others (Schmitter 2000; Arnull and Wincott 2002; Harlow 2002; Lord 2004; Bogdanor 2007). We define accountability as: 'a relationship between an actor and a forum, in which the actor has an obligation to explain and to justify his or her conduct, the forum can pose questions and pass

2 This section is based on Bovens et al. 2010.

judgement, and the actor may face consequences'. Depending on the nature of the forum, one can distinguish between political, legal, administrative, or social accountability (Bovens 2007). Executive institutions, such as the European Commission, are subject to various accountability relations simultaneously, such as political accountability to the European Parliament, legal accountability to the European Courts, and administrative accountability to the European Anti-Fraud Office (OLAF), the European Ombudsman, and the European Court of Auditors. In this chapter, we only concentrate on political accountability, on accountability to political forums. We will limit ourselves to two types of political forums, the European Parliament and its various committees, and the national parliaments.

When studying these political accountability relations, it helps to distinguish between accountability in the books – *de jure* accountability – and accountability in practice – de facto accountability. We will first describe what formal provisions for executive political accountability have been put in place. Secondly, we will explore how these operate in practice. In doing so, we will distinguish three different elements or stages.

First of all, we want to know to what extent the actor is obliged to *inform the forum about his or her conduct*, by providing various sorts of data about the performance of tasks, about outcomes, or about procedures. Often, and particularly in the case of failures or incidents, this also involves the provision of explanations and justifications (Bovens et al. 1999; Hearit 2005; Hood et al. 2007). Informing can be done in a general way, directed at the general public, for example, through online disclosure or freedom of information provisions. However, it also can be done as part of specific accountability relations, for example, by providing explicit information to parliamentary committees.

The second stage is *debate*. For a relation to qualify as an accountability relation, there needs to be a possibility for the forum to interrogate the actor and to question the adequacy of the information or the legitimacy of the conduct – hence, the close semantic connection between 'accountability' and 'answerability'.

Thirdly, in a full accountability relationship the forum may *pass judgment* on the conduct of the actor. It may approve of an annual account, denounce a policy, or publicly condemn the behavior of an official or an agency. In passing a negative judgment, or following it, the forum may impose *consequences* on the actor. These consequences can be highly formalized, such as fines, disciplinary measures, civil remedies, or even penal sanctions, in case of a negative judgment, but they can also be based on historical conventions, such as a vote of non-confidence by a parliament, or on informal practices, such as naming and shaming.

Given this analytical framework, our main question is: *to what extent can we observe (emerging) formal and informal accountability relations between the selected three executive actors and the European Parliament and/or (some) national parliaments?*

In answering this general question, we focus on three sub-questions:

(1) *Informing*. To what extent are there formal obligations and informal practices regarding the active provision of information by each of these three executive actors to the European Parliament and to the national parliaments?
(2) *Debate*. To what extent are there formal possibilities and informal practices regarding the questioning of each of these three executive actors by the European Parliament or the national parliaments?
(3) *Judgment*. To what extent are there formal possibilities and informal practices regarding the approval or denouncement of the conduct of these three executive actors by either the European Parliament or the national parliaments?

We try to answer these questions by mapping the emerging formal political accountability provisions that are in place for each of the three executive actors. Also, we have made an explorative analysis of the actual accountability practices in various settings in the European Parliament, involving these three presidents, in the post-financial crisis years (2009–14). In the latter exercise, we distinguish between the Presidents appearing before the committees (mainly the Economic and Monetary Affairs Committee, occasionally the Constitutional Affairs Committee) and in the Plenary.[3] We have also gathered information – to the extent that it is available – on debates and hearings of each of the three Presidents before some national parliaments and have undertaken an explorative and selective analysis in this regard on aspects of information, debate, and judgment, as well as considering the inter-parliamentary dimension.

3 This was based on an analysis of the minutes of all the meetings of the Plenary and the various committees, which Van Rompuy, Rehn and Trichet/Draghi attended within the parliamentary term of 2009–14.

The political accountability of the President of the European Council: informal bits and pieces

President Van Rompuy and the European Parliament

The *de jure* accountability arrangement between the European Parliament and the European Council is traditionally very limited. Only the obligation to inform the European Parliament after a summit has taken place is laid down at Treaty level (Art. 15(6)(d) TEU). The European Council shall submit a report after each of its meetings and a yearly written report on the progress achieved by the Union. To fulfill this obligation, the President must attend plenary sessions (Van der Steeg 2009: 5). There have been some further *de jure* developments in some of the (legislative) measures adopted to combat the crisis. The Regulations of the 'Six Pack' provide inter alia for the President of the European Council to come before a committee of the European Parliament, in particular the ECON, and to inform it and engage in an 'economic dialogue' (Fasone 2014: 175–76).[4]

These economic dialogues give the competent committee the opportunity to invite, among others, the President of the European Council to discuss different topics mentioned in the specific Regulation. Attending these meetings is not mandatory but facilitative. Besides, the Committees have the right to invite any person to attend and to speak at a meeting (Rule 193 of European Parliament Rules of Procedure).[5] Rule 110 of the Rules of Procedure allows the Presidents of the Institutions to give statements, after which the President of the Parliament may invite them to join in a debate on the content of the statements. The nature of all these rights is facilitative and informative, rather than obligatory and pressuring. The Parliament holds no real formal powers. It can table a motion according to Rule 120 of its Rules of Procedure, but it cannot attach real negative consequences (Van der Steeg 2010: 130).

4 Regulation 1177/2011 amending Regulation (EC) No. 1467/97 on speeding up and clarifying the implementation of the excessive deficit procedure, OJ 2011, L306/33, Article 2a; Regulation 1176/2011 on the prevention and correction of macroeconomic imbalances, OJ 2011, L306/25, Article 14; Regulation 1175/2011 amending Regulation 1466/97 on the strengthening of the surveillance of budgetary positions and the surveillance and coordination of economic policies, OJ 2011, L306/12, Article 2-ab; Regulation 1174/2011 on enforcement measures to correct excessive macroeconomic imbalances in the euro area, OJ 2011, L306/8: Article 6; Regulation 1173/2011 on the effective enforcement of budgetary surveillance in the euro area, OJ 2011, L306/1: Article 3.

5 Rules of Procedure of the European Parliament, 7th Parliamentary Term, March 2014 version, available at www.europarl.europa.eu/sides/getDoc.do?pubRef=-//EP//NONSGML+RULES-EP+20140310+0+DOC+PDF+V0//EN&language=EN.

Overall the *de jure* accountability arrangement between the European Parliament and the European Council is weak, and mainly covers, to a limited extent, the first aspect of our definition of accountability (information) and not debate or judgment and consequences. Moreover, it is scattered across a number of legal sources (Treaties and secondary legislation) with some salient variations among them.

The story is somewhat richer when one looks at the de facto political accountability of the European Council President to the European Parliament. In the pre-Lisbon years, the rotating Presidents of the European Council occasionally visited the European Parliament to give a statement (Crum 2009; Van de Steeg 2010). Since 1997, some informal accountability practices vis-à-vis the European Parliament emerged (Van de Steeg 2010: 142). After the Lisbon Treaty (which instituted the full-time Presidency) and the financial crisis, these practices have developed further.

During the parliamentary terms of 2009–14, Van Rompuy attended 15 debates in plenary. These were almost exclusively meetings on *Conclusions of the European Council* as well as some on *Economic Governance.* Van Rompuy often started with an introductory speech. Afterwards, the Parliamentarians reacted. At the end of the meeting, Van Rompuy almost always took the opportunity to respond to the questions and comments given by the Parliamentarians in the meeting.

During these meetings before Plenary, the Parliamentarians mainly used the opportunity to ask questions and express their views by adding pressure on Van Rompuy to take effective steps to overcome the crisis. The questions and comments directed at Van Rompuy during these meetings were both informative and criticizing. Usually he did not specifically react to all questions, but used his final speech to summarize the most important points raised and answered by telling what had been done to improve the situation with regard to these points and what work still had to be done. In some meetings Van Rompuy extensively reacted to the 'you need to act, you need to act now' type suggestions in his final speech. He stipulated what had been done and justified any delays by referring to the difficult circumstances. He said that both the member states and the institutions should take the blame and that the crisis had been underestimated. He ended by summarizing what steps were to be taken and by reassuring them that he would work hard. In that regard he really responded to the major line of criticism and concerns. Nevertheless, he was not eager to admit that he or the European Council in general had made a mistake. He acknowledged problems, referred to difficulties and other factors and, in very general terms, reiterated what had been done and explained how he wanted to continue to solve the remaining problems.[6] The setting of the meetings did not stimulate a really intensive debate, owing to the structure of introductory speech followed by questions and a concluding speech, and owing to the fact that the blue card procedure[7] was never used on or by Van Rompuy.

Occasionally, some form of judgment could be perceived. For example, European Parliament member Swoboda accused Van Rompuy of adopting legislation without consulting the Parliament.[8] Van Rompuy acknowledged this issue in a short but summarizing speech in which he addressed the general topics of the meeting. After this, the President of Parliament reiterated that Van Rompuy was wrong in not consulting the Parliament and underlined the importance of democratic legitimacy through the European Parliament.

Van Rompuy visited and debated with ECON only three times during the parliamentary term of 2009–14. During these three meetings, Van Rompuy (and others) gave a speech. Twice the speeches were followed by exchanges of views and a Q&A session. The nature of these exchanges of views and the Q&A was more than just informative, but not of an accusatory or strongly criticizing nature. During the session of 30 January 2013, Van Rompuy (and, in fact, almost all speakers) left the meeting directly after their speeches. European Parliament member Servaas expressed his disappointment because under those circumstances the meeting could not lead to a debate (although one Commission representative and another speaker did stay). The exchange of views was, therefore, limited to the views of the different Parliamentarians. Van Rompuy did not respond to comments and questions.

President Van Rompuy and the national parliaments

The European Council has two parliamentary political accountability relations – the national and the European. Here lies the nub: only the European Parliament can (in a very limited fashion) hold the collective

6 For example, Van Rompuy's speech half way into the European Parliament plenary debate of 23 June 2010, Brussels.

7 Rule 149 of the European Parliament Rules of Procedure, n. 5 above.

8 Hannes Swoboda's statement during the European Parliament debate of 3 July 2012, Strasbourg, in which he is being supported by Rebecca Harms and Sylvie Goulard, who (together with Kathleen van Brempt and Phillippe Lamberts) had already made this point during the debate of 16 November 2011, Strasbourg.

European Council to account. At the national level, individual national parliaments can hold only their individual Prime Minister or Minister to account depending on their national constitutional arrangements. Apart from the French President (and the President of the Commission), each member of the European Council is a head of government and formally accountable as such to his respective national parliament. All national parliaments have developed to some extent specific structures and procedures (Wessels et al. 2013: 14). However, these were on the whole designed for the ordinary legislative procedure and not for the very different context of European summits. Thus, the fact that national parliaments may have the right to be informed and to give their opinion on draft regulations or draft directives as part of the traditional EU law-making process will not assist in holding Prime Ministers to account in the context of the rapidly evolving role of the European Council. Generally there are no specific rules and procedures aimed at controlling Euro summits. In fact, in the overwhelming majority of the member states, there is no differentiation between the various kinds of European Council meetings. In several countries a debate occurs only before and after *ordinary* European Council meetings even though the rules do not specify this focus (Wessels et al. 2013: 31).[9]

Likewise, the provisions of the Lisbon Treaty (Art. 12 TEU and subsidiarity protocol), which installed new opportunities for an 'early warning mechanism' on subsidiarity issues, do not bite in the explicitly non-legislative context of the European Council. Article 10 TEU merely states the formal nature of the accountability relationship of Prime Ministers in the European Council with national parliaments. The implication is that the ensuing obligations of information, debate, and sanctioning are purely a matter for national (constitutional) law and practice. In the end, there are in fact 28 different national accounts with very different views as to the required and or desirable relations between national parliaments and the European Council.

There are no specific rules and procedures to control the President of the European Council either in the Treaties or in national laws. Yet the fact that since the entry into force of the Lisbon Treaty the European Council is a formal institution with a semi-permanent President has brought about some changes to de facto political accountability to the national parliaments. We can observe the new phenomenon of the President of the

9 In Austria, however, committees debate also the extra-ordinary European Council meetings as well as Euro summits.

European Council appearing before individual national parliaments in order to inform, explain, and justify decisions that are being taken by the European Council or in implementation of European Council decision-making. Van Rompuy has visited a number of national parliaments over the course of the past few years (for example, Cyprus, Malta, Romania, Estonia, Slovenia, and France).[10] On the whole these are 'set' speeches, and there seems to be little opportunity for real dialogue or debate and there is certainly no possibility of any sanctioning or other consequences.

President Van Rompuy and inter-parliamentary forums

Inter-parliamentary cooperation is encouraged through COSAC (Conference of Parliamentary Committees for Union Affairs of Parliaments of the European Union).[11] Van Rompuy has attended and engaged in a dialogue on a number of occasions.[12]

In addition, a plethora of inter-parliamentary meetings have been arranged outside the formal framework of the Treaties. They may be organized at the initiative of the relevant committees of the European Parliament, who invite their counterparts in national parliaments. For example, the meeting held on 27–28 February 2012 addressed the so-called 'European Semester for Economic Policy Coordination'. In the words of Van Rompuy during this event, the 'growing interweaving of European and national politics' was illustrated by an Inter-Parliamentary Committee meeting on the European Semester for Economic Policy Coordination.[13] In this context, the President of the European Council engaged in a dialogue with representatives of both the European Parliament and the national parliaments jointly.

10 Van Rompuy's speech at the Parliament of Cyprus, Nicosia, 28 May 2012; speech at the House of Representatives of Malta, Valletta, 11 July 2013; speech at the Joint meeting of the Chamber of Deputies and of the Senate of Romania, Bucharest, 25 April 2012; speech at the Estonian Riigikogu, Tallinn, 26 February 2013; speech at the National Assembly of Slovenia, Ljubljana, 25 May 2012; speech at the French Assemblée Nationale, Paris, 9 October 2013.

11 Articles 9 and 10 of Protocol No. 1 on the Role of National Parliaments in the European Union (annexed to the Lisbon Treaty).

12 See Van Rompuy's speech at the COSAC meeting of 26 October 2010, Brussels.

13 Van Rompuy's speech of 27 February 2012, Brussels. See too a number of other inter-parliamentary meetings which he has attended, in particular: speech of 30 January 2013 during European Parliamentary Week 2013; and speech of 20 January 2014 during European Parliamentary Week 2014.

Article 13 of the Stability Treaty provides for the installation of an inter-parliamentary meeting. Two meetings of this 'Conference of Parliaments' have taken place, with Van Rompuy addressing both. In his words at the second one on 20 January 2014: 'although each national parliament remains responsible for its country's own economic policy and its own budget, these powers are now exercised in a context of enormous inter-dependence and in a framework that we are developing together to manage that interdependence'.[14] Through a forum like this, which unites all national parliaments, the President of the European Council is able to provide information and engage in some dialogue – although again in a context devoid of any judgement or consequences.

The political accountability of the Commission: extensive information, a bit of debate, no consequences

'Tsar' Rehn and the European Parliament

The European Parliament does have some formal powers to hold the Commission accountable. Article 230 TFEU obliges the Commission to answer all written and oral questions asked by the Parliament. Article 121(5) TFEU lays down the obligation for the President of the Commission (as well as the President of the Council of Ministers) to submit a report on the results of multilateral surveillance to the Parliament.

The most important tool for the Parliament in this respect is the economic dialogue. This gives the competent committee the opportunity to discuss certain issues with the Commission. Article 15 of Regulation (EU) No 473/2013,[15] for example, confers on Parliament the power to invite the Commission to discuss certain budgetary matters. Besides, the Parliament must be duly involved in the European Semester. The purpose of this economic dialogue explicitly is to ensure more transparency and accountability.[16] Attending the dialogues is not obligatory, although the ECJ can, in exceptional circumstances, be involved under Article 265 TFEU (Fasone 2014: 176). In other words, the Parliament can ask the (Vice-) President of the

14 See Van Rompuy's speech of 20 January 2014, n. 13, above.

15 Regulation 473/2013 on common provisions for monitoring and assessing draft budgetary plans and ensuring the correction of excessive deficit of the member states in the euro area OJ 2011, L140/11.

16 The other examples are Article 3 of Regulation 472/2013; Section 1 A of Regulation 1177/2011; Article 14 of Regulation 1176/2011; Section 1 Aa of Regulation 1175/2011; Article 6 of Regulation 1174/2011; and Article 3 of Regulation 1173/2011.

Commission to answer some questions and elaborate certain choices, but that is, in principle, as far as it goes.[17] Rule 110 of the European Parliament Rules of Procedure[18] gives the Presidents of the Institutions the right to give statements after which the President of the Parliament may ask them to elaborate these statements during a debate. Rule 111 gives the President of the Parliament the right to invite the President of the Commission or another Commissioner to make a statement to explain decisions taken during a meeting and to take part in a debate on this decision with the Parliament. Rule 114 prescribes that the Commission must present its recommendation on the broad guidelines of economic policy to the relevant committee. Rule 115 grants the parliamentary committees the right to ask the Commission questions, and provides the possibility for oral answers and a debate. Rule 116 arranges Question Time with the Commission, the questions of which are bound by some strict requirements (laid down in Annex II of the Rules of Procedure). The answers, however, must be concise and relevant. This seems to be one of the only clear obligations.

All these rights to be informed and to participate in a debate with the Commission representative, however, lack pressuring power because there are few real consequences attached to these meetings. The Parliament does hold the power to table a motion for a resolution according to Rule 120 and a motion for censure under Article 234 TFEU. The latter article probably contains the strongest tool for Parliament, containing a voting procedure which might result in the resignation of members of the Commission.

As to the de facto accountability of the Commission to the European Parliament: during the parliamentary term of 2009–14, Olli Rehn attended no fewer than 44 plenary meetings.[19] The nature of these meetings in general was a mixture of informative statements and comments by members of Parliament, sometimes followed by a short dialogue. During most meetings, Rehn stayed somewhat in the background. He gave a speech in which he reacted to some of the comments and in which he sketched the objectives and ideas of the Commission. There were no extensive debates between him and members of the European Parliament.

17 An additional tool 'to be informed' is Rule 193 of the European Parliament Rules of Procedure (n. 5, above), which allows a committee to organize a hearing with experts, where this is considered essential to its work on a particular subject. This rule must be read in line with point 50 of the Framework Agreement on relations between the European Parliament and the European Commission [2010] OJ L304/47.

18 European Parliament Rules of Procedure, n. 5, above.

19 For an overview of the attendances see: www.europarl.europa.eu/plenary/en/home.html.

Six of these meetings were part of the European Semester. The nature of these meetings was also informative.[20] During these debates, different Parliamentarians asked questions and gave statements. Sometimes, a European Parliament member used the so-called 'blue-card'[21] immediately to ask another speaker a question or perhaps to interrupt him or her with a comment. Rehn, however, was not really participating in the debates. He provided an opening speech and sometimes an additional speech to finalize his contribution.[22] This contained a summarizing note in which he formulated a general reaction to the points raised during the meeting. In between these two speeches he did not really participate. Mostly the Parliamentarians asked for the vision, opinion, or strategy of the Commission or of Rehn. Some questions, however, went a bit further. In those cases, European Parliament members pointed out to Rehn and others the (mostly negative) facts, asking them (although not explicitly) to justify or at least explain what had caused these facts to occur. On other occasions, they suggested that the focus should lay on these facts and that action must be taken. An example is the question of Hannes Swoboda during the meeting of 25 February 2014.[23] In general, Rehn did not immediately react. He gave rather extensive speeches and broad answers, but they were often not really to the point or were insufficiently detailed. There were no, or very few, consequences or other means of serious pressure and Rehn was able to leave the sittings without responding to questions addressed to him.

Rehn and the national parliaments

Olli Rehn was heard by the Commission for European Affairs, the Commission of Foreign Affairs, the Commission of Finances of the French Assemblée Nationale,[24] and then by the Commission for Finances

20 For example, during the European Parliament debate of 12 March 2014, Strasbourg. The questions asked to Rehn were informative in general, however, Rehn didn't stay to answer them. He only gave an introductory speech. It was a debate at times, but Rehn wasn't really involved in it.

21 Laid down in Rule 149(8) of the European Parliament Rules of Procedure, n. 5, above.

22 For example, during the European Parliament debate of 5 February 2013, Strasbourg.

23 Hannes Swoboda, during the European Parliament debate of 25 February 2014, Strasbourg.

24 18 June 2013. Transcript available in French at www.assemblee-nationale.fr/14/europe/c-rendus/c0069.asp.

and Budgetary Control of the French Sénat.[25] Rehn spent one hour at the Assemblée and probably one hour at the Sénat, and gave the same speech to both institutions. He also visited a number of other national parliaments – for example, the Greek one in 2010 and the Italian one in 2013.[26] In the Netherlands it seems there were several meetings (and a live recording) with the Dutch parliament in the context of the European Semester, but transcripts of these meetings are not available.[27]

The transcripts that do exist (such as for the French parliament) suggest two key insights: first, the dialogue between national parliaments and EU leaders enables the latter to explain the policy choices made at the EU level, thus permitting information to reach the benches of parliament. Secondly, it is the opportunity for parliamentarians to question EU representatives, notably concerning the evolution of the EMU, even though the time allotted to such dialogues is often too short. For example, in France Rehn came to explain and defend the 2013 CSRs addressed to France. He presented the recent achievements of the EU (the economic governance, the banking union, fiscal consolidation, and the renewed credibility of the EU on the markets) and its objectives (an autonomous EU able to manage internal crisis without the help of the IMF and sustainable growth). Rehn went a bit into the details of the ESM, EFSF, and the EMU when asked by Jean Arthuis, a centrist Senator, but his answer was rather brief.

Rehn and inter-parliamentary forums

In the past years, Rehn has attended a number of inter-parliamentary forums. The Inter-Parliamentary Committee Meeting on the European Semester which took place on 27–28 February 2012 is one of them. In his speech at that event,[28] Rehn argued that while economic policies were a matter of common concern, national governments remained in charge of these policies; therefore, there was a need ‘to ensure that national

25 Transcript available in French at www.nossenateurs.fr/seance/9555#table_40124.

26 Rehn's speech at the Italian Parliament, Rome, 17 September 2013; Rehn's speech at the Greek Parliament, Athens, 9 December 2010.

27 Advisory Council on International Affairs (AIV), *Public Support for the European Union: Building Trust*, Advisory Report No. 88, April 2014, 29–30, citing H. Beun (2014), Tweede Kamer voert al dialoog met Europese Commissie (House of Representatives, already in dialogue with the European Commission), *Internationale Spectator*, no. 45, 44–45.

28 Rehn's speech of 28 February 2012, Brussels.

parliaments [were] completely involved in the whole cycle of economic policy-making at the European level'. According to Rehn, ownership and democratic accountability at the national level was indispensable for success on the European level.

Another key inter-parliamentary event which Rehn attended was the European Parliamentary Week (EPW) on the European Semester which took place on 28–30 January 2013. Rehn's speech, delivered at the opening plenary session of the event,[29] was followed by a brief exchange of views with MEPs and national parliamentarians.[30] A recent COSAC report, however, points out that some national parliaments were dissatisfied with the level of engagement with representatives of EU institutions during the 2013 EPW.[31] For instance, the Czech *Poslanecká sněmovna* argued that there was a 'lack of opportunities for a dialogue and debate with the Presidents of the European Union Institutions', while the Czech *Senát* complained of a lack of genuine dialogue on semester-related topics, with the 'EU representatives showing up only to read their short speeches and then leaving the event without engaging in any dialogue with national Parliaments'. The French *Sénat* referred to the debates as simply a juxtaposition of speeches with no conclusions, while the Dutch *Tweede Kamer* claimed that these types of meetings tended to result in 'unrelated monologues'.[32]

Rehn also attended the 2014 EPW which took place on 20–22 January and hosted within its framework the second Inter-Parliamentary Conference on Economic Governance along with inter-parliamentary committee meetings on the European Semester.[33] During this event, Rehn addressed the parliamentarians on two separate occasions, and his speeches were followed by an exchange of views of more than one hour.[34]

29 Rehn's speech of 29 January 2013, Opening Plenary Session Parliamentary Week, Brussels.

30 Based on the EPW 2013 event programme available at www.europarl.europa.eu/webnp/webdav/site/myjahiasite/users/malfons/public/week%202013/EPW%20FINAL%20programme.pdf.

31 COSAC, 'Nineteenth Bi-annual Report: Developments in European Union Procedures and Practices Relevant to Parliamentary Scrutiny' (May 2013), 17–18.

32 Ibid.

33 Created on the basis of Article 13 TSCG.

34 Based on the EPW 2014 provisional event programme available at www.europarl.europa.eu/webnp/webdav/site/myjahiasite/shared/EPW%202014/European%20Parliamentary%20Week%202014%20EN%20-%20draft%20100114.pdf.

The political accountability of the European Central Bank: informative and intensive dialogues, some critical debates

President Draghi and the European Parliament

In the context of monetary policy, the legal basis for the ECB's accountability to the European Parliament is Article 284(3) TFEU (ex-Article 113(3) TEC), which provides that the ECB will send the European Parliament an annual report on the activities of the ECB and on the monetary policy of both the previous and current year. Moreover, the President of the ECB is to present this report to the European Parliament which then may hold a general debate on the basis of this report. In addition, it is provided that the President of the ECB and the other members of the Executive Board may, at the request of the European Parliament or on their own initiative, be heard by the competent committees of the European Parliament. While Article 113(3) TEC only mandated the presentation of the annual report to the European Parliament, Rule 113 of the European Parliament Rules of Procedure created the additional requirement of the ECB President appearing before the ECON committee at least four times a year (Fasone 2014: 175).[35] These appearances of the ECB President before the European Parliament – in plenary and in the ECON committee – is what became known as the Monetary Dialogue (ibid.). Finally, according to Rule 118 of the European Parliament Rules of Procedure, any Member of the European Parliament may also submit a question for written answer to the ECB.

Article 284(3) TFEU provides that not just the President but also the other members of the Executive Board may be heard by ECON, but it makes no reference to the members of *the Governing Council*. The Governing Council is composed of the six members of the Executive Board *and the governors of the national central banks of the 18 euro-area states*. As Article 284(3) TFEU makes no mention of the Governing Council, there is no Treaty obligation for the national central bank presidents to appear before the ECON committee (Amtenbrink 2002: 161). Thus, 18 out of the 24 members of the Governing Council are shielded from accountability at the European level, and it is doubtful whether this accountability gap is properly filled by national parliaments. According to Amtenbrink, 'it seems difficult to imagine that an individual central bank governor [...] would be held accountable for the conduct of the Governing Council as a whole' (ibid.). Moreover, the argument that presidents of national central

35 European Parliament Rules of Procedure, n. 5, above.

banks should be accountable only to national parliaments does not hold because when they act as members of the Governing Council, they perform ECB-related tasks (ibid.) and take decisions, which affect the euro area as a whole.

As to the de facto accountability of the ECB to the European Parliament on monetary policy, in the post-financial crisis years (2009–14), the ECB Presidents Trichet and Draghi attended five meetings in plenary. These were all meetings to discuss the *ECB Annual Report*. Trichet attended the meetings on the reports of 2008[36] and 2009,[37] while Draghi attended the meetings on the reports of 2010,[38] 2011,[39] and 2012.[40] Both Trichet and Draghi gave an introductory speech and concluded with general remarks on what was discussed during the meetings. The Parliamentarians expressed their views, gave comments, and asked questions. Trichet and Draghi did not answer them immediately, but made a selection and commented on this selection during the concluding speech. The majority of the contributions by the Parliamentarians consisted of political statements. Most of them did not contain explicit criticism or accusations, with some exceptions.[41] The structure of the meetings did not really allow for a debate to take place. In that regard the meetings were very similar to those with Van Rompuy and Rehn. There was an opening speech, the Parliamentarians expressed their views and concerns and asked the Presidents to elaborate and, in some instances, to justify certain decisions. The Presidents ended the meeting with concluding remarks which covered most of the topic but almost never included specific responses to the critiques. Apart from some individual members of parliament, there were no strong negative judgements expressed.

Trichet and Draghi also engaged in a *monetary dialogue* with the Economic and Monetary Affairs Committee four times a year. Between 2009 and 2014, they attended these monetary dialogues 21 times. According to the minutes on the website of ECON, Draghi only visited the Committee one other time as President of the ECB. The same goes for Trichet.[42] The nature of the monetary dialogues, in general, is informative, but with some room for critique and debate. Draghi usually starts with a speech, followed

36 (25-03-2010).
37 (22-11-2010).
38 (01-12-2011).
39 (16-04-2013).
40 (12-12-2013).
41 For example, the European Parliament debate of 22 November 2010, Strasbourg.
42 They did attend public hearings as Chairman of the ESRB.

by Parliamentarians asking questions, which are immediately answered by Draghi. This setting is rather informal and allows Parliamentarians to react immediately to a response given by Draghi, thereby creating opportunities for more genuine political debates.[43] This occurs during most of the meetings, although not always.[44] Parliamentarians ask mostly informative questions. They seek to know Draghi's (and the ECB's) position on certain matters and (possible) developments. They want Draghi to explain how some words are going to be put into action.[45] These questions are mostly combined with their own views, suggestions, or speculations. The responses given by Draghi are mostly extensive and detailed. He explains the views and strategies of the ECB and does not go into the negative speculations and scenarios expressed by Parliamentarians. Sometimes a critical question[46] or a comment forces Draghi to take a defensive position,[47] and in very rare instances Draghi is asked to give some sort of justification.[48] It also occurs that a Parliamentarian is not satisfied with the answers given by Draghi and asks additional questions.[49] Draghi always responds to these questions. For Trichet the analysis is almost entirely the same: the majority of questions were informative and concerned the views,

43 For example, during the Monetary Dialogue of 3 March 2014, Brussels, where Sampo Terho, Pablo Zalba Bidegain, and Markus Ferber used this opportunity, or the Monetary Dialogue of 23 September 2013, Brussels, where Sylvie Goulard wouldn't stop after one answer. The best example is the dialogue between Draghi and Philippe Lamberts during the Monetary Dialogue of 9 July 2012, Brussels (which was in fact partly on the accountability of the ECB/Draghi).

44 Indeed, in some meetings the structure was more like those of the economic dialogues with Olli Rehn: 3 questions – reaction, 3 questions – reaction, etc. See, for example, the Monetary Dialogue of 9 October 2012, Brussels.

45 For example, Arlene McCarthy during the Monetary Dialogue of 17 December 2012, Brussels.

46 See, for example, Nikolas Chountis and the Chair during the Monetary Dialogue of 23 September 2013, Brussels; Derk Jan Eppink during the Monetary Dialogue of 25 April 2012, Brussels, or during the Monetary Dialogue of 8 July 2013, Brussels, where he sketches a possible negative scenario that would be caused (at least partly) by a decision taken by Draghi, or the question asked by Wolf Klinz during the Monetary Dialogue of 16 December 2013, where he ascertains that the ECB policy might not be functioning.

47 For example, Pascal Canfin during the Monetary Dialogue of 25 April 2012, Brussels, or Olle Schmidt during this same meeting.

48 For example, Astrid Lulling during the Monetary Dialogue of 16 December 2013, Brussels.

49 For example, Nikolas Chountis and Astrid Lulling during the Monetary Dialogue of 8 July 2013, Brussels or Werner Langer, Pablo Zalba Bidegain and Anni Podimata during the Monetary Dialogue of 23 September 2013, Brussels.

expectations, and strategies of Trichet and the ECB. Critical questions and debates were very rare.

Overall the structure of the monetary dialogues provides a good platform for an intensive debate with the President of the ECB. The Parliamentarians ask many questions to Draghi and Trichet and never debate with each other. The questions are mostly of an informative nature. Draghi and Trichet answer almost all questions, although sometimes they avoid commenting on the core issue (especially with regard to speculations and comments made by others). As one of them said, 'they comment on facts only'. In addition to informative questions, sometimes doubts and criticisms are expressed, but these tend to be rather mild and remain limited to individual members. In some instances, a debate takes place between the President of the ECB and a European Parliament member. The member mostly asks follow-up questions, but in some instances reacts with comments and mild countering ideas. The Presidents both respond to almost all follow-up questions and comments.

In addition to such 'immediate' responses it seems that there may be a delayed response in the sense of the ECB incorporating points raised during the European Parliament dialogue in its further monetary policy-making (Eijffinger and Mujagic 2004). Earlier qualitative work found that the ECB is in fact 'highly responsive' to the ECON and some changes were implemented (ibid.). There is clearly scope for the monetary dialogue to evolve and improve further especially when account is taken of its national equivalents in the USA and in the United Kingdom (Claeys et al. 2014).

The ECB is now empowered in addition to monetary policy with specific tasks concerning the prudential supervision of credit institutions established in participating member states. It carries out these tasks within a Single Supervisory Mechanism (hereafter: SSM) composed of the ECB and the national competent authorities. Accountability to the European Parliament within this framework is governed by Article 20 of the SSM Regulation[50] and an Interinstitutional Agreement signed by the ECB and the European Parliament.[51] The requirements of accountability with regard to the prudential supervisory role of the ECB are more demanding than

50 Regulation 1024/2013 conferring specific tasks on the European Central Bank concerning policies relating to the prudential supervision of credit institutions, OJ 2013, L 287/63.

51 Interinstitutional Agreement between the European Parliament and the European Central Bank on the practical modalities of the exercise of democratic accountability and oversight over the exercise of the tasks conferred on the ECB within the framework of the Single Supervisory Mechanism [2013] OJ L 320/1.

those in relation to its monetary policy function. Thus, under Article 20 SSM Regulation, the Chair of the Supervisory Board is not only required to present an annual report to the European Parliament in plenary, reply to questions from MEPs, and appear before the ECON committee upon request, but she must also divulge sensitive information – although in 'confidential oral discussions behind closed doors' – and cooperate with European Parliament investigations.

The Interinstitutional Agreement between the European Parliament and the ECB provides for more detailed arrangements regarding the requirements spelled out in Article 20 SSM Regulation. The agreement requires the Chair of the Supervisory Board to attend two *ordinary public hearings* at the ECON committee 'in the course of the following year',[52] that is during the transition period from 3 November 2013 to 4 November 2014. No reference is made to a specific number of meetings following the transition period – once the ECB formally assumes its supervisory tasks. Accordingly, it is still to be seen whether these meetings will take place twice a year or more frequently, as is the case for the ECB President who attends four monetary dialogues annually. What is also striking is that only the Chair and the Vice-Chairs of the ECON committee may attend the *confidential meetings* with the Chair of the Supervisory Board.[53] Moreover, the Interinstitutional Agreement states that: 'No minutes or any other recording of the confidential meetings shall be taken. No statement shall be made for the press or any other media. Each participant to the confidential discussions shall sign every time a solemn declaration not to divulge the content of those discussions to any third person'.

These strict confidentiality requirements make it difficult to assess the de facto accountability arrangements at the time of writing this article (and perhaps permanently). Even though the Interinstitutional Agreement provides room for more accountability to the European Parliament as such, the extensive emphasis on secrecy and confidentiality with regard to all the information supplied by the ECB to the European Parliament does not leave much room for public discussion or debate on this information in plenary or even in the ECON committee. This in turn removes the raw ingredients for accountability – information and deliberation – from public space. The question whether this is justified in a general fashion and the wider context of parliaments (in this instance the European Parliament) agreeing to non-public accountability processes is beyond the scope of this

52 Section I.2, first para. of the EP-ECB Interinstitutional Agreement.
53 Section I.2, tenth para. of the EP-ECB Interinstitutional Agreement.

chapter. For now, the SSM web presence under the heading accountability is (much) thinner than its monetary dialogue counterpart with only the quarterly reports submitted by the ECB to the European Parliament during the preparatory phase available at the time this chapter was written (in addition to answers to MEPs' written questions).

President Draghi and the national parliaments

It was explicitly stated by the ECB in its response to a recent European Parliament questionnaire that, '[t]he ECB is not accountable to national parliaments'.[54] This statement applies to its activities in the areas of both monetary policy and banking supervision. However, when it comes to reporting obligations and an exchange of views, there are differences between these two distinct spheres of activity of the ECB. In the context of monetary policy, there is no legal framework for scrutiny by the national parliaments, nor are there any reporting obligations on the ECB. In contrast, the supervisory functions of the ECB entail certain formal reporting obligations towards the national parliaments along with the possibility to invite the Chair or a member of the Supervisory Board to appear before a national parliament. This is laid down in Article 21 of the SSM Regulation.[55]

Jean-Claude Trichet, former President of the ECB, was heard once within the framework of a French parliamentary commission of inquiry concerning tax avoidance. He explained how and why the financial crisis of 2008 emerged, and notably advocated for an international entity responsible for the enforcement of international standards for supervision of banks.[56] He refused (7 May 2014) to attend the *Oireachtas* Committee of Inquiry into the Banking Crisis arguing that there was no responsibility to the national level or need to account. This attitude seems a bit out of kilter with newer practices of his successor and may have to do with a (secret) letter he sent to the Irish Finance Minister just before Ireland bailed out Anglo Irish Bank.

In recent years, the ECB President has visited several national parliaments. Draghi's first visit to the German *Bundestag* took place on 24 October

54 'ECB response to the questionnaire of the European Parliament on the Troika' published on the ECB website on 10 January 2014. www.ecb.europa.eu/pub/pdf/other/140110_ecb_response_troika_questionnaireen.pdf.

55 Regulation 1024/2013, n. 50, above.

56 16 July 2013. Transcript available in French at www.senat.fr/rap/r13-087-2/r13-087-224.html#toc35.

2012. In his speech Draghi stated that '[i]t was rare for the ECB President to speak in a national parliament' and that the ECB was accountable to the European Parliament.[57] However, he stated that the purpose of his visit was to 'explain ECB's policies' and to listen to the views of the parliamentarians. The remainder of his speech was devoted to the explanation of the rationale behind ECB's introduction of the Outright Monetary Transactions (OMTs) and addressed the potential concerns of German observers over the impact of this policy. He also emphasized that the ECB was acting within its mandate and that it was still fully independent. He concluded by stating that he looked forward to the discussion with the MPs.

Draghi appeared before the Spanish *Congreso de los Diputados* on 12 February 2013. His speech focused on three subjects: the state of the economy, the ECB's monetary policy, and its long-term vision on the economic and monetary union.[58] Regarding the state of the economy, he stated that there were some improvements (also in Spain), but that he was aware of the heavy social costs of the adjustments. However, he argued that 'the reforms should not be seen in isolation: they aim[ed] to create stronger, better functioning and [...] fairer economies, for the benefit of all citizens'. Regarding the ECB's monetary policy, he discussed the provision of liquidity to banks through long-term refinancing operations (LTROs) and the ECB's bond-buying activities through OMTs, arguing that these measures had led to improvement in the financial environment. Finally, as to the longer-term vision of the EMU, he talked about the financial, fiscal, economic aspects and eventually a 'deeper political union'. He mentioned the SSM and the SRM as the steps towards a financial union and the need to restore competitiveness in order to achieve a genuine EMU. He concluded the speech by opening the floor to opinions and questions.

Draghi visited the French *Assemblée Nationale* on 26 June 2013. His speech to the French parliament was very similar to the one delivered before the Spanish congress.[59] He discussed the same three topics: ECB's monetary policy, growth and adjustment in the euro area, and progress towards a deeper EMU. In the final part of his speech, he also spoke of increasing democratic legitimacy parallel to the transfer of greater authority to the EU level, stating that the European Parliament and national parliaments had a key role to play in this respect.

57 Opening Statement at Deutscher Bundestag by Mario Draghi, Berlin, 24 October 2012.

58 Introductory Statement at the Congreso de los Diputados de España, Madrid, 12 February 2013.

59 Introductory Remarks at the French Assemblée Nationale, Paris, 26 June 2013.

To sum up, Draghi's visit to the German Bundestag was primarily aimed at explaining and justifying the ECB's unconventional measures, while his Spanish and French visits focused greatly on underlining the positive effects of the unconventional measures and emphasizing the importance of structural reforms. Moreover, in both the Spanish and the French speeches, he advocated the banking union, a deepening of the EMU in all other dimensions of economic policy, and the achievement of a political union. In this respect, the speech before the French assembly was much more ambitious than the one before the Spanish congress, as Draghi made explicit references to a transfer of power to the EU and even to a United States of Europe.

President Draghi and inter-parliamentary forums

There seems to be no track record of the ECB attending inter-parliamentary conferences organized by the European Parliament.[60] The bi-annual reports of COSAC barely mention the ECB and there is no record of President Draghi engaging with them.

Conclusion: emerging post-crisis political accountabilities

Some Presidents are more accountable than others

We can observe the emergence of some formal and informal accountability relations between the trinity of executive actors and the European Parliament and (some) national parliaments in the post-crises years. However, the emerging political accountability regime is denser for some presidents than for others.

Contrary to our expectations, the political accountability relations of Draghi, the ECB President, are the most developed.[61] The structure of the monetary dialogues provides a good platform for an intensive debate with the President of the ECB. The Parliamentarians ask many questions

60 See the European Parliament webpage on Relations with National Parliaments: www.europarl.europa.eu/webnp/cms/pid/11;jsessionid=8F715C78DF5D938D3F1FA12F9200BE00.

61 It must be noted that despite our conclusion that compared to Rehn and Van Rompuy, Draghi is more accountable to the European Parliament, we do not claim that the ECB is a very accountable institution as such. The criticisms voiced by Claeys, Hallerberg and Tschekassin (2014)regarding the European Parliament's lack of sanctioning powers and its merely consultative role in the appointment of the ECB executive board are certainly valid. The European Parliament does have the right to approve the Chair and Vice-Chair of the SSM Supervisory Board but the ECB selects the candidates. The long-standing criticism regarding the publication of the minutes of the Governing Council is currently being addressed by the ECB: www.ecb.europa.eu/press/pr/date/2014/html/pr140703_1.en.html.

to Draghi and Trichet and some forms of political debate do develop. Secondly, the requirements of accountability with regard to the supervisory role of the ECB are more demanding than those in relation to its monetary policy function. The Chair of the ECB Supervisory Board is not only required to present an annual report to the European Parliament in plenary, to reply to questions from MEPs and appear before the ECON committee upon request, but she must also divulge sensitive information and cooperate with European Parliament investigations. Some preliminary steps have been taken to engage in a dialogue with national parliaments.

Olli Rehn, Vice-President of the European Commission and Commissioner for Economic and Monetary Affairs and the euro, comes in second. The European Parliament has several formal powers to oblige him to provide information and to engage in debate. The most important tool for the European Parliament in this respect is the economic dialogue. Accountability in the books is not yet fully matched by accountability in practice. During the parliamentary term of 2009–14, Olli Rehn attended no fewer than 44 plenary meetings. However, the nature of these meetings is rather informative. The European Parliament does not confront Rehn and he can get away with rather extensive speeches and broad answers. There are no, or very few, consequences or other means of serious political pressure. With regard to national parliaments, while Rehn has made several visits, they appear to be more informative in nature rather than of the kind that entail genuine debate, let alone judgement by parliamentarians.

Van Rompuy, the president of the European Council, has been the least accountable of the trinity in the post-crises years. The *de jure* accountability arrangement between the European Parliament and the European Council is traditionally very limited and basically only covers the provision of general information. Van Rompuy appeared in the European Parliament only three times a year on average and the setting of the meetings does not stimulate a real and intensive debate. The accountability relationship with national parliaments is still in its infancy and was restricted to occasional visits and 'set' speeches with very little debate and no opportunities for judgement or sanctioning.

Evolving supranational, very-limited intergovernmental political accountability

Most accountability relations that have evolved are with the European Parliament and with its committees. Particularly the economic and monetary dialogues with the Economic and Monetary Affairs Committee provide promising venues for political executive accountability. Accountability relations with national parliaments are non-existent or very limited. Some of these presidents have visited some national parliaments, but there are no formal requirements to do so and the informal practices are fragmented and incidental. There are some inter-parliamentary initiatives, such as COSAC, that may provide a road towards future executive intergovernmental accountability. However, these are still in their infancy and do not go beyond informing.

An important question for further research is how EU executive accountability compares with national executive accountability. This first exploration suggests that the political accountability of the presidents of the ECB comes out most favourably. Trichet and Draghi often appeared in the European Parliament and its committees and they have been quite forthcoming, compared to some of their national counterparts.[62] The political accountability of the EU Commission and its (Vice-)President vis-à-vis the European Parliament is gradually 'normalising' (Wille 2013) and step by step starts to resemble executive accountability to parliaments at the national level. However, there are still many steps to be taken. Vice-President Rehn visited the European Parliament no fewer than 44 times, but the accountability relation did not go much beyond informing. The political accountability of the President of the European Council compares the least favourably with national political leaders. There is virtually no regime of political accountability to the European Parliament, or to national parliaments, and in this respect this President is still 'out of control'.

The new executive powers that have been put in place at the EU level after the financial crises have not yet been followed by an equally robust set of formal accountability institutions and informal accountability practices. There are some provisions 'in the books', particularly regarding the relation between the Commission and the European Parliament, but these have not yet given rise to mature practices of political account giving. This is, to some extent, a natural course of affairs. In many member states it took years before parliamentary practices of political accountability fully matured. Often, accountability trails behind the establishment of executive power and it may take a while before we can observe a full 'normalization' of political-administrative relations (Wille 2013). However, given

62 For the relationship with parliament of the Banque de France, the Bank of England, the Bundesbank, the Nederlandsche Bank, among others, see Amtenbrink 1999: 286–308.

the outcome of the 2014 European Parliament elections and the strong parliamentary involvement in the formation of the new Commission, it is to be expected that the new European Parliament will exercise more of its accountability powers towards Moscovici, the new 'budget-tsar', and that the process of normalization will evolve further.

The desired level of political accountability of the ECB President is a point of vehement debate between the 'German' and the 'French' schools of thought. In past years, the ECB Presidents have been more forthcoming towards the European Parliament than some of their national counterparts towards their respective parliamentary forums.

The 'youngest' of the three presidencies, the President of the European Council, is by far the least accountable. The intergovernmental nature of this institution stands in the way of the development of substantive accountability practices. Twenty-eight national parliaments are too fragmented an institutional architecture to provide real countervailing powers. The EU presidency is, in practice, a form of supranational executive power and is very difficult to control by solitary intergovernmental forums. In the long run, either some sort of assembly of national parliaments will have to be developed that can act as an intergovernmental forum of parliamentary accountability or the European Parliament has to step in here too. Time will tell if Donald Tusk remains 'out of control' or even if it matters.

References

Amtenbrink, F. (1999) *The Democratic Accountability of Central Banks: A Comparative Study of the European Central Bank*, Oxford: Hart Publishing.

(2002) 'On the Legitimacy and Accountability of the European Central Bank: Legal Arrangements and Practical Experiences', in A. Arnull and D. Wincott (eds), *Accountability and Legitimacy in the European Union*, Oxford: Oxford University Press.

Arnull, A., and Wincott, D. (eds) (2002) *Accountability and Legitimacy in the European Union*, Oxford: Oxford University Press.

Bogdanor, V. (2007) *Legitimacy, Accountability and Democracy in the European Union*, London: Federal Trust.

Bovens, M. (2007) 'Analysing and Assessing Accountability: A Conceptual Framework', *European Law Journal*, 13(4), 447–68.

(2010) 'Two Concepts of Accountability: Accountability as a Virtue and as a Mechanism', *West European Politics*, 33(5), 946–67.

Bovens, M., Curtin, D., and 't Hart, P. (eds) (2010) *The Real World of EU Accountability: What Deficit?*, Oxford: Oxford University Press.

Bovens, M., 't Hart, P., Dekker, S., and Verheuvel, G. (1999) 'The Politics of Blame Avoidance: Defensive Tactics in a Dutch Crime-fighting Fiasco', in H. Anheier (ed.), *When Things Go Wrong: Failures and Breakdowns in Organizational Settings*, Thousand Oaks: Sage.

Bovens, M., 't Hart, P., and Schillemans, T. (2008) 'Does Public Accountability Work? An Assessment Tool', *Public Administration*, 86(1), 225–42.

Chalmers, D. (2012). 'The European Redistributive State and a European Law of Struggle', *European Law Journal*, 18(5), 667–93.

Claeys, G., Hallerberg, M., and Tschekassin, O. (2014) 'European Central Bank Accountability: How the Monetary Dialogue Could be Improved', Bruegel Policy Contribution, 2014/04, Brussels.

Crum, B. (2009) 'Accountability and Personalisation of the European Council Presidency', *Journal of European Integration*, 31(6), 685–701.

Curtin, D. (2009) *Executive Power of the European Union. Law, Practices and the Living Constitution*, Oxford: Oxford University Press.

(2014) 'Challenging Executive Dominance in European Democracy', *Modern Law Review*, 77(1), 1–32.

Day, P., and Klein, R. (1987) *Accountabilities: Five Public Services*, London: Tavistock.

Decision of the European Central Bank of 4 March 2004 on Public Access to European Central Bank Documents, OJ L 80/42 (as amended by Decision ECB/2011/6 of the European Central Bank of 9 May 2011, OJ L 158/37).

Dubnick, M. (2002) 'Seeking Salvation for Accountability', paper presented at the Annual Meeting of the American Political Science Association, Boston, 29 August–1 September.

Eijffinger, C., and Mujagic, E. (2004), 'An Assessment of the Effectiveness of the Monetary Dialogue on the ECB's Accountability and Transparency: A Qualitative Approach', *Intereconomics*, 39(4), 190–203.

European Commission (2001) 'European Governance: A White Paper', COM (2001) 428 final.

(2003) *Report from the Commission on European Governance*, Luxembourg: Office for Official Publications of the European Communities.

Fasone, C. (2014) 'European Economic Governance and Parliamentary Representation. What Place for the European Parliament?', *European Law Journal*, 20(2), 164–85.

Fossum, J. (2014) 'The Structure of EU Representation and the Crisis', in S. Kroger (ed.), *Political Representation in the European Union: Still Times of Crisis?*, London: Routledge.

Habermas, J. (2012) *The Crisis of the European Union: A Response*, Cambridge: Polity Press.

Harlow, C. (2002) *Accountability in the European Union*, Oxford: Oxford University Press.

Hearit, K. (2005) *Crisis Management by Apology: Corporate Response to Allegations of Wrongdoing*, London: Taylor & Francis.

Hood, C. et al., (2007) *The Tools of Government in the Digital Age*, London, Palgrave Macmillan.

Koppell, J. (2005) 'Pathologies of Accountability: ICANN and the Challenge of "Multiple Accountabilities Disorder"', *Public Administration Review*, 65(1), 94–107.

Lord, C. (2004) *A Democratic Audit of the European Union*, Basingstoke: Palgrave Macmillan.

Mair, P. (2005) 'Popular Democracy and the European Union Polity'. European Governance Papers, C-05-03. www.connex-network.org/eurogov/pdf/egp-connex-C-05-03.pdf.

Meijer, A., and Schillemans, T. (2009) 'Fictional Citizens and Real Effects: Accountability to Citizens in Competitive and Monopolistic Markets', *Public Sector Management - An Interactive Journal.*

Mulgan, R. (2003) *Holding Power to Account: Accountability in Modern Democracies*, Basingstoke: Palgrave Macmillan.

Pollitt, C. (2003) *The Essential Public Manager*, London: Open University Press/McGraw-Hill.

Scharpf, F. (2011) 'Monetary Union, Fiscal Crisis and the Pre-emption of Democracy', MPIfG Discussion Paper 11/11.

Schillemans, T. (2008) 'Accountability in the Shadow of Hierarchy: The Horizontal Accountability of Agencies', *Public Organization Review*, 8(2), 175–94.

Schmitter, P. (2000) *How to Democratize the European Union: And Why Bother?* Lanham, MD: Rowman & Littlefield.

Scott, C. (2000) 'Accountability in the Regulatory State', *Journal of Law and Society*, 27(1), 38–60.

Van de Steeg, M. (2009) 'Public Accountability in the European Union: Is the European Parliament Able to Hold the European Council Accountable?', European Integration online papers. http://eiop.or.at/eiop/index.php/eiop/article/view/2009_003a.

(2010) 'The European Council's Evolving Political Accountability', in M. Bovens, D. Curtin, and P. 't Hart (eds), *The Real World of EU Accountability: What Deficit?* Oxford: Oxford University Press.

Wessels W., et al. (2013) 'Democratic Control in the Member States of the European Council and the Euro Zone Summits'. www.notre-europe.eu/media/democraticcontrol-rozenberg-kreilinger-et-al-ne-jdi-tepsa-mar13.pdf?pdf=ok.

Wille, A. (2013) *The Normalization of the European Commission: Politics and Bureaucracy in the EU Executive*, Oxford: Oxford University Press.

9

The limits of collective action and collective leadership

GIANDOMENICO MAJONE

The paradoxical logic of collective action

It is commonly assumed that if all the members of a group agree on some common interest, then there would be a tendency for the group to seek to further this interest, i.e., the group would also act in a self-interested or group-interested manner. Mancur Olson's important contribution to political economy has been his proof that this familiar assumption is basically wrong (Olson 1971). This proof depends on the argument that the members of the group will not provide as much of the collective good as it would be in their common interest to provide. Such a tendency towards sub optimality is due to the fact that by definition a collective good, such as economic integration, is available to all members of a group once it has been provided by any member. Since an individual member gets only part of the benefit of any expenditure he makes to obtain more of the collective good, he will discontinue his purchase of it before the optimal amount for the group as a whole has been obtained.

In some small groups (like the original Six of the 1951 Paris and 1957 Rome Treaties) one or two members may find that they would be better off if the collective good were provided – even if they had to pay the entire cost of providing it themselves – than they would be if it were not provided at all. In such situations there is a presumption that the collective good will be produced. Thus in small groups, where each member gets a substantial portion of the total gain simply because there are few others in the group, a collective good can often be produced by the voluntary, self-interested action of the members of the group. Actually, the greatest likelihood that a collective good will be provided occurs in the case of small groups of members of unequal size (again, the situation of the original Six); for the greater the interest of any single member in the collective good, the greater the likelihood that this member will get such a significant portion of the total benefit from the provision of the good that she will gain from seeing that the good is produced, even if she has to pay the entire cost herself. Even in the smallest groups, however, the members of the group will not provide as much of the good as it would be in their common interest to provide. This less than optimal provision of the collective good is again due to the fact that, by definition, a collective good is such that other members of the group cannot be kept from consuming it once any group member has provided it.

The logic of collective action operates not only in groups of individuals but also in the case of states. An interesting example of this is provided by the well-known historian Heinrich August Winkler in the first volume of his *Geschichte des Westens* (Winkler 2012: 760). According to the 1821 'federal war constitution' (*Bundeskriegsverfassung*) of the German confederation, no state was allowed to participate with more than three army corps to the confederate army. This rule was dictated by the desire to avoid even 'the appearance of the supremacy of one member state over the other members of the *Bund*'. The Prussian state was a member of the *Bund*, but important Prussian territories – East and West Prussia, and Posen – were not part of the German confederation. For this reason the Prussian state was allowed to have nine, rather than three, army corps. Because of this, the other states of the *Bund* could assume that in case of a foreign threat Prussia would mobilize its entire military might. As a consequence they kept their contribution to the common defence well below the limit allowed by the federal constitution.

In sum, the size of the group is a key element in the logic of collective action, and '*the larger the group, the further it will fall short of providing an optimal amount of a collective good*' (Olson 1971: 35; italics in the original). Olson concludes that if larger groups/organizations do in fact exist this is not because of the collective good they provide but because of the power of coercion they may enjoy (as in the case of the state) or because of selective (positive or negative) incentives that voluntary organizations may provide. A selective incentive is one that applies selectively to the individuals (or subgroups) depending on whether they do or do not contribute to the provision of the collective good. A well-known example of selective incentive in the context of the EC/EU is the Common Agriculture Policy, a positive incentive offered to France for its support of European integration.

Unfortunately, the larger the group the more difficult it becomes to provide suitable selective incentives to all the members of the group. The availability of such incentives is limited, in case of the EU, not only by the size of the group but also by the socio-economic heterogeneity of its members. An even more basic problem in organizing and maintaining socially and economically heterogeneous groups is due to the fact that the members are less likely to agree on the exact nature of whatever collective good is at issue or on how much of it is worth 'buying'. In the EU context we have the traditional cleavage between the countries that wish to limit integration to the economic sphere and those that support also political integration. Consensus on such matters is especially difficult because the defining characteristic of collective goods – that they go to everyone in the group if they are provided at all – entails that all the members of the group have to accept whatever level and type of the good is provided. It follows that political entrepreneurs who attempt to organize collective action will be more likely to succeed if they strive to organize relatively homogeneous groups. Thus some of the most serious problems the European Commission is experiencing today, particularly in the area of policy harmonization (see, e.g., Piris 2011: 8–12), originated in the 'big bang' enlargement of 2004–07—an enlargement which the Commission, paradoxically, eagerly supported.

The applicability of Mancur Olson's analysis to the case of European integration could be demonstrated by a number of other examples. It is therefore rather surprising that the concepts developed in the present section seem to have been generally ignored by political scientists, legal scholars and even by economists writing about the EU. Given the importance of the limits of collective action for understanding the causes of the present crisis of EU-style integration it may be useful to list here Mancur Olson's key propositions, as summarized by Cornes and Sandler (1996: 324–6):

(1) Large groups may not provide themselves a collective good.
(2) The larger the group, the lower the collective provision level.
(3) Large, well-endowed members will bear a disproportionate burden of collective provision, so that the small will exploit the large.
(4) Asymmetric groups (including both well-endowed and poorer members) are more apt to contain at least one member or subgroup whose benefits from collective action will exceed the associated costs, even if these costs are solely born by the individual member or the subgroup.
(5) Collective action can be promoted, up to a point, by selective incentives and/or institutional design.

Olson's *Logic of Collective Action* was first published in 1965. Since the mid-1970s, neo-institutional economists have provided important insights into other dimensions of the logic of collective action. Key to the understanding of these broader aspects of collective action is the notion of transaction costs.

Political transaction costs

Transaction costs are the costs of operating an economic, political, or social system. Thus the costs of using the market system have been classified as: (1) costs of preparing contracts, i.e., search and information costs, narrowly defined; (2) costs of concluding contracts: bargaining and other decision-making costs; and (3) costs of monitoring and enforcing the contractual obligations. Such costs are clearly different from the costs of producing goods and services – the only costs considered by neoclassical economics – but they are as real and significant as production costs. Following Williamson (1985), we can think of transaction costs, whether they arise in economic, political, or social systems, as the equivalent of friction in physical systems.

The idea of studying political processes in the transaction-cost mode seems to have originated with Douglass North (1990), who, however, focused on a particular kind of transaction cost, namely failure of 'instrumental rationality' for participants in the political process. Furubotn and Richter (2000: 47) define political transaction costs as the costs of supplying public goods by collective action. Specifically, these are: (1) the costs of setting up, maintaining, and changing a system's formal and informal political organization; and (2) the costs of running a polity. Actually, most forms of economic transaction costs appear also in political processes; but political processes are likely to be even more beset by transaction costs than are economic processes and relationships. This observation suggests that a transaction-cost politics perspective should take advantage of the main results of transaction-cost economics, but move beyond them if it is to provide new insights. This is precisely the research programme sketched by the distinguished Princeton economist Avinash Dixit in *The Making of Economic Policy* (Dixit 1996).

The most significant transaction costs of EU-style integration are best understood as costs of collective ownership, i.e., by thinking of the member states as the 'owners' of the EU – in the same sense in which the members of a producer or consumer cooperative are, in fact, its owners. Ownership, as the term is conventionally used, has two essential attributes: the exercise of formal control and the receipt of residual gains. Formal control does not necessarily mean effective control. Thus, in business corporations, cooperatives, and mutual enterprises, formal control generally involves only the right to elect the firm's board of directors and to vote directly on a small set of fundamental issues, such as mergers or the dissolution of the firm (Hansmann 1996). The costs of ownership, and of collective ownership in particular, have received only limited attention by the new institutional economics of organization, while they have been either ignored or not recognized as such by writers on European integration. The costs of collective ownership may be broken down into three categories: the owners' costs of decision-making; the costs of delegation (or agency costs); and the costs of risk bearing.

To grasp intuitively the nature of decision-making costs in cases of collective ownership, think of a worker-owned firm. When many persons share ownership of a firm there are likely to be differences of opinion concerning the firm's policies and programmes. Serious problems arise especially when the outcome of the collective decision will affect different owners differently. Thus, if a worker-owned firm must shut down one of its two plants, the workers at the two plants are likely to have very different preferences about which plant should be chosen. When the interests of the individual owners differ, mechanisms for collective choice, such as voting, engender costs, known as 'costs of collective decision-making'.

The costs of collective decision-making are logically distinct from the agency costs discussed below. The latter costs arise in the context of a principal(s)–agent relation and include the costs of monitoring the agent and the costs resulting from the failure to monitor the agent with perfect effectiveness. On the other hand, the costs of collective decision-making can be significant even in modest-sized organizations, in which there are no hired managers and hence no significant agency costs. The costs associated with collective choice mechanisms are of two broad types. First, there are the costs resulting from decisions whose outcomes fail to maximize the aggregate welfare of the owners themselves as a group, favouring instead the interests of some subgroup. During the current euro crisis, for example, a number of key collective decisions were deemed to favour the interests of the creditor countries rather than the interests of the other members of the Eurozone, not to mention the interests all the members of the EU. Second, there are the costs of the decision-making process itself.

Examples of the second type of costs of collective decision-making are bargaining and influence costs. Bargaining costs are the costs involved in negotiations among different parties. They include not only the opportunity costs of bargainers' time, but also resources expended trying to improve one's bargaining position, the costs of monitoring and enforcing the agreement, and the losses from failure to reach an agreement. A most important source of bargaining costs at the supranational level is the opportunistic behaviour of bargainers mainly interested in national (rather than 'European') benefits and costs. Influence costs are the costs incurred in attempts to bias the decisions of the central institutions in a self-interested fashion; in attempts to counter such influence activities by others; and by the resulting degradation of the quality of decisions. Students of economic organizations have suggested that influence costs are one important reason why many, if not most, merged organizations cannot do everything the separate components did, and more (Williamson 1985; Milgrom and Roberts 1992). Judging from the extensive literature on interest groups in the EU, influence costs are at least as pervasive, and potentially even more serious, than bargaining costs in their distorting consequences. Influence costs are particularly significant when decisions are taken at the level of the European Council or of the EU Council of Ministers.

One of the main causes of high decision-making costs in the EU is the need to reach a collective decision satisfying different, even contradictory, national interests. As a result, many important issues might remain unresolved or are even completely neglected. Agreement on EMU, for example, was celebrated as a turning point in European integration. However, the Maastricht Treaty left unanswered a number of fundamental policy questions concerning monetary union. In order to make political agreement possible, the question of measures to coordinate economic policies, or to provide compensatory budgetary transfers, was sidestepped. Also, issues of external monetary policy, unitary external representation of the monetary union, exchange-rate policy, and political accountability were left unsettled. Even the basic question, whether it made economic sense to adopt a 'one-size-fits-all' monetary policy for structurally very different economies, was never properly discussed. As a result, EMU turned out to be a high-risk project with no easy exit option when things go wrong.

Delegation, or agency, costs are the second category of costs of collective ownership. One of the most significant features of the institutional architecture of the EC/EU is the extensive delegation of powers to the supranational institutions. According to Miles Kahler, the member states 'have delegated more important and extensive functions to European institutions than has been the case with the members of other international or regional institutions. The Commission, for example, surpasses even the strongest secretariat of an international organization' (Kahler 1995: 85). Agency costs are particularly significant in the case of multiple owners, or principals, all of whom have some power to influence the actions of the agent. What in the literature is known as 'common agency' is a situation where multiple principals try to influence the agent. In the usual case, i.e., when the principals have different preferences and priorities, the delegation produces results that are significantly inferior to what could be achieved by one truly unified principal. In part this is because the results that can be achieved when each principal offers a particular incentive to the agent tend to cancel each other out (for a formal proof of this and related results concerning multi-principal agencies, see Dixit 1996: 157–71).

The costs of risk bearing have been deliberately ignored in the EU before the seriousness of the euro crisis had to be officially admitted. As I argue elsewhere (Majone 2014), the political culture of European leaders, until recently, has been one of total optimism. The traditional approach to European integration (generally known as the Monnet strategy of *fait accompli*) implies that the success of a collective decision is determined by the decision-makers themselves – by the very fact that they agreed on the decision – rather than by those who will be affected by the eventual outcomes. This emphasis on the process of decision-making rather than on actual results excludes a priori the possibility of failure. For this reason the question of feasibility has been systematically ignored by integrationist leaders. Thus, there is no indication that the feasibility of the goal of the 1970 Werner Plan – monetary union by 1980 – was ever seriously considered. The so-called 'bicycle theory' of European integration – according to which integration must keep moving forward, especially in a crisis, for the bicycle (that the EU is seen to be) not to fall – provides the conceptual justification of the strategy of *fait accompli*. As noted above, the costs of risk bearing are today recognized and accepted (however reluctantly) by all EU leaders. It is, however, important to realize that, in the words of an economist at Goldman Sachs, Dirk Schumacher, 'as long as the main political legitimacy rests on the national level, there are limits to how much international risk-sharing is possible' (*Wall Street Journal*, 20–22 December 2013, p. 4).

A strong institutional leadership could reduce, if not annul, many of the costs mentioned above. However, the idea that leadership may be provided by a single country or institution is incompatible with the principle of 'collective leadership', hence with the assumption of the essential equality of all the member states. To understand the problem of leadership in the context of EU-style integration, it may be helpful to keep in mind that there are different kinds of leadership.

Three kinds of leadership

John Plamenatz (1973: 83–90), distinguishes three activities, all of them leadership in the broad sense of the word, which are important in the sphere of governance and politics: management; government; and leadership in the strict sense. Managers provide leadership by directing the work of others. Government, as distinct from management, consists, not in directing the work of others but in making rules for their guidance and applying those rules to them. Finally, leadership in the strict (political) sense consists in promoting or defining some goal that the people (or a section of them) share, or that the promoter hopes to get them to share. This kind of leadership consists, not in ruling or managing others, but in speaking for them. Speaking for people in the sense relevant here means, above all, giving expression to aims, beliefs, and feelings that people are willing to endorse, though they may never have thought about them until they were adopted by some trusted leader. To be a leader in this sense is to have a large say in defining goals, principles, and attitudes which are, or are supposed to be, shared.

Plamenatz's taxonomy allows us to identify situations that require leadership in the political sense of the term. In his classic study, *Leadership in Administration*, the well-known American sociologist Philip Selznick points out that when leadership (in Plamenatz's strict sense) fails, it is more often by default than by positive error. One type of default is the failure to set goals. Selznick writes:

> Once an organization becomes a 'going concern', with many forces working to keep it alive, the people who run it can readily escape the task of defining its purposes [...] there is the wish to avoid conflicts with those in and out of the organization who would be threatened by a sharp definition of purpose, with its attendant claims and responsibilities. (Selznick 1957: 25–26)

Much administrative analysis, he adds, takes the goal of the organization as given, whereas in many crucial instances this is precisely what is problematic. It is therefore important to emphasize the leader's responsibility to define the mission of the enterprise. A related type of default of leadership occurs when goals, however neatly formulated, enjoy only a superficial acceptance and do not really influence the total structure of the enterprise and its specific activities. It follows that the task of building special values and a distinctive competence into the organization is a prime function of leadership. Selznick's analysis of leadership relies heavily on the distinction between 'organization' and 'institution'. While the term 'organization' refers to an 'expendable tool', an 'institution' is a responsive, adaptive organism, heavily dependent on its social or political embedding, and on its contacts with the outside world. Keeping this distinction in mind, it becomes clear why the default of leadership shows itself in an acute form when organizational survival – or even organizational achievement in terms of resources, procedures, and stability – is confounded with institutional success.

The EU may be the clearest illustration of Selznick's thesis that, for the bare continuity of organizational existence, leadership in the strict sense is often dispensable. The greatest challenges to institutional leadership, on the other hand, arise when goals are not well defined, and when fluid situations require constant adaptation. Many of the present problems of European governance can be traced back to the scarcity of institutional leadership *relative to the scope of the powers transferred to the supranational level.* The fact that the need of leadership grows with the scope of institutional commitments should be as obvious as the point that the need of democratic legitimation grows with the scope of competences transferred to the supranational level. In fact, both needs are seldom recognized explicitly and hence deserve to be emphasized here. The 1957 Treaty of Rome did not require much institutional leadership since its most important articles were concerned with negative integration, i.e., the removal of obstacles to the free movement of people and goods (Majone 2009: 138–43). Given these limited objectives, the kinds of leadership discussed by Plamenatz under the labels of management, and of government as rule-making, were sufficient. The default of institutional leadership became increasingly apparent as successive treaties kept expanding supranational competences without a statement of mission more specific than 'ever closer union'; without robust popular support; and even without a corresponding increase in institutional resources. Indeed, the strategy of *fait accompli*, traditionally used to expand the activities of the EC/EU, represents the clearest admission of the absence of institutional leadership at the European level. This strategy consists in pushing ahead with ambitious integration projects without worrying too much about either feasibility or democratic legitimacy. The rationale behind this strategy, as Pascal Lamy clearly understood long ago, was the realization that the people were not ready to accept the steady expansion of supranational powers. Thus, instead of trying to rally the people in support of some clearly defined goals, Jean Monnet and his followers preferred, in Lamy's words, 'to get on without telling [the people] too much about what was happening' (cited in Ross 1995: 194). Such lack of trust is incompatible, not only with the notion of institutional leadership but also with the ideology of collective leadership.

The European Commission as would-be leader

A key element of the ideology behind the post-Second World War model of European integration was the basic equality and equal dignity of all members of the would-be community of nations, from the smallest to the largest: no leader but a 'collective leadership'. This principle of formal and (to the extent possible) substantive equality of the member states has inspired all the European treaties and also the day-to-day practice. It is also reflected in the design and *modus operandi* of EU institutions. Indeed, an important, if tacit, responsibility of the Commission is to ensure that the interests of the smaller member states are sufficiently taken into consideration – which explains why the strongest supporters of the Commission have always been the smaller countries. Clear evidence of the importance the smaller member states attach to being directly represented in this body is the promise made by the European Council, after the failure of the first Irish referendum on the Lisbon Treaty (June 2008) to abandon the planned reduction of the number of Commissioners – a promise meant to facilitate the success of the second referendum. The problem is that a return to the old rule of one Commissioner per member state would result in too high a number of Commissioners for the institution to work efficiently. With a membership of 28 states (with more to come in the future) at very different levels of socio-economic development and with quite different needs and priorities, it is increasingly difficult to follow the traditional 'one-size-fits-all' approach ('harmonization') to policymaking.

As a consequence of this diversity, in a number of important policy areas the Council does not receive enough proposals because the Commission itself cannot agree on what is needed or desirable. The problem is aggravated by the fact that the member states, old and new, increasingly see 'their' Commissioner as their own representative in the Commission. To avoid these and other difficulties, decisions are made by consensus, which means that with so many members the Commission can hardly take decisions (Piris 2011). Under such conditions this institution is unable not only to use its monopoly of legislative and policy initiative but even to exercise the weaker forms of leadership mentioned in a preceding section.

Thus the Commission, which many euro-enthusiasts used to see as the kernel of the future government of a politically united Europe, in fact looks more and more like an international bureaucracy and less and less like a proto-government. Even the European Council – the most likely candidate to provide leadership at the supranational level – is only able to achieve what the member states want it to achieve, with agreements hammered out, often bilaterally, beyond its walls (Peterson and Shackleton 2012). There are good reasons to believe that, short of a radical transformation, political leadership will always be an extremely scarce commodity in the EU. The problem is that in most circumstances a leaderless group will provide a less than optimal supply of a collective good – even if every member of the group desires that good. In a later section of this chapter we shall see how recent attempts to overcome the crisis of monetary union have undermined the principle of equality both within the euro group and between this group and the other members of the EU. This development is closely related to the steady loss of influence of the European institution, which, in the intentions of the founding fathers, should have provided all three kinds of leadership mentioned by Plamenatz. Indeed, the Commission is, or was meant to be, 'a distinct hybrid: the European Union's largest administrator and main policy manager, as well as a source of political and policy direction' (Peterson 2012: 96).

Walter Hallstein, the first president of the Commission from 1958 to 1967 stressed particularly the political function of this hybrid institution, often referring to himself as the equivalent of a European prime minister. Also Jacques Delors envisioned an economically and politically united Europe, with the Commission as the federal executive. Both Hallstein's and Delors's activism illustrate the pitfalls and risks of such analogies. Hallstein's attempt to turn the Commission into an embryonic government of the European Economic Community put him on a collision course with French president de Gaulle, who bitterly opposed any extension of the Commission's powers. The showdown came in early 1965, when Hallstein introduced proposals to link completion of the financial arrangement of the Common Agricultural Policy with greater executive authority for the Commission and budgetary powers for the European Parliament. The 'Empty Chair' crisis, which paralyzed the Community for seven months, was eventually resolved at a foreign ministers' meeting in Luxembourg on 28 and 29 January 1966, where agreement was reached to adopt an interim financial regulation for the CAP, deferring the question of additional powers for the Commission and the European Parliament. Both sides approved the famous Luxembourg Compromise, which maintained the principle of majority voting, but acknowledged that 'when very important issues are at stake, discussions must be continued until unanimous agreement is reached'. The Commission was in a marginalized position during the crisis and in finding a solution to it. In the words of Piers Ludlow (2006: 90), 'Community crisis and the need for political decisions brought the member states to the fore and minimised the scope for the Commission to use the vast technical expertise it had built up of the EEC's day-to-day operations'. The Commission was not invited to the ministerial discussions among the other five member states, and was even excluded from some of the meetings of the committee of permanent representatives. The regularity and frequency of such encounters during the period of the French boycott 'did graphically underline how completely the Commission had been pushed to the margins of a dispute it was widely – if rather unfairly – blamed for starting' (ibid.: 91).

Jacques Delors took over as president of the European Commission in January 1985. The new president was looking for a key project around which the process of European integration could be relaunched. After rejecting a number of possibilities that might fail to attract the unanimous support of the member states, Delors settled on the completion of the internal market as the central plank of his *rélance* of the integration process – the White Paper on *Completing the Internal Market* listed the obstacles to free movement within the Community and identified the types of action necessary to overcome these obstacles. All the approximately 300 measures of the legislative programme were to be adopted no later than by the end of 1992. More than 20 years after the 'Europe "'92'"' target, however, the single market is still far from being a reality. The most serious problem area when it comes to completing the single market was, and remains, the services sector. Since in all modern economies the services sector accounts for at least 70 per cent of GDP and 50 per cent of employment, the free movement of goods is no longer sufficient to ensure market integration. Most services are still regulated at the national level, while socio-economic conditions vary so much across the Union – income inequality, as measured by the Gini concentration coefficient, is far greater in the enlarged Union than in the USA – that centralized harmonization of national laws and regulations is likely to reduce aggregate welfare, while ex post harmonization, via regulatory competition, continues to meet strong political opposition from EU institutions and most member states. The aim of Delors's Single Market project was to open the EU internal borders to the free movement of all the factors of production and exchange, as within a nation state. This aim is generally supposed to have been more or less achieved but the truth is rather different: 'In many areas the Single Market exists in the books but, in practice, multiple barriers and regulatory obstacles fragment intra-EU trade and hamper economic initiative and innovation' (Piris 2011: 15).

Another aim of Delors was to advance political integration in Europe on the back of a programme of market liberalization. This goal has been missed even more patently than the single market for services. 'Delors wanted a politically integrated Europe. The first step was the single market, once you have a single market you have a single currency, and then the door is open to political integration'. This is how Alexandre Lamfalussy, at the time general manager of the Bank for International Settlements, summarized the grand strategy of the president of the European Commission in an interview with David Marsh in May 2007 (Marsh 2010: 122). In 1988 – almost 20 years after the initial announcement of the Werner Plan for achieving economic and monetary union by 1980 – Delors began a new campaign for EMU, and persuaded the European Council to set up a committee composed of central bankers and economic experts, under his (Delors's) chairmanship. Echoing the proposals of the 1970 Werner plan, the Delors Committee Report recommended a three-stage move to EMU, starting with closer economic and monetary coordination. Unfortunately, the document left many important questions open, supposedly to be settled by the governments later on. As explained by Delors himself to David Marsh in 2007, 'fundamentally EMU was a political issue that could only be decided by the governments. In the report, I wanted to draw attention to the need for sufficient economic coordination as a precondition for EMU' (ibid.).

What Delors called the 'acceleration of history' in Central and Eastern Europe in 1989 and 1990 made differences of opinion concerning monetary union appear relatively unimportant. Germany's attention was now focused on national reunification rather than European affairs, and this fact may have facilitated final agreement on EMU. At the same time, the geopolitical events of those years seemed to revive interest in European Political Union, but the most visible result of two years of frenetic discussions about the nature, scope, and competences of EPU was the three-pillar 'temple' of the Maastricht Treaty. Delors had vainly opposed this arrangement in favour of a 'tree' whose different functions would be connected to a common Community 'trunk' (Ross 1995). In fact, the Commission had very little influence over the negotiations on political union. Maastricht marked the end of the post-1985 *rélance* of European integration, rather than the big leap forward that Delors had wanted. George Ross has correctly identified the basic flaw in Delors's strategy: the failure of the French leader to realize that the traditional Monnet method of 'integration by stealth' could only work as long as Europe did not impact significantly on the daily lives of ordinary Europeans. After monetary union this method could not work anymore.

Delors was followed by Jacques Santer as Commission president. Presiding over an administration that had become inefficient, in some respects even chaotic, the Santer era culminated in the dramatic mass resignation of the entire Commission in March 1999, after the publication of a report of a Committee of Independent Experts, convened by the European Parliament, on charges of fraud, mismanagement, and nepotism. Since the resignation of Santer and his Commissioners, the institution that was supposed to drive integration forward has become increasingly weak. Thus the Commission was marginalized first in the negotiations that led to the Treaty of Nice, and then in the Convention on the Future of Europe that drafted the Constitutional Treaty. Romano Prodi, the new Commission president (1999–2004), proposed without success a constitutional structure in which almost all decisions would be taken by majority vote; closer cooperation among some member states would be excluded; and the Community method would be extended to apply to most policy areas, including the common foreign and security policy. Unsurprisingly, a former member of the Commission later lamented the Prodi Commission's 'astonishing weakness' (citation in Peterson 2012: 117). As noted above, today the Commission is unable, not only to use its monopoly of legislative and policy initiative, but even to exercise the weaker forms of leadership mentioned in a preceding section.

The euro crisis and the problem of the reluctant hegemon

In his classic study of the 1929–39 world depression, Charles Kindleberger writes: 'for the world economy to be stabilized, there has to be a stabilizer, one stabilizer' (Kindleberger 1973: 305). He goes on to note that in the 1970s leadership was a word with negative connotations, while collective decision-making was regarded as more 'aesthetic'. In those years the leadership of the USA was beginning to slip, and the American scholar doubted that 'the rising strength of Europe in an enlarged European Economic Community will be accompanied by an assertion of leadership [...] and assumption of responsibility for the stability of the world system' (ibid.: 307–08). In fact, neither the EEC nor the EU ever tried to assume responsibility for the stability of the world system. The present crisis of EMU has made clear that only Germany could provide the needed leadership – if not for the world system then at least for the Old Continent; not necessarily on a permanent basis but at least in the present predicament and in equally serious crisis situations of the future (see below). The attempt to establish a sort of French–German duopoly or diarchy – in the short *Merkozy* interlude – did not work, as Kindleberger would have predicted. Actually, this author could call attention to his discussion of the role of France in the great depression of the 1930s, to point out analogies with the present euro crisis:

> Not big enough to have responsibility forced on it, nor small enough to afford the luxury of irresponsibility the French position in the inter-war period was unenviable. It had the power to be a destabilizer, but was

> insufficiently powerful to stabilize [...] France could be (and was) blamed for upsetting the system when she had no capacity to take it over and run it in the presence of two larger powers, one feeble [the United Kingdom], the other irresponsible [the USA]. (Kindleberger 1973: 303)

Today's Germany is neither feeble like the United Kingdom in the interwar period nor irresponsible like the USA in the same period. However, in spite of its active role in the euro crisis, it is extremely reluctant to play the role of a true leader – for very good reasons having to do with history but also with the ideology of the European integration project. As far as history is concerned, one should always keep in mind Ludwig Dehio's conclusion that the only occasion on which the peoples of Europe seem to display solidarity is when they oppose the hegemonic aspirations of one of the states of the continent (Dehio 1961: 25). This historical legacy explains why the basic equality and equal dignity of all the member states is a key element of the ideology of European integration, as noted above. Given the level of mutual mistrust, especially in crisis situations, it is thus almost unimaginable that the members of the EU, large or small, would be willing to accept a German hegemony, even though Germany, de facto, already conditions the economies of the other member states in important respects.

A common currency was supposed to accelerate the process of economic and political convergence towards a common model of European governance. Paradoxically, one unanticipated consequence of monetary union has been the extent to which the competitive position of the members of the Eurozone have diverged. Italy, Spain, Portugal, Greece, and, more recently, France have lost a significant amount of competitiveness, while Germany, Austria, the Netherlands, and a few other northern countries have gained a significant amount of competitiveness. The other unanticipated consequence of EMU is the general acknowledgment of the infeasibility of political union, now and in the foreseeable future. The possible consequences of the present state of affairs have been drawn by the Hungarian-born American financier George Soros who, in an essay published in September 2012, argued that in order to avoid a definitive split of the Eurozone into creditor and debtor countries, and thus a likely collapse of the EU itself, Germany must resolve a basic dilemma: either assume the role of the 'benevolent hegemon' or else leave the Eurozone.

If Germany were to give up the euro, leaving the Eurozone in the hands of the debtor countries, all problems that now appear to be insoluble could be resolved through currency depreciation, improved competitiveness, and a new status of the ECB as lender of last resort. The common market would survive, but the relative position of Germany and of other creditor countries that might wish to leave the Eurozone would change from the winning to the losing side. Both groups of countries could avoid such problems if only Germany were willing to assume the role of the benevolent hegemon. However, this would require the more or less equal treatment of debtor and creditor countries, and a much higher rate of growth, with consequent inflation. These may well be unacceptable conditions for the German leaders, for the Bundesbank, and especially for the German voters. At any rate, both conditions could be satisfied only with significant progress on the road to a political union, in which Germany would accept the responsibilities implied by its leadership role (Soros 2012). In a later essay, Soros (2013) added that the present problems are the consequences of the fatal flaw of the European monetary union: in creating the ECB as a fully independent central bank the member states effectively indebted themselves in a currency which they cannot control. As a consequence, when the risk of a Greek default became concrete, the financial markets reacted by reducing the status of all heavily indebted members of the Eurozone to that of developing countries with large debts in a foreign currency.

Also, some German commentators have recently maintained that their country should agree to play a hegemonic role, and not just in the present crisis. One of the clearest statements of this view is an essay by Christoph Schoenberger, 'Hegemon wider Willen' [Unwilling hegemon] (Schoenberger 2012). The author argues that the crisis of the Eurozone has made clear what people have been reluctant to acknowledge in the past, namely that Germany has become the hegemonic power in Europe. While this leading role provides a unique possibility to influence the future of the Old Continent, it also entails duties and burdens. Unfortunately, German political leaders and public opinion are quite unprepared to meet this challenge. In fact, as the old East–West conflicts and the post-war division of Germany pass into history, awareness of the precarious situation of the country, placed as it is at the heart of Europe, seems to recede. And yet German guidance is precisely what Europe needs in order to face up to the uncertainties and challenges of the twenty-first century, according to Schoenberger. The largest, most populous and economically most powerful member of the EU cannot evade this responsibility. To speak of German hegemony is not to advocate Germany's dominance over the rest of Europe, but only to recognize the fact that there are no strong and democratically legitimated institutions at the European level. Those who criticize the European Commission for its alleged interference in domestic affairs, for example, do not realize that very little can happen in Brussels without the agreement of the governments and the bureaucracies of the member states. Even the European Parliament tends to be ignored by voters who see no connections between national and European politics. The steadily decreasing turnouts in European Parliament elections provide the clearest proof of the people's indifference towards the institution that should represent them at the European level. In fact, the crisis of the Eurozone, with its sequel of summits of the heads of government following one another, has emphasized the intergovernmental features of the Union. On the other hand, the difficulty of finding a solution of the present crisis at the intergovernmental level, under the assumption of the basic equality of all the member states, can only lead to the conclusion that what the EU needs is a hegemonic power – a need usually concealed by the search for consensus which characterizes decision-making in Brussels.

Unfortunately, the argument continues, Germany is not mentally prepared to assume the burden of a hegemonic role in Europe, and also its institutions were not designed for such a task. Thus, the Bundestag, under the pressure of public opinion and the influence of recent decisions of the German Constitutional Court, has developed a tendency to limit more and more the freedom of action of the federal government in foreign and European affairs, pretending that the decisions of the executive in this area should depend on explicit parliamentary mandates. What, then, are the alternatives to a German hegemony? The only reasonable alternative, according to Schoenberger, would be a strengthening of the supranational institutions to make them dependent, not on the agreement and directions of the national governments, but on the support of European voters. Unfortunately, such a solution is impossible since the EU has been designed around an inter-governmental core, as the present crisis has amply demonstrated. Thus we are back to the need of a 'wise' German hegemony – unless we are prepared to accept the break-up of the Union.

It is refreshing to read such a crisp analysis of an issue that most Germans, in all walks of life, prefer to ignore. Unfortunately, the analysis is far from being either entirely convincing or complete. First, the author starts from the traditional notion of hegemony as preponderance of material resources. Other, more refined, notions of hegemony and hegemonic stability do not assert an automatic link between power and leadership (see below). But even the cruder notion does not seem to fit the facts. While it is certainly true that Germany is larger, more populous, and economically more powerful than any of its European partners, its superiority is hardly as clear as in historically undisputed cases of international hegemony. In the nineteenth century, the *Pax Britannica* was based not only on Britain's naval supremacy but also on Britain's pioneering role in the first industrial revolution, on the higher productivity of its industry, at least until the 1870s, and on the role of London as the financial centre of the world. The *Pax Americana* of the 1950s and 1960s was based on the absolute superiority of the USA in production, services, research and development, technological innovation, not to mention military might. Today Germany does not play any comparable role, even on the modest European scale. In particular, this country is hardly a leader in the services sector, which, as we know, accounts for more than 70 per cent of the GDP of all modern economies. In the case of financial services, for example, the European leader is Britain, not Germany.

The more sophisticated notion of hegemony emphasizes the importance of domestic attitudes, political structures, and decision-making processes: 'Decisions to exercise leadership are necessary to "activate" the posited relationship between power capabilities and outcomes' (Keohane 1984: 35). Schoenberger is fully aware that this kind of 'force activation' is still lacking in Germany; unfortunately, he gives no idea of how this limitation could be overcome, or how hegemonic stability could be maintained once the present crisis of the Eurozone is somehow resolved. The most serious flaw in the analysis of the German scholar, however, is the implicit assumption that, barring a total collapse of the EU, European integration will remain stable at the present level, or even resume its march towards 'more Europe' once the crisis is over. In fact, integration is becoming more differentiated, and there are also clear indications of a retrograde movement in several respects. Thus, the goal of a truly integrated European market appears to be less and less feasible; and it can even be argued that the European market is actually less integrated today than twenty or thirty years ago. This is because of the growing importance of services, which, as was noted above, are still largely regulated domestically; but also because growing socio-economic heterogeneity within the Union makes policy harmonization increasingly problematic.

Again, monetary union was originally meant to be a public good, shared by all member states, while it turned out to be a club good (see the following section). Recent proposals of two-speed integration (e.g., by Piris 2011 and by Bofinger et al. 2012) go in the same direction of differentiated integration. At the end of this process of opting out, making exceptions, and separating avant-gardes and rear guards, we may reach a situation where a hegemon leading the entire membership of the EU is no longer needed: either the aims of European integration are redefined to include a few, limited, and widely shared goals – a return to the spirit of the Rome Treaty with few, concrete commitments, and collective leadership; or else the EU becomes a 'club of clubs', with the supranational level mainly responsible for monitoring competition among different territorial and/or functional clubs (Majone 2014). As noted above, it seems to be highly unlikely that European integration can remain stable at the present level. In fact, the crisis of monetary union and the remedies so far adopted have already deeply transformed the nature of the EU.

European integration: from collective good to club good

The cost of adhering to the principle of the essential equality of all the member states keeps growing as the membership of the EU expands and more and more competences are transferred to the supranational level. As mentioned in an earlier section, the incentives for group action diminish as group size increases, so that larger groups are less able to act in their common interest than small ones. This is why participation in large voluntary organizations depends, not on the collective benefits but on the individualized incentives these organizations provide. For the EU, however, it is increasingly difficult to provide such incentives since its resources do not grow in proportion to its expanding membership and to the growing scope of its competences.

If neither the leadership nor the incentives and sanctions that make collective action possible is available, then one may well doubt whether EU-style integration may still be properly considered to be a collective good. Thus, monetary union, initially conceived as a collective good to be shared by all the member states of the EU, was quickly transformed into a 'club good' by the British and Danish *de jure* opt-outs and by Sweden's de facto opt-out. According to the economic theory of clubs (Buchanan 1965), a 'club good' is a public good from whose benefits individuals may be (or may wish to be) excluded; an association established to provide an excludable public good is a 'club'. The same definitions apply if, instead of individuals, we consider independent states. Associations of independent states, such as confederations, are typically voluntary, and their members are exclusively entitled to enjoy certain benefits produced by the association. The club goods in question may be collective security, policy coordination, common technical standards – or a monetary union limited to a subset of members. The important point is that as an association of states expands the cost of uniformity in the provision of collective goods can escalate dramatically. The economic theory of clubs predicts an increase in the number of voluntary associations to meet the increased demand of goods more precisely tailored to the different requirements of various subsets of more homogeneous states. Aggregate welfare is maximized when the variety in preferences is matched by a corresponding variety of institutional arrangements.

Buchanan's economic theory of clubs provides a good conceptual foundation for the functional (rather than territorial) approach to supranational governance – an approach advocated by David Mitrany in the 1940s and by Ralph Dahrendorf in the 1970s. The essential principle of a functional organization of supranational activities, according to Mitrany, 'is that activities would be selected specifically and organized separately, each according to its nature, to the conditions under which it has to operate, and to the needs of the moment' (citation in Eilstrup-Sangiovanni 2006: 57). At the same time, Mitrany was sceptical about the advantages of political unions. His main objection to schemes for continental unions was that the closer the union the more inevitably would it be dominated by the more powerful member – a point which has been hardly considered by later writers on European integration but is becoming highly relevant today, as suggested by the above discussion of Germany as potential, if reluctant, hegemon.

The economic theory of clubs emphasizes the advantages of institutional pluralism, and implies that an efficient assignment of tasks between different levels of governance need not coincide with existing national boundaries: there may be significant externalities and a need for coordination between some, but not all, regions within a country or group of countries. The theory also explains why a number of tasks which used to be assigned to central governments are today performed by private, increasingly transnational, organizations. Although there is a strong historical correlation between standardization and the emergence of the sovereign territorial state (Spruyt 1994), current views on standardization have changed radically as a result of the advance of globalization, the development of technology, and the growing variety and sophistication of technical standards. As Alessandra Casella (1996) has argued, the fact that in today's integrating world economy the relevant community of standards users need not be territorially defined, distinguishes the traditional approach from the contemporary understanding of standards as a special class of club goods. Moreover, as the complexity of a society increases, the number of clubs tends to increase as well. This is because greater diversity of needs and preferences makes it efficient to produce a broader range of club goods. The general implication of Casella's argument is that top-down harmonization may be desirable when the market is relatively small and homogeneous. In a large market, on the other hand, harmonization tends to be brought about by the recognition of similar demands or needs, rather than by a policy imposed from the top. Hence a multiplicity of club goods tends to replace harmonized policies.

A Europe of clubs organized around functional tasks would not exclude the possibility of large projects supported by all the member states – as long as there is clear evidence (through referendums, supermajorities in national parliaments, etc.) of sufficient popular support. This is precisely the point Dahrendorf wished to emphasize with his statement that 'everyone does what he wants and [...] no one must participate in everything', a situation that 'though far from ideal is surely much better than avoiding anything that cannot be cooked in a single pot' (cited in Gillingham 2003: 91–92). Concretely this meant that there would be common European policies in areas where the member states have a common interest, but not otherwise. This, said Dahrendorf, must become the general rule rather than the exception if we wish to prevent continuous demands for special treatment, destroying in the long run the coherence of the entire system.

The view of Europe as a 'club of clubs', far from being new, has deep roots in the history of the Old Continent. As several distinguished historians have argued, the European global dominance of the past was made possible not by centralization but by fragmentation and by the competition stimulated by fragmentation. In turn, political rivalry facilitated the commercial revolution of the Middle Ages by making it possible for the mercantile community to bypass, where necessary, the rules of this or that city or state. The Hanseatic League, which has been viewed by some scholars as a major unifying force in northern Europe, developed from being an association of merchants to a league of towns on the Baltic and the North Sea. One of the tasks of the league was to facilitate the exchange of information between merchants, but the Hansa was not merely an economic association. Like a state, it waged wars, and on occasion it could make or break kings. In fact, the Hansa was an alternative to the sovereign state (Spruyt 1994: chap. 6). The 'European miracle' made possible by a unique combination of competition and cooperation continued in later centuries. The states of early modern Europe were surrounded by actual or potential competitors. Hence the fairly rapid diffusion of policy and institutional innovations throughout the continent in the period preceding the full development of the nation state. In its state-system, writes Eric Jones (1987:115), 'Europe had a portfolio of competing and colluding polities whose spirit of competition was adapted to diffuse best practice'. But as the national states of Europe became more self-conscious they began to impede the movement of capital and people by closing their borders and enforcing cultural and legal homogeneity on their people. The long century of nationalism that followed was an aberration in European history, and the integration process started after the Second World War was a healthy, indeed a necessary, reaction to the catastrophic consequences of nationalist ideology. In the early stages of the integration process it was not unreasonable to assume that the European Economic Community would evolve, sooner or later, into a politically integrated bloc, perhaps even into something like a federation. That assumption is no longer tenable in a Union of 28 members at vastly different stages of socio-economic development, with different geopolitical concerns, and correspondingly diverse policy priorities. A Europe of clubs seems to be the only solution of the present crisis of European integration that is both feasible and historically justified.

References

Bofinger, P., Habermas, J., and Nida-Ruemelin, J. (2012) 'Einspruch gegen die Fassendemokratie' [Protest against a would-be democracy], *Frankfurter Allgemeine Zeitung*, 4 August.

Buchanan, J. (1965) 'An Economic Theory of Clubs', *Economica*, 32(1), 1–14.

Casella, A. (1996) 'Free Trade and Evolving Standards, in J. Bhagwati and R. Hudec (eds), *Fair Trade and Harmonization*, vol. 1, Cambridge, MA: MIT Press, 119–56.

Cornes, R., and Sandler, T. (1996) *The Theory of Externalities, Public Goods and Club Goods*, Cambridge: Cambridge University Press.

Dehio, L. (1961) *Deutschland und die Weltpolitik im 20. Jahrhundert*, Frankfurt: Fischer Bücherei.

Dixit, A. (1996) *The Making of Economic Policy*, Cambridge, MA: MIT Press.

Eilstrup-Sangiovanni, M. (2006) *Debates on European Integration*, New York: Palgrave Macmillan.

Furubotn, E., and Richter, R. (2000) *Institutions and Economic Theory*, Ann Arbor: University of Michigan Press.

Gillingham, J. (2003) *European Integration, 1950–2003*, Cambridge: Cambridge University Press.

Hansmann, H. (1996) *The Ownership of Enterprise*, Cambridge, MA: Belknap Press.

Jones, E. (1987) *The European Miracle*, 2nd edn, Cambridge: Cambridge University Press.

Kahler, M. (1995) *International Institutions and the Political Economy of Integration*, Washington, DC: Brookings Institution.

Keohane, R. (1984) *After Hegemony*, Princeton, NJ: Princeton University Press.

Kindleberger, C. (1973) *The World in Depression*, Berkeley and Los Angeles: University of California Press.

Ludlow, P. (2006) 'De-Commissioning the Empty Chair Crisis: The Community Institutions and the Crisis of 1965-66', in J.-M. Palayret, H. Wallace and P. Winand (eds), *Visions, Votes and Vetoes*, Brussels: Peter Lang, 79–96.
Majone, G. (2009) *Europe as the Would-be World Power: The EU at Fifty*, Cambridge: Cambridge University Press.
(2014) *Rethinking the Union of Europe post-Crisis – Has Integration Gone Too Far?* Cambridge: Cambridge University Press.
Marsh, D. (2010) *The Euro*, New Haven, CT: Yale University Press.
Milgrom, J., and Roberts, P. (1992) *Economics, Organization and Management*, Englewood Cliffs, NJ: Prentice-Hall.
North, D. (1990) 'A Transaction Cost Theory of Politics', *Journal of Theoretical Politics*, 2(4), 355–67.
Olson, M. (1971) *The Logic of Collective Action*, Cambridge, MA: Harvard University Press.
Peterson, J. (2012) 'The College of Commissioners', in J. Peterson and M. Shackleton (eds), *The Institutions of the European Union*, 3rd edn, Oxford: Oxford University Press, 96–123.
Peterson, J., and Shackleton, M. (2012) 'Conclusion', in J. Peterson and M. Shackleton (eds), *The Institutions of the European Union*, 3rd edn, Oxford: Oxford University Press, 382–402.
Piris, J.-C. (2011) 'It is Time for the Euro Area to Develop Further Closer Cooperation among its Members', Jean Monnet Working Paper 05/11, NYU School of Law.
Plamenatz, J. (1973) *Democracy and Illusion*, London: Longman.
Ross, G. (1995) *Jacques Delors and European Integration*, London: Polity Press.
Schoenberger, C. (2012) 'Hegemon wider Willen' [Unwilling hegemon], *Merkur*, 66(1), 25–33.
Selznick, P. (1957) *Leadership in Administration*, New York: Harper & Row.
Soros, G. (2012) 'Deutschland muss führen oder aus dem Euro austreten' [Germany must lead or else give up the euro], *Spiegel*, 9 September.
(2013) 'Falls Jemand den Euro verlässt, sollte es Deutschland sein' [If anybody should leave the euro it ought to be Germany], *Spiegel*, 9 April.
Spruyt, H. (1994) *The Sovereign State and its Competitors*, Princeton, NJ: Princeton University Press.
Williamson, O. (1985) *The Economic Institutions of Capitalism*, New York: Free Press.
Winkler, H. A. (2012) *Geschichte des Westens*, vol. 1, 3rd edn, Munich: Verlag C. H. Beck.

10

Europe's legitimacy problem and the courts

DIETER GRIMM

How the Court of Justice revolutionized the European Union and thereby enhanced its own power

It is well known that the European Union (EU) became what it is today, a unique political entity somewhere between an international organization and a federal state, mainly through the jurisprudence of its Court of Justice. It is also known that, at times, the progress of European integration was propelled more by judgments of this court than by political decisions of the heads of state and government of the member states or the Council of Ministers of the EU. The discreet way in which courts used to operate was a precondition of this type of progress. Meanwhile, however, it became apparent that this 'integration by stealth' is a source of the legitimacy problem that the EU has been facing for quite some time (Majone 2005; Rose 2014). It seems that this path toward integration reached its limits. The role of the Court has to be reconsidered.

The jurisprudence that revolutionized the EU began with two seminal judgments of 1963 and 1964 whose impact extended far beyond their immediate cause. In *Van Gend and Loos*, decided six years after the foundation of the European Economic Community (EEC) upon a referral by a Dutch court, the Court had to answer the question whether an individual was entitled to bring an action based on an alleged violation of the Treaty of Rome against a member state in a national court.[1] The EEC started as a customs union; the then Article 12 of the Treaty forbade the member states to introduce new customs or increase the existing ones. The Netherlands had done just that and the logistic enterprise *Van Gend and Loos* had been asked to pay the increased tariff. It challenged the order in the Netherlands, based on Article 12.

1 *Van Gend en Loos*, EU:C:1963:1.

It was not controversial that the Netherlands had violated the Treaty. Controversial was the remedy. On the one hand, there could be no doubt that individuals affected by a state act that violated the Treaty had no access to the Court. On the other hand, it was equally clear that the Commission could start a Treaty violation procedure in the Court against a defaulting member state. The question was whether an individual could claim a treaty violation by a member state before this member state's courts. The Treaties remained silent with regard to this question. But that did not mean that the Court could leave it open. Rather, the answer had to be derived from more general considerations about the nature and the purpose of the Treaty.

The Treaty of Rome was a treaty under international law concluded by sovereign states. In the Treaty the states had transferred a number of sovereignty rights to the EEC, including the right to levy customs. The provisions were binding for the parties to the Treaty under international law, but the violation of an obligation under international law did not trigger immediate consequences in domestic law. In the absence of a clear will of the contracting parties, international treaties, according to general understanding, would not convey individual rights against a member state on private persons. This was the position taken by the governments of three member states that participated in the litigation. And this was also the opinion of Advocate General Roemer in this case.

The Court, to the contrary, found that the Treaty applied directly in the member states and had to be enforced by their courts. In its view the clear and unambiguous prohibition to increase existing tariffs created direct relations between the member states and the individuals submitted to their authority. This result could have hardly been reached under the traditional understanding of the scope of international law. The Court departed from this understanding and set out to declare the European Treaties 'a new legal order of public international law'. The new element was just the inclusion of the individuals. The Court derived this from the purpose of the Treaty to establish a common market whose functioning directly affects the citizens of the member states and therefore exceeds traditional international relations.

In *Van Gend and Loos*, the Court had remained silent about the question what the judgment meant with regard to contradicting national law. It could leave this question open because the Dutch Constitution, different from the other member states' constitutions, granted international law primacy over domestic law. It was clear that the Treaty imposed an obligation on the member states to adjust national law to European requirements. But was it also self-executing in the sense that in the case of a conflict the national law automatically lost its applicability? In *Costa* v. *ENEL* the Court answered this question in favor of the second alternative.[2] No national court or other agency was permitted to apply it. In cases of doubt, national courts had to refer the question of compatibility to the Court whose decision was binding for them.

What remained open after *Costa* v. *ENEL* was the question whether the primacy or European law was confined to ordinary law of the member states of whether it extended also to the national constitutions. This had been denied in particular by the Italian Constitutional Court. In *Internationale Handelsgesellschaft* the Court of Justice declared in 1970 that national constitutions were not exempted from the primacy of European law and confirmed in 1978 in *Simmenthal II* that domestic courts had to leave contradicting domestic law unapplied without prior involvement of the national constitutional courts.[3] Since then, Article 100 of the German Basic Law, which reserves the power to the Federal Constitutional Court to declare a German law void or inapplicable, is no longer true.

The path to these findings had been paved by a preliminary methodological turn of the Court of Justice. Up to then, the guideline for interpreting international treaties had always been the will of the contracting states. Every provision that limited their sovereignty had to be construed narrowly unless a clear intent to the opposite existed. The Court, in accordance with the idea that the Treaty of Rome was an autonomous new legal order that had emancipated itself from the national sources, departed from the traditional methodology and interpreted the Treaty in a constitutional mode, namely more or less detached from the member states' will and instead according to an objectivized purpose (Annweiler 1997; Grundmann 1997; Buck 1998; Beck 2013).

Part of this methodological turn was the so-called '*effet utile*', which rounds out the direct effect and the supremacy of European law. *Effet utile* meant that, among the possible interpretations of community law provisions, the understanding had to be chosen that allowed the EEC to exhaust its powers in the most extensive way. By the same token, the *effet utile* restricted the scope of application of national law. It had to be applied narrowly wherever it came in touch with European law. The Court understood the *effet utile* not only as a guideline for its own interpretation of the Treaty, but also for the national courts when they had to determine the scope and meaning of European law.

2 *Costa*, EU:C:1964:66.

3 *Internationale Handelsgesellschaft*, EU:C:1970:114; *Simmenthal*, EU:C:1978:49.

The judgments have rightly been called revolutionary (Weiler 1994). What the Court derived from the Treaty had not been agreed upon explicitly by the founding states, and it seems doubtful whether the Treaty would have been adopted had it explicitly contained provisions as to this result. Revolutionary was also the method of interpretation that allowed the Court to reach this result, and revolutionary were above all the effects of the judgments. They transformed the European Community from an international organization among many, albeit with larger powers and a denser organizational structure, into a supranational entity *sui generis* and its law into a superior order above all national law.

The first ones to discover the true dimension of the judgments were American scholars of European law (in particular, Weiler 1991: 2413). They interpreted the development as a 'constitutionalization' of the Treaty. In its legal nature the Treaty continued to be a treaty under international law, which can be amended only by a unanimous decision of the member states. Its source is not a European *pouvoir constituant*. The member states are the 'Masters of the Treaties'. But in its application the Treaty became independent from the will of the member states and bound them not like international law but like a constitution. They were no longer able to determine the meaning of their product and even lost the power to guarantee the applicability of their own law.

Van Gend and Loos and *Costa* v. *ENEL* are widely regarded as an act of self-empowerment of the Court, not in the sense that it acted on its own initiative – after all, the questions had been referred to it by Dutch and Italian courts – but in the sense that the way it answered the questions enhanced its own power. Nevertheless, it seems too easy to explain this in terms of institutional self-interest of judges, as some political scientists would have it. This explanation does not sufficiently consider the logic of judicial decision-making. Rather, one has to distinguish between intent and effect. The Court's intent was clearly actively to promote the purpose of the Treaty, namely to establish a common market. At the same time, however, this had the effect of an extension of its own powers at the expense of the member states.

How the Court used its newly acquired power

As an immediate consequence of the two revolutionary judgments the member states and their European organ, the Council, were no longer needed to establish the single market. Direct effect and supremacy of European law allowed the Commission (as the organ charged with enforcing the treaties vis-à-vis the member states) and the Court (as the organ charged with determining the meaning of the Treaties in concrete cases) to take the task of implementing economic integration in their own hands. If they declared that national law impeded the common market, it became inapplicable without the member states having a realistic chance to defend the domestic law. Everything depended then on which concept of integration the Court had and whether it got a chance to realize it.

The most important instrument to provide the Court with opportunities to realize its concept was the referral procedure. Yet, the instrument could only be used by national courts. They decided whether to refer questions of compatibility between national and European law to Luxembourg. Lower courts may do that, last instance courts have to do it. But the Court was not in a position to enforce this duty. The European Court depended on the cooperation of the national courts. However, national courts were generally willing to cooperate. So, the referral procedure, not the treaty violation procedure initiated by the Commission, became the centerpiece of the Court's activity. Again, we owe the explanation of this by no means evident behavior of national courts to American observers (Alter 2001; Stone Sweet 2004).

In substance, the Court pursued the goal of market integration with considerable zeal, subordinating other concerns to this goal. It was a Court with an agenda (Streinz 2010; Wahl 2013: 248). Although designed as an arbiter between the EU and the member states – each side had the right to appeal to the Court because of an alleged Treaty violation of the other side – the Court sided with the EU. Based on the *effet utile*, it expanded the European competences and to the same extent limited the range of national law. Powers transferred to the EU were interpreted broadly, powers retained by the member states narrowly. The same is true for the principle of proportionality. It is applied with a double standard. The member states' laws are submitted to strict scrutiny, while a lenient standard of review is applied to European law.

The beneficiaries of the ensuing jurisprudence were the four economic freedoms (free movement of goods, services, labor and capital). Originally, they were understood as guidelines for legislative measures to establish the Common Market. The member states were obliged to abolish market-detrimental law. Harmonized market-conforming EU law could be enacted by the Council. The Court transformed the four freedoms from objective legal principles into fundamental rights of the economic actors who thus got an instrument to pursue their economic interests judicially. The economic integration no longer depended on the willingness of the member states to adapt their law to the four freedoms. The Court itself could eliminate all impediments to market integration that it discovered in the laws of the member states. There is a detailed account of the consequences for national law so that a few remarks may suffice here (Mangold 2011).

While the Court had originally interpreted the Treaty provisions that prohibited national tariffs and protectionist measures in an anti-discriminating way, it later on underlay the Treaties with an anti-regulatory ratio. Thus, all national laws that in some way or other impeded the exercise of the four economic freedoms became a target for the Court. The Treaty prohibitions thereby lost their contours since any national law may, under certain circumstances, impede the free movement, social law, educational law, divorce law etc. As a consequence, domestic law that had no discriminative motive, not even an economic motive at all, but pursued some other goal such as health, product safety, workplace safety etc., could be declared incompatible with the Treaties.

In a similar vein, the Treaty prohibition of state aids to economic enterprises, which distorted or threatened to distort the competition, were extended to public institutions that rendered services to the population. The motives for establishing a public service and the capacity of the market to provide this service in a satisfactory manner played no important role. It is true that all these Treaty prohibitions contain exceptions in the interest of public morality, public policy, public security etc. But they were usually interpreted narrowly. On the other hand, the understanding of the Treaty allowed the Court to extend the scope of European law into areas where the EU lacked legislative powers like labor law, social security law, tax law, so that here the member states were no longer free to use legislative powers that they had not transferred to the EU.

What the Court could not do, however, was replace the abolished national law by European law and regulate the privatized services. This required European legislation. It was, however, easier to abolish law of the member states than to enact European law. Deregulation at the national level happens by the stroke of a pen of the Commission or the Court. Re-regulation on the European level is a difficult procedure with many veto players and high hurdles. It worked in some fields like environmental law, not in others. The consequence was the well-known asymmetry between negative and positive integration, negative integration meaning the elimination of domestic law, positive integration meaning the creation of European law (Scharpf 1999: 43; Majone 2005: 143).

This asymmetry accounts for the liberalizing tendency of European integration as pursued by the Commission with the backing of the Court

(Scharpf and Schmidt 2000; Höpner and Schäfer 2008; Joerges and Rödl 2009; Scharpf 2010: 221 and 352; Schmidt and Thatcher 2013). It leaves a gap between national deregulation and European reregulation. The privatization of public services does not only concern the ownership (sometimes the owner remains the state), but the logic these institutions follow: from public service to profit orientation. National regulation of privatized services in the interest of the public that depends on them are regarded with suspicion in Brussels. Even the social policy, although not transferred to the EU, comes under pressure. In a liberalized economy a high standard of social protection disadvantages the national economy and therefore meets political obstacles.

This is not to say that, regarding the choice between a social-market economy and a liberal-market economy, the Court deliberately took sides for the neo-liberal program. Such opinions exist (references in Kokott 2011). But they miss the difference between intent and effect. As far as intent is concerned, the Court pursued a legal goal, the establishment and maintenance of the common market. However, because of the Court's decision to constitutionalize the Treaties and to transform the economic freedoms from objective principles to subjective rights of the economic actors, combined with their extensive interpretation, its jurisprudence developed a liberalizing *effect.*

As a consequence of the interpretation of the economic freedoms as subjective rights of the market participants, the vast majority of cases in Luxembourg developed out of claims of economic actors who found national regulations detrimental to their economic activities. If the claims were successful – and, because of the pro-European attitude of the Court, they often were – they led to measures of negative integration whereas the Court was unable to fill the regulatory gaps that it had opened nor could it require the legislative organs of the EU to compensate for the loss created by its jurisprudence. In turn, the liberalization that was the consequence of this jurisprudence made it more difficult for the member states to uphold their standards of social policies.

But there are still more means to reduce the space for national legislation. One is the interpretation of the effect of European directives (Prechal 2005). Different from EU regulations, directives leave room for national decisions as to the ways and means of implementation. However, this space has been constantly narrowed. The Court ruled that, in the case of non-compliance or insufficient compliance, the directive applies directly within the member states, provided it is clear and precise enough. In addition, the Court required national courts to interpret domestic law in conformity with directives, regardless of whether the specific law implements a directive or depends on a directive and even regardless of the legislative competence of the EU. Directives are declared applicable even before the deadline for implementation ends.

The most recent example of an elimination of national law can be observed in the field of basic rights (for a survey, see Kühling 2009). Already before the adoption of the European Charter of Fundamental Rights the Court had begun to determine the scope of the judge-made rights broadly and even extended them into areas where the EU had no competences. In order to limit the application of the Charter, the member states declared in Article 51 that EU fundamental rights apply to the institutions of the EU, but to the member states 'only' when they are implementing European law. In addition, Article 51 stated that the Charter 'does not extend the field of application of Union law beyond the powers of the Union'. According to the Court's understanding, implementing European law implies the application of national law provided that this is somehow connected to Union law. Moreover, it holds on to its view that the member states have to observe the economic freedoms also when they exercise national competences.[4]

This would not matter greatly if the Charter and the member states' bills of rights were more or less the same. This is true to a large extent regarding the textual level. The European Charter contains more rights than most constitutions of the member states, but avoids contradictions to the national Bills of Rights. Yet, considerable differences appear on the level of interpretation. While the national constitutional courts tend to give priority to personal and communicative rights over economic rights, the Court does it the other way round. There are examples to the contrary. But they are not sufficient to indicate a change in trend. Where the member states enjoy the greatest freedom to regulate according to their constitutional law they are most strictly limited by EU law as understood by the Court.

Why the jurisprudence creates a legitimacy problem

'Integration through law' is usually told as a success story in which the Court appears as the hero. And a success story it is, at least insofar as the economic integration is concerned. But the economic perspective is not the only possible one. The success had a legitimacy drawback whose deeper reasons are still not sufficiently noticed. The focus of the article is on those reasons. It does not aim at answering the question whether the

4 In fields like data protection that permeate many legislative areas this opens a door for a particular wide influence of EU beyond its powers (Grimm 2013).

two judgments of 1963 and 1964 and the jurisprudence based on them were right or wrong from a legal point of view. Direct effect and supremacy of EU law are meanwhile generally accepted and the question is only whether they apply unconditionally or whether there are certain '*contro limiti*'[5] derived from the constitutions of the member states.

As an immediate effect of the jurisprudence, there are now two paths toward integration instead of one. The first path was opened by the Treaty itself. It consists of a transfer of powers from the member states to the EU. This path requires a unanimous decision in the conference of heads of state and government, followed by ratification in each member state, which has to be compatible with the national constitution. No member state can be ignored. The power shift that takes place on this path is rooted in the explicit will of the member states. Because this will is formed democratically, the power shift can be ultimately attributed to the peoples of the member states. Should they no longer agree, the member states may reverse the power shift by the same procedure or leave the Union.

The second path is not explicitly provided by the Treaty. It was opened by the Court through the two judgments of 1963 and 1964. It can be used by the EU itself, namely by its executive and judicial organs, the Commission and, in the last instance, the Court. The means is the interpretation of the Treaty. It excludes the member states and the EU organ in which they are represented, the Council, but also the European Parliament. They have no say in it. While the transfer of powers on the first path is actively promoted by the member states, they suffer a loss of powers on the second path. Since the original path toward integration was blocked until the Single European Act of 1987 because of the French obstruction, the new path became dominant. During this period the Court was the driving force of European integration.

The two paths do not only differ with regard to actors and procedure. They also differ in nature. The first is political, the second administrative and judicial. As far as legitimation is concerned, this difference is crucial. The actors on the first path are democratically legitimized and accountable in their respective states. Their decision to transfer powers to the EU will usually be accompanied by a public debate in which the national government has to justify its measures. The people and their representatives thus get a chance to influence the decision. If the citizens do not agree with the decisions of the government and the political parties supporting it in parliament they can express their disagreement in the next election.

5 Expression used by the Italian Constitutional Court (Cartabia 1995: 95).

The actors on the second path have a weaker democratic legitimation than those acting on the first path and they are not accountable to an electorate. Rather, their decisions are immunized from the outcome of elections. They do not have to fear public protest. They are smaller in number and more homogeneous, due to their professionalization as lawyers. They do not face veto players, as is the case on the first path. The limits set to a transfer of powers by the national constitutions play no role for the European institutions. The people of the member states and their representatives are not involved. If a judgment of the Court attracts public attention, the attention follows the judgment rather than preceding it. All this makes the second path smoother than the first.

However, the non-political mode of decision-making on the second path does not deprive the decisions themselves of their political character. The agreement of the member states to establish a common market can be implemented in many ways. The Treaties do not determine the way. They leave choices. Which model is chosen, a liberal-market or a social-market model, is of high political impact. The same is true for the decision how to divide the private and the public sector and which standard of social security is aimed at. The question here is not what is preferable. This is contested. The issue is whether decisions of this kind should be taken in a democratic process or by democratically not accountable agents.

Moreover, the second path does not simply supplement the first one. It rather leaves deep marks on it. While the member states retain the exclusive power to amend the text of the Treaties, they no longer control the power drift by way of judicial interpretation of the Treaties. Fundamental principles of the Treaties are thereby affected. Undermined is the rule that extensions of community powers require an amendment to the Treaties. The principle of conferral that reserves public power to the member states unless explicitly transferred to the EU is undermined. Undermined is also the *Kompetenz-Kompetenz* that authorizes the member states to regulate the division of powers between themselves and the EU. The difference between treaty amendment and treaty interpretation becomes blurred.

If this is discussed not just in terms of efficient integration but also in terms of democratic legitimation, a legitimacy gap comes to the fore. The loss of democratic substance on the side of the member states does not correspond with a democratic gain on the side of the EU. There is rather a power shift from the political institutions of the member states to the non-political European institutions. Vis-à-vis these institutions the political means to secure democratic legitimation and accountability fail. Neither the Council nor the European Parliament is involved. Elections on the national level as well as on the European level do not matter for the judicial power. In the field of Treaty application the executive and the judicial organs of the EU are uncoupled from the democratic processes and remain among themselves. European politics are largely depoliticized.

The non-political mode can also explain why the legitimacy problem remained hidden for quite some time. Originally, the European project enjoyed broad support among Europeans. In the wake of the Second World War integration was embraced as a means to overcome the nationalism that had caused so much harm to losers and winners of the war alike. Meanwhile, the threat of war among the European states no longer exists and the original enthusiasm is fading away. What remained of the European project was the common market, neither an object for enthusiasm nor for disapproval. Economic integration seemed to be non-political and contributed to prosperity. The common market was legitimized by the growing welfare it produced.

Yet, the jurisprudence of the Court had done much more than establishing a common market. It had transformed the EEC into a political community, but this had happened by stealth. The turning point is marked by the Maastricht Treaty of 1992. Intended to open a new chapter in the process of European integration, the Treaty all of a sudden disclosed that the integration had left its economic stage and become a political project. The people became aware how many political problems were no longer solved in the national capitals but by the European Communities without involvement of the citizens. The Europe that the Maastricht Treaty wanted to secure and advance was not the Europe to which the acceptance by the citizens referred. Maastricht was a gain for the integration, but a loss for its acceptance by the citizens.

Different from the legitimacy gap that opened up with the Single European Act of 1987, the gap opened by the jurisprudence of the Court has not been closed. The Single European Act allowed for majority decisions in the Council and thus interrupted the legitimation chain that runs from the member states to the European institutions. It was now possible that a member state was submitted to laws that it had not agreed to in the Council and perhaps explicitly rejected in its domestic democratic process. Yet, the transition to majority decisions in the Council was accompanied by legislative powers for the European Parliament. The democratic legitimacy which the elected and controlled governments of the member states could no longer provide if they were outvoted was compensated for by a genuine European legitimacy, the participation of the European Parliament.

The fact that also the jurisprudence of the Court created a legitimacy gap remained largely unnoticed. This reveals a deep ambivalence that is characteristic for European integration. On the one hand, stealth was a precondition of successful integration in the past. Many of the integration steps brought forth by judgments of the Court would not have succeeded in the political mode. But the same stealth is responsible for the low acceptance of the European project now. The citizens were not asked whether this is the type of integration they wanted and they did not get a chance to express their will, as was possible for the integration progress in the political mode. A return to the political mode may, however, threaten to thwart or at least slow down further process or provoke a return to intergovernmentalism.

What makes it so difficult to solve the problem?

All this does not explain, however, why the member states did not react to a jurisprudence that shifted the power more and more from them to the EU. Are they not the 'Masters of the Treaties'? Are they not in a position to reverse the judicial power shift if they are not happy with it? After all, they decide in the European Council on the direction, extent and pace of integration and they are the main actors of EU legislation in the Council of Ministers. This should give them the opportunity to reprogram the jurisprudence of the Court if they do not recognize their intentions in the Court's interpretation of the treaties or observe detrimental effects caused by that interpretation. Why did they not use it?

The discreet way in which courts act may have played a role (Venzke 2013). Courts decide individual cases according to rules set by the political branches of government. The language in which the decisions are presented more or less conceals the choices that the judges made. This is particularly so in the judgments of the Court, which are highly apodictic and do not allow dissenting opinions. Quite often cases that give rise to far-reaching consequences lack conspicuousness. A case may seem politically irrelevant and thus go unnoticed. The national governments may have the impression that the case affects only a single member state so that the rest does not see a reason to intervene. If the result of a decision satisfies the member states they often do not pay attention to the reasoning and the consequences it may entail in the future. Whether a single decision lays the ground for a whole line of jurisprudence can only be ascertained in retrospect.

Warnings from outside were rare. The nonpolitical mode of decision-making lowered public attention. Enthusiasts of European integration liked it because it was what they desired. So they did not care much about the question whether it was the appropriate actor who achieved it. National politicians paid little attention to European politics. Likewise, the media did not realize what was going on. Court decisions from Luxembourg were not of interest for a long time. Even legal science failed to act as a critical observer. The scholars of domestic law left EU law to a few specialists. The specialists of European law identified themselves with their object. They regarded their discipline as part of the European project and refrained from criticism in order not to endanger it.

But even if there had been a will to alter a line of jurisprudence it would not have been so easy to realize it, as the former German President Roman Herzog had to learn when he launched his appeal to 'Stop the European Court of Justice' (Herzog 2008). Courts operate under the umbrella of judicial independence. They are independent of political directives and they are independent of elections. This is a precondition of their function to enforce the law. The independence is democratically tolerable because courts are submitted to other bonds, namely the law which is made by the political branches of government in a democratic process. However, nothing shows more clearly than the jurisprudence of the Court that the binding force of legislative texts is limited.

Legal norms are written for an indefinite number of future cases. This is why they are formulated in more or less general and abstract terms. The cases to which they are applied are individual and concrete. The gap has to be bridged by interpretation. The judge must find out what the general norm means with regard to a concrete problem. This requires a concretization of the text in view of the case at hand. The concretization is never fully determined by the text of the norm. It leaves space for the construction of the meaning. Doctrine and method narrow the space, but they are unable to eliminate it. It is beyond the reach of politics to regulate the process of interpretation or to dictate or prohibit a certain method of interpretation. This is true for every law, not only for European law.

What is neither impossible nor prohibited, however, is legislative change of the law. Laws can be repealed, amended and specified. Otherwise the law would petrify and lose its capacity to meet new challenges or new preferences of an elected majority. It is by no means illegitimate to legislate with the intent to change the way courts deal with the law, even though only for the future. The content of the law is determined in the political process. Only the interpretation and application of the law have to be free from political influence and go on according to legal, not political criteria. Without the distinction between the (political) making of the law and its (juridical) application to cases the benefits of the rule of law are put at risk.

However, the most important cause for the limited power of politics to redirect the Court is the least noticed one. It lies in the constitutionalization of the Treaties (Grimm 2016). To explain this, a brief look to the function of democratic constitutions seems helpful. Constitutions legitimate and limit political power. In order to achieve this, they must enjoy primacy over government acts. What has been regulated on the constitutional level is no longer open for political regulation. This is why constitutions serve as a framework in which politics act, not as a replacement for politics. They regulate political decision-making formally and materially, but leave the decisions themselves to the political process. This difference is crucial for constitutionalism. It is a precondition of democracy. If disregarded democracy pays the price. More constitutional law equates with less democracy and more power of the judiciary at the expense of the democratic institutions.

The European Treaties were not written as a constitution in the sense of state constitutions. It was the jurisprudence of the Court that elevated them to the constitutional level. But the Treaties have little in common with a constitution. They regulate lots of subject matters that would be ordinary law in a state. This is why the Treaties are so voluminous. In Europe, the difference between constitutional law and ordinary law has been largely levelled. The constitutionalization of the Treaties would not have caused a democratic problem had they contained only provisions that are functionally constitutional law. Since this is not the case, the EU is overconstitutionalized.

With the constitutionalization of the Treaties the interpretation and application of EU primary law gained the quality of enforcement of the quasi-constitution. This means that the political branches of the EU and the member states are not only unnecessary to establish the common market. They are also unable to correct the administrative and judicial branches of the EU in their way to establish the common market. The constitutionalization of the Treaties thus immunizes the Commission and in particular the Court against any attempt by the democratically responsible institutions of the EU to react to the Court's jurisprudence by changing the legal program. Likewise, they are immunized against public pressure. As far as the Treaty extends, elections do not matter. The constitutionalization is at the origin of the independence of the executive and the judiciary from the democratically legitimized and accountable organs.

It is true that the member states have the right to bring an action if they think that the EU institutions acted *ultra vires*, however, but this is only against the Commission and not against the Court which is entitled to decide in the litigation. The Commission, in turn, acts under the umbrella of the Court. Because of the Court's agenda, lawsuits by the member states were not very promising. The Court saw its role neither in protection of the Treaty rights of the member states nor as a neutral arbiter between them and the Commission. As a tendency, the Commission could count on winning the case if it sued the member states for a violation of the Treaties. If a member state brought an annulment action against the Commission for exceeding the powers conveyed on it by the Treaties, a defeat was likely. Again, there are cases that point to the opposite direction, but they do not seem to change the tendency.

Under these circumstances, the only possibility the member states have to redirect the Court are amendments of the Treaties, just as the member states can redirect their constitutional courts by constitutional amendments. For good reasons, constitutional amendments are more difficult than ordinary legislation. Since the constitution contains the rules on which political competitors have agreed, their change usually requires a super-majority. But amendments are by no means impossible. The USA is a rare exception. For instance, the German Basic Law has been amended 60 times in 65 years, and many amendments concerned more than just one article.

But it is extremely difficult to reach Treaty amendments in the EU. The requirement of unanimity among 28 member states plus ratification in each state and the great efforts that are necessary to build a consensus make amendments almost unavailable for the rather minor purpose of reacting to a line of jurisprudence. Unhampered by political interference, the Court could often do what would not have been allowed or viable for politics. Because of the self-empowering effects of constitutionalization created by the Court in combination with the fact that the Treaties are full of rules of a non-constitutional character, the Court is freer than any national court. This explains the concerns of the German Constitutional Court and the safeguards it wants to establish. Self-interest of a national Court may be involved, but basically it is a resistance against the erosion of democracy.[6]

How international and national courts differ and what follows from that

Courts have a mandate to apply the law, not to make it. This is why they act under conditions other than those for lawmakers. They do not formulate general policies but decide individual cases according to pre-established

6 BVerfGE 123, 267 *Lisbon Treaty*, Judgment of 30 June 2009 (Grimm 2009).

principles and rules. Their horizon is therefore limited by the legal issue at hand. Their informational resources are restricted compared to those of the political branches. The judicial procedure does not lend itself to broad participation. Only the parties to a lawsuit have the right to be heard. Only the legal aspects of the conflict may be discussed and only legal arguments count. Externalities or repercussions of the judgment cannot be introduced into the judicial process unless they affect the purpose of the norms.

This is nothing specific to the Court. It is more or less the same for all courts. It is also inevitable that courts, in applying the law, are not completely determined by the text of the law, but have room for choices. If the Court is blamed for exceeding the limits of adjudication it is often argued that national constitutional courts show a similar behavior and interpret their constitutions in creative and self-empowering ways, deriving results from the text that the founders had not intended and could not have foreseen. This is undeniably so. Therefore, the question arises whether there are differences between national and international courts that would justify or even require different standards regarding judicial activism or deferentialism.

One obvious difference is that the political constraints emanating from constitutional interpretation are smaller in the member states than in the EU because the national constitutions do not claim to regulate as much as the Treaties do. They are more or less confined to rules that are functionally constitutional law and do not resemble ordinary law. Hence, the space for political change of the law, also in reaction to jurisprudence, is bigger on the national level than on the European level. Another reason is that amendments to the national constitutions are easier than amendments to the European Treaties. National constitutional courts or courts with constitutional adjudication are thus less protected against the amendment power than the Court.

But these are not the only differences between the national and the international judiciary which might justify the application of different standards. More important differences can be found in the contextual circumstances of national and international adjudication. What context and how does it matter? Judges and courts operate in an institutional and social framework that precedes the individual judgments and determines them not less than the text of the provisions applied by a court to individual cases (Voigt 1999; Vanberg 2005; Volkmann 2013: 167 et seq.). Like other institutions, courts are path-dependent. Precedents play a considerable role, regardless of whether the legal system attributes binding effect to them or not. It takes much more effort to change an established line of jurisprudence than to follow long standing practice. Consistency, not only within a judgment but also between judgments, is a legal value, as it guarantees legal certainty and reliability.

In addition to precedent, doctrine provides the judge with a number of accepted solutions or argumentations which, because of their general acceptance, do not need further reflection or reasoning. Part of this context is also a methodology for the interpretation of legal texts that guides judicial decision-making and distinguishes between legal and non-legal arguments. Moreover, courts are under constant observation by legal science. Scholars evaluate and criticize judgments from a legal point of view, disclose the implications of judgments and offer alternatives to traditional solutions. It makes a difference whether judges are inclined to listen to legal writing or whether contacts between legal science and legal practice are rare.

These contextual elements are nowhere laid down, let alone prescribed. They are not immune against change, but if they change they do so slowly and subtly. The change happens, it cannot be ordered. All attempts of legislators to prohibit or at least regulate the interpretation of their statutes have been in vain. Not always are judges aware of the contextual elements. The less conscious they are the greater is their effect. Usually they come to the fore only if a judgment seems to go beyond the consensus or if a deep break in the political and legal system occurs so that the traditional way of handling legal issues is no longer appropriate or if a total new set of judges is appointed. Conversely, if a revolutionary regime decides to leave the old judges in place this may well affect the realization of the new order.

However, the context is not only legal. The legal norms of a country are deeply grounded in its social norms. The jurisprudence is accompanied and influenced by social conditions as well. The perception a society has about the law plays a role. Is it understood as purely instrumental for political purposes or does it represent a set of values of a society with the effect that it is not only instrumental in the hands of politicians but also guides and limits them in their actions? Is it more or less accepted to circumvent the law or is insisting on legal obedience the general attitude within a society? Which role does a society attribute to judges? Is judicial review regarded as a threat to or as a safeguard of democracy? The reputation of judges and the scope of their activity depend to a large extent on these prerequisites.

These are also viewpoints for the public observation of judicial activities that exists next to the professional observation. Courts act within a 'communicative arrangement' (Komárek 2014: 538). It is maintained and fueled by the media of mass communication. In observing the judiciary the general public is guided by criteria different from those of the professional observer. Usually, it is less interested in the legal reasoning of courts than in the outcome of a decision. But this may well reflect a general sense of justice in a society. The way in which the media report on court decisions is an important factor in shaping this sense of justice.

Judges are not insensitive to these elements (Vanberg 2005). Even if they are not prepared to decide cases according to the interests of politicians or the expectations or emotions of the general public and not according to the law, the way they fill the leeway that the law leaves is influenced by such considerations. Courts are aware of their vulnerability. They decide what is legal and illegal. But they do not dispose of the means to enforce their judgments. This is up to the executive. It disposes of the use of legitimate force. How these means are handled depends among others on the backing that the judiciary enjoys in a society. Judges will therefore hesitate to render judgments that undermine the legitimacy of the judiciary or whose acceptance and enforcement is highly unlikely.

In spite of the increasing internationalization of the law the context in which courts operate remains largely a matter of national legal and general culture. It differs from country to country and from legal system to legal system. Every legal system is a product of the national culture and, in turn, constantly reproduces this culture. Foreign influences and cross-border exchanges are by no means excluded (Choudhry 2006). But they are adapted to national traditions and needs. The legal and social context keeps courts in touch with the society for which they administer justice. It is of importance for the recognition and acceptance of the judiciary, even if one disagrees with certain judgments. This is the more important since courts are for good reasons not accountable for the decisions they render.

In our context, it is important to realize that the conditions which keep the judiciary in touch with society are different in a nation state and in an international setting. The more international a court is, the weaker the contextual constraints. In the EU they are thinly developed or missing. The Court could for a long time act largely without criticism by the legal science and unobserved by the media and consequently escaped the attention of the general public. The various mechanisms that mitigate judicial review do not take effect vis-à-vis the Court. Its range of interpretations of the law is less determined by a legal culture. It can exploit the various legal cultures, but the societal roots of the mix are low.

As compensation for the greater freedom that the international courts enjoy compared to national courts, more self-restraint can be expected from international courts than from domestic courts. Some international courts have developed instruments to limit their power in the interest of national diversity. The European Court of Human Rights recognizes a 'margin of appreciation' for the member states of the Council of Europe. The Court of Justice has not developed a similar device. The *effet utile* of the Court is the opposite of the margin of appreciation of the European Court of Human Rights. Although cases can be cited where the Court was willing to accord a member state the right to uphold certain domestic standards even if they restricted the four economic freedoms,[7] this has not yet become the usual attitude. In general it is its methodological instrument combined with the mission that it feels that accounts for the activism of this Court.

By the constitutionalization of the Treaties, which were not intended to be a constitution in the traditional sense of the term, the Court laid the ground for the alienation of the non-political organs of the EU from the democratically legitimized and accountable organs. The failure to develop a method of interpretation that would respond to the consequences of the jurisprudence for the legitimacy of the EU aggravated the problem (Weiler 2012). By applying a lenient standard of review to these decisions and at the same time severely restraining the democratically taken decisions of the member states the Court continues to uphold the system. Whereas domestic (constitutional) courts have the potential to contribute to the legitimacy of the (national) political system, the Court is part of the legitimacy problem of the EU (Weiler 2012: 263).

What can be done?

Judicial self-restraint comes to mind first when this question is asked. However, the call for judicial self-restraint is as ubiquitous as it is ineffective. It appeals to the professional ethics of judges, which cannot be transformed into formal legal rules for individual behavior. If the appeal works it works informally by conviction. But it is not easy to convince a judge not to rule what, according to his best knowledge, the law requires. There are maximalist and minimalist ways to determine what the law requires.

7 The most frequently cited case is *Omega*, EU:C:2004:614. But *Omega*, although praised in Germany, is quite ambivalent. The Court agreed that the prominent role of human dignity in the German Basic Law (Article 1) justifies a restriction of the free movement of goods (Article 26 TFEU). Yet, it did this after a balancing between the two rights, whereas in Germany dignity is protected absolutely and hence not subject to limitation and balancing.

Which way prevails is rather a question of a legal culture than of deliberate choice. Self-restraint is either rooted in a country's political and legal culture or it will be neglected. An effective solution must work independently of the judges' attitude toward adjudication.

The search must be guided by a clear notion of the evil that should be remedied and the goal that should be reached. The evil lies in the depoliticization of the decision-making process in the EU, the integration by stealth. The goal can therefore only be a repoliticization of this process (Vauchez 2014). As an obstacle the constitutionalization of the Treaties has been identified, with which the Court enhanced its powers and at the same time immunized itself against the democratic processes in the EU as well as in the member states. To be sure, the question is not whether the jurisprudence of the Court is right or wrong in legal terms, good or bad in political, social or economic terms. These are legitimate questions, but they are not pursued here. What is not at question either is the independence of the Court. The evil cannot be remedied by another evil. The grievance is the invulnerability of the Court's jurisprudence. How can a repoliticization be achieved without endangering the independence of the judiciary?

Some authors place their hope in the principle of subsidiarity. But this principle applies to the European legislature, that is the Commission, the Council and the European Parliament, and not to the Court. To the contrary, the Court is the institution to rule on alleged violations of the principle. Up to now the principle has remained without any legal effect. The reason is not so much an unwillingness to apply it than its extreme vagueness. Subsidiarity is suitable for designing political systems, not for deciding concrete conflicts about the allocation of powers. The fact that under the Treaty of Lisbon national parliaments have gained the power to challenge a Union law before the Court on grounds of subsidiarity will not make up for its emptiness. Should the Court nevertheless start to apply it this would be another step toward depoliticization of political questions.

Others have suggested the withdrawal of the power to decide conflicts of competences between the EU and its member states from the Court and transferring it to a specialized European court (Weiler 1999: 322; Herzog 2008). Different from the pro-integrationist Court of Justice, this court should act as a true arbiter between the EU and the member states. It should therefore be composed by an equal number of judges from the Court of Justice and national constitutional courts and only sit ad hoc, not permanently. This might indeed be a way to reach a more balanced jurisprudence in conflicts of competences. It would probably limit the creeping power shift from the member states to the EU. But it remains within the sphere of the judiciary and would thus not contribute to a repoliticization of decisions on the European level.

Some authors hope to achieve this by lowering the binding force of judgments of the Court of Justice (Scharpf 2009: 198 et seq.). The idea is some sort of an override clause in the Treaties, which permits the Council or the European Parliament or the member states to disregard Court decisions under certain conditions. This is not without precedent. Override clauses exist for instance in the Canadian Charter of Rights and Freedoms and in the British Human Rights Act. In both countries, they were a condition for the adoption of the Bill of Rights. Practically they play no role. This could not be taken for granted in Europe. Therefore, some proposals contain safeguards against abuses. These solutions avoid the illegality of non-compliance. But they would convey only a formal, not a substantive legality to the refusal and therefore seem problematic in terms of legitimacy.

Others place their hope in the national constitutional courts and their power to declare European legal acts including decisions of the Court of Justice of the European Union (CJEU) inapplicable on grounds of the national constitution. Some courts indeed claim this power. The German Court justifies this claim explicitly with the argument that the national constitutional courts are the only remaining bulwark against *ultra vires* acts of the EU and infringements of the identity of the national constitutions. However, the national constitutional courts' power is limited in how it protects national democracy against erosion by the EU and its Court. What it cannot achieve is repoliticizing European decision-making and thus strengthening the European democracy.

But even if one finds a legal basis for this power in Article 4 (2) TEU one should not overestimate this possibility. It is unable to change the whole judicial practice but is limited to bar extreme outliers. The German Constitutional Court itself declared that it will exercise its power only in cases of obvious Treaty violation, provided they result in a structural power shift from the member states to the EU.[8] However, it will be extremely rare that a single decision of the Court of Justice causes such a power shift. A power shift is usually the result of an accumulation of cases of which none alone would seem to justify the intervention of a national court. The accumulation, however, will never be the object of litigation in a court.

8 BVerfGE 126, 286 *Honeywell*, Judgment of 6 July 2010 (Payandeh 2011; Grimm 2012: 178).

Courts can only render verdicts in single cases and not adjudicate about the overall result of a whole line of jurisprudence.

If the primary goal is not the limitation of the CJEU but the repoliticization of the European process of decision-making that has been de-politicized by the jurisprudence of the Court, the solution can only be sought on the European level. The proposal in which the idea of a repoliticization most frequently finds expression is the parliamentarization of the EU. The European Parliament shall be endowed with all powers national parliaments usually have. This can, however, not be achieved without consequences for the other organs of the EU. The plan therefore includes the postulate to upgrade the Commission to a parliamentary government and to downgrade the Council to a second house of the European Parliament. This is recognizable as the pattern of national democracies and, as a matter of fact, it would come close to a transformation of the EU into a federal state.

If realized, this reform would largely cut off the EU from the legitimation that it still receives from the member states and therefore open a new legitimacy gap (Weiler 2012; Grimm 2015). However, in our context it is more important that a parliamentarization of the EU would leave the source of the problem, its over-constitutionalization, completely untouched. For, also, the European Parliament is below and not above the constitution. In all subject matters that have been regulated in the Treaties the European Parliament would not have a say and the outcome of European elections would not matter. The preferences of the citizens could not be translated into political decisions. In other words, although endowed with all powers national parliaments enjoy the European Parliament would nevertheless not reach the position of the national parliaments because it could use its power only in the non-constitutionalized area. In all matters regulated in the Treaties the Court would remain the principal actor that could be redirected only by amendments to the Treaties.

If the obstacle to a repoliticization of European politics is not the limited role of the European Parliament but the constitutionalization of the Treaties, although these are not confined to constitution-like provisions, but contain lots of rules that would be ordinary law in a state, the solution to the problem must be sought here. As long as the Treaties were regarded as international agreements of states their volume did not pose a legitimacy problem. The fulfillment of Treaty obligations by the member states were left to them and their democratic processes, whereas the Commission and the Court could only require the states to fulfill their obligations but not replace them by European decisions. It became a legitimacy problem when the Court constitutionalized the Treaties and thereby gained the power to pursue the integration itself, bypassing the member states and their democratic processes and bypassing the Council and the European Parliament as the European legislators.

How can that be prevented? My suggestion is not to reverse the constitutionalization of the Treaties but rather to draw consequences from it. If the Treaties have been elevated to constitutional rank, which was not their original destination, they should be confined to those norms that reflect the function of constitutions whereas all other provisions would be levelled down to the rank of ordinary law (Scharpf 2015). This would not require a revision of the provisions of the Treaties. But it would give the political branches of the EU, Council and European Parliament the power to change the downgraded part of the Treaties by way of legislation and so to redirect the jurisprudence of the Court if they find that it does not reflect their intentions as legislators or produces undesirable effects.

The jurisprudence of the Court is certainly not the only source of the European legitimacy problem. But it is an important and neglected source. And it is easier to remedy this problem than many other legitimacy problems in Europe, mainly those that stem from the weakness or absence of the societal preconditions of a vibrant democracy, which would keep the European Parliament in touch with the citizenry. The conditions for vibrant democracy are still much better (albeit by no means always satisfactory) in the member states than in the EU. For the time being and for the foreseeable future the EU depends to a large extent on the legitimacy that it receives from the member states. The financial crisis confirms this (Weiler 2012: 268). For this reason the EU must have a self-interest in a strong democracy of the member states. It does not seem to be aware of this. Repoliticization could be a means to change that.

References

Alter, K. (2001) *Establishing the Supremacy of European Law*, Oxford: Oxford University Press.

Annweiler, J. (1997) *Die Auslegungsmethoden des Gerichtshofs der Europäischen Gemeinschaften*, Frankfurt: Peter Lang.

Beck, G. (2013) *The Legal Reasoning of the Court of Justice of the EU*, Oxford: Hart Publishing.

Buck, C. (1998) *Über die Auslegungsmethoden des Gerichtshofs der Europäischen Gemeinschaft*, Frankfurt: Peter Lang.

Cartabia, M. (1995) *Principi inviolabili e integrazione europea*, Milan: Giuffrè.

Choudhry, S. (ed.) (2006) *The Migration of Constitutional Ideas*, Cambridge: Cambridge University Press.

Grimm, D. (2009) 'Defending Sovereign Statehood against Transforming the European Union into a State', *European Constitutional Law Review*, 5(3), 353–73.

(2012) *Die Zukunft der Verfassung II: Auswirkungen von Europäisierung und Globalisierung*, Berlin: Suhrkamp.

(2013) 'Der Datenschutz vor einer Neuorientierung', *Juristenzeitung*, 68(12), 585–92.

(2015) 'The Democratic Costs of Constitutionalization: The European Case', *European Law Journal*, 21(4), 460–73.

(2016) *Europa ja – aber welches?*, Munich: Beck.

Grundmann, S. (1997) *Die Auslegung des Gemeinschaftsrechts durch den Europäischen Gerichtshof: Zugleich eine rechtsvergleichende Studie zur Auslegung im Völkerrecht und im Gemeinschaftsrecht*, Konstanz: Hartung-Gorre.

Herzog, R. (2008) 'Stop the European Court of Justice' *Frankfurter Allgemeine Zeitung*, 8 September.

Höpner, M., and Schäfer, A. (eds) (2008) *Die politische Ökonomie der europäischen Integration*, Frankfurt: Campus.

Joerges, C., and F. Rödl (2009) 'Informal Politics, Formalised Law and the "Social Deficit" of European Integration: Reflections after the Judgments of the Court in Viking and Laval', *European Law Journal*, 15(1), 1–19.

Kokott, J. (2011) 'Der EuGH – eine neo-liberale Institution?', in *Grundrechte und Solidarität: Durchsetzung und Verfahren. Festschrift für Renate Jaeger*, Kehl: Engel, 115–34.

Komárek, J. (2014) 'National Constitutional Courts in the European Constitutional Democracy', *International Journal of Constitutional Law*, 12(3), 525–44.

Kühling, J. (2009) 'Fundamental Rights', in A. Von Bogdandy and J. Bast, *Principles of European Constitutional Law*, 2nd edn, Oxford: Hart, 479–514.

Majone, G. (2005) *Dilemmas of European Integration: The Ambiguities and Pitfalls of Integration by Stealth*, Oxford: Oxford University Press.

Mangold, A. (2011) *Gemeinschaftsrecht und deutsches Recht*, Tübingen: Mohr Siebeck.

Mayer, F. (2000) *Kompetenzüberschreitung und Letztentscheidung*, Munich: Beck.

Payandeh, M. (2011) 'Constitutional Review of EU law after Honeywell', *Common Market Law Review*, 48(1), 9–38.

Prechal, S. (2005) *Directives in EC Law*, 2nd edn, Oxford: Oxford University Press.

Rose, R. (2014) *Representing Europeans*, Oxford: Oxford University Press.

Scharpf, F. (1999) *Governing in Europe: Effective and Democratic?*, Oxford: Oxford University Press.

(2009) 'Legitimacy in the Multi-level European Polity', *European Political Science Review*, 1(2), 173–204.

(2010) *Community and Autonomy, Institutions, Policies and Legitimacy in Multilevel Europe*, Frankfurt: Campus.

(2015) 'After the Crash: A Perspective on Multilevel European Democracy', *European Law Journal*, 21(3), 384–405.

Scharpf, F., and Schmidt, V. (eds) (2000) *Welfare and Work in the Open Economy*, Oxford: Oxford University Press.

Schmidt, V., and M. Thatcher (eds) (2013) *Resilient Liberalism in Europe's Political Economy*, Cambridge: Cambridge University Press.

Stone Sweet, A. (2004) *The Judicial Construction of Europe*, Oxford: Oxford University Press.

Streinz, R. (2010) 'Die Rolle des EuGH im Prozess der Europäischen Integration', *Archiv des öffentlichen Rechts*, 135, 1.

Vanberg, G. (2005) *The Politics of Constitutional Review in Germany*, Cambridge: Cambridge University Press.

Vauchez, A. (2014) *Démocratiser l'Europe*, Paris: Seuil.

Venzke, I. (2013) 'Understanding the Authority of International Courts and Tribunals', Amsterdam Law School Research Paper, 2013-29.

Voigt, S. (1999) *Explaining Constitutional Change*, Cheltenham: Elgar.

Volkmann, U. (2013) *Grundzüge einer Verfassungslehre der Bundesrepublik Deutschland*, Tübingen: Mohr Siebeck.

Wahl, R. (2013) 'Das Recht der Integrationsgemeinschaft Europäische Union', in C. Franzius (ed.), *Beharren - Bewegen, Festschrift für Michael Kloepfer*, Berlin: Duncker & Humblot.

Weiler, J. (1991) 'The Transformation of Europe', *Yale Law Journal*, 100(8), 2403–83.

(1994) 'A Quiet Revolution: The European Court of Justice and its Interlocutors', *Comparative Political Studies*, 26(4), 510–34.

(1999) *The Constitution of Europe*, Cambridge: Cambridge University Press.

(2012) 'Europe in Crisis – On Political "Messianism", "Legitimacy" and the "Rule of Law"', *Singapore Journal of Legal Studies*, 248–69.

11

Crisis reconfiguration of the European constitutional state

DAMIAN CHALMERS

Introduction

Public finance laws govern some of an administration's most significant powers: its powers to tax, borrow and spend. These powers allow administrations to redistribute, consolidate their own capacity and address individual and collective well-being, and have, thus, provided a central context to the formation of the modern European constitutional state (Steinmo 1993). After briefly setting out how they have shaped, inter alia, modern understandings of sovereignty, citizenship and parliament–executive relations, this chapter shall argue that EU law is unique in subjecting budgets and taxation to formally superior legal structures which claim the authority to reshape these. The initial lax application of EU law in this field obscured how it could, consequently, resettle understandings of sovereignty, citizenship and parliament–executive relations. This changed with the crisis which put in play two central EU legal narratives: those of risk regulation and bonded government. The former requires the public finances or economies of the euro-area not to impose undue risks on neighbouring states or future generations whilst the latter requires states whose economies or finances are in trouble to redeem this through covenanting certain action to other euro-area states.

The next section argues that each of these narratives poses demands on conventional understandings of sovereignty, citizenship and parliamentary powers. The narrative of risk regulation reconfigures sovereignty so that a precondition for the entitlement to tax is that it does not impose undue risks on others outside its territory so that it now involves a commitment to citizens in other euro-area states and to future generations even if this dilutes commitments to citizens within the national territory. Parliamentary power is, correspondingly, reduced wherever it is seen as a source of risk. Bonded government, by contrast, divides sovereign power with the pan-Union administrative structures responsible for securing repayment of the bond acquiring sovereign powers of their own as they have to have the power to require whatever it takes to secure redemption. Such a world finds no place for notions of citizenship or representative democracy, and the logic of the bond leads to a consequent displacement of these.

The final section will argue that these narratives are partial. They sit alongside each other and more conventional national narratives about sovereignty, citizenship and parliamentary power. The relationship between all these is both fluid and unclear. The earlier period of the crisis, thus, suggested that the narratives of risk regulation and bonded government were discrete, with the latter confined to those seeking financial support from other euro-area states and the ECB. The post-crisis world suggests a coming together in which the degree of sovereign power exercised by euro-area institutions over individual states will depend on the degree of risk their economies and finances are deemed to pose. Alongside this, different states will have to decide how they translate these narratives into their domestic constitutional vernaculars with different approaches to risk, for example, shaping these processes. Finally, there can be resistance to these narratives of risk regulation and bonded governed. This has, indeed, begun to occur with a new incipient Europeanised praxis emerging whereby national constitutional courts develop thresholds for citizenship and national parliaments network and explore opportunities for influence within these panoramas. Whether this will be sufficient to safeguard the constitutional authority of euro-area states remains one of the great uncertainties of the post-crisis era.

Taxation and the modern European constitutional settlement

Sovereignty acts as the identifier for who has the right to tax with the consequence that sovereignty and the power to tax have long contributed to each other's development. A distinction was thus made as early as the fourteenth century between the monarch's private capacity and his fiscal role, which went to matters that affected the community as a whole (the *fisc*). The latter allowed him to demand money for its benefit (the *res fisci*), but this could only be made in relation to something which was to be considered a quasi-sacred common utility, a *res quasi sacri*. The King could not give it away and it endowed the Crown with traits which today would be identified as the common good. This allowed a division which is central to modern sovereignty, that of the King's Bodies, in which the sovereign represents both the corporeal presence of the monarch and the body politic (Kantorowicz 1985: 171–91). This, in turn, served to move European states from domain states, based around patronage and ownership, to fiscal states identified by the collection of taxes in the name of the body politic (Grappenhaus 1998: 21–53). This tradition has persisted into modernity. The nineteenth-century *Wohlfahrstaat*, the precursor of the modern European welfare state, set out the 'requirement that the members in their totality have the obligation to care for the single individual, just as the single individual has the obligation to care for the totality' (Nauwerck 1844: 5). In like vein, early British descriptions of the welfare state differentiated it from the power state as it required the state to give effect to a notion of community (ibid. 44–47). If other meanings emerged of the welfare state as a form of social insurance, the link between taxation, welfare and the sovereign as body politic continued into the twentieth century, notably in interpretations of the *Sozialstaat* that root it in civil society, which integrates civic values of individual self-determination and mutual commitment, on the one hand, and social practices, on the other, into some form of collective presence that the state must develop (Bockenförde 1991: 165–67; Heinig 2008: 73–75).

Sovereignty placed no limits on the extent of this power to tax. This was problematical even in the Middle Ages, with claims that the sovereign did not have the power to impose excessive or arbitrary taxation, and that subjects must consent to it (Bodin 1955: 193–97; Sacks 1994; Veneendaal 1994). The emergence of budgets exacerbated this as these extended and formalised the sovereign's fiscal power (Bonney 1999). The etymology of the term, from the French word *bougette* (leather purse), therefore indicated something taken for hidden and mistrusted reasons. It was first used pejoratively in 1730 in Britain to challenge excise duties seen as regressive (Scott 2009: 26–27). The response was pressure for the participation of all taxpayers in decisions about the levying and spending of taxes, most emblematically in the 'contributions publiques' developed in the wake of the French Revolution (Kwass 2000: 255–310). The emergence of the budget was tied, thus, to the development of a second central institution of the constitutional imaginary, to wit, citizenship. Citizenship rooted taxation in the idea of consent, that it should be tied to representation and that the amount levied be related to the different material circumstances of individuals (Rousseau 1999: 33). This linking of taxation to the membership of a community, in turn, reshaped notions of citizenship as the argument could be applied as much to how fiscal receipts were used as it could to how taxes were levied. Citizenship, thus, evolved to incorporate the idea that membership allowed the citizen social rights (Marshall 1950). However, these social rights did not involve a *juste retour* from the market or an entitlement to expect a duty of care from strangers but rather a right to benefit from social policies administered by the state and financed by taxation (Korpi 1989: 309).

Finally, the contentiousness of taxation was central, therefore, to the emergence of the central institutional relations which dominate perceptions on the modern European state, those between parliament and the executive. Since the seventeenth century, parliaments ate into or overturned royal prerogatives to levy taxes. The onset of the budget marks this rise to parliamentary supremacy with parliaments seen as having a monopoly over the adoption of budgets. As Wehner (2006: 767) has observed, 'the requirement for legislative approval of financial measures is a democratic foundation stone that is enshrined in constitutions around the world'. The power of the purse is seen as central to granting parliaments power over the executive and to their power having material consequences in that it allowed them the resources to have their preferences enforced (Einzig 1959: 59–62; Congleton 2011; Fisher 2014: 223–24). Furthermore, this fiscal power secured parliaments a power over society, as redistributive conflicts between different social actors now came to be channelled through parliament, and this, in turn, allowed parliaments to be seen as the place that brought these actors into mutual political dependence (Webber and Wildawsky 1986). The monopoly over the discharge of the budget (i.e., the collection of revenue, borrowing, and the spending of resources) held by the executive has been equally central to the executive's control over public administration. This division has led to budgetary politics being marked by jockeying between parliament and executive. The latter has, in some jurisdictions, invoked effective discharge of the budget to reduce parliaments to ratifying chambers which can neither veto a budget nor introduce amendments without bringing down the government, whereas, in others, parliaments have increasingly extended their power of oversight over the executive implementation of budgets (Schick 2002: 15; Posner and Park 2007: 1).

The European narratives of risk regulation and bonded government

There are many styles of fiscal and welfare regime in Europe, but few, if any, without sovereignty, citizenship and these parliament–executive roles at their centre. This constancy is in large part because economic, financial, party political and social pressures are seen as environmental ones which can inform preferences, political dynamics and institutional micro-processes, but do not fundamentally reshape the semantics of public finances as they do not claim a substituting authority for any of the phenomena mentioned above. EU law changed this. It established a legal regime, the Stability and Growth Pact, which overlooked national systems of public finances, and claimed a pre-eminent substituting legal authority for this regime. National systems were to be subject to it and thus could be legally redefined by it. This redefinition of public finances also instrumentalised them. Their role was to support and, above all, not disrupt the functioning of monetary union. Most emblematically, Article 119(3) TFEU, requires all Union and national activities to comply with the 'guiding principles' of stable prices, sound public finances and monetary conditions, and a sustainable balance of payments. These are not valued as ends in themselves but for the 'purposes set out in Article 3 TEU' – in particular, the establishment of an economic and monetary union. Institutionally, this entailed both mechanisms to address the risks of disruption, such as the Excessive Deficit Procedure, and EU legal norms that would discipline states more widely to limit the incidence of these risks, most notably the Broad Economic Policy Guidelines.

Prior to the crisis, the level of oversight and disciplining was weak. Union oversight was confined to monitoring annual budget deficits in a manner which did not place undue pressures on them.[1] Beyond this, it had weak disciplining effects (Beetsma et al. 2009; Rauch et al. 2011). As a consequence, the potential constitutional transformations were obscured. The reforms introduced subsequent to the crisis changed this.[2] There was, first, to be much more extensive oversight. In addition to oversight of the annual budget deficit, total public debt, macroeconomic performance and the structural budget balance of euro-area states (in short, all the central

1 Prior to 2009, budget deficits were only declared excessive if they were either significantly above 3% of GDP and projected to rise for the subsequent year or occurred in conditions of strong economic growth. In addition, many headings of expenditure could be discounted. Regulation 1467/97/EC on speeding up and clarifying the implementation of the excessive deficit procedure, OJ 1997, L 209/6, as amended by Regulation 1056/2005, OJ 2005, L 174/5, Article 2(3).

2 This chapter does not describe the reforms introduced since the crisis in any detail. For discussion, see Chalmers et al. 2014: 714–25 and 740–53.

areas of economic and fiscal policy) were now to be policed.[3] Secondly, this oversight was to be more intensive. New sanctions procedures were introduced for macroeconomic imbalances and significant observed deviations from the progression of states to balanced budgets,[4] and pre-existing excessive deficit procedures were changed to facilitate the imposition of sanctions.[5] Thirdly, a reformation of national administrative structures was to take place to ensure that more robust systems of statistics, fiscal rules and public accounts were established.[6] These were to be reinforced by stronger institutional processes through the establishment of independent statistical agencies, independent fiscal councils and the alignment of budgetary procedures.[7] Fourthly, to emphasise the pre-eminence of this transformation and national commitment to budgetary stability, euro-area states must grant quasi-constitutional status to the norm of securing a balanced budget within their domestic settlements.[8]

The transformations are even more significant for those states – Cyprus, Greece, Ireland, Portugal and Spain – which have had to seek financial support as a result of a collapse in their public finances.[9] As is well known, a condition for such support has been a commitment to programmes, set out in memoranda of understanding, which have not only involved heavy oversight of the implementation of the reforms outlined above, but

3 Regulation 1173/2011 on the effective enforcement of budgetary surveillance in the euro area, OJ 2011, L 306/1; Regulation 1175/2011 amending Regulation 1466/97 on the strengthening of the surveillance of budgetary positions and the surveillance and coordination of economic policies, OJ 2011, L 306/12; Regulation 1176/2011 on the prevention and correction of macroeconomic imbalances, OJ 2011, L 306/25.

4 Regulation 1174/2011 on enforcement measures to correct excessive macroeconomic imbalances in the euro area, OJ 2011, L 306/8; Regulation 1175/2011, supra n. 3, Article 6(2); Regulation 1173/2011, n. 3, above, Article 4.

5 Regulation 1177/2011 amending Regulation 1467/97 on speeding up and clarifying the implementation of the excessive deficit procedure, OJ 2011, L 306/33.

6 Directive 2011/85 on requirements for budgetary frameworks of the member states, OJ 2011, L 306/41; Regulation 1466/97 on the strengthening of the surveillance of budgetary positions and the surveillance and coordination of economic policies, OJ 1997, L 209/1, as amended by Regulation 1175/2011, n. 3, above, Article 10a.

7 Regulation 1466/97, n. 6, above, Article 10a. Regulation 473/2013 on common provisions for monitoring and assessing draft budgetary plans and ensuring the correction of excessive deficit of the member states in the euro area, OJ 2013, l 140/11, Articles 5 (fiscal councils) and 6–8 (budgetary alignment).

8 Article 3(2) TSCG.

9 The financial support offered to Spain was distinctive as it focused exclusively on reforms to the banking sector. Mention should also be made of balance of payments programmes which did not differ markedly in the terms required of states, which were granted to Hungary and Latvia at the beginning of the financial crisis in 2008 and 2009.

also reforms to their administration more generally, spending cuts, privatisations, increases in taxation and significant deregulation of their labour markets. Furthermore, these states are placed on a treadmill where they are subject both to heavy oversight and to a tightly structured programme whereby support is only gradually released as and when they are deemed to have met the conditions of that programme.[10] If these latter processes could initially be framed as exceptional ones granted, outside the framework of EU law, temporarily to states which had fallen off the cliff financially,[11] this illusion was peeled away both by EU institutions being at the centre of their operation and by provision for any future support to be offered fully within an EU legal framework.[12]

Cumulatively, these reforms transformed the demands of EU law on public finances from aspirational ones into prescriptive and detailed visions. If the 70 pages of reform of the so-called 'Six Pack' and 'Two Pack' hemmed states in with a hedgerow of constraints and procedures, it is, however, the broader ethoi underpinning these which has served to resettle domestic constitutional settlements. These ethoi have a constitutive dimension insofar as, by establishing new rationales for public finances, they require the existing processes to be restructured to secure this rationale. They also have an epistemic dimension insofar as sense can only be made of complex domestic and Union processes in place when these are placed and interpreted against these ethoi. The value of individual requirements lies not in their own sake but in how they enable these ethoi to be realised, and, conversely, these ethoi can be turned around by states to justify non-compliance with or reinterpretation of these individual requirements.

The crisis did not so much lead to an implementation of the objectives in Article 119(3) TFEU but set out two new ethoi: those of risk regulation and bonded government. These reconfigured ideas of sovereignty, citizenship and the balance of powers between parliament and executive.

The trajectory of *risk regulation* is set out in the 'Six Pack' and the Fiscal Compact. It involves, first, the provision of a series of public goods: low debt, balanced budgets and balanced economic performance,[13] and are characterised by what the public finance literature has termed a common

10 On the public health effects of these programmes, see Vandoros et al. 2013.

11 As of 1 November 2014, only Cyprus and Greece were still subject to programmes.

12 Regulation 472/2013 on the strengthening of economic and budgetary surveillance of member states in the euro area experiencing or threatened with serious difficulties with respect to their financial stability, OJ 2013, L 140/1, Article 7.

13 On these, see, respectively, Protocol on the Excessive Deficit Procedure, Article 1; Article 3(1) TSCG; Regulation 1176/2011, n. 3, above, Article 2.

pool resource problem (von Hagen and Harden 1995; Velasco 2000). Those contributing to the good are significantly greater than those who can degrade the good, and there are strong incentives for the latter to do this: be they the direct recipients of taxes at the expense of taxpayers in the case of public debt; current generations at the expense of future generations in the case of structural deficits; or particular sectors or actors at the expense of the wider economy in the case of macroeconomic imbalances. The European Union has a tradition of regulating public goods, notably market externalities. It also has credibility to mediate these tensions as its members – be they finance ministers of other euro-area states or the Commission –sit independently from the domestic parties at the centre of this conflict and are strongly affected by any significant externalities which may arise. Secondly, threshold norms, rather than legal prohibitions, are used as indicators of a risk to these public goods. One feature of threshold norms is that, as they are only indicators, their breach warrants intervention only if further evidence can be provided of the risk. Violation of the norm is not egregious per se. Macroeconomic imbalances are only problematical, for example, if they show a 'trend giving rise to macroeconomic developments which are adversely affecting, or have the potential adversely to affect, the proper functioning of the economy of a member state or of the economic and monetary union, or of the Union as a whole'.[14] A further feature of threshold norms is that the identification of a risk does not lead to immediate sanction but rather to more intensive regulation. States found to incur an excessive deficit etc. are subject to adjustment or correction plans and monitored by the Commission, and only if they are found not to perform these satisfactorily is there any move to a sanctions stage. These plans are subject to no legal controls, and, indeed, have never led to sanction. Indeed, the state is not required to meet the thresholds before it can be released from the process, but, rather, merely needs to have abated the risk in the eyes of the EU institutions (Chalmers 2012: 682–84).

Thirdly, a non-majoritarian institution monitors the risks posed by national activities to these goods on the grounds that it has credibility, expertise and is not affected by the pressures posed by electoral processes (Majone 1997: 139). The Commission is charged with the initial determining of the presence of an excessive deficit etc. but the traditional division in EU law between risk assessment and risk management is maintained with the Council formally declaring the presence of these and the enactment

14 Regulation 1176/2011, n. 3, above, Article 2(1).

of sanctions. However, its discretion is constrained. If, in other fields of EU law, they have to provide reasons for not following the assessment,[15] the constraint is a more explicitly proceduralised one with the Council only able to overturn a proposal for sanctions (except with the excessive imbalance procedure) through reverse qualified majority voting (QMV) (Palmstorfer 2014).

Fourthly, organisational rules, processes and forms of expertise are introduced to discipline domestic structures (i.e., statistics, fiscal rules or public accounts) to inculcate a self-policing culture of regulatory obedience. Alongside this, a political economy of constraint is introduced in which new domestic actors emerge, such as independent fiscal councils, to institutionalise this expertise and discipline or independent actors, such as constitutional courts and statistical offices, are granted new powers in the name of these public goods. These powers are granted formally to police administrations but their dramatic nature makes such policing unlikely. Instead, these are used to signal the credibility of the regulatory procedures to wider audiences by setting out sanctions whose dramatic nature emphasises the value attached to the protected public goods (Kelemen and Teo 2014).

Fifthly, these processes are dominated by regulatory conversations between EU institutions and national finance ministries about the setting and meeting of individual targets. For states which have not breached any threshold, these conversations take two forms. Budgets must be vetted by the Commission and ECOFIN prior to presentation for adoption by national parliaments, and macroeconomic and medium-term budgetary performance is, within the framework of the European Semester, subject to recommendations by the Commission and ECOFIN. For states which have breached these thresholds, conversations take place within the context of adjustment or correction plans. They are, thus, more targeted and more structured in that they operate under the shadow of a regulatory pyramid of sanctions, namely, escalating systems of warnings, public warnings, temporary sanctions, financial sanctions and, finally, increased sanctions in the event of non-compliance (Braithwaite 2002: 12). This leads, finally, to a quality of democratic engagement which is associated with regulatory democracy (Armstrong 2013). A system of stakeholder input, a system of notice and comment, is established in which stakeholders and national parliaments can express opinions which can feed into the

15 *Pfizer*, T-13/99, EU:T:2002:209, para. 199.

European Semester for Economic Coordination. As with other regulatory processes, these inputs feed into policy but are excluded from enforcement as they do not touch the sanction processes.

The second trajectory formalised by the European Stability Mechanism (ESM) and Regulation 472/2013 is that of *bonded government*. The bond describes not merely a commitment to repay a debt but also, from the old Indo-European word *bhendh*, something which ties parties together in a relationship of tight mutual dependence. The *bhendh* is used to preserve or maintain a particular place or object (Roy 2009: 177), and also, in Viking legend, to embody elements of the supernatural or fantastical to material things so that they cannot be lost. The bond is used, in other words, to secure, first, a relationship dedicated to restore a reality which embodied an imaginary moral equilibrium and which the bonded party is to feel great guilt for breaching. As something imagined, there is, to be sure, a fantastical element to this reality. It marks, secondly, a relationship of dependence (and, therefore, of possible abuse) which acts as the vehicle for this restoration in which one party has authority but no responsibility, while the other has responsibility but no authority. As this relationship exists to restore a treasured (but distorted) mutual commitment, it is characterised not merely by the dominance of one party but by a distorted moral economy in which the duty to repay is projected as going to a party's sense of who they are (Esterci 1996: 130–35).

Applying this to the ESM, we see, first, that the projected way of life is the 'financial stability of the euro area'.[16] Relative poverty or levels of suffering are not preconditions for financial support, but, rather, whether the state of that state in question's public finances poses a risk to the euro area's stability.

In principle, support should only be given if it is indispensable to protect this stability.[17] This imaginary has played out in debtor states where default would be to retreat from modernity itself (Featherstone 2011: 193). It has also played out more generally with the sovereign debt crisis being seen as a 'crisis of confidence in [...] Europe itself' (Barroso 2011). Repayment of debt by the states whice were offered financial support is central to restoring this and to securing a form of redemption. A second feature is the quality of the commitment entered into by debtor states. These do not rest in simple compliance with formal legal structures, but with malleable notions. It is hard to characterise the memoranda of understanding

16 ESM Treaty, Article 3.
17 ESM Treaty, Articles 12 and 13.

setting out the conditions to be followed as legal documents.[18] It is not clear what legal sanctions are prompted by formal breach and they are continually revisited. The first Greek memorandum was altered five times, for example, in its first year of operation (Tuori 2012: 12). Furthermore, a whole range of other instruments characterised by their non-legal qualities have been used to support these arrangements, prevent default and secure repayment of debt (Wilsher 2014: 257–66).[19] Indeed, it is not clear that compliance with these would secure the debtor state's position. This rests on how it is perceived by financial markets, and, if they perceive its performance as insufficient to regain sufficient trust for investment, new financial support will be have to found for that state and new conditions will have to be imposed. The third feature of this relationship is that it is founded on administrative decision rather than clear legal competence. The ESM grants EU institutions, notably the Commission and the ECB, powers to negotiate and monitor agreements governing a range of welfare and fiscal activities which are not granted by the TEU, but this has been held to be fine providing it is granted by the decision of some national governments and provided that it does not alter the 'essential character' of their EU powers.[20] Fourthly, the illusion of full restoration, however iniquitous the consequences, is maintained. No form of debt relief, direct or indirect, can be offered on the financial support provided to these states.[21]

If, in 2011 and 2012, these two trajectories started off as discrete, with the former intended to discipline all euro-area states and the other to redeem those requiring financial support, their trajectories have increasingly intertwined in the period since. At a formalistic level, this has taken place through the bringing of future financial support programmes firmly within EU law.[22] These programmes may still be discrete from the rest of the regulatory package governing states' public finances and macroeconomies, but they cast an ever-lengthening shadow. Similar structures now apply where a state is found to have an excessive deficit. It must now

18 They have been characterised as not generating legal commitments by the Greek Council of State, 668/2012, *First Memorandum of Understanding*, Judgment of 20 February 2012.

19 These have included purchase of debt on the secondary market by the ECB (the Securities Market Programme), the use of the TARGET2 payment system within the euro as a form of credit between national central banks, and the extension of loans on equal terms to all commercial banks by the ECB (Long-Term Refinancing Operation), and most recently the purchase of recovered bonds.

20 *Pringle*, EU:C:2012:756, para. 158.

21 2 BvR 2728/13 *ECB/ESM*, Judgment of 14 January 2014 (German Constitutional Court).

22 Regulation 472/2013, n. 12, above, Article 7(1).

put forward an 'economic partnership programme' describing the policy measures, structural reforms and measures to improve competitiveness that will be taken, and these will be duly policed.[23] The narrative of bonded government is also being extended beyond that of policing deviant states, and is seeping more generally into the language of the risk regulation. The 'Report of the Four Presidents' setting out a road map for deeper integration within the euro area proposed that individual contractual arrangements be established between each euro-area state and the EU institutions (van Rompuy et al. 2012). These arrangements would cover activities which are considered to pose risks for the euro area (European Commission 2013a: 4–6) and would set out fiscal and structural policies to be carried out by each state with 'temporary, targeted' financial support offered as an incentive for compliance with these arrangements (14–16).[24] The Commission set this out more specifically in a call for a Convergence and Competitiveness Instrument, which would set out individual contractual arrangements with individual states containing measures to be adopted and timelines for adoption, with financial support for implementation to be provided by the Union (European Commission 2013b: 2–3). In December 2013, the European Council renamed the arrangements 'Partnerships for Growth, Jobs and Competitiveness'. It stated individual contractual arrangements were to be embedded in the European Semester and would apply to all euro-area states except those subject to a macroeconomic adjustment programme. They would cover:

> a broad range of growth and job-enhancing policies and measures, including the performance of labour and product markets, the efficiency of the public sector, as well as research and innovation, education and vocational training, employment and social inclusion. (European Council 2013: para. 34)

Alongside this, associated solidarity mechanisms would be established to provide support for meeting these arrangements (European Council 2013: paras. 30–36). The controversial nature of such arrangements has, to date, meant that further elaboration has stalled. For the moment, it is better to see this as a stymying of this logic than a rejection of it. The draft Franco-German proposals for further Eurozone integration, leaked to *Die Zeit* in June 2015, proposed therefore a more powerful euro group with better resources which would impose stricter

23 Ibid., Article 9.

24 All euro area states would be required to enter such arrangements. It would be a matter of choice for non-euro area states.

controls over national governments (*Die Zeit* 2015). All these arrangements are clearly regulatory ones intended to abate risks to the euro area from perceived poor economic or fiscal performance and to prevent states from being subject to correction plans under the excessive imbalance procedure. However, they contain strong elements of bonded government, with the power of these depending on the individual state's need for support and the strenuousness of the conditions imposed. The consequence is the emergence of a spectrum. At each end sits the ideal types of risk regulation and bonded government. Very few states will be subject to either narrative exclusively, with elements of each touching on how institutional procedures or conditions are articulated or executed. The constitutional resettlement will also, to be sure, be highly uneven as the mix between these narratives and the strength with which they bear down will depend greatly on the circumstances of each individual euro-area state.

Communities of risk and divided sovereignty

Risk regulation touches the question of sovereignty insofar as it frames euro-area states as forming a *community of risk*. The grounding for Union power over public finances set out in the 'Six Pack' and Fiscal Compact is based on recognition of risks that euro-area economies and public finance pose to each other and a mutual commitment to manage these risks. The notion of risk is too transient a concept to supplant sovereignty. Its assumption is that sovereigns can establish conditions for the realisation of these public goods. They may not be able to do this consistently in a reliable manner, and it is this which has to be regulated. Both the German Constitutional Court and the French Constitutional Council, thus, found the Fiscal Compact constitutionally unproblematic, notwithstanding that it requires quasi-constitutional change to entrench the balanced budget rule.[25] The former held that it did not over-constrain budgetary policy, a field central to German constitutional identity whose content has to be agreed by the German parliament.[26] In like vein, the French Constitutional Council found that the Fiscal Compact did not compromise the essential conditions for the exercise of national sovereignty

25 Article 3(2) TSCG.

26 2 BvR 1390/12 *ESM Treaty/Fiscal Compact*, Judgment of 9 September 2012, paras. 301–316.

as protected by the French Constitution.[27] These judgments are paralleled by the European Council Conclusions of December 2013 which stated that the new partnerships on growth, jobs and competitiveness must respect budgetary sovereignty (European Council 2013: para. 36). However, sovereignty is destabilised, as a community of risk introduces the idea of *balance* to the body politic: be it a balanced macroeconomy, a balanced budget or a deficit which should not be excessive. If, historically, the sovereign as a body politic was indivisible and immutable, this idea of balance now characterises it as permeable to the external environment with there being a duty on the legal system to recalibrate this body politic in response to external jolts. This is not only economically and politically challenging, as this external environment is a source of constant instability but also requires states to constitutionalise the world of risk cultures.[28] They have to take a stance on how to anticipate the possibility of adverse events.

Some have taken a strategic approach, seeing this as a chance for them to gain advantage. In its Basic Law, Germany has sought a 'beggar thy neighbour' policy by committing itself to a lower budget deficit (0.35 per cent of GDP) than that required by EU law in the hope that this will enable easier borrowing for itself than the rest of the euro area.[29] Others with relatively strong fiscal positions have taken a stance that this risk is insufficiently grave to warrant change. There has been little constitutional response or debate about such an amendment in Estonia, Finland, Luxembourg or the Netherlands. Another group took a more tactical stance: reactive, defensive and hesitant. In some instances, the idea of a balanced budget is left highly generalised,[30] to be defined subsequently by the national legislature[31] or by the Union – one with a constitutional commitment in the last case to do what that state is told in the hope that this will placate capital markets.[32] There is a final group, which contains Portugal and France, where significant debates took place about constitutional amendments, and this was indeed proposed by the national government but it was

27 Decision no. 2012-653 DC, *Treaty on Stability, Coordination and Governance in the Economic and Monetary Union*, Judgment of 9 August 2012, paras. 16 and 30.

28 On the responses of national constitutions, see the excellent EUI resource. http://eurocrisislaw.eui.eu/topic/national-law-changes/.

29 This is now contained in Article 115(2) Basic Law. For criticism, see Truber and Will 2012.

30 Article 81(6) Italian Constitution.

31 Article 148 Slovenian Constitution.

32 Article 135(2) Spanish Constitution.

unable to secure the necessary parliamentary majority. Legislation was, nevertheless, passed to meet the balanced budget rule. In such instances, the risks are recognised but the commitment to meeting them is of a non-constitutional nature, thereby suggesting no wider resettlement to meet the demands of this risk community.[33]

This world of constitutional risk cultures has shaped government responses to the unfolding of the crisis. The German position, whilst securing it more flexibility internationally, constrains it domestically. There is simply a formal rule to be met. The government has, thus, called for others to adopt a similar stance.[34] However, this position has a deeper element. It sees economic stability secured by formal procedures and norms as the foundation for the German constitutional settlement. This has a narrative which harks back to *Brunner*, the judgment on the constitutionality of the Maastricht Treaty, which found that, although monetary policy was a significant and wide-ranging power, it did not need to be subject to German democratic controls, as economic stability was the rock upon which democracy was built. In this way, economic stability has become a form of *raison d'état* which pre-empts democracy.[35] By contrast, the Italian constitutional position requires its government to agitate as much as possible for a change in EU rules, as only that will allow it the freedom to escape austerity.[36] Its position is, paradoxically, the most Europeanised, as it has transferred the power of decision over what is a balanced budget to EU decision-makers. The French position, by contrast, lends itself to defiance. There is little constraint, and, therefore, when EU burdens became unduly imposed there is every incentive for governments to challenge them.[37]

In a bonded universe, a straightforward division of sovereignty takes place. On the one hand, the sovereignty of states participating in the ESM or similar arrangements persists. On the other, the memoranda of

33 An intermediate position is that of the Irish Fiscal Responsibility Act 2012. This is a statute but is protected from constitutional challenge.

34 'Merkel Defends Fiscal Rules as Paris and Rome Put Growth First', *Financial Times*, 16 October 2014. www.ft.com/cms/s/0/fedbfcfc-5518-11e4-b616-00144feab7de.html#axzz3Gn4hW4K3.

35 *Brunner* v. *TEU* [1994] 1 CMLR 57, paras. 95–96.

36 The Italian Prime Minister, Matteo Renzi, not only advocated greater budget flexibility, but, it was reported, made it a condition of his support for the appointment of the new Commission President. Bloomberg, 'Renzi Backs Juncker on Budget Flexibility', 18 June 2014. www.bloomberg.com/video/renzi-backs-juncker-on-italian-budget-flexibility-BiugYK9jQAqBRvJYQlxifw.html.

37 'France to Miss EU Budget Deficit Target', *Guardian*, 10 September 2014. www.theguardian.com/business/2014/sep/10/france-miss-eu-budget-deficit-target.

the ESM have gone to those activities, which, in Agamben's words, enable 'bare life', namely, those activities which allow us to exist as biological organisms, be these social assistance programmes that allow people to be housed and fed, health care spending or pensions. This control over bare life, the power to let live, is a hallmark of sovereign power (Agamben 1998: 142). The ESM is exercising powers historically associated with the sovereign. As a consequence, debates about the ESM and other financial support arrangements have been marked by whether these excessively encroached on state sovereignty. The Supreme Court of Estonia was most explicit. It found the offering of financial support within the framework of the ESM compromised Estonia's financial sovereignty, and that the ESM was only compatible with the Estonian constitution because it pursued a legitimate purpose, namely, protecting against financial instability and endangerment of the economy, and did so in a proportionate manner.[38] In addition, the German Constitutional Court ruled that excessive sovereign powers in the field of budgetary policy had been transferred to Union institutions which threatened Germany's constitutional identity and the ESM would only be constitutional if the German parliament participated in the exercise of these powers.[39] More recently, the Greek Council of State found that a wage cut in the salaries of military personnel agreed under the memorandum violated the Constitution because the Greek state had a special duty towards these personnel by virtue of their mission in securing defence, public order and preventing crime: a mission which it deemed to be an expression of state sovereignty.[40]

A governmentalisation of sovereignty has also taken place within the Europeanised side of this division of sovereignty. This requires some explanation. Historically, sovereignty – be it vested in the monarch, parliament, the nation or the people – has acted as a counterpart to government. The sovereign ordained government, thereby indicating its limited and authorised qualities. It was also something for which government worked (Maiolo 2007: 151–53; Agamben 2012: 109–43). Sovereignty, thereby, acted to limit government, expose the insufficiency of its performance and, as a consequence, expose it to contestation (Lindahl 2003: 87–90 and

38 Case 3-4-1-6-12 *Request of the Chancellor of Justice to declare Article 4(4) of the Treaty establishing the European Stability Mechanism in conflict with the Constitution*, Judgment of 12 July 2012.

39 Case 2 BvR 1390/12 et al. *ESM Treaty (Temporary Injunctions)*, Judgment of 12 September 2012.

40 CTE 2192/2014, *Salaries of Military Personnel*, Judgment of 23 June 2014. www.ste.gr/councilofstate/index_gr.jsp.

101–10). Sovereignty was also to be contrasted with the notion of sovereign powers, which were powers over the individual that could be transferred to the administration. They were distinct from sovereignty, which was irreducible and non-transferrable (Loughlin 2010: 186–96). This distinction is not present at a pan-Union level as the Union does not claim sovereignty. It has acquired sovereign powers for its institutions, however. As there is no residual notion of sovereignty to limit or structure these and no distinction between sovereignty and sovereign power in EU (or ESM) law, this leads to a risk that EU government and sovereignty become conflated (Chalmers 2013: 204–10).

The consequence of this governmentalisation was exposed in *Pringle*, where the legality of the ESM was challenged.[41] The Court of Justice characterised the ESM in three important ways. First, with regard to the provenance of its power, it was sufficient that this was done by national executives collectively. They could entrust tasks to the institutions outside the framework of the Treaties provided that these tasks do not alter the essential character of what these do under the Treaties.[42] Administrative decision could find legal authority. Secondly, this power could be almost limitless. This limitlessness could involve EU institutions having very wide-ranging powers, as the only constraint is that these powers do not affect the 'essential character' of the institutions. In the case of the Commission, this character is merely to promote the general interest of the Union, a sufficiently broad cachet to allow almost anything.[43] This limitlessness also comprises a lack of institutional checks on the exercise of this power. Thus, in response to the claim that the ESM should be subject to fundamental rights and judicial review, the Court stated that, as the ESM operated outside the framework of EU law, it was not subject to EU legal controls.[44] The third characteristic of the ESM is that an institutional settlement was established which provides for no arena for discussion or contestation of its power. Discussion in other arenas was to be curtailed by there being no duty on the part of ESM bodies to disclose internal deliberations or reasons for decisions.

The other side of this division of sovereignty, the side described in national terms, acts as a counterpoint to EU action, and serves to found legal resistance against EU measures. However, in this case, it is peculiarly

41 *Pringle*, EU:C:2012:756.
42 Ibid., para. 158.
43 Ibid., paras. 163–164.
44 Ibid. paras. 178–181.

evacuated. There are no judgments from states seeking financial support where a constitutional court has ruled that the terms of a memorandum excessively encroach on national sovereignty. This is possibly due to the particular moral economy of the bond in which it is a peculiar form of redemption on the part of the debtor. Thus, when the issue was raised before the Greek Council of State, it ruled that there had been no violation of sovereignty as the memorandum had been something autonomously assumed by the Greek government.[45] In legal terms, it involved a wholly domestic pre-commitment: even if this flew in the face of the financial reality. By contrast, this moral economy does not apply in the case of creditor states. In its *ECB/ESM* decision, the German Constitutional Court used analogous reasoning to that of sovereignty to rule on the legality of the system of Outright Monetary Transactions.[46] It found that the system of bond purchases was *ultra vires*, as it constituted an act of economic policy and the ECB had no powers in this field beyond supporting the economic policies of the euro-area states. The Constitutional Court then stated that OMT would only have to be annulled if, inter alia, the breach was structurally significant. It would have to transgress either on German constitutional identity or particularly affect German democratic discourse: something that was the case here, as OMT had considerable implications for German fiscal policy.[47] This reasoning of structurally significant breach uses an identical grammar to that deployed by other courts when they complain about excessive encroachment on national sovereignty. In both instances, there is an idea of a domestic body politic – a collective human order which may be designated a nation, people, public or society – deprived, by the Union, of a freedom to take measures to set out what it is about. The point was made even more explicitly in the German Constitutional Court's final ruling on the ESM where it ruled that democratic self-government required that 'as representatives of the people' the Bundestag retain control of fundamental budgetary decision.[48]

45 668/2012, *First Memorandum of Understanding*, Judgment of 20 February 2012.

46 The programme of Outright Monetary Transactions (OMT) was founded on a power of administrative decision without regard to competence, European Central Bank press release of 6 September 2012: 'Technical Features of Outright Monetary Transactions'. www.ecb.europa.eu/press/pr/date/2012/html/pr120906_1.en.html. It committed the ECB to open-ended purchase of securities on the secondary market of those states which had entered a financial support programme where this was necessary to support the public finances of that state.

47 2 BvR 2728/13 *ECB/ESM*, Judgment of 14 January 2014, paras. 37–40.

48 2 BvR 1390/12 *ESM/Fiscal Compact*, Judgment of 18 March 2014, para. 162.

Destabilisation of this control by the Union went not merely to this institution's prerogatives, but also to a notion that the German people were no longer free, and, implicitly, sovereign.

A challenge with this reasoning is the asymmetries it generated. The German Constitutional Court has, thus, been criticised for making unilateral decisions for Europe and for failing to acknowledge this in its reasoning. The Court's decisions affect Greeks, Portuguese, etc., arguably more than Germans, but there is no recognition of their voice or needs in its judgments (Everson and Joerges 2013: 17–18; Wilkinson 2014). The force of this argument would be softened if other national constitutional courts expressed themselves as freely about the legality of these arrangements. However, as we have seen, even if this is formally possible, this has not taken place.

Sovereignty operates across a spectrum, consequently, in a post-crisis world. At one end, there are states which have ignored the world of constitutional risk cultures and do not seek financial support. For these states, the changes have been minimal. If invoked at all, sovereignty goes, *pace* the judgment of the Estonian Supreme Court, to how much support they are to offer. It acts as a constraint on redistribution. There are then states which do not require financial support but through internalising the balanced budget rules and the like into their constitutional settlements have entered a world of constitutional risk cultures in which sovereignty becomes about a particular constitutional disposition to risk: be it complete formal avoidance in the German commitment to economic stability, to institutional adaptability in the case of Spain or explicit defiance in the case of France. And, finally, there are states requiring financial support. These enter into a bifurcated world in which sovereignty involves both external institutions having uncircumscribed powers over them and also a foundation for resistance.

Attenuated citizenship and a Europeanised citizenship of resistance

There is no direct language on citizenship in either the 'Six Pack' or the Fiscal Compact. At one level, this is unsurprising, as these configure institutional arrangements around a series of policy goals. The language of risk, however, extends the range of commitments owed by the citizens of a state. These have duties to limit the risks imposed on citizens of other euro-area states, and, insofar as risk goes to restricting the incidence of future adverse events, those on future generations. The compact at the heart of the citizen is, thus, reconfigured. If, conventionally, it was a compact owed between current members of a community identified with a national territory, the narrative of risk regulation distends this so it is now something owed also to citizens outside the territory and to future citizens. Such a compact would travel in the opposite direction from that traditionally journeyed by modern citizenship, which has granted members entitlements of freedom and equality backed by community commitments as bulwarks against the instability and injustices of the wider socio-economic environment. Turner has, thus, argued that citizenship should increasingly turn its attention towards rooting personal security and sense of self in opposition to transnational flows which destabilise individual identities and senses of place (Turner 2001: 189). Notwithstanding its extension of benign duties of guardianship, a citizenship characterised by an open-ended commitment towards a highly underspecified group of others vitiates such a project. This is all the more so, as the objects of this commitment are artefacts. Future generations can offer the current generation no mutual commitment as the former do not exist yet. The quality of the mutual commitment between citizens in different states is unsteady as the distribution of future adverse consequences is unclear. Nobody knows, for example, which other EU citizens would suffer in the event of a Greek default. The consequence is an unsteady dilution of national citizenship.

The commitment to future generations does this most starkly through the use of fiscal rules. These set numerical targets for budgetary policy generally and for its different components. They can set targets in terms of the revenue to be obtained, expenditure, budget deficits, total debt or structural deficits, and can be applied not just to government generally but to central, local or regional government. They are seen by advocates as setting a commitment between generations by making the externalities for future generations of current debt clear (Wyplosz 2013: 502–03). However, it was only in the 1990s that fiscal rules began to be applied as at national level, largely as signals of fiscal commitment to the financial markets, and the evidence of their policy effectiveness is far from clear (Kennedy and Roberts 2001; von Hagen 2006: 26–27).

EU law requires that each state adopt numerical fiscal rules specific to it which promote compliance with Union reference values on deficit and debt (e.g., a structural deficit not greater than 0.5 per cent of GDP, a budget deficit not greater than 3 per cent of GDP or total debt not more than 60 per cent of GDP) and are calculated over a multi-annual fiscal planning horizon.[49] These rules provide a detailed web setting out

49 Directive 2011/85, n. 6, above, Article 5.

micro-calculations over revenue and expenditure, how these reference values will be met and standards against which performance is to be reviewed. To this end, this web is strengthened by states also being required to set out the targets and scope of these rules; systems for compliance; independent bodies to provide reliable and independent analysis of whether there has been compliance; and the consequences of compliance.[50] However, as even their advocates have admitted, fiscal rules are deeply undemocratic. They enact highly artificial numerical values which restrict the tax and spend choices available to representative democracies (Wyplosz 2013: 504–07). Choices cannot be made because they breach a numerical value, and the further these numerical values stretch into the future – as they do with a multi-annual framework – the more constraining these decisions become. The central space for the enactment of citizenship, namely, the coming together in representative institutions to determine the extent and quality of mutual provision within a society, has been shrunk. The scale of this shrinkage is illustrated by EU legal detail hidden away in other legislation. For states with a balanced budget, annual growth in expenditure must not exceed potential growth unless the difference is matched by corresponding revenue measures.[51] For other states (most states), increased expenditure must be at a rate lower than the rate of growth in their GDP,[52] and, if they reduce government revenue (i.e., through lower taxes), they must make matching expenditure reductions.[53]

The commitment to citizens in other states is present wherever a state has to engage with actors from other EU states or with other EU institutions over its fiscal, welfare or economic policies. Famously, this can occur as a corrective process where it is subject to additional policing or sanction because it has run an excessive deficit or macroeconomic imbalance or where it has significantly deviated from its path towards a balanced budget. This policing and sanctioning is done by administrative actors, however, namely, the Commission and economic and finance ministers in the ECOFIN Council. It is difficult to argue that these are suitable relays for a wider compact between citizens in different territories. Instead, through their policing and sanctioning, they act to restrict what

50 Ibid., Article 6. Subsequent legislation further required independent bodies to be established to monitor compliance with the fiscal rules. Regulation 473/2013, n. 7, above, Article 5.

51 Regulation 1466/97 as amended by Regulation 1175/2011, n. 6, above, Article 5(1)(a).

52 Ibid., Article 5(1)(b).

53 Ibid., Article 5(1)(c).

states may offer to their citizens. Alongside the corrective process, there is a preventive process. This now largely happens within the context of the European Semester. The Semester involves surveillance and assessment of national economic, employment, fiscal, climate change and welfare policies. The Commission makes recommendations on an individual state's budgetary, economic and social policy, with the Council endorsing these recommendations.[54] States are expected to take due account of these in the formulation of their policies in the succeeding years.[55] However, once again the central accountability is to administrative actors in the form of the Commission and the Council. To be sure, the European Parliament is to be involved in the passing of a resolution and debate on the Recommendations.[56] It can also ask questions of the Presidents of the Commission, Council, European Council and euro group about it.[57] Stakeholders may also seek involvement in accordance with prior EU legal procedures.[58] However, this is weak stuff, which does not displace the dominance of the Commission and the Council. It provides a thin veneer over the compressing of the space for the development of the national citizenship compact by the latter institutions.

Neither the EU law on fiscal rules, nor that on the corrective processes, nor that on the European Semester, makes any explicit mention of citizenship. To be sure, this allows these to subvert national citizenship draconically. It also results in their effects being unsteady, which, in turn, allows for ad hoc ring-fencing of national institutions from its effects. Macroeconomic imbalance procedures are required therefore to respect national practices and institutions for wage formation and collective bargaining.[59] This is an isolated example, however. Beyond this, restrictions on the enactment of national citizenship occur as and when states are considered to implement and to observe the fiscal rules and other EU disciplines concerning their fiscal, economic and welfare policies.

On its face, the situation regarding citizenship is even more unforgiving where the narrative of bonded government applies. The various financial support mechanisms, be they those of the ESM or of the ECB, make no provision for involvement in any form by a citizen of any euro-area state.

54 Ibid., Article 2-a(3).
55 Ibid., Article 2-a(3).
56 Ibid., Article 2-a(4).
57 Ibid., Article 2-ab.
58 Ibid., Article 2-a(4).
59 Regulation 1176/2011, n. 3, above, Article 1(3).

Furthermore, as the Court has stated in *Pringle*, given that the ESM, at least, does not have to observe EU fundamental rights law,[60] it is equally not required to observe (under EU law at least) any constraints imposed by either EU or national citizenship laws. The combination of the division of sovereignty mentioned earlier, which allows national laws to emerge as points of resistance to this exercise of EU sovereignty, and this absence of constraint, have resulted, however, in an emergence of a *Europeanised citizenship narrative*, which is being developed by national constitutional courts. As these have seen the operation of the ESM violate tenets of domestic citizenship which go to the heart of both the national body politic (as they have seen it) and domestic constitutional identity, across the euro area there has been strident and increasingly generalised resistance from those states which have been offered financial support as well as those offering it.

This narrative began when the German Constitutional Court stated that the right to vote for representatives in the Bundestag, arguably the most central tenet of German citizenship, was violated if the latter did not have the power to determine a policy, such as budgetary policy, which went to the heart of German constitutional identity. Decisions made by the ESM or other support arrangements with significant budgetary effects in Germany must involve the Bundestag, therefore, and the latter must be given sufficient information to discharge this task.[61] If the need for citizen representation was set out in Germany, in states receiving financial support, there is increasingly concern to secure a certain equality of burden shared between citizens and a minimum level of well-being for them. With regard to the former, the Portuguese Constitutional Tribunal has twice found that Portuguese implementation of its memorandum of understanding was unconstitutional, as reductions in public remuneration unconstitutionally discriminated between public-sector and private-sector workers with regard to who should bear the costs of the measures it violated, thereby breaching the principles of equality and proportionality in the Portuguese Constitution.[62] On the latter, decisions have taken two routes. The Portuguese Constitutional Tribunal has conveyed that decisions must allow time for citizens to reorganise their lives when significant costs are

60 *Pringle*, EU:C:2012:756.

61 2 BvR 987/10 et al. *Euro Rescue Fund*, Judgment of 7 September 2011, paras. 124–125; 2 BvR 1390/12 et al. *ESM Treaty (Temporary Injunctions)*, Judgment of 12 September 2012, paras. 208–215.

62 Acordão 187/2013, *State Budget 2012*, Diário da República, 1.ª série N.º 78 22 April 2013; Acordão 413/2014 *State Budget 2014*, Judgment of 30 May 2014. www.tribunalconstitucional.pt/tc/acordaos/20140413.html.

imposed on them. Whilst it allowed that the administration could reduce public pensions, it found that cuts made to public pensions, with insufficient warning for recipients to make alternative provision, breached the Portuguese constitutional principle of mutual trust: the Portuguese constitutional counterpart for legitimate expectations.[63] The other route taken was that adopted by the Greek Council of State in its *EYDAP* judgment, where it set out that there is a minimum threshold of substantive rights which measures cannot fall below.[64] The challenge was to the privatisation of a water and sewage company. The Greek court found that this privatisation violated Articles 5(5) and 21(3) of the Greek Constitution, which respectively granted individuals a right to protection of their health and imposed a duty on the state to secure it. It reasoned that the provision of clear water and sanitation was central to public health, and privatisation gave no certainty as to the continuity of the provision of these at an affordable level.

These judgments are scattered, and it is currently only possible to talk of an incipient Europeanised citizenship narrative. This narrative would not be developed out of Court of Justice case law, but from national judicial responses to EU institutional interventions in the field of economic, fiscal and social policy. (On the important role of national courts, see Komárek 2014.) Reasons for believing it might emerge are twofold. In the first place, it will be difficult for EU institutions to ask something of one state when it has been found to go against the constitution of another state. Politically, the inequality of treatment would be picked upon by opponents as evidence of the egregiousness of the measure. In the second place, it is possible that national courts will look to the practice of courts in other states to work out the meaning of their own constitutional provisions in the light of the novel contexts in which these must be interpreted in a post-crisis world. This has been done most recently by the German Constitutional Court when it cited the position of the supreme courts of ten other Union states to help develop its view on the idea that EU law should respect the constitutional identity of member states.[65] Courts may do this because these provide insights. They may also do it because it bolsters their position. Criticism of a position is harder when it is one adopted across Europe. And the benefits of this are also twofold. It allows the combined wisdom

63 Ruling 862/13 *State Pensions*, Judgment of 18 December 2013, paras. 21–45. www.tribunalconstitucional.pt/tc/acordaos/20130862.html.

64 8 Cte 1906/2014 Olom *EYDAP*, Judgment of 4 June 2014.

65 2 BvR 2728/13 *ESM/ECB*, Judgment of 7 February 2014, para. 30.

of euro-area courts to come together to develop a common, albeit not unified, narrative on what citizenship means in the euro area. Alongside this, insofar as the euro area constitutes a large laboratory comprised of many jurisdictions in which a diversity of challenges will be made to notions of citizenship, one would expect, as a corollary, a commensurately nuanced and detailed vision of citizenship to emerge in response to these challenges.

Europeanised parliamentary opportunism

The dominant trope under both the regulatory and the bonded government narratives is that the crisis significantly accelerated executive dominance over parliaments in respect of budgetary policy to the extent where the influence of the latter is significantly eviscerated (Habermas 2011; Chalmers 2012; Crum 2013; Dawson and de Witte 2013; Majone 2014). The reason for such consensus lies in the formal structures which institutionalise these narratives.

Parliaments are seen within the risk regulation narrative as a threat to those public goods protected by the 'Six Pack' and Fiscal Compact, be they a balanced economy or balanced budget. The need for re-election incentivises opportunism and short-termism. If reference is made to the need for their 'closer and more-timely involvement' in the governance arrangements of the 'Six Pack', actual provision is scant.[66] Within the preventive part of the arrangements, there is provision that states should involve them within the European Semester but only in line with their legal and political arrangements.[67] States are also required to provide information to the Council on whether the programmes setting out their fiscal and economic projections (and assumptions on which these are based) for the following three years, and how they plan to move towards a balanced budget, were presented to the national parliament, whether the latter had approved it and whether it had had the opportunity to discuss the Council's opinion on the previous programme.[68] However, this is only a reporting requirement and there is no actual duty on national governments to involve national parliaments in any of these ways at all (House of Lords European Union Committee 2013: para. 167). There is absolutely no provision for national parliamentary involvement in the corrective processes where the states are subject to additional policing and can be sanctioned for breach

66 Regulation 1175/2011, n. 3, above, Preamble, alinea 11.

67 Ibid., Preamble, alinea 15.

68 Regulation 1466/97, n. 6, above, Article 3(4).

of budgetary or macroeconomic norms. As mentioned earlier, the process is an administrative triangle between the national administration, the Commission and the finance ministers of the ECOFIN Council with policy subject to negotiation between the national administration and the Council in the first place, with the Council intervening only if this breaks down. This parliamentary deficit in both the preventive and corrective processes is not neutral as these processes are, in turn, used by national administrations to counter parliament suggestions or preferences.

The diminishing of parliamentary status within budgetary policy is more vividly drawn, however, in Regulation 473/2013, one half of the 'Two Pack'. This aligns euro-area budget processes. Budgets for central government for the forthcoming year are to be fixed not later than 31 December.[69] Draft plans are to be presented to the Commission by 15 October.[70] It is to assess whether these comply with that state's EU budgetary obligations by 30 November, and can ask a state to revise its draft within two weeks of submission if serious non-compliance with these obligations is identified.[71] In addition, the euro group shall discuss these Commission opinions on the drafts.[72] As these are drafts which might have to be revised, national parliaments cannot adopt budgets until the process is completed. This might be as late as the end of November, giving them only a month to adopt the budget. This is an absurdly short time, and a consequence of this is that debate between the Commission and the national administration may supplant that within the parliament as the central arena for debate over the budget (para. 152).

The narrative of bonded government provides even less mention of national parliaments. There is no provision in the ESM either for national parliaments to participate in the workings of it or that they must approve the memorandum of understanding agreed by any state receiving financial support. The moral economy of the bond requires that the bonded party take not just formal ownership but also a moral responsibility for the debt. Payment is done because it is the right thing to do. This taking of ownership has required invariably that states seeking financial support have had to secure parliamentary assent for the programmes agreed under the memorandum of understanding. In many cases, this appears to be no more than the granting of hollow acclaim to a *fait accompli*. The successful challenges

69 n. 7, above, Article 4(3).
70 Ibid., Article 6(1).
71 Ibid., Article 7(1) & (2).
72 Ibid., Article 7(5).

before both the Greek Council of State and Portuguese Constitutional Tribunal bear witness to parliaments which were unable to influence egregious measures sufficiently. Notwithstanding that, this power of acclaim is technically a power of veto which grants a small space to secure some variation in the terms, the most notable of which was that secured in March 2013 when the Cypriot parliament voted against and secured the removal of a term in the Cypriot memorandum which would have placed a levy on all deposit accounts. However, this space is very small. The memoranda were subject to considerable debates in the parliaments of all the states securing support and the Cypriot example of variation is an isolated one. The space granted is a space for resistance but at an uncertain cost. The parliament does not know what the costs of seeking variation will entail, be they a refusal to grant any support or the imposition of more draconian terms.

All this makes a powerful case for the asphyxiation of parliamentary democracy by the crisis. However, for all this, a *Europeanised parliamentary opportunism* has emerged which has recreated a certain room for parliamentary democracy (Jančić 2014). Opportunities were provided by the fluid qualities of both the risk regulation and bonded government narratives. To be sure, each provides a legal superstructure which puts procedures in play, allows for selective institutional interventions and prescribes a large number of substantive constraints. However, neither provides a closed legally constituted space for budgetary policy to take place nor sets out a legal system of checks and balances which fully governs institutional relations. This results in many institutional interventions taking place in situations which are either not fully governed by EU legal procedures or fall largely outside them. This has, inter alia, created space for parliamentary opportunism.

First, there is now considerable parliamentary debate of Union government of economic, fiscal and welfare policy. It is, indeed, the dominant subject in parliamentary debates about the European Union. In a study of parliamentary debates between 2010 and 2012, Auel and Hönig (2014: 1184–88) found that there were 998 hours of plenary debate across the Union on these topics, 47.4 per cent of all EU related plenary debates. In like vein, Jančić (2014) has noted, in a study of British, French and Portuguese parliaments, increased parliamentary overview of European Council meetings, with debates prior to and subsequent to every European Council meeting prompted by the sense of the importance of that institution in the government of the crisis.

Secondly, some advantage has been taken of the establishment of new arenas, notably the European Semester. A study found that plenary debates on the European Semester were relatively limited. Equally, there was little parliamentary tradition across the Union of discussing multi-annual budgetary plans by governments (Hallerberg et al. 2012: 68–75). However, the Semester had led to parliamentary committees debating the programmes (which contain multi-annual plans) which are submitted to the European Semester in the overwhelming majority of states, with a 2014 COSAC Report finding that 29 chambers out of a sample of 38 did so (COSAC 2014: 42). Equally, Commission evaluation of national draft budgets has also provided some opportunities for parliaments, with 21 out of a sample of 37 chambers stating parliamentary committees had considered these evaluations with the corollary implication that these evaluations provided more information and another perspective through which to consider their national budgets (44).

The final practice is that of inter-parliamentary networking. The TSCG provided for a conference of national parliaments and the European Parliament to consider budgetary policy and issues covered by the Fiscal Compact.[73] Potentially, this conference could give voice to a collective view of national parliaments of the compact states, and would thus have considerable authority. Notwithstanding the fact that it has met three times, it has been bedevilled by arguments about internal organisation and has yet to acquire this voice (Cooper 2014). A more powerful actor has been COSAC, the established body for national parliamentary voice. In 2013, it set out the range of national parliament views on the report of the 'Four Presidents' proposing greater fiscal and financial integration (COSAC 2013: 5–6). It went further in 2014 by making active recommendations of its own that the social dimension be better integrated into economic and monetary union, and, in particular, that there should be greater use of social and employment indicators (COSAC 2014: 32–34). It was helped by there being near unanimity amongst national parliaments on this, but it is possible, and this is argued very tentatively, that this may be a starting point for the exercise of collective parliamentary voice to inform Union decision-making in these fields.

This Europeanised opportunism is an inchoate and weak surrogate for parliamentary democracy. As Puntscher Riekmann and Wydra (2013: 565) have observed, national parliaments are placed in a situation in which their role is to debate and expose EU policies, but, ultimately, still to ratify them.

73 Article 13 TSCG.

In a world where parliaments become debating chambers – there to expose the follies of policy and allow critique to be forcefully expressed – it is not surprising that they look for all avenues to continue debate and allow review. However, the tolerance of this by executives is also telling. It suggests the institution of an empty proceduralism in which parliaments are accorded these avenues at the expense of any real influence over budgetary agendas or choice over budgetary ratification.

Conclusion

It is too early to tell how the crisis will reconfigure European constitutional democracy. Interpretations of citizenship and innovative forms of parliamentary involvement may flourish across Europe in vibrant ways. Notwithstanding their formal claims, pan-euro-area legal structures may be insufficiently resilient to bring about the sort of change they claim to effect. More pessimistically, it may be that the logic of risk regulation and bonded government are followed through with the consequent evisceration of traditional understandings of sovereignty, citizenship and parliamentary democracy. This is speculative because much is dependent on future institutional action, but this uncertainty is increased by a change already brought about. Historically, constitutions and political settlements provided the insulation for democracy. They provided structures which shielded it from wider social, economic or political pressures. Notwithstanding the wider inequalities and pressures, the political arena instituted a place of civility in which everybody stood as equals. The narratives of risk regulation and bonded government internalise these wider pressures and inequalities into legal norms which then strip away these protections. The quality of citizenship or parliamentary democracy present in a state will depend on the latitude allowed by these legal norms, whose content, in turn, is a response to the perceived position of that state's economy and its status in global capital markets. And the dismantling of this insulation is the corrosion of the proud European tradition of political autonomy and political equality.

References

Agamben, G. (1998) *Homo sacer: Sovereign Power and Bare Life*, Stanford, CA: Stanford University Press.

(2012) *The Kingdom and the Glory*, Stanford, CA: Stanford University Press.

Armstrong, K. (2013) 'The New Governance of EU Fiscal Discipline', *European Law Review*, 38(5), 601–17.

Auel, K., and Hönig, A. (2014) 'Parliaments in the Euro Crisis: Can the Losers of Integration Still Fight Back?', *Journal of Common Market Studies*, 52(6), 1184–93.

Barroso, J.-M. (2011) 'European Renewal – State of the Union Address 2011, European Parliament', Strasbourg, 28 September 2011, speech 11/607. http://europa.eu/rapid/press-release_SPEECH-11-607_en.htm.

Beetsma, R., et al. (2009) 'Planning to Cheat: EU Fiscal Policy in Real Time', *Economic Policy*, 24, 753.

Bockenförde, E. (1991) *State, Liberty and Society*, trans. J. Underwood, New York and Oxford: Berg.

Bodin, J. (1955) *Six Books of the Commonwealth*, trans. M. Tooley, Oxford: Blackwell.

Bonney, R. (1999) *The Rise of the Fiscal State in Europe, 1200-1815*, Oxford: Oxford University Press.

Braithwaite, J. (2002) 'Rewards and Regulation', *Journal of Law and Society*, 29(1), 12–26.

Chalmers, D. (2012) 'The European Redistributive State and a European Law of Struggle', *European Law Journal*, 18(5), 667–93.

(2013) 'European Restatements of Sovereignty', in R. Rawlings, P. Leyland and A. Young (eds), *Sovereignty and the Law: Domestic, European and International Perspectives*, Oxford: Oxford University Press.

Chalmers, D., Davies, G., and Monti, G. (2014) *European Union Law*, 3rd edn, Cambridge: Cambridge University Press.

Congleton, R. (2011) *Perfecting Parliament: Constitutional Reform, Liberalism, and the Rise of Western Democracy*, Cambridge: Cambridge University Press.

Cooper, I. (2014) 'Parliamentary Oversight of the EU after the Crisis: On the Creation of the "Article 13" Interparliamentary Conference', LUISS Guido Carlo Working Paper Series 21/2014.

COSAC (2013) *Nineteenth Bi-annual Report: Developments in European Union Procedures and Practices Relevant to Parliamentary Scrutiny*, Brussels: COSAC Secretariat.

(2014) *Twenty-first Bi-annual Report: Developments in European Union Procedures and Practices Relevant to Parliamentary Scrutiny*, Brussels: COSAC Secretariat.

Crum, B. (2013) 'Saving the Euro at the Cost of Democracy?', *Journal of Common Market Studies*, 51(4), 614–30.

Dawson, M., and de Witte, F. (2013) 'Constitutional Balance in the EU after the Euro-Crisis', *Modern Law Review*, 76(5), 817–44.

Einzig, P. (1959) *The Control of the Purse*, London: Secker & Warburg.

Esterci, N. (1996) 'Imobilização por Dívida e Formas de Dominação no Brasil de Hoje' *Lusetopie*, 4, 123–38.

European Commission (2013a) 'Towards a Deep and Genuine Economic and Monetary Union Ex Ante Coordination of Plans for Major Economic Policy Reforms', COM (2013) 166.

(2013b) 'Towards a Deep and Genuine Economic and Monetary Union: The Introduction of a Convergence and Competitiveness Instrument', COM (2013) 165.
European Council (2013) 'Conclusions of the Presidency of 20 December 2013', EUCO 217/13.
Everson, M., and Joerges, C. (2013) 'Who is the Guardian for Constitutionalism in Europe after the Financial Crisis?', London School of Economics LEQS Working Paper 63/2013.
Featherstone, K. (2011) 'The Greek Sovereign Debt Crisis and EMU: A Failing State in a Skewed Regime', *Journal of Common Market Studies*, 49(2), 193–217.
Fisher, L. (2014) *The Law of the Executive Branch: Presidential Power*, Oxford: Oxford University Press.
Grapperhaus, F. (1998) *Tax Tales from the Second Millennium: Taxation in Europe (1000 to 2000)*, Amsterdam: IBFD.
Habermas, J. (2011) 'Europe's Post-Democratic Era', *Guardian*, 10 November.
Hallerberg, M., et al. (2012) *An Assessment of the European Semester*, Brussels: Bruegel.
Heinig, H. (2008) *Der Sozialstaat im Dienst der Freiheit*, Tubingen: Mohr.
House of Lords European Union Committee (2013) 'The Role of National Parliaments in the European Union, Session 2013–14', 9th Report, Stationery Office.
Jančić, D. (2014) 'National Parliaments and EU Economic and Financial Governance: Battling/Combatting the Euro Crisis' (mimeograph).
Kantorowicz, E. *The King's Two Bodies: A Study in Mediaeval Political Theology*, Princeton, NJ: Princeton University Press.
Kelemen, D., and Teo, T. (2014) 'Law, Focal Points, and Fiscal Discipline in the United States and European Union', *American Political Science Review*, 108(2), 355–77.
Kennedy, S., and Roberts, J. (2011) 'The Role of Fiscal Rules in Determining Fiscal Performance', Banca di Italia Workshop on Fiscal Rules, Rome.
Komárek, J. (2014) 'National Constitutional Courts in the European Constitutional Democracy', *International Journal of Constitutional Law*, 12(3), 525–44.
Korpi, W. (1989) 'Power, Politics, and State Autonomy in the Development of Social Citizenship: Social Rights during Sickness in Eighteen OECD Countries since 1930', *American Sociological Review*, 54(3), 309–28.
Kwass, M. (2000) *Privilege and the Politics of Taxation in Eighteenth-Century France*, Cambridge: Cambridge University Press.
Lindahl, H. (2003) 'Sovereignty and Representation in the European Union', in N. Walker (ed.), *Sovereignty in Transition*, Oxford: Hart.
Loughlin, M. (2007) *Foundations of Public Law*, Oxford: Oxford University Press.
Maiolo, F. (2007) *Medieval Sovereignty: Marsilius of Padua and Bartolus of Saxoferrato*, Delft: Eburon.

Majone, G. (1997) 'From the Positive to the Regulatory State: Causes and Consequences of Changes in the Mode of Governance', *Journal of Public Policy*, 17(2), 139–67.

(2014) 'From Regulatory State to a Democratic Default', *Journal of Common Market Studies*, 52(6), 1216–23.

Marshall, T. (1950) *Citizenship and Social Class: And Other Essays*, Cambridge: Cambridge University Press.

Nauwerck, K. (1844) 'Über den Verein zur Hebung der untern Volksklasse, 15 Berliner Blätter', quoted in K. Peteren and J. Petersen, 'Confusion and Divergence: Origins and Meanings of the Term "Welfare State" in Germany and Britain, 1840–1940', *Journal of European Social Policy*, 23(1), 37–51.

Palmstorfer, R. (2014) 'The Reverse Majority Voting under the "Six Pack": A Bad Turn for the Union?' *European Law Journal*, 20(2), 186–203.

Petersen, K., and Petersen, J. (2013) 'Confusion and Divergence: Origins and Meanings of the Term "Welfare State" in Germany and Britain, 1840–1940', *Journal of European Social Policy*, 23(1), 37–51.

Posner, P., and Park, C.-K. (2007) 'Role of the Legislature in the Budget Process: Recent Trends and Innovations', *OECD Journal on Budgeting*, 7, 1–15.

Puntscher Riekmann, S., and Wydra, D. (2013) 'Representation in the European State of Emergency: Parliaments against Governments?', *Journal of European Integration*, 35(5), 565–82.

Rauch, B., et al. (2011) 'Fact and Fiction in EU-Governmental Economic Data', *German Economic Review*, 12(3), 243–55.

Rousseau, J.-J. (1999) *Discourse on Political Economy and The Social Contract*, trans. C. Betts, Harmondsworth: Penguin.

Roy, C. (2009) 'Practical Fastenings of the Supernatural', *Viking and Mediaeval Scandinavia*, 5, 177–212.

Sacks, D. (1994) 'The Paradox of Taxation, Fiscal Crises, Parliament and Liberty in England, 1450–1640', in P. Hoffman and K. Norberg (eds), *Fiscal Crises, Liberty, and Representative Government, 1450–1789*, Stanford, CA: Stanford University Press.

Schick, A. (2002) 'Can National Legislatures Regain an Effective Voice in Budget Policy?', *OECD Journal on Budgeting*, 3, 15–42.

Scott, H. (2009) 'The Fiscal Military State and International Rivalry during the Long Eighteenth Century', in C. Storrs (ed.), *The Fiscal Military State in Europe: Essays in Honour of PGM Dickson*, Aldershot: Ashgate.

Steinmo, S. (1993) *Taxation and Democracy*, New Haven, CT: Yale University Press.

Truber, A., and Will, H. (2012) 'The German "Debt Brake" – A Shining Example for European Fiscal Policy', Working Paper 15/2012, Institute for International Political Economy, Berlin.

Tuori, K. (2012) 'The European Financial Crisis – Constitutional Aspects and Implications', EUI Law Working Paper 2012/28.

Turner, B. (2001) 'The Erosion of Citizenship', *British Journal of Sociology*, 52(2), 189–210.

Vandoros, S., et al. (2013) 'Have Health Trends Worsened in Greece as a Result of the Financial Crisis? A Quasi-Experimental Approach', *European Journal of Public Health*, 23(5), 727–31.

Velasco, J. (2000) 'Debts and Deficit with Fragmented Fiscal Policymaking', *Journal of Public Economics*, 76(1), 105–25.

Veneendaal, A. (1994) 'Fiscal Crises and Constitutional Freedom in the Netherlands, 1450–1795', in P. Hoffman and K. Norberg (eds), *Fiscal Crises, Liberty, and Representative Government, 1450–1789*, Stanford, CA: Stanford University Press.

von Hagen, J. (2006) 'Fiscal Rules and Fiscal Performance in the European Union and Japan', *Monetary and Economic Studies*, 24(1), 25–60.

von Hagen, J., and Harden, I. (1995) 'Budget Processes and Commitment to Fiscal Discipline', *European Economic Review*, 39(3), 771–79.

von Rompuy, H., et al. (2012) 'Towards A Genuine Economic and Monetary Union'. www.consilium.europa.eu/uedocs/cms_Data/docs/pressdata/en/ec/134069.pdf.

Webber, C., and Wildawsky, A. (1986) *A History of Taxation and Public Expenditure in the Western World*, New York: Simon and Schuster.

Wehner, J. (2006) 'Assessing the Power of the Purse: An Index of Legislative Budget Institutions', *Political Studies*, 54(4), 767–85.

Wilkinson, M. (2014) 'From Karlsruhe, with Love? Questioning the Constitutionality of Unconventional Monetary Policy', LSE Law Policy Briefing Paper No. 6.

Wilsher, D. (2014) 'Law and the Financial Crisis: Searching for Europe's New Gold Standard', *European Law Journal*, 20(2), 241–83.

Wyplosz, C. (2013) 'Fiscal Rules: Theoretical Issues and Historical Experiences', in A. Alesina and F. Giavazzi (eds), *Fiscal Policy after the Financial Crisis*, Chicago: University of Chicago Press.

Die Zeit (2015), 'Merkel strebt an Euroreform radikale', 2 June.

12

Integration through law and the crisis of law in Europe's emergency

CHRISTIAN JOERGES

Structuring the argument

'Constitutional Emergency!' (*Verfassungsnot!*) – this is the notion which Paul Kirchhof, who had been *judge rapporteur* for the Second Senate of the *Bundesverfassungsgericht* in the proceedings challenging the compatibility of the Treaty of Maastricht of 1992 with Germany's Basic Law 1992,[1] used in his comment in the *Frankfurter Allgemeine Zeitung* (Kirchhof 2012) on the state of the Union after the financial crisis. Kirchhof did not consider the influence of the proclamation of a stability union (*Stabilitätsemeinschaft*) in the Maastricht-*Urteil* on the unfortunate developments in Europe. Ernst-Wolfgang Böckenförde, his renowned former colleague in the Second Senate, had been more explicit. In a contribution in the *Neue Züricher Zeitung* (Böckenförde 2010), he had recalled that the Court had, indeed, been made aware of the risks inherent in the establishment of a 'monetary union without a simultaneous or immediately subsequent political union'.[2] The Court had considered that the decision to incur such a risk was a matter of high politics for which 'the institutions with competence [...] must take political responsibility'. The responses we are witnessing two decades later, he added, are, legally speaking, outrageous (*abenteuerlich*). This, however, may be the price that we have to pay: 'Necessity knows no law'. Böckenförde added a question mark to this remark, later observers who share his concerns, are less ambivalent (Dyson 2013: 211; White 2013).

Our analysis will not engage in exegetic exercises about Schmittian notions (Schmitt 1989). It will nevertheless follow Böckenförde in his search for an explanation and understanding of the (mis-)treatment of

1 *Manfred Brunner and Others* v. *The European Union Treaty* (Cases 2 BvR 2134/92 & 2159/92, BVerfGE 89, 155), [1994] 1 CMLR 57.

2 *Brunner et al.* v. *The EU Treaty*, n. 1, above, para. 93.

law in Europe's crisis. Our search will focus on the political dimension of the economy. After the financial crisis, after the renaissance of Karl Polanyi's work in economic sociology, and the recent attention paid both by students of the 'varieties of capitalism' and economic historians to the institutional infrastructures and social fabric of northern and southern European economies (Iversen and Soskice 2013; Abelshauser 2014; Hall 2014; Manow 2015), this focus should hardly be surprising. It signals, nevertheless, a critical intention, namely, a break with the benign neglect of 'the economic' in the mainstream of European constitutionalism, on the one hand, and the widespread refusal or inability in the social sciences and economics to take 'the legal' seriously, on the other. The following enquiries will proceed in five steps.

(1) The first section will deal with the so-called foundational period of the integration project.[3] The objective here is to reveal how the reliance on the 'integration through law' agenda and its doctrines have furthered a specific neo-liberal economic tilt of the integration project.
(2) The second section will proceed to explore the reconfiguration of the law–politics relationship after the Commission White Paper on completion of the internal market of 1985,[4] the turn to majority voting after the Single European Act of 1986, attempts to establish a new synthesis between market building, and law-mediated politics in particular in all realms of social regulation. These efforts were innovative in many respects, but their legitimacy remained precarious. They increasingly had to rely on technocratic regimes and governance structures in which expertise substituted the rule of law and democratic legitimation. Such developments fostered and foreshadowed what was to happen under the impact of the financial crisis.
(3) The third section will turn to the most important and most problematic move of the integration project, namely, the establishment of EMU by the Treaty of Maastricht of 1992 and its complementation by the Stability and Growth Pact (SGP) in 1997. In our reconstruction we will argue that EMU and the SGP were a conceptually incoherent German–French compromise which failed to provide for effective solutions of the conflict constellations they were to generate. Implicit in that analysis is the assertion that the problems of EMU we are witnessing

3 European Commission, 'Completing the Internal Market', COM (85) 310 final.
4 Ibid.

in the crisis cannot be resolved by means of more rigid enforcement mechanisms.

(4) The fourth section will characterise and evaluate the responses to the crisis. We will endorse Böckenförde's diagnosis: Europe is in an emergency and its responses are born out of 'grim necessity' (Dyson 2013). It follows from our critical reconstruction of the history of the law–politics relationship that a safe harbour into which the European project should or could return is simply unavailable. The choice, then, becomes one between a 'normalisation' and 'muddling through', on the one hand, and 'contestation', on the other.

(5) This alternative will be examined in the concluding section. We will proceed from the hardships which the crisis imposes on so many European citizens, and explain why Europe's present (un)constitutional constellation is, in our view, unsustainable. We will add, however, that a reliable recipe is not available. What we will submit, instead, will be an account of the conflict constellations which the crisis has generated and some conjecture on the law's potential to contribute to civilised settlements with constructive perspectives.

Integration through law and economic constitutionalism

'Integration through law' has, for good reasons, become the trademark of the European project both within and beyond its foundational period. This success story is phenomenal. It has been retold so often that it should suffice here to restate the core messages of the two judgments that have framed its normative validity and were meant, understood and recognised as a 'constitutionalisation' of the EEC Treaty. This recognition, however, remains puzzling. We will address, in the following subsection, three queries, and then discuss in some detail a fourth one, which is of obvious importance in the present context, namely, the not-so-widely noticed relationship between the constitutionalisation of the Treaty and economic constitutionalism.

Integration through law as constitutionalisation

To restate, first, the well-known judicial messages: in *Van Gend en Loos*, handed down on 5 February 1963,[5] the ECJ held that European rights

5 *Van Gend en Loos*, EU:C:1963:1.

can be directly effective and thereby become 'the law of the land in each Member State':

> [T]he Community constitutes a new legal order of international law for the benefit of which the states have limited their sovereign rights, albeit within limited fields, and the subjects of which comprise not only member states but also their nationals. Independently of the legislation of member states, Community law therefore not only imposes obligations on individuals but is also intended to confer upon them rights which become part of their legal heritage.

In *Costa* v. *ENEL* the ECJ spelled out the implications:

> It follows that the law stemming from the Treaty, an independent source of law, could not, because of its special and original nature, be overridden by domestic legal provisions, however framed, without being deprived of its character as Community law and without the legal basis of the Community itself being called into question.[6]

These statements are the creed of European law. Scepticism as to their normative wisdom is rare; the most prominent and insisting exception is Dieter Grimm (2015). This is phenomenal in view of – in particular – four queries to which the constitutionalisation paradigm has never delivered convincing responses:

(1) Direct effect and supremacy are meant to ensure the efficacy of European law. Why should this type of effect deserve to be equated with the validity that the constitutional law of democratic states is expected to ensure? The tensions between (economic) integration and democratic legitimacy seem obvious and their resolution via uniform legal rules simply inconceivable.
(2) The famous characterisation of law as the 'object and the agent of integration' (Dehousse and Weiler 1990: 243) was coined at the height of the American law and society movement which advocated the study of 'law in its context' and all sorts of interdisciplinary 'law and ... ' explorations. How could European law scholarship defend views and visions on the potential of 'law as such' which looked so outmoded and were long since discredited? The integration through law agenda had to insist on a drastic disembedding of law and its operation from its social contexts.
(3) The assumption of the unity doctrine that 'one size fits all' was not as implausible in the foundational period of the ECC as it has become in the Union of 28. However, even in the relatively homogenous orders of

6 *Costa*, EU:C:1964:66.

the former EEC, any unification at European level had disintegrative effects within national legal orders, which European law is unable to cure because it cannot reach the sphere of social norms within which the law operates and on which its social legitimacy and its functioning depend (Joerges 1997; Ladeur 2014).

(4) The fourth intriguing query concerns the normative dimensions of economic governance. The social responsibility of the economy is in constitutional democracies ensured by democratic rule. That type of control over the European economy in its entirety was not envisaged. Beneficial effects on the welfare of all Europeans through economic integration were apparently taken for granted. The opening of the national economies and the commitment to free movement could rely on a solid consensus throughout a broad political spectrum. Economic integration was not perceived as a challenge to the national welfare states. Or was it? It seems highly likely that influential stakeholders expected from early on what seems by now common wisdom, namely, that the in-built economic liberalism of the integration project would keep welfarist tendencies at bay (Von Hayek 1948).

Economic constitutionalism

This assumption is anything but daring from a German perspective. What happened through the constitutionalisation of the treaty provisions – most notably, through the conceptualisation of the economic freedoms as basic rights which Europe's market citizens could invoke against their home states – was very much to the liking of Germany's ordoliberalism, the one and only contemporary school of thought that took the legal dimensions of the economy really seriously. This school of thought by no means represented the majority of Germany's domestic *Staats- und Verfassungsrecht* and early European law scholarship. Economic constitutionalism was a theory residing in the private law compartments of our discipline, whereas European law was understood as a new sub-discipline of public law. The young Federal Republic had witnessed an intense debate on the notion of an economic constitution which concerned its core *problématique*, namely, the conceptualisation of the ordering of the economy as a self-legitimating *ordo* which required a legal institutionalisation beyond the reach of politics. In this debate, the ordoliberal school and its adherents in the German *Staatsrecht* were confronted with the quest for *democratic* legitimacy and the primacy of the legislative authority in the ordering of the 'economy and society', which was defended at the time by a clear majority of Germany's constitutional lawyers, who insisted upon the primacy of the legislature, and won their case with the *Investitionshilfe-Urteil* handed down on 20 July 1954,[7] a good number of years prior to the ratification of the Treaty of Rome. The tension between the national commitment to democracy and the primacy of democratic legitimated legislation, on the one hand, and the ordoliberal reading of the constitutionalisation of the EEC-Treaty, on the other, are obvious. How plausible is it that the concept of an economic constitution which represented a minority view within Germany's public law scholarship and also in the new European law community, and which was hardly known anywhere outside the Federal Republic, could have operated in tandem with the proponents of the constitutionalisation paradigm? Historians have still some work to do here. But some conjectures may be submitted: Germany's post-war academia felt committed to both the European project and the democratic order established by the Basic Law. The idea of an economic constitution with its vision of a supranational legitimacy which did not depend upon democratic credentials seemed to offer a way out of such loyalty dilemmas. Much more important is the enormous, but apparently not widely noticed, influence of ordoliberalism at important political turning-points and at all levels of governance. Strangely enough, Billy Davies (2007) does not even mention ordoliberalism in his very instructive reconstruction of the early German debates on the democratic deficit of the integration project, but lists the leading proponents of the school from, for example, the Commission's first president Walter Hallstein, Commissioner Hans van der Groeben to the learned diplomat Carl-Friedrich Ophüls. Antoine Vauchez (2013) wonders why 'law professors and employers in France who saw in Articles 85–86 of the Rome Treaties no more than a simple roadmap that would have to bend to political winds and to particular national circumstances' did not impress the Commission; but he realises and documents the strong linkages between the German Cartel Office in Berlin and their colleagues in DG IV (see, in more detail, Wigger 2008).

The neo-liberal tilt of the European project – no alternatives?

The Treaty of Rome establishing the EEC was certainly not a deliberate assault on the welfare-state legacy of post-war Europe. National social

7 BVerfGE 4, 7 *Investitionshilfegesetz*, Judgment of 20 July 1954. The Court held that Germany's Basic Law was not committed to a particular economic model, but entrusted the democratically legitimated legislation with the ordering of the economy. A more widely known setback was the seminal BVerfGE 50, 290 *Mitbestimmungs-Urteil*, Judgment of 1 March 1979, which confirmed the compatibility of Germany's co-determination legislation with the Basic Law.

models in all their variety were expected to coexist peacefully with the gradual integration of European economies. The Ohlin Report (1956) had endorsed the welfare-enhancing credentials of the EEC and John G. Ruggie's famous argument about 'embedded liberalism' provided pertinent theoretical backing (Ruggie 1982; see also Steffek 2006). *Tempora mutantur*, however. What Fritz Scharpf (2002) was to characterise some 20 years later as a 'decoupling' of Europe's economic governance from its state-based social legacy had indeed been fostered by the institutional design of the EEC and then gradually deepened continuously (Höpner 2014).

The price to be paid for this kind of progress was to become more readily visible with the various rounds of enlargement and the ever-greater socio-economic diversity and political salience of integrationist moves. 'Integration through law', with its reliance upon a 'one-size-fits-all' assumption, was to become a strikingly inadequate response to the challenges of European diversity and an ever more implausible response to the quest for legitimacy of European rule.

Was all this really unavoidable? There are countless examples that confirm the decoupling thesis in the encounters of European law with the regulatory concerns of the member states. But there are also important counter-examples and the author of the decoupling-theorem himself has submitted a counter-vision in which he pleaded for an integration strategy which would be respectful of the political autonomy of the member states while at the same time requiring them to choose Community-friendly policies (Scharpf 1994). The pattern of pertinent conflicts and tensions was recurring over and over again: the European market-building agenda intruded into spaces that the member states had exempted from market governance on the grounds of competences that they had not conclusively or only partly conferred to the European level. In such 'diagonal' conflict constellations, European law cannot plausibly claim 'supremacy' or resort to the doctrine of 'pre-emption'. The two levels of governance could instead be expected to coordinate their agendas cooperatively. In many instances, the ECJ has indeed found innovative responses to such complex conflict constellations solutions.[8] These responses departed from the 'one-size-fits-all' philosophy of the integration through law tradition and resorted, instead, to the development of procedural frames within which the EU and the concerned jurisdictions could accommodate their concerns and

8 Famous examples include *Albany International*, EU:C:1999:430; *Altmark Trans*, EU:C:2003:415; *Centros*, EU:C:1999:126, versus most recently *Ålands Vindkraft*, EU:C:2014:2037.

interests (see, in some detail, Joerges and Schmid 2004: 293 ff.; Azoulai 2013).

The turn to regulation and governance

The integration project entered its most dynamic phase after the Single European Act,[9] with its turn to majority voting and the subsequent European-wide support for the Jacques Delors' Single Market Programme (European Commission 1985). The implementation of this programme generated a range of innovations which transformed the Economic Community and its law through new regulatory endeavours. This process, however, was never legally consolidated; it was, instead, followed by a turn to informal modes of governance and a renewal of the technocratic legacy of the European project in which the idea of law-mediated governance gradually eroded both of these moves. Their obvious importance for the functioning of the economy notwithstanding, this did not affect the complacency of European legal scholarship towards the economy.

Social regulation in the European economy

The Internal Market Programme of the Delors Commission was an innovative project. It synthesised the market-building agenda with new regulatory techniques in the entire spheres of 'social regulation' (consumer protection, safety at work and environmental policy). This novel type of Europeanisation was arguably an unavoidable implication of the Europeanisation process. Was it at all conceivable that the establishment of European regulatory bodies would avoid technocratic modes of governance and thereby deepen Europe's democratic deficit? The concept of 'deliberative supranationalism' sought to overcome that objection by a turn to 'horizontal constitutionalisation', arguing that legitimate policies should and could be based on deliberative decision-making processes (Joerges and Neyer 1997), a suggestion that was to become ever more difficult to defend with the enormous expansion of European regulatory activities (Joerges and Neyer 2014; Weimer 2015; see also below). Not only the modes of transnational decision-making but also the implications of their contents need to be considered and justified. Policy preferences in the realms of social regulation tend to mirror the diversity of socio-economic

9 OJ 1987, L 169/1.

conditions, and transnational prerogatives affect the competitive conditions of national economies within the Union (Scharpf 1997). Because of these implications the legitimacy *problématique* of the Europeanisation of social regulation was bound to remain on the political agenda. The difficulties that these debates have to address are very considerable. They concern tensions between national and European regulatory powers, the delimitation of legislative and executive powers, the integration of expert knowledge into regulatory decision-making, and the cooperation of governmental with non-governmental actors. It is obvious that these challenges could not be meaningfully addressed on the conceptual premises of the integration through law agenda. 'Law' could no longer provide normative orientation autonomously. It was, from now on, the normative quality of decision-making processes, rather than its uniformity, which could ensure the legitimacy of European rule.

The intense debate among lawyers and political scientists on the efficacy and legitimacy of these practices remains of principal importance. It remains theoretically challenging as an attempt to come to terms with the steadily increasing interdependence, socio-economic diversity, and, by the same token, the dramatically intensifying difficulty of arriving at common political positions (Höpner 2014).

The turn to governance

The turn to governance which the White Paper of the Prodi Commission announced in 2001 occurred nearly a decade prior to the establishment of EMU.[10] This move seemed to respond quite convincingly, in principle, to widely shared perceptions of the *impasses* of the 'old' community method and the enormously increasing burdens on the EU system. The governance initiative did, in fact, generate manifold innovations that were accompanied by enormous research activities. Any one-dimensional assessment of these activities would be misplaced. But the liberation of the European *praxis* from the bedrock of the 'integration through law' agenda and the discipline of the rule of law was risky and went, in a particularly glamorous instance, a step too far. It was the Lisbon European Council of 2011 which recommended resort to the Open Method of Co-ordination (OMC) in areas of social policy where the Treaty had failed to confer legislative powers. The OMC became regarded as the new mode of governance

10 European Commission, 'European Governance: A White Paper', COM (2001) 428 final of 25 July 2001, OJ 2001, C 287/5.

par excellence. Its advocates expected that it would open opportunities to cure Europe's notorious 'social deficit' (Trubek and Trubek 2005; de Búrca and Scott 2006; Sabel and Zeitlin 2007; Sabel and Zeitlin 2012).

With the benefit of hindsight, the affinities between the new modes of 'integration through de-legalisation' (Joerges 2007), the post-crisis turn to the 'Union method' and the transformation of economic and social governance are readily apparent. The pre-crisis turn to governance replaced legal enforceability of legislative and administrative acts by coordination processes, procedures of multilateral supervision upon the basis of guidelines or benchmarks laid down by the European Council, the Council and the Commission. Public support for this policy of the coordination and comparison of best practices was intended to provide the necessary incentives to ensure success and performance which would inevitably lead to adaptation and change of national policies at member-state level. The evidence on which such positive expectations were based has always been slim. What seems much more unsettling, however, are the deeper institutional and political defects which the turn to governance has revealed rather than cured. What the proponents of the OMC sought to accomplish was nothing less than a transformation of Europe's constitutional constellation (its *Verfassungswirklichkeit*) by what in the post-crisis euro-speak today would be called 'unconventional' means. They did not consider, let alone advocate, the authoritarian turn to austerity politics that we are witnessing in Europe's current emergency. What they also failed to consider were alternatives to their unconventional moves towards 'more Europe'.

That point will be taken up below in the concluding section. As an interim summary, we have to conclude that the early sceptical comments on the governance White Paper (Joerges et al. 2002) were well-founded. What is left of the turn to governance since then is a rise of executive power and the strengthening of technocratic rule. The original aspirations and hopes gradually eroded. This holds true even for the new approach to harmonisation and standards which had initially – for good reasons – been praised as a legitimate novel form of private transnationalism (Schepel 2013). Similarly disappointing is the development of the comitology system into which this author had projected the potential of a 'deliberative' correction of orthodox supranationalism (Joerges and Neyer 1997). The Commission had already in its 2001 White Paper indicated its dislike in particular of the regulatory and management committees in which the influence of member states was considerable, and pleaded, instead, for the establishment of 'executive agencies' that would use 'external executive agencies', albeit 'under the Commission's control'.[11] This striving for a European administrative system guided by the Commission was not successful. The committee system continued its irresistible growth – to date, some 270 committees with thousands of representatives of the member state deliver some 1,800 implementing legal acts per year which amount to 65 per cent of the Union's legislative output. But comitology, as we had portrayed it in 1997, experienced a normative degeneration (Joerges and Neyer 2014; Falke 2014). The steady increase of decisions that have to be taken has protected the system against hierarchical centralisation. By the same token, its rationalisation via comprehensive 'scientification' is simply inconceivable.[12] What we observe, instead, is mostly routinised administrative backstage decision-making and occasional tough bargaining over sensitive issues (Blom-Hansen and Brandsma 2009).

European agencies, once designed as a merely informational mode of governance, experienced a spectacular upgrading. At the time of writing (January 2015), some 40 agencies are in operation, each of them designed to accomplish some task of its own. The formal legal framework of these bodies seemed for decades to be governed or squeezed by the principles of the two landmark *Meroni* judgments,[13] which had explained that the delegation of powers to an agency cannot go beyond the powers of the delegating authority, a restraint that was substantiated by the famous reserve against the exercise of discretionary powers that would amount to policy-making. In a judgment of 14 May 1981, the ECJ added that agencies (at the time, bodies 'established by secondary law') 'may not be empowered by the Council to adopt acts having the force of law'.[14] This legal straitjacket had been developed long before the European turn to regulation and governance occurred so intensively. It is hence unsurprising that the proponents of regulatory policies felt invited and compelled to design frameworks within which non-legal means could accomplish, indirectly or informally, what was legally foreclosed. One particularly striking example is the much discussed authorisation of genetically modified organisms (GMOs) by the European Food and Safety Authority (EFSA). Maria Weimer (2015) has,

11 Ibid., 30–31.

12 The European Parliament continued nevertheless with its relentless efforts to strengthen its influence. The new regulatory procedure with scrutiny is acclaimed as a success of this agenda. It is a success only in the books. Until the end of 2012, the European Parliament only objected three times (0.4 per cent) and the Council 10 times (1.4 per cent) to draft measures (Falke 2014: 274).

13 *Meroni*, EU:C:1958:7; *Meroni*, EU:C:1958:8.

14 *Romano*, EU:C:1981:104, para. 20.

in a comprehensive analysis of the pertinent legislative framework, discerned a striking asymmetry between that framework and its implementation. While the framework seems to foster deliberative decision-making, European decision-making processes have continuously ended with the authorisation of GMOs in spite of persisting scientific controversies and strong political opposition both by and within the member states. This outcome she explains by an authoritarian scientification strategy pursued by EFSA.[15]

Truly disquieting seems the type of departure from the *Meroni* and *Romano* doctrines which the Court has proclaimed in its judgment of 21 January 2014.[16] This judgment has redefined the modes of 'agencification' under the amended provisions of Articles 290 and 291 TFEU on the delegated powers to adopt non-legislative acts. It concerned Europe's recently amended system of financial supervision, in particular, the empowerment of the European Securities and Markets Authority (ESMA) to intervene by legally binding acts in member-state financial markets in the event of a 'threat to the orderly functioning and integrity of financial markets or to the stability of the whole or part of the financial system in the Union'.[17] Two steps taken by the Court seem particularly noteworthy, and deserve, indeed, to be called 'revolutionary' (Adamski 2014: n. 67). The first concerns the interpretation of Article 114 TFEU, which provides for 'measures for the approximation of the provisions laid down by law, regulation or administrative action in member states which have as their object the establishment and functioning of the internal market'. By this provision, so the Court explained, 'the authors of the TFEU intended to confer on the Union legislature, depending on the general context and the specific circumstances of the matter to be harmonised, discretion as regards the most appropriate method of harmonisation for achieving the desired result, especially in fields with complex technical features'.[18] This message did not merely replicate quite widely shared insights into the dependence of the proper functioning of modern markets on adequate regulatory

15 An at least partial revision of this unfortunate mode of decision-making is now in sight. After years of discussions on the amendment of Directive 2001/18/EC by an opt-out clause which would not legalise import restrictions but the prohibition of cultivation of genetically modified organisms, a political agreement was reached in the Council on 12 June 2014.

16 *United Kingdom* v. *Parliament and Council*, EU:C:2014:18.

17 Regulation 236/2012 on short selling and certain aspects of credit default swaps, OJ 2012 L 86/1, Article 28. Article 24(3) defines such threats in much detail.

18 *United Kingdom* v. *Parliament and Council*, n. 16, above, para. 102.

frameworks as recommended by the protagonists of European regulatory policies. It concluded that, in the present context, Articles 290 and 291 are not applicable in the first place. Instead, Article 28 of Regulation 236/2012:

> must be perceived as forming part of a series of rules designed to endow the competent national authorities and ESMA with powers of intervention to cope with adverse developments which threaten financial stability within the Union and market confidence. To that end, those authorities must be in a position to impose temporary restrictions on the short selling of certain stocks, credit default swaps or other transactions in order to prevent an uncontrolled fall in the price of those instruments. Those bodies have a high degree of professional expertise and work closely together in the pursuit of the objective of financial stability within the Union.[19]

This is nothing less than an emergency doctrine, as the Court realises in its characterisation of the 'measures taken by several Member States'.[20] Emergency measures are generally held to include discretionary powers. The Court, however, refrains from an explicit adoption of this implication. It explains, instead, that 'Article 28 of Regulation No 236/2012 vests ESMA with certain decision-making powers in an area which requires the deployment of specific technical and professional expertise'.[21] Can it really be expertise in the sense of knowledge that can be acquired and shared by an expert community as the Court's formula assumes? If this were so, national authorities could be persuaded by better arguments, and resorting to authoritative decision-making would be superfluous. There is, of course, time pressure that excludes extensive deliberation. But it is precisely this constellation that indicates that decisions have to be taken in uncertainty and properly phrased as 'emergency measures' in the preamble to Regulation 236/2012.

The technocratic alternative to economic constitutionalism

From the inception of the European project, functionalist and technocratic ideas have been serious candidates for its legitimation. 'The technocrats' were an innovative movement in the USA; David Mitrany had elaborated functionalism as a mode of transnational governance (Steffek 2014). The technocratic legacy of the European project, its historic basis and conceptual elaboration are distinct (Möllers 1999: 397 ff.). An influential contribution was the work of Hans Peter Ipsen with its conceptualisation of

19 Ibid., para. 85.
20 Ibid., para. 109.
21 Ibid., para. 82.

the European Communities as special-purpose organisations with functionally defined objectives (*Zweckverbände funktionaler Integration*). Ipsen rejected both further-reaching federal ambitions *and* earlier interpretations of the Community as a mere international organisation. Community law was defined as a *tertium* between federal or state law, on the one hand, and international law, on the other, an order constituted by its 'objective tasks' and adequately legitimated by their solution that could rely on '*Wissensbildung*' (expertise) and hence to depend on political '*Willensbildung*' (will formation) (see Kaufmann 1997: 312–19).

When Europe initiated the 'completion of the internal market', technocratic visions seemed far better prepared to understand and guide the new synthesis of market building and social regulation than the ordoliberal tradition with its old defence of a 'system of undistorted competition' and its new focus on the critique of anti-competitive regulation. The dynamics of the integration project and the drastically expanding scope of its activities, however, made the technocratic efforts to play down 'political will formation' ever more implausible. These challenges have been addressed in the intensive debates on the institutionalisation of the older and new modes of European governance, and they continue to date in the search for new forms of administrative accountability (Curtin 2009).

It is apparent from our sketch of the development of European regulatory politics in the previous sections that our account of what has actually occurred is critical. This is not to say that these developments were without alternatives. At present, however, the prospect of institutionalising such alternatives is overshadowed by the responses to the financial crisis. To these responses, we have to turn now, albeit not immediately, but only after a reconstruction of what happened with the establishment of the EMU by the Treaty of Maastricht.

Economic and monetary union as diagonal conflict constellation

The Treaty of Maastricht of 1992 is an extremely important turning-point in the development of the integration project. Its new provisions were widely perceived at the time as both a continuation and a deepening of what had been accomplished, as a move towards 'an ever closer union', marked by an opening of new policy fields and the crowning of the completion of the internal market by monetary union (for a more nuanced reading, see Dehousse 1994). By now, we realise that the warnings against institutional insufficiencies were justified and we are exposed to the bitter consequences. Three aspects that deserve highlighting in the following sub-sections are: first, the affinities of the EMU with ordoliberal economic constitutionalism; second, the unfortunate promotion of this perception by the Second Senate of the German Constitutional Court (GCC) in its Maastricht-*Urteil* of 1993; and third, the alternative reading of the EMU as a 'diagonal' conflict constellation.

The EMU as a pyrrhic victory of ordoliberalism

'One market, one money!' The famous slogan which the Commission used in 'An evaluation of the potential benefits and costs of forming an economic and monetary union', published in 1990,[22] insinuated continuity with the internal market programme and an understanding of EMU as its consummation. The background was far more complex. One widely told narrative portrays the EMU 'as the product of an "intergovernmental" [...] deal whereby Western Germany was allowed to reunify with Eastern Germany in exchange for ensuring its partners that it would remain firmly anchored in the EU. And that meant giving up the Deutsch Mark in exchange for a common European currency' (Lefkofridi and Schmitter 2015: 7–8; cf. Leaman 2001: 220 ff.). Such evaluations are for historians to examine. Even though the political deal between France and Germany could not be rationalised in economic terms, the expectation that the common currency would foster economic convergence and even force Europe into deeper political integration was still widespread (Eichengreen 2015: 90–93). Lawyers, however, need conceptual grounds for their understanding of the rules and principles they are expected to apply. On which premises, on what theoretical paradigm, could they build? On paper, the EMU has much in common with ordoliberal economic constitutionalism: the new exclusive European competence for monetary policy, its anti-inflationary dedication to price stability, the establishment of an independent central bank far removed from all political influence and placed firmly outside the institutional structures of the Union – this ensemble seemed to militate for such a reading. Leading representatives of the ordoliberal tradition, however, were disappointed by the Treaty of Maastricht. The reserves were manifold. They not only concerned the provisions on monetary union, but also the conferral of new competences, in particular, in the new Title on industrial policy (Article 157 TEU; now Article 173 TFEU). It seemed no longer plausible to assign a constitutive

22 Available at http://ec.europa.eu/economy_finance/publications/publication7454_en.pdf.

function to the 'system of undistorted competition' when the promotion of that system is only one among many other competing objectives. The relative weight of competition law and policy had more clearly than ever to be determined in political processes (Streit and Mussler 1995). Even the institutional framework of monetary union did not look really trustworthy. Ordoliberals are well aware of the dependence of an institutionalised project upon its internal organisational norms and the mindset and convictions of its leaders. The procedural norms which assigned one vote of equal weight to each Member of the ECB Council were a risk for the defence of the statutory commitment. Even more precarious was the autonomy of member states in the fields of fiscal and economic policy. The provisions on coordination were vague and the obligation of member states to 'regard economic policy as a matter of common concern' not particularly instructive. The Stability and Growth Pact adopted in 1997 openly provided room for political manoeuvring.[23] One cannot but conclude that 'the Maastricht macroeconomic constitution granted the law but a minor role' (Tuori and Tuori 2014: 243). Even this is a euphemistic account. What was left of the project of an 'economic constitution' had been politicised, but that move towards bargaining and compromise was camouflaged by 'soft law' (Adamski 2012). To be sure, scholars indebted to the Freiburg School have continued to pursue their vision of legitimate economic governance (Feld 2012). But such appeals illustrate Hegel's '*Ohnmacht des Sollens*' (the powerlessness of the ought) as we will argue below. But first, we will observe how Germany's *Bundesverfassungsgericht* has sought to avoid that conclusion.

The fictitious stability union of the Maastricht-Urteil

In the community of European lawyers, the judgment of the GCC of 12 October 1993 on the Treaty of Maastricht attracted enormous, mostly critical attention.[24] Tellingly enough, the critics hardly ever dealt with the passages on EMU. They underlined, instead, that the Court has misstated the views of Hermann Heller, were irritated by the characterisation of the Union as a '*Verbund*', rather than a '*Gemeinschaft*', and found a touch of Schmittianism in the judicial reasoning (Weiler 1995). What the Court had to say about the economy seemed less interesting. But these

23 OJ 1997, C 236/1.

24 *Brunner* v. *The European Union Treaty* [1994] 1 CMLR 57.

passages were, in fact, the most irritating pronouncements in the lengthy judgment. The GCC found that it was precisely the substitution of politics and policies by legal rules and the independence of the ECB which ensured the compatibility of the EMU with the Basic Law. This pronouncement was the Court's response to the submission of the plaintiffs that the EU was about to acquire such wide-ranging competences that nation states could no longer act as the masters of their 'democratic statehood'. Economic integration, so the Court argued, was an autonomous and *apolitical* process, which might, and indeed should, operate beyond the reach of member state political influence. By virtue of a constitutional commitment to price stability and rules that guarded against inappropriate budgetary deficits, MU seemed hence well structured. Accordingly, doubts about the democratic legitimacy of economic integration were diverted. To rephrase the argument slightly: yes, the Treaty *is* compatible with the Basic Law. But this is true only because it is inspired by Germany's stability philosophy and only as long as this stability pact is actually respected.[25]

The Court had been warned explicitly 'by important contributors to the debate that a currency union, especially between States which are oriented towards an active economic and social policy, can ultimately only be realised in common with a political union (embracing all essential economic functions) and cannot be realised independently thereof or as a mere preliminary stage on the way to it'.[26] It could hence not take the sustainability of the 'stability community' for granted. And, indeed, Ernst-Wolfgang Böckenförde, one of the renowned judges of the deciding Second Senate, has recently underlined that the judges were fully aware of the fragility of the *Stabilitätsgemeinschaft* [stability community], which they defended as a constitutional command. Böckenförde (2010) refers to a passage in which the GCC seeks to distinguish its constitutional guardianship of essentially political decisions:

> The decision to agree on a monetary union and put it into operation without a simultaneous or immediately subsequent political union is a political

25 Para. 90 of the judgment reads: 'This conception of the currency union as a community based on stability is the basis and subject-matter of the German Act of Accession. If the monetary union should not be able to develop on a continuing basis the stability present at the beginning of the third stage within the meaning of the agreed mandate for stabilisation, it would be abandoning the Treaty conception'.

26 Ibid., para. 92.

one, for which the institutions with competence on the matter must take political responsibility.[27]

One remains perplexed. The judges must have known that it would be simply inconceivable to correct politically the deal to which they had given their legal blessing. And they decided accordingly when they were confronted with the request to prevent monetary union from entering the third stage.[28] Under the common currency, the financial interdependencies in a socio-economically ever more heterogeneous Union were deepened, but the new exclusive European competence for monetary policy was too weak an instrument to govern the European economic sphere. It was strong enough to deprive the member states of their former crucially important governmental powers. Europe continued to be a 'market without a state', while the former masters of the treaties had become 'states without markets'.[29]

EMU as a 'diagonal' conflict constellation

The argument of those 'important contributors to the debate' to which the GCC referred has, by now, become common wisdom: the separation of monetary policy from fiscal and economic policy which the Maastricht Treaty enacted was a design failure. But, contrary to the assertions dominating Europe's present crisis management, it does not follow that stricter rules would have worked post 1992 or would now be able to repair the damage done. The reasons have remained the same and the errors committed in Maastricht and during the crisis continue to follow the patterns that were institutionalised in the foundational period: the political dimensions of 'the economic', the 'social embeddedness' of markets, the insights of economic sociology, the research on the varieties of capitalism, in short:

27 Böckenförde is referring to para. 93 of the judgment. The passage reads in full: 'This does not raise a question of constitutional law, however, but of politics. The decision to agree on a monetary union and put it into operation without a simultaneous or immediately subsequent political union is a political one, for which the institutions with competence on the matter must take political responsibility. If it emerges that the desired monetary union cannot in reality be achieved without a (not yet desired) political union, a fresh political decision will be required as to how to proceed further. There is room for such a decision as a matter of law, because under the present Treaty the monetary union is no more able to give rise automatically to a political union than to an economic union; that would require an amendment of the Treaty, which could not happen without a decision of the national state institutions, including the German Bundestag. Whether that decision is taken is again – in the context of what is constitutionally permissible – a political matter.'

28 2 BvR 1877/97 und 2 BvR 50/98 *German Participation in EMU*, Judgment of 31 March 1998.

29 See, in more detail, Joerges 1996.

the socio-economic, institutional and political heterogeneity of Europe is disregarded, the 'one-size-fits-all' philosophy is renewed and the insulation of legal and administrative rule from democratic political processes continued. Barry Eichengreen (2015: 337–63) has recently summarised concisely the varieties of crisis patterns in the so-called 'PIIGS' countries (i.e., Portugal, Italy, Ireland, Greece and Spain). This variety mirrors the very considerable differences in these five economies and, so Eichengreen adds, errors on the part of both Europe's crisis managers and policy makers in the countries in difficulties. This critical assessment does not dispense us from the task of defining a notion which adequately characterises the constellation which was actually established. We understand the simultaneity of (1) a Europeanised monetary policy (Article 3(1)(c) TFEU), for which the Union claims supremacy; (2) the continuance of national autonomy in the fields of fiscal and economic policy; (3) and the type of coordination provided for in Articles 119 and 121 TFEU as a 'diagonal' conflict constellation. This constellation is not governed by 'supremacy', while 'horizontal' conflicts between the member states persist. No authority has been entrusted with powers which would ensure that the policies pursued at both levels of governance would be coordinated effectively. Again, the failure to provide such a framework is neither wilful nor accidental. The economic and fiscal policies of member states reflect the specifics of their economies and societal conditions. This heterogeneity did not dissolve under the common currency. The uniformity of European monetary policy was to become ever more dysfunctional. What we have observed, instead, namely, the resort to intergovernmental bargaining, soft supervision and tentative coordination, is hence unsurprising. It is, by the same token, a deep crisis of the 'integration through law' project.

Emergency Europe: the law in crisis

The fragility of the European constellation under the EMU and the de-legalisation of European economic governance was not perceived or not taken seriously until it unfolded so dramatically in the financial crisis. Within a time-span of half a decade, we have been witnessing the establishment of a rhapsody of new modes of economic governance and regulatory mechanisms: In March and May 2010, the Commission developed the 'Europe 2020 Strategy,'[30] and the 'European Semester,'[31] respectively.

30 'Communication from the European Commission of 3 March 2010', COM (2010) 2020 final.

31 'Communication from the European Commission of 12 May 2010', COM (2010) 250 final.

These were followed by the European Financial Stability Facility (EFSF) Framework Agreement[32] in June 2010, and by the European Council's 'Euro Plus Pact'[33] in March 2011. Simultaneously, upon the basis of the simplified revision procedures laid down in Article 48(6) TEU, the European Council also decided on 25 March 2011 to add a new Paragraph 3 to Article 136 TFEU, which permitted the establishment of a stability mechanism and the granting of financial assistance, effective 1 January 2013.[34] This was followed in November 2011 by a bundle of legislative measures aimed at re-enforcing budgetary discipline on the part of the member states. The package is supposed to go down in history under the catchy title of the 'Six Pack', and entered into force on 13 December 2011.[35] The high point of all this is the Treaty on Stability, Co-ordination and Governance (TSCG), drafted in December 2011, approved at an informal meeting of the European Council on 30 January 2012, and signed on 2 March 2012 by 25 out of the then 27 member states. A debt brake according to the German model has been introduced, and will be subject to judicial review by the CJEU in the form of institutional borrowing, with one member state bringing action against another. Support from the European Stability Mechanism (ESM) – a permanent crisis fund – will be available only to countries in the euro area that have signed the pact. The TSCG has been ratified by the required number of member states and entered into force on 1 January 2013. Two further Regulations submitted back in November 2011 – the 'Two Pack' – were adopted with parliamentary blessing in March 2013. They provide 'for monitoring and assessing draft budgetary plans and ensuring the correction of excessive deficit of the member states in the euro area' and 'the strengthening of economic and budgetary surveillance of member states experiencing or threatened with serious difficulties with respect to their financial stability in the euro area'.[36]

32 Confirmed in the conclusions of the European Council, Brussels, 17 June 2010, EUCO 13/10, CO EUR 9, CONCL 2. The Framework Agreement was concluded by the ECOFIN Council and confirmed by the European Council, Brussels on 17 June 2010.

33 Conclusions of the European Council, Brussels, 24/25 March 2011, EUCO 10/11, CO EUR 6, CONCL 3 (Annex I).

34 Decision 2011/199 amending Article 136 TFEU with regard to a stability mechanism for member states whose currency is the euro, OJ 2011, L 91/1.

35 The five Regulations 1173–1177/2011 and Directive 2011/85. These are contained in OJ 2011, L 91/1.

36 www.europarl.europa.eu/pdfs/news/expert/infopress/20130312IPR06439/20130312 IPR06439_en.pdf.

All of this is comprehensively documented and updated by the Commission.[37] Its functioning is described and analysed, and debated meticulously by legal academics and practitioners. 'Constitutional Change through Euro Crisis Law' is the title of a project at the EUI Law department that has started with the study of 'the legal instruments adopted at European or international level in reaction to the Eurozone crisis at the national legal and constitutional structures of the 28 member states of the European Union'.[38] The notion of 'crisis law' is revealing. It indicates that there is much more at stake than an assessment of the legality of the ongoing transformations which could rely on the methodology lawyers use in their readings of legal materials. 'Crisis law' has affected fundamental accomplishments and principles that seemed firmly established (see Joerges and Weimer 2014; Joerges 2014c). To begin with the classics:

- 'The states have limited their sovereign rights, albeit within limited fields', has been held in *Van Gend en Loos*[39] and confirmed over and over again, e.g., in Article 5/2 TFEU. This principle has been thoroughly disregarded (Ruser 2014) and then replaced by the comprehensive legalisation of measures seeking to rescue the financial stability of the monetary union.[40]
- The member states have 'created a body of law which binds both their nationals and themselves', concluded *Costa* v. *Enel*.[41] But what is left of supremacy if the member states remain empowered to establish an '*Ersatzunionsrecht*' (Lorz and Sauer 2012),[42] through which they reorganise Europe's *Verfassungswirklichkeit* (the real operation of the Union) via international cooperative action?
- The judicial establishment of human rights, which complements the economic freedoms of the EEC Treaty, has been one of Europe's most cherished constitutional innovations that the EU charter consolidated. This promise has been held not to cover Europe's '*Ersatzunionsrecht*'.[43]
- The budgetary power of parliaments used to be regarded as a core institution of constitutional democracies. This power has been negotiated

37 http://ec.europa.eu/economy_finance/publications/legal_texts/compendium2014_en.htm.
38 http://eurocrisislaw.eui.eu/about.
39 *Van Gend en Loos*, EU:C:1963:1.
40 *Pringle*, EU:C:2012:756, para. 136.
41 *Costa*, EU:C:1964:66.
42 Cited by the German Constitutional Court in 2 BvR 1390/12 *ESM/Fiscal Compact*, Judgment of 18 March 2014, para. 226.
43 See *Pringle*, n. 40, above, paras. 179–180.

away by the Fiscal Compact and is now supervised continuously in the context of the European Semester.

- Article 3 TEU commits the Union to 'a highly competitive social market economy, aiming at full employment and social progress, and a high level of protection' – these have been downgraded to long-term objectives at best. The 'European social model' has become invisible in crisis law and politics.[44] Under the conditions of monetary unity, member states can, indeed, respond to the objective of a strengthened competitiveness only through 'internal devaluations', i.e., austerity measures such as reductions of wage levels and/or social entitlements.
- 'The granting of any required financial assistance' under the ESM Treaty has been 'made subject to strict conditionality by the Council decision of 25 March 2011 which amended Article 136 TFEU'.[45] The Memoranda of Understanding which proceed accordingly have suspended the political autonomy of the 'Member States in difficulties' very significantly.
- The ECB has redefined its mandate profoundly and became a key political actor in the management of the crisis and is operating in areas beyond what used to be understood as 'monetary' policy[46]

Is all this legal? Is the infamous 'secret' letter about the reform of Italian politics which the ECB sent on 5 August 2011 to the Italian government within the Bank's mandate?[47] Does it still make sense to raise such questions? Their *lege artis* discussion would require a valid yardstick. We have argued above that the Maastricht arrangement cannot be called a legal framework, let alone one of constitutional validity. What Maastricht has established can neither be saved nor repaired. EMU is an unruly conflict constellation. Its unruliness is the result of both a normative evaluation and sociological observations. The only conceivable conceptual rational of the EMU on offer is that of the Freiburg tradition. But the ordoliberal vision that remained has *not* been realised by the Treaty of Maastricht. Contemporary proponents of the Freiburg tradition and their sympathisers underline that they do not expect an implementation of ordoliberal rules and principles (Feld 2011; Konrad 2014). We have to conclude that

44 Suffice it here to point to European Commission 2012.

45 OJ 2011, L 91/1.

46 Ibid.

47 In this letter Italy is ordered to deregulate its economy, introduce more work flexibility and increase privatizations. The Italian version was published in the *Corriere della Sera* of 29 September 2011; an English version is available at www.voltairenet.org/article171574 .html.

there is, sadly, no law available which would provide a reliable yardstick for the assessment of the spectacular transformation of Europe's constitution constellation.

All this is not meant to justify that ongoing transformation, nor its prescriptive elements, nor the form in which it proceeds. The quests for more competitiveness through so-called structural reforms which are the officious conceptual basis of the new modes of economic governance do not seem to be based upon any coherent paradigm. The *ductus* and prose which sounds ordo- and/or neo-liberal to many critical observers (e.g., Guérot and Dullien 2012; Biebricher et al. 2013) is misleading. The discretionary and authoritarian managerial mode of Europe's crisis politics not only disregards all recognised notions of political accountability and democratic legitimacy; it is also incompatible with the ordoliberal and the Hayekian commitment to the rule of law and the guidance of economic policy by justiciable criteria (Mestmäcker 1973). Fritz W. Scharpf has pointed to this twofold fallacy with particular clarity. The excessive imbalance procedure as adopted in the 'Six Pack' and the 'Two Pack' regulations[48] are the strongest conceivable illustration of his critique. It is the very logic of this procedure that 'dictates that it must operate without any pre-defined rule and that the Commission's *ad hoc* decisions must apply to individual member states in unique circumstances rather than to EMU states in general. Regardless of the comparative quality of its economic expertise, the Commission lacks legitimate authority to impose highly intrusive policy choices on Member States' (Scharpf 2013: 139). Precisely, this is foreseen for an undefined range of policy areas in which the EU still lacks hard-law competences. To be sure, Europe's 'crisis law' is geared towards a strengthening of economic 'competitiveness' in Europeanising and globalising markets. Even if this objective may one day be achieved more stringently, the disregard of Hayek's philippic against the 'pretence of knowledge' (Von Hayek 1989) remains as obvious as the lack of justiciable criteria of the new modes of economic governance.

At this point, we have to return to the guiding question of this chapter and Böckenförde's characterisation of the financial crisis as a state of emergency (Böckenförde 2010). Böckenförde did not explicitly refer to Carl Schmitt in that comment. But this he had done some decades earlier in his Freiburg inaugural lecture which was dedicated to Carl Schmitt's ninetieth

48 See for a lucid summary of the pertinent documents by the Commission: http://ec.europa.eu/economy_finance/economic_governance/sgp/index_en.htm.

birthday on 11 July1978 (Böckenförde 1978).[49] The lecture dealt with the fierce debate in the Federal Republic on the German *Notstandsgesetzgebung* (emergency legislation).[50] A breakdown of the correlation between the situation implicitly presupposed in the law ('*Normallage*') as the reference point of its regulatory objectives ('*der intendierten Regulierungskraft der Norm*' (1884), a striking discrepancy and tension between conferred powers and means, on the one hand, and the irrefutable challenges of a state of emergency, will, Böckenförde submitted, provoke the quest for exceptional powers and means to cope with such emergencies.[51]

Böckenförde's definition illuminates the discrepancy between the ordoliberal conceptual premises of EMU, on the one hand, and its hybrid construction and operation, on the other. What follows from that insight? Does the law end where necessity governs? Böckenförde did not answer this question. His comment in the *Neue Züricher Zeitung* is a description, rather than a justification, of the outrageous treatment of the law. Do we have to accept the new 'crisis law' as a functional necessity and comply with its commands or are we to insist on a return to a constitutional condition. The second alternative is obviously 'better'. What is unfortunately not so obvious is the availability of this option. The decision to establish the EMU was a mistake that can neither be undone nor repaired. What we are witnessing, instead, are hectic managerial activities, accompanied and challenged by a broad debate in which no such thing as a consolidated alternative is likely to emerge. 'Normalisation' versus 'contestation' is a framing of emergency constellations which has become quite widely used in the American emergency debates after 9/11 (Frankenberg 2010: 235 ff.; Kuo 2014). Normalisation designates an arrangement with the transformation of Europe's constitutional constellation as a *factum* (more or less) *brutum* which the new 'crisis law' will govern for the time being. Contestation characterises efforts to regain a new constitutional condition in a constellation of high uncertainties and political struggle. We will, in the concluding section, explore this alternative.

49 On Böckenförde's indebtedness to Carl Schmitt, see the interview with Dieter Gosewinkel (2010: 359–91).

50 Enacted through an amendment of the Basic Law on 24 June 1968; the text is accessible at www.documentarchiv.de/brd/1968/grundgesetz-notstandsgesetze.html.

51 '[E]ine *grundsätzliche* Diskrepanz zwischen den vorgesehenen Befugnissen/Modalitäten und einer Erfolgreichen Wahrnehmung der Aufgabe [...] angesichts einer unvorhergesehenen ernsten Gefahr' (ibid., 885).

Unfreezing the law–politics relationship through conflicts law

'Contestation' is not an established legal concept. It characterises an unsettled constellation and signals the need to regain a legal condition which deserves recognition. Is a legal framing of such transformative processes conceivable, a 'law of struggle' (Chalmers 2012)? The following tentative deliberations build on a reconceptualisation of European law as a new type of conflicts-law approach, which I started to develop a long while ago (Joerges 2005) and have since then elaborated continuously (e.g., Joerges et al. 2011; Joerges 2014a). The links to and affinities with 'contestation' are manifold: most importantly, the conflicts-approach takes the heterogeneity of the Union into account and provides framework for the conflict constellations which that heterogeneity is bound to generate; equally significant, the responses to such conflicts cannot build upon ready-made substantive rules but must be achieved through productive innovations and fair compromises; last but not least, there is no in-built guarantee that such resolutions will actually be reached; quite to the contrary, the conflicts-approach envisages irresolvable 'true' conflicts and their undecidability. This is implied in its core message: Europe's *finalité* is not a unity realised through uniformity but *unitas in pluralitate.*

The premises of conflicts-law constitutionalism in a nutshell

In the present context, it is not necessary to go into the conflicts-approach in any detail. It should suffice to underline two assumptions:

(1) The openness and interdependence of the member states within the Union affect their democratic orders considerably. National decision-making processes cannot be Europeanised and their policies reflect national concerns and interests. But their decisions regularly affect neighbouring polities whose citizens have had no voice in these processes. That observation is the basis for a reconceptualisation of the ordering functions of European law: European law must require the member states of the Union to take their neighbours' concerns seriously – in this respect, it aims at compensating the structural democratic deficits of nation-statehood. Here lies an inherently *democratic* potential of EU law, which is categorically different from that of nation states. Under the impact of Europeanisation, our societies are experiencing an ever-greater gulf between decision-making in and by individual polities and the impact of such decisions on foreign citizens. This schism is a normative challenge to democratic orders because

the very notion of democratic self-legislation requires that citizens who are the addressees of a law and affected by them can, in the last instance, interpret themselves as its authors.[52] The core problem of this dimension of conflicts law is to determine the legitimacy of the restrictions of national political autonomy and to substantiate principles and mechanisms of mutual consideration.

(2) On the other hand, European societies, furthermore, experience in ever more domains that they are not, or are no longer, in a position to ensure responses to their concerns autonomously, but, instead, depend on transnational cooperation. European conflicts-law has, therefore, a vocation to structure cooperative problem-solving in such fields. The core problem here is the quality of such cooperative modes. Inter-democratic cooperation cannot be equated with the democracies of sovereign states but is nevertheless a democratic command, which, like the premise just underlined, is a consequence of the mutual interdependence of the European polities (similarly, Innerarity 2015; Preuß 2013).

The reconceptualisation of European law as a 'new type of conflicts law' was designed as an exercise in critical theory with normative perspectives that would not confront the state of the integration project with merely normatively attractive ideas but which, in the tradition of the Frankfurt School of Critical Theory, would identify aspects of the integration process that had a potential for institutional innovations, and might, thanks to the ingenuity of committed actors, be transformed in a constructive way. In less troubled times it seemed possible that conflicts-law constitutionalism could eventually be elaborated further and proceed as a *reconstructive* project, i.e., a reconceptualisation of European law that would, to a considerable degree, be compatible with European law as it stood and be able to orient its further development. The reconstructive status was based upon its sociological premises that reflect the conflict-laden European constellation more adequately than the orthodoxy of European law. All that seemed necessary, and, indeed, overdue, was to reconsider the integration project in the light of Europe's ever-growing diversity, to take the conflicts which this diversity generated into account, and to reorient Europe's agenda

52 In a recent more authoritative restatement: 'Nation-states [...] encumber each other with the external effects of decisions that impinge on third parties who had no say in the decision-making process. Hence, states cannot escape the need for regulation and coordination in the expanding horizon of a world society that is increasingly self-programming, even at the cultural level' (Habermas 2007: 176).

from harmonisation and unity to the management of complex conflict constellations.[53]

The two core premises just outlined remain normatively valid. The transformation of Europe's constitutional constellation by its new 'crisis law', however, has affected the reconstructive potential of the approach. What is left of it?

Contestation

Conflicts-law constitutionalism had assumed that European law would provide frameworks within which conflicting interests and claims could be resolved constructively. 'Crisis law' can be understood as a response to 'grim necessity' (Dyson 2013). Even though it must not, without further ado, be called a wilful and unwarranted abuse of power, it cannot, contrary to Poiares Maduro (2012), be rationalised and justified as a response to democracy failures of the European nation states. It is rather, for the many reasons listed above, exposed to bitter normative objections. What is so difficult to predict is the impact of these objections. What we can safely, albeit sadly, assume, however, is that, under Europe's crisis law, well-known conflict configurations will persist and new ones are being generated. The ambition of the following deliberations is a modest one. They seek to outline a series of spheres of contestation in which law might be invoked to endorse justified claims. This is by no means to suggest that out of such contestation and '*Kampf ums Recht*' (the struggle for law) a new, let alone coherent, constitutional architecture might emerge. What is conceivable is a civilising impact of law on European crisis management, political processes and practices.

The European Parliament and national parliaments

'The lack of parliamentary politics is [...] the most disturbing element of European democracy' (Pollak 2014: 37). The European Parliament, as the most visible institutional embodiment of the Union's democratic commitments, tends to be marginalised in Europe's state of emergency

53 I refrain here from discussing affinities with the theory of demoi-cracy, which envisages 'a Union of peoples, understood both as states and as citizens, who govern together but not as one' (Nicolaïdes, 2013: 311) or with 'republican' as opposed to 'liberal' intergovernmentalism' (Bellamy 2013). Both of these approaches are challenged by the crisis in much the same way as conflicts law constitutionalism.

by the new transgovernmentalism of the European Council (Fossum 2014: part I, sect. 3). National parliaments, too, are in difficulties, albeit of different kinds. The debtor countries under the ESM, which signed the so-called memoranda of understanding, have to pay with the loss of their political autonomy for access to financial funds – and their parliaments are forced to accept what they cannot like. Parliaments are, nevertheless, powerful institutions. There are indicators that they join forces to defend their constitutional status and strengthen cooperative links (Benz 2013). The recent Greek uprising against the austerity politics reveal that transnational intergovernmentalism can be seriously irritated by the outcome of national elections which legitimise the quest of national governments for a reopening of the negotiations over the conditions of financial assistance. It is hardly a constellation conceivable in which the contingencies and risks of the European project could come to the fore more drastically. At stake is a contest between technocratic rule and democratically legitimated claims. The rationality and the efficacy of the former are anything but convincing. The readiness and the potential of the Greek government to engage transformative processes that generate acceptance of its constituency are difficult to evaluate. And yet this conflict constellation could lead to a transformation of authoritarian conditionality into cooperative reforms and problem-solving. It could even foster the development of procedures guiding these processes in conformity with legal standards ensuring their fairness and legitimacy.

Constitutional Courts could become more active in the defence of democratic principles and the rule of law. They could move towards a new Europeanised understanding of their vocation. This is a normative vision which the GCC has thoroughly failed to pursue. In its judgment of 12 September on the rescue package for Greece,[54] the Court responded to the quest for solidarity on the part of the member states in difficulty by making the signing of the memoranda contingent upon the approval of the *Bundestag*. This requirement is a two-edged sword. Anybody aware of the time constraints under which such decisions have to be taken will wonder about the quality of such supervisions (Hassemer 2012; Maurer 2013). Even more irritating is the Court's failure to consider how the practice of conditionality affects the constitutional principles of the member states concerned. The position of a parliament preserving its budgetary

54 Judgment of 12 September 2012, BVerfG, 2 BvR 1390/12, available at www.bverfg.de/entscheidungen/rs20120912_2bvr139012en.html.

autonomy at the cost of those who experience the constraints of 'conditionality' mirrors nothing better than the power asymmetries in the Union. The attitude of the GCC and the kind of disrespect which it has exercised in its ESM judgment is precisely the opposite of what conflict-law constitutionalism would suggest. The GCC is not legitimated to curtail the political autonomy of democratic institutions of other member states. Its task would have been to define principles which ensure the accountability of those imposing hardship and which ensure a fair debate on the affected polities and with their representatives. Why shouldn't Constitutional Courts reconceptualise 'conditionality' and insist on its transformation into truly cooperative problem-solving, as envisaged by conflicts-law constitutionalism?

Similar conflict constellations seem quite likely in the context of the European Semester. As far as this procedure seeks to coordinate budgetary and economic policies *ex ante*, it can be understood as a mechanism which makes parliaments aware of mutual responsibilities which then constrain their political autonomy of national parliaments. But this cannot justify a delegation, *de jure* or de facto, to the experts and technocrats in DG Economy and Finance in the European Commission. A recent study on the legitimacy and effectiveness of the European Semester commissioned by Policy Department A of the European Parliament (Hallerberg et al. 2012) concludes that output legitimacy cannot be accomplished under the uncertainties of the crisis while input legitimacy will depend, first and foremost, on the involvement of the parliaments. The potential of national parliaments to exert influence remains considerable as long as they retain their so-called 'ownership' of the national contributions to the semester process. It is hence not only conceivable, but also quite likely, that, in the not too distant future, the new policy coordination within the annually repeating European Semester, the reporting and multilateral surveillance obligations, the macroeconomic imbalance procedures and the responses to country-specific recommendations, will lead to new assessments of the weight of socio-economic diversity, insights into the social embeddedness of the markets, acknowledgement of the different regulatory, social and economic cultures in the member states and a search for innovative responses to complex conflict constellations. All this is not to say that the law could build upon, let alone offer, new conceptual guidance. The point is, rather, that law may be better advised to become sensitive to political contestation and learning, rather than opting to operate upon the basis of discredited assumptions.

The urgency of the social question

The 'structural reforms' which Europe's new modes of governance seek to realise have been under way for quite some time and the same is true for the abandonment of the 'European social model'. More than a decade ago, Fritz Scharpf, in his discussion of the Open Method of Co-ordination, observed that the policies promoted under this flag had to respect the priority of the internal market objectives and of the EMU (Scharpf 2002: 655). Alternative accounts have continued to argue that high labour standards would foster quality production, skill formation and cooperation. After the Eastern enlargement, however, these debates were overshadowed by Europe's deepened socio-economic diversity and the quest for the accession states to gain access to the labour markets of 'old Europe'. The response was the judgments of the ECJ in *Viking* and *Laval*, both handed down in December 2007.[55] By now, the imperative of euro survival has radicalised the pressures on welfare-state traditions. The Euro Plus Pact of 2011[56] listed the measures which the signatories were expected to undertake in order to adapt their employment regimes to the exigencies of competitiveness. The Pact relied on the Open Method of Co-ordination so that the member states were left with considerable leeway. The memoranda of understanding that countries receiving bail-out funds had to sign are much more intrusive, however (Barnard 2012; Rödl and Callsen 2014). They are an essential element of the new economic governance and revoke the promise of a European social model which would sooner or later complement, harmonise, renew or replace the variety of national traditions.

Again, however, the envisaged transformations were met with resistance. Popular protests on the streets of Athens, Madrid, Lisbon and, to a lesser extent, Dublin, indicate indignation. At the same time, the asymmetries in social hardship, not just within national societies but, more visibly, between debtor- and creditor-states, create new tensions rather than solidarity commitments among the citizens of Europe. The responses to the Greek protest against European 'rescue' measures have shown again how unlikely it is that the imposition of austerity will generate re-orientation beyond the stereotypes of 'ever more Europe', on the

55 *International Transport Workers' Federation* v. *Viking*, EU:C:2007:772; *Laval*, EU:C:2007:809.

56 Conclusions of the European Council, Brussels, 24/25 March 2011, EUCO 10/11, CO EUR 6, CONCL 3 (Annex I).

one hand, and populist defences of national accomplishments and sentiments, on the other.

This lack of transnational solidarity is not so difficult to explain: the socio-economic diversity of the Union excludes the construction of one uniform social model. European citizens would have to distinguish between domestic and inter-state justice, between the solidarity in its various societies and the solidarity among its *demoi* (Joerges 2014b). This is not so easy to translate into a transnational social agenda. Constitutional Court could nevertheless intervene where austerity politics affect human and social rights. One signal has been sent by Portugal's Constitutional Court,[57] which has examined the compatibility of the austerity measures of the Portuguese government with the Portuguese Constitution. The Court explicitly recognised:

> [T]he seriousness of the current economic/financial situation and the need to attain the public-deficit goals included in the specific economic policy conditions laid down in the memoranda of understanding between the Portuguese government, the European Union and the International Monetary Fund.

However, it then objected to the implementation of these requests because of their disregard for the principles of equality and proportionality.[58] This may not be much, but it is more than nothing – and much more is conceivable (Fischer-Lescano 2014).

Distributional conflicts are the most sensitive of all controversies in Europe. They can be observed within and between European societies. They are the background of social unrest and of populist movements. Seemingly paradoxically, the most important and most powerful organiser of distributional politics is by now the ECB, Europe's non-majoritarian institution par excellence. Redistribution occurs as a collateral damage or benefit through the banks' extensive understanding of monetary policy, most notably through its Open Market Transactions Programme. Equally paradoxically, two other non-majoritarian institutions are involved in

57 Acórdão No. 187/2013, Processo no. 2/2013, 5/2013, 8/2013 e 11/2013, Plenário, English translation available at www.tribunalconstitucional.pt/tc/en/acordaos/20130187s.html; for an encouraging commentary, see Barnard 2013: sect. C, text accompanying nn. 37 et seq.)

58 Ioannidis (2014: nn. 183 et seq.) points to a more audacious judgment of the Greek Supreme Administrative Court. The court found that the cuts imposed on public sector pensions 'violate the principles of a social state, but also lead to its destruction since they deteriorate the pensioners situation to such a level that the principle of human dignity according to the Constitution is jeopardised' (see Akrivopoulou 2013).

the contest over this programme, namely, the GCC[59] and the CJEU. Their contest can be observed, but the conflict cannot be resolved: the matter is legally undecidable, but courts are unlikely to admit that.

Constitutional guardianship through interactive adjudication?

Regaining a constitutional condition, this is the challenge to which the tensions between the European commitments to the rule of law and democracy, on the one hand, and the practices of its crisis management, on the other, are exposing parliaments, the European publics, civil society and trade unions. But these institutions and actors have no common agenda and it is simply inconceivable that they could coordinate their resistance or initiatives. This may be a good reason for the recent tendency in European law scholarship to explore the potential of interactive or even cooperative adjudication (Viellechner 2012; Wendel 2013).[60] The much criticised GCC has given nurture to such visions in a passage of its ESM order which redefines the eternity clause of Article 79(3) of the Basic Law in the following way:

> Article 79(3) of the Basic Law does not guarantee the unchanged existence of the law in force, but those structures and procedures *which keep the democratic process open* and, in this context, safeguard parliament's overall budgetary responsibility [...] If the monetary union cannot be achieved in its original structure through the valid integration programme, new political decisions are needed as to how to proceed further. It is for the legislature to decide how possible weaknesses of the monetary union are to be counteracted by amending European Union law.[61]

Franzius (2013) and Everson (2014) infer from this passage the insight that the future constitutional gestalt of the Union cannot be shaped democratically upon the basis of or from within one single national order, through the judicial supervision of the European constitutionalisation process

59 2 BvR 1390/12 *ESM/Fiscal Compact*, Judgment of 18 March 2014.

60 Does the GCC decision 2 BvR 2728/13 *ESM/ECB*, Judgment of 15 January 2014 signal the court's readiness to engage in such discourses? It has been widely noted that the German Court has, for the first time, made use of the reference procedure. It does not mean, however, that the court has subjected itself without further ado to the authority of the Court of Justice. It has made it so abundantly clear that, in its view, the ECB has taken action outside its mandate that it is difficult to see how the latter could come up with arguments that would lead the German court to believe that there was no 'manifest and structurally significant transgression of powers'.

61 2 BvR 1390/12 *ESM/Fiscal Compact*, Judgment of 18 March 2014, para. 206 (emphasis added).

or, by the same token, as a reserve against an exclusive responsibility of the Court for the defence of constitutionalism in the Union. This process must, instead, involve the constitutional courts of the Union in their entirety and build upon their interactions with the Court. How realistic are such expectations? Is this late nineteenth-century *Kathedersozialismus* (professorial Marxism or socialism) of Germany's Historical School of National Economics reloaded as *Katheder-Konstitutionalisms*? Interactive adjudication would break with the orthodoxy of integration through law. It would also break with the respect for high politics which both courts have shown so far. This time high politics speaks with different voices.

References

Abelshauser, W. (2014) 'Europa in Vielfalt einigen. Eine Denkschrift'. www.homes.uni-bielefeld.de/wabelsha/Denkschrift.pdf.

Adamski, D. (2012) 'National Power Games and Structural Failures in the European Macroeconomic Governance', *Common Market Law Review*, 49(4), 1319–64.

(2013) 'Europe's (Misguided) Constitution of Economic Prosperity', *Common Market Law Review*, 50(1), 47–86.

(2014) 'The ESMA Doctrine: A Constitutional Revolution and the Economics of Delegation', *European Law Review*, 39(6), 812–34.

Akrivopoulou, C. (2013) 'Facing l'état d'exception: The Greek Crisis Jurisprudence', *International Journal of Constitutional Law Blog*, 11 July 2013. www.iconnectblog.com/2013/07/facing-letat-dexception-the-greek-crisis-jurisprudence.

Azoulai, L. (2013) 'The European Court of Justice and the Duty to Respect Sensitive National Interests', in M. Dawson, B. de Witte and E. Muir (eds), *Judicial Activism at the European Court of Justice: Causes, Responses and Solutions*, Cheltenham: Edward Elgar, 167–87.

Barnard, C. (2012) 'The Financial Crisis and the Euro Plus Pact: A Labour Lawyer's Perspective', *Industrial Law Journal*, 41(1), 98–114.

(2013) 'The Charter, the Court – and the Crisis' (6 August 2013), University of Cambridge Faculty of Law Research Paper No. 18/2013.

Bellamy, R. (2013) 'An Ever Closer Union among the Peoples of Europe: Republican Intergovernmentalism and Demoicratic Representation within the EU', *Journal of European Integration*, 35(5), 499–516.

Benz, A. (2013) 'An Asymmetric Two-level Game: Parliaments in the Euro Crisis', in B. Crum and J. Fossum (eds), *Practices of Inter-Parliamentary Coordination in International Politics – The European Union and Beyond*, London: Routledge, 125–40.

Biebricher, T., Hien, J., Jabko, N., and Chari, A. (2013) 'Critical Exchange on Neoliberalism and Europe: Europe and the Political Philosophy of Neoliberalism', *Contemporary Political Theory*, 12(4), 338–75.

Blom-Hansen, J., and Brandsma, G. (2009) 'The EU Comitology System: Intergovernmental Bargaining and Deliberative Supranationalism?', *Journal of Common Market Studies*, 47(4), 719–40.

Böckenförde, E.-W. (1978) 'Der verdrängte Ausnahmezustand. Zum Handeln der Staatsgewalt in außergewöhnlichen Lagen', *Neue Juristische Wochenschrift*, 31, 1881–90.

(2010) 'Kennt die europäische Not kein Gebot? Die Webfehler der EU und die Notwendigkeit einer neuen politischen Entscheidung' [Does necessity not know rules? Design flaws of the EU and the necessity of a new political decision], *Neue Züricher Zeitung*, 21 June.

Chalmers, D. (2012) 'The European Redistributive State and a European Law of Struggle', *European Law Journal*, 18(5), 667–93.

Curtin, D. (2009) *Executive Power of the European Union: Law, Practices and the Living Constitution*, Oxford: Oxford University Press.

Davies, B. (2007) 'The Constitutionalisation of the EEC/EC: West Germany between Legal Sovereignty and European Integration 1949–1974', PhD thesis, King's College London.

de Búrca, G., and Scott, J. (eds) (2006) *New Governance, Law and Constitutionalism*, Oxford: Hart Publishing.

Dehousse, R. (ed.) (1994) *Europe after Maastricht: An Ever Closer Union?*, Munich: Beck.

Dehousse, R., and Weiler, J. (1990) 'The Legal Dimension', in W. Wallace (ed.), *The Dynamics of European Integration*, London: Pinter, 242–60.

Dyson, K. (2013) 'Sworn to Grim Necessity? Imperfections of European Economic Governance, Normative Political Theory, and Supreme Emergency', *Journal of European Integration*, 35(3), 207–22.

Eichengreen, B. (2015) *Hall of Mirrors: The Great Depression, The Great Recession, and the Uses and Misuses of History*, Oxford: Oxford University Press.

European Commission (1985) 'White Paper on Completion of the Internal Market', COM (85) 310 final.

(2012) 'A Blueprint for a Deep and Genuine Economic and Monetary Union: Launching a European Debate', COM (2012) 777/Final 2.

Everson, M. (2014) 'An Exercise in Legal Honesty: Rewriting the Court of Justice and the Bundesverfassungsgericht', Institute for Advanced Studies, Vienna, Political Science Series, 136/2014.

Falke, J. (2014) 'Comitology After Lisbon: What is Left of Comitology as we Have Praised it?', in C. Joerges and C. Glinski (eds), *The European Crisis and the Transformation of Transnational Governance: Authoritarian Managerialism versus Democratic Governance*, Oxford: Hart Publishing, 271–92.

Feld, L. (2011) 'Ein Scheitern ist nicht eingeplant, oder: Ordnungspolitische Prinzipien der Europäischen Währungsunion', Impulsrede zur Sozialen Marktwirtschaft, Wirtschaftspolitischer Club Deutschland e.V.

www.wpcd.de/fileadmin/user_upload/Impulsreden_2011_und_2010_Schriftenreihe_WPCD.pdf.

(2012) 'Europa in der Welt von heute: Wilhelm Röpke und die Zukunft der Europäischen Währungsunion', Hamburgisches Weltwirtschaftsinstitut Policy Paper 70. http://roepke.hwwi.de/.

Fischer-Lescano, A. (2014) 'Human Rights in Times of Austerity Policy: The EU Institutions and the Conclusion of Memoranda of Understanding', legal opinion commissioned by the Chamber of Labour, Vienna, Baden-Baden. www.jura.uni-bremen.de/institute/zentrum-fuer-europaeische-rechtspolitik/aktuelles.

Fossum, J.-E. (2014) 'The Structure of EU-representation and the Crisis', in Sandra Kröger (ed.), *Political Representation in the European Union: Still Democratic in Times of Crisis?*, Abingdon and NewYork: Routledge, 140–75.

Frankenberg, G. (2010) *Staatstechnik: Perspektiven auf Rechtsstaat und Ausnahmezustand*, Frankfurt: Suhrkamp.

Franzius, C. (2013) 'Demokratisierung der Europäischen Union', *Europarecht*, 655–67.

Gosewinkel, D. (2010) '"Beim Staat geht es nicht allein um macht, sondern um die staatliche Ordnung als Freiheitsordnung". Biographoisches Interview mit Ernst-Wofgang Böckenförde', in E.-W. Böckenförde, 'Kennt die europäische Not kein Gebot? Die Webfehler der EU und die Notwendigkeit einer neuen politischen Entscheidung', *Neue Züricher Zeitung*, 21 June, 305–86.

Grimm, D. (2015) 'The Democratic Costs of Constitutionalization: The European Case', *European Law Journal*, 21(4), 460–73.

Guérot, U., and Dullien, S. (2012) 'The Long Shadow of Ordo-Liberalism: Germany's Approach to the Euro Crisis'. www.ecfr.eu/page/-/ECFR49_GERMANY_BRIEF_AW.pdf.

Habermas, J. (2007) *The Divided West*, Oxford: Polity Press.

Hall, P. (2014) 'Varieties of Capitalism and the Euro Crisis', *West European Politics*, 37(6), 1223–43.

Hallerberg, M., Marzinotti. B., and Wolff, G. (2012) 'An Assessment of the European Semester', study commissioned by the European Parliament, Brussels. www.europarl.europa.eu/studies.

Hassemer, W. (2012) 'Is There No Time for the Law?', *Frankfurter Allgemeine Zeitung*, 28 June.

Höpner, M. (2014) 'Wie der Europäische Gerichtshof und die Kommission Liberalisierung durchsetzen: Befunde aus der MPIfG-Forschungsgruppe zur Politischen Ökonomie der europäischen Integration', MPIfG DP 2014/8, Cologne.

Innerarity, D. (2015) 'Images of Europe around the Crisis', *The European Legacy: Toward New Paradigms*, 20(1). www.tandfonline.com/doi/abs/10.1080/10848770.2014.984981#.VM4FTy6AqT0.

Ioannidis, M. (2014) 'EU Financial Assistance Conditionality', *Heidelberg Journal of International Law*, 74(1), 61–104.

Ipsen, H-P. (1969) 'Zur Verfassung der fusionierten Gemeinschaft', *Integration*, 1(1), 3–22.

Iversen, T., and Soskice, D. (2013) '*A Structural-Institutional Explanation of the Eurozone Crisis*', Cambridge, MA: Harvard University, Department of Government.

Joerges, C. (1996) 'The Market without a State? States without Markets? Two Essays on the Law of the European Economy', San Domenico di Fiesole, EUI Working Paper Law 1/96.

(1997) 'The Impact of European Integration on Private Law: Reductionist Perceptions, True Conflicts and a New Constitutional Perspective', *European Law Journal*, 3(4), 378–406.

(2005) 'Rethinking European Law's Supremacy: A Plea for a Supranational Conflict of Laws' (with comments by Damian Chalmers, Rainer Nickel, Florian Rödl and Robert Wai), San Domenico di Fiesole, EUI Working Paper Law 12/2005.

(2007) 'Integration through De-legislation? An Irritated Heckler', European Governance Papers (EUROGOV) No. N-07-03.

(2014a) 'Conflicts-Law Constitutionalism: Ambitions and Problems', in M. Cremona, et al. (eds.), *Reflections on the Constitutionalisation of International Economic Law: Liber Amicorum for Ernst-Ulrich Petersmann*, Leiden: Martinus Nijhoff, 111–37.

(2014b) 'Legitimacy without Democracy in the EU? Perspectives on the Constitutionalization of Europe', in M. Poiares Maduro, K. Tuori and S. Sankari (eds), *Transnational Law: Rethinking European Law and Legal Thinking*, Cambridge: Cambridge University Press, 248–68.

(2014c): 'Europe's Economic Constitution in Crisis and the Emergence of a New Constitutional Constellation', *German Law Journal*, 15(5), 985–1028.

Joerges, C., and Glinski, C. (eds) (2014) *The European Crisis and the Transformation of Transnational Governance: Authoritarian Managerialism versus Democratic Governance*, Oxford: Hart Publishing.

Joerges, C., and Neyer, J. (1997) 'From Intergovernmental Bargaining to Deliberative Political Processes: The Constitutionalisation of Comitology', *European Law Journal*, 3(2), 273–99.

(2014) 'Deliberativer Supranationalismus in der Krise', in O. Flugel-Martinsen, et al. (eds), *Deliberative Kritik – Kritik der Deliberation. Festschrift für Rainer Schmalz-Bruns*, Wiesbaden: Springer, 353–72.

Joerges, C., and Schmid, C. (2004) 'Towards Proceduralization of Private Law in the European Multi-Level System', in A. Hartkamp, et al. (eds), *Towards a European Civil Code*, The Hague: Kluwer Law International, 4th edn, 277–310.

Joerges, C., and Weimer, M. (2014) 'A Crisis of Executive Managerialism in the EU: No Alternative?', in G. de Búrca, C. Kilpatrick and J. Scott (eds), *Liber Amicorum for David M Trubek*, Oxford: Hart Publishing, 295–322.

Joerges, C., Kjaer, P., and Ralli, T. (2011) 'Conflicts Law as Constitutional Form in the Postnational Constellation', *Transnational Legal Theory*, 2(2) 152–85.

Joerges, C., Mény, Y., and Weiler, J. (2002) 'Mountain or Molehill? A Critical Appraisal of the Commission White Paper on Governance', European University Institute-Robert Schumann Centre/ NYU School of Law Jean Monnet Center.

Kaufmann, M. (1997) *Europäische Integration und Semokratieprinzip*, Baden-Baden: Nomos.

Kirchhof, P. (2012) 'Verfassungsnot!', *Frankfurter Allgemeine Zeitung*, 20 July.

Konrad, K, (2014) 'Balancing Austerity and Strategies for Growth', *CFA Institute Conference Proceedings Quarterly*, 31(2), 1–8.

Krieger, T, (2012) 'Es geht nicht ohne internationalen Ordnungsrahmen - Zum Verhältnis von Markt und Staat im Angesicht der Finanzkrise', *Amos international: Internationale Zeitschrift für christliche Sozialethik*, 6, 8–14.

Kuo, M.-S. (2014) 'The Moment of Schmittian Truth: Conceiving of the State of Exception in the Wake of the Financial Crisis', in C. Joerges and C. Glinski (eds), *The European Crisis and the Transformation of Transnational Governance: Authoritarian Managerialism versus Democratic Governance*, Oxford: Hart Publishing, 83–100.

Ladeur, K.-H. (2014) 'Conflicts Law as Europe's Constitutional Form … and the Conflict of Social Norms as its Infrastructure', in C. Joerges and C. Glinski (eds), *The European Crisis and the Transformation of Transnational Governance: Authoritarian Managerialism versus Democratic Governance*, Oxford: Hart Publishing, 203–26.

Leaman, J. (2001) *The Bundesbank Myth: Towards a Crique of Central Bank Independence*, Basingstoke: Palgrave Macmillan.

Lefkofridi, Z., and Schmitter, P. (2015) 'Transcending or Descending? European Integration in Times of Crisis', *European Political Science Review*, 7(1), 3–22.

Lorz, A., and Sauer, H. (2012) 'Ersatzunionsrecht und Grundgesetz. Verfassungsrechtliche Zustimmungsgrundlagen für den Fiskalpakt, den ESM-Vertrag und die Änderung des AEUV', *Die öffentliche Verwaltung*, 573–82.

Majone, G. (1993) 'The European Community between Social Policy and Social Regulation', *Journal of Common Market Studies*, 31(1), 153–70.

(2014) *Rethinking the Union of Europe Post-Crisis – Has Integration Gone Too Far?* Cambridge: Cambridge University Press.

Manow, P. (2015) 'Social Protection, Capitalist Production: The Bismarckian Welfare State in the German Political Economy 1880–2010', unpublished habilitation thesis, Constance (forthcoming).

Maurer, A. (2013) 'From EMU to DEMU: The Democratic Legitimacy of the EU and the European Parliament', IAI Working Papers 13/11 (April).

Mestmäcker, E.-J. (1973) 'Power, Law and Economic Constitution', *German Economic Review*, 2, 177–98.

(2011) 'Der Schamfleck ist die Geldverachtung' [The shaming flaw is the disdainfulness of money], *Frankfurter Allgemeine Zeitung*, 18 November.

(2012) 'Ordnungspolitische Grundlagen einer politischen Union' [Foundational principles for the ordering of a political union], *Frankfurter Allgemeine Zeitung*, 12 November.

Möllers, C. (1999) *Staat als Argument*, Munich: C. H. Beck.

Müller, J.-W. (2003) *A Dangerous Mind: Carl Schmitt in Post-War European Thought*, New Haven, CT: Yale University Press.

Nicolaïdes, K. (2013) 'European Demoicracy and its Crisis', *Journal of Common Market Studies*, 51(2), 311–39.

Ohlin Report (1956) 'International Labour Organisation, Social Aspects of European Economic Co-operation, Report by a Group of Experts' (summary), *International Labour Review*, 74, 9–123.

Poiares Maduro, M. (2012) 'A New Governance for the European Union and the Euro: Democracy and Justice', European Parliament, September 2012. www.europarl.europa.eu/studies.

Pollak, J. (2014) 'Compounded Representation in the EU: No Country for Old Parliaments?', in S. Kröger (ed.), *Political Representation in the European Union: Still Democratic in Times of Crisis?* Abingdon and NewYork: Routledge, 37–69.

Preuß, U. (2013) 'Gibt es eine völkerrechtliche Demokratietheorie?', in H. Heinig and J. Terhechte (eds), *Postnationale Demokratie, Postdemokratie, Neoetatismus : Wandel klassicher Demokratievorstellungen in der Rechtswissenschaft*, Tübingen: Mohr Siebeck, 169–84.

Rödl, F., and Callsen, R. (2014) 'The Struggle for Union Rights under the Euro and the Dialectics of Social Integration', in C. Joerges and C. Glinski, *The European Crisis*, Oxford, Hart, 101–22.

Ruggie, J. (1982) 'International Regimes, Transactions and Change: Embedded Liberalism in the Postwar Economic Order', *International Organization*, 36(2), 375–415.

Ruser, A. (2014) 'The EU's New Economic Governance is Blurring the Boundaries between European Competences and Domestic Sovereignty', LSE. http://blogs.lse.ac.uk/europpblog/2014/01/30/the-eus-new-economic-governance-is-blurring-the-boundaries-between-european-competences-and-domestic-sovereignty.

Sabel, C., and Zeitlin, J. (2007) 'Learning from Difference: The New Architecture of Experimentalist Governance in the European Union', EUROGOV Working Paper No. C-07-02. http://edoc.vifapol.de/opus/volltexte/2011/2466/pdf/egp_connex_C_07_02.pdf.

(2012) Experimentalism in the EU: Common Ground and Persistent Differences, *Regulation and Governance*, 6(3), 410–26.

Scharpf, F. (1994) 'Autonomieschonend und gemeinschaftsverträglich: Zur Logik der europäischen Mehrebenenpolitik', in F. Scharpf (ed.), *Optionen des Föderalismus in Deutschland und Europa*. Frankfurt am Main: Campus, 131–55.

(1997) 'Introduction. The Problem-solving Capacity of Multi-level Governance', *Journal of European Public Policy*, 4(4), 520–38.

(2002) 'The European Social Model: Coping with the Challenges of Diversity', *Journal of Common Market Studies*, 40(4), 645–70.

(2013) 'Monetary Union, Fiscal Crisis and the Disabling of Democratic Accountability', in W. Streeck and A. Schäfer (eds), *Politics in the Age of Austerity*, Cambridge: Polity, 108–42.

Schepel, H. (2013) 'The New Approach to the New Approach: The Juridification of Harmonized Standards in EU Law', *Maastricht Journal of European and Comparative Law*, 12(4), 521–33.

Schmitt, C. (1989)[1921] *Die Diktatur. Von den Anfängen des modernen Souveränitätsgedankens bis zum proletarischen Klassenkampf*, 5th edn, Berlin: Duncker & Humblot.

Steffek, J. (2006) *Embedded Liberalism and its Critics: Justifying Global Governance in the American Century*, New York: Palgrave Macmillan.

(2014) 'The Cosmopolitanism of David Mitrany: Equality, Devolution, and Functional Democracy beyond the State', *International Relations*. http://ire.sagepub.com/content/early/2014/07/17/0047117814526608.abstract.

Streit, M., and Mussler, W. (1995) 'The Economic Constitution of the European Community. From "Rome" to "Maastricht"', *European Law Journal*, 1(1), 5–30.

Trubek, D, and Trubek, L. (2005) 'Hard and Soft Law in the Construction of Social Europe: the Role of the Open Method of Co-ordination', *European Law Journal*, 11(3), 343–64.

Tuori, K, and Tuori, K. (2014) *The Eurozone Crisis: A Constitutional Analysis*, Cambridge: Cambridge University Press.

Vauchez, A. (2013) 'Brokering Europe Euro-Lawyers and the Making of a Transnational Polity', LSE Law, Society and Economy Working Papers 19/2013.

Viellechner, L. (2012) 'Berücksichtigungspflicht als Kollisionsregel: Zu den innerstaatlichen Wirkungen von völkerrechtlichen Verträgen und Entscheidungen internationaler Gerichte, insbesondere bei der Auslegung und Anwendung von Grundrechten', in N. Matz-Lück and M. Hong (eds), *Grundrechte und Grundfreiheiten im Mehrebenensystem: Konkurrenzen und Interferenzen*, Berlin and Heidelberg: Springer, 109–59.

von Hayek, F. (1948) 'The Economic Conditions of Interstate Federalism', in F. Von Hayek, *Individualism and Economic Order*, Chicago: University of Chicago Press, 255–72.

(1989) 'The Pretence of Knowledge', *American Economic Review*, 79(1), 3–7.
(2002) 'Competition as a Discovery Procedure', *Quarterly Journal of Austrian Economics*, 5(1), 9–23.
Weiler, J. (1991) 'The Transformation of Europe', *Yale Law Journal*, 100(8), 2403–83.
(1995) 'Does Europe Need a Constitution? Reflections on Demos, Telos and the German Maastricht Decision', *European Law Journal*, 1(1), 219–58.
Weimer, M. (2015) *Constitutionalising EU Administrative Risk Governance*, Oxford: Oxford University Press.
Wendel, M. (2013) 'Richterliche Rechtsvergleichung als Dialogform: Die Integrationsrechtsprechung nationaler Verfassungsgerichte in gemeineuropäischer Perspektive', *Der Staat*, 52(3), 339–70.
White, J. (2013) 'Emergency Europe', *Political Studies*, 61(1), 1–19.
Wigger, A. (2008) 'Competition for Competitiveness: The Politics of the Transformation of the EU Competition Regime', PhD thesis, VU Amsterdam.

INDEX

Lightning Source UK Ltd.
Milton Keynes UK
UKOW06n2027190416

272589UK00002B/55/P

9 781107 107182